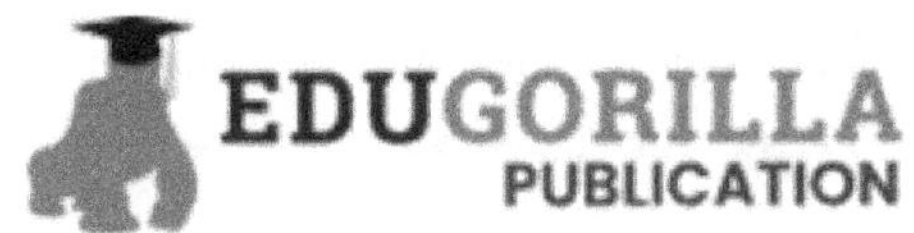

Delhi Police

Constable Recruitment Exam

Latest Edition
Practice Kit

10 Tests
10 Mock Test

Based On Real Exam Pattern

✓ Thoroughly Revised and Updated

✓ Detailed Analysis of all MCQs

<table>
<tr><td>Title</td><td>: Delhi Police Constable Recruitment Exam</td></tr>
<tr><td>Author Name</td><td>: Mr. Rohit Manglik</td></tr>
<tr><td>Published By</td><td>: EduGorilla Community Pvt. Ltd.</td></tr>
<tr><td>Publishers Address</td><td>: 12/651, First Floor Opp. Arvindo Park, Near Jama Masjid,
Indira Nagar, Lucknow, Uttar Pradesh-226016, India</td></tr>
</table>

Copyright EduGorilla

Disclaimer EduGorilla

Compiled and created by EduGorilla Community Pvt. Ltd

Printed By EduGorilla Community Pvt. Ltd.

ROHIT MANGLIK
CEO, EduGorilla

Dear Applicants,

People say *"Success comes to those who work hard."* But I've seen people working hard for their exams day in and day out for marginal success. While others succeed in their examinations by putting in just half the work. So are they God Gifted? No! I believe that it's because they work *smart* and not just *hard*. Similarly, for your exams, you should strategize your preparation so as to increase the likelihood of success. Well with EduGorilla get ready to increase your *chances of selection* in your exam by *16x*.

EduGorilla helps you in not only working *hard* but also working in a *smart and strategic* manner. With EduGorilla's preparation package, you get a chance to make your exam preparation easy, and a fun learning path towards selection. Finding the right path to your preparations can be difficult if you don't know in which direction to head. Don't worry, we have you covered! EduGorilla will be your guide to success in your journey. With our Preparation Package, you can prepare strategically and beat the exam in just one attempt.

EduGorilla's Preparation Package includes-

- **Test Series**
- **Books**

Our preparation package is handcrafted as per the latest changes, expert opinions, and students' discretion. Thus, enabling you to get through each stage of the selection process for your exam.

Our Books are designed by the teachers and experts of the respective exam with a combined 150+ years of experience; to provide you with easy, efficient, and effective learning. Our books are smart, in the sense that not only do they give you the answers to the questions but also provide similar questions for practice.

EduGorilla's competent Test Series gives you real-time experience and confidence through which you can clear your offline or online exam in just one attempt. We currently host 83,000+ mock tests for 1,440+ competitive and academic exams.

Thus, EduGorilla misses no chance to assist you in your preparation and covers all stages of the exam, so that you don't have to look anywhere else.

We provide complete preparation packages for defense, banking, teaching, and other National & State-Level exams. Hence, it doesn't matter which exam you aspire to because you will reach your success.

ALL THE BEST !

Let EduGorilla be your Guide to Success.

Rohit Manglik,
Founder and CEO, EduGorilla

INTRODUCTION

EduGorilla focuses on guiding students to succeed in their examinations. With that in mind, our book, titled "Delhi Police : Constable Recruitment Exam", has been drafted through the collective efforts of our distinguished experts with 150+ years of combined experience. This book consists of questions that are created following the latest changes in the syllabus and exam pattern. We compiled the book on the basis of questions that are most likely to appear in the Delhi Police Constable Exam. Through EduGorilla's "Delhi Police : Constable Recruitment Exam" your chances of success will increase 16x.

EduGorilla does this through our Complete Preparation Package. This package consists of well-conceptualized and structured content in the form of questions that are tailor-made according to your needs and will help you practice for exams in a smart way by pinpointing all the necessary information. It also provides hints and solutions, along with a smart answer sheet for your self-evaluation. You can assess your shortcomings and work accordingly on areas that may require more of your attention.

EduGorilla promises to help you succeed in your examination and accomplish your dream goals. We believe in our aspirants and see them at the top of the merit list. And the first step towards the top is to start preparing with us. EduGorilla's "Delhi Police : Constable Recruitment Exam" includes the following attributes.

➤ Well-Researched Content

➤ Top-Notch Quality

➤ Detailed Answers and Analysis

➤ Smart Answer Sheet

➤ Exam Relevant Questions

Therefore, EduGorilla fortifies your preparation and makes it durable enough to help you stand tall and beat the examination.

Delhi Police Constable Exam

Scan QR code for Eligibility, Exam Pattern, Syllabus and more.

Book ID: 0183

TABLE OF CONTENTS

General Knowledge/Current Affairs

Q.1 Which among the following is also called as 'Powerhouse' of the cell?

A. Plastids **B.** Mitochondria
C. Golgi bodies **D.** Cell walls

Q.2 Which organism has the maximum approximate life span?

A. Crow **B.** Parrot
C. Tortoise **D.** Crocodile

Q.3 Carbon monoxide poisoning can be cured by:

A. Exposing the affected person to fresh oxygen
B. Eating butter
C. Drinking lemon-water
D. Consuming multi-vitamin tablet

Q.4 At room temperature, the metal that remains liquid is-

A. Mercury **B.** Platinum **C.** Lead **D.** Zinc

Q.5 Which of the following is not present in a matter?

A. Proton **B.** Neutron **C.** Electron **D.** Positron

Q.6 An electric motor converts _____ energy to mechanical energy.

A. Sound **B.** Thermal
C. Chemical **D.** Electrical

Q.7 A solid cannot change its shape easily compared to liquid because of :-

A. Stronger intermolecular force in solid
B. Larger intermolecular separation in solid
C. The bigger molecular size of solid
D. The lower density of solid

Q.8 Who is the father of Geometry?

A. Aristotle **B.** Sushruta
C. Pythagoras **D.** Euclid

Q.9 The percentage of earth surface covered by India is :

A. 2.4 **B.** 5.4 **C.** 3.4 **D.** 6.4

Q.10 Which is the smallest state in India(smallest land area)?

A. Kerala **B.** Madhya Pradesh
C. Goa **D.** Assam

Q.11 Ice glacier's melting is a common phenomenon linked to the rise in seawater level. The glaciers are predominantly present in

A. Greenland **B.** Antarctica
C. Himalayas **D.** Arctic

Q.12 Who has been called Napoleon of India?

A. Samudra Gupta **B.** Chandra Gupta
C. Kumar Gupta **D.** Harsha Vardhana

Q.13 Swaraj Party was formed by _________?

A. Motilal Nehru and Mahatma Gandhi
B. Motilal Nehru and Chittaranjan Das
C. Vipin Chandra Pal
D. Subhash Chandra bose and Motilal Nehru

Q.14 Who appoints the Comptroller and Auditor General of India under Article 148?

A. Vice President of India
B. President of India
C. Prime Minister of India
D. Chief Justice of India

Q.15 Which of the following is associated with the phrase 'bicameral legislature'?

A. A legislature consisting of 10 members
B. A single assembly
C. A legislature consisting of a lower and upper chamber
D. A legislature consisting of two members of the Supreme Court

Q.16 Which one of the following is not a method of estimating National Income?

A. Expenditure method
B. Product method
C. Export-import method
D. Income method

Q.17 When was the first Round Table conference held?

A. November 1930 **B.** December 1931
C. January 1932 **D.** December 1932

Q.18 The Kannada language was the mother tongue of which of the following empire?

A. The Rashtrakutas **B.** The Senas
C. The Pratiharas **D.** The Shunga Empire

Q.19 Which of the following kingdoms were associated with the life of the Buddha?

1. Avanti
2. Gandhara
3. Kosala
4. Magadha

A. 1, 2 and 3 **B.** 2 and 3 only
C. 1, 3 and 4 **D.** 3 and 4 only

Q.20 Who invented the safety brake, which stops the elevator from crashing?

A. Thomas Edison **B.** Eli Whitney
C. Henry Ford **D.** Elisha Otis

Q.21 India ranked ______ rank in IMD's competitiveness rankings:

A. 44th **B.** 45th **C.** 49th **D.** 43rd

Q.22 The 44th session of the World Heritage Committee of UNESCO held in ____
A. Fuzhou, Fujian province China
B. Tbilisi, Georgia
C. Yerevan, Armenia
D. Kyiv, Ukraine

Q.23 Which country has unveiled a new political map that includes Jammu and Kashmir as part of the country's territory for the first time?
A. China   **B.** Afghanistan
C. Nepal   **D.** Pakistan

Q.24 Who was recently reappointed as the Inspector General of Border Security Force (BSF)?
A. V K Johri
B. Abhinav Kumar
C. Rajeev Rai
D. Arun Kumar Sharma

Q.25 In August 2020, the Defence Ministry has signed an MoU with which IIT and DARPG to develop artificial intelligence and machine learning techniques to conduct predictive analysis of public grievances?
A. IIT Kanpur   **B.** IIT Kharagpur
C. IIT Madras   **D.** IIT Roorkee

Q.26 Who has been appointed as New York City's new health commissioner by Mayor Bill de Blasio in August 2020?
A. Dr. Subhash Jain
B. Dr. Dave A Chokshi
C. Dr. Valluvan Jeevanandam
D. Dr. Rahul Kumar Nath

Q.27 Which of the following has launched a new platform, 'Secure Connected Digital Experience', to help enterprises adopt and rebuild their organizations in a post-COVID-19 world?
A. Airtel
B. Reliance Industries
C. MTNL
D. Tata Communications

Q.28 Which of the following has announced the launch of its Favipiravir in India under the brand name Covihalt for the treatment of mild to moderate COVID-19?
A. Sun Pharma   **B.** Lupin Limited
C. Biocon   **D.** Aurobindo Pharma

Q.29 Indian Railways has further revised its Freight Policy during Unlock 3 to promote economical activities. A concession of how much percent is given for loading in open wagons covered with Tarpaulin?
A. 30   **B.** 35   **C.** 40   **D.** 45

Q.30 Name the American computer scientist who worked in the 1960s on Computer Time-Sharing System which allowed multiple users in different locations to access a single computer simultaneously through telephone lines, passed away recently.

A. Dennis Ritchie   **B.** Fernando Corbato
C. Larry Page   **D.** John McCarthy

Q.31 In which state, HRD Minister Ramesh Pokhriyal Nishank and the CM of the state have laid the foundation stone of IIM?
A. Himachal Pradesh   **B.** Bihar
C. Punjab   **D.** Uttar Pradesh

Q.32 Autistic pride day recognizes the importance of pride for autistics and understands it not as a disease but as a difference. It is being observed on which date every year?
A. 19th June   **B.** 17th June
C. 18th June   **D.** 12th June

Q.33 The Government of which state has constituted its State Finance Commission recently?
A. UP   **B.** Andhra Pradesh
C. Orissa   **D.** Telangana

Q.34 DD Assam 24×7 channel has been launched by whom through video conferencing in August 2020?
A. Amit Shah   **B.** Arvind Kejriwal
C. Piyush Goyal   **D.** Prakash Javadekar

Q.35 Ebrahim Alkazi passed away in August 2020. He was related to which of the following fields?
A. Politics   **B.** Theatre
C. Real Estate   **D.** Cricket

Q.36 Since its inception in 1974, World Environment Day is celebrated every year on:
A. 04th June   **B.** 08th June
C. 06th June   **D.** 05th June

Q.37 The World Bank retained its forecast of India's growth rate at ____________ for the current financial Year 2020-21.
A. 7.1%   **B.** 7.6%   **C.** 7.2%   **D.** 3.2%

Q.38 What is the theme of World Environment Day 2020?
A. Air pollution
B. Seven Billion People, One Planet, Consume with Care
C. Raise Your Voice Not the Sea Level
D. Biodiversity

Q.39 Indian Army has developed India's first indigenous 9mm Machine Pistol along with which among the following organizations?
A. DRDO
B. HAL
C. Mahindra
D. TATA Advanced Systems

Q.40 The report on 'Benchmarking India's Payment Systems' which was released mentions that the country is "strong" in areas like having necessary laws and cash in circulation per capita. Which organization has releases the report on 'Benchmarking India's Payment Systems'?
A. SEBI   **B.** Finance Ministry
C. NABARD   **D.** RBI

Q.41 Name the person, who got the red carpet treatment at Japan's Imperial Palace where he made history, becoming the first world leader to meet with the new emperor of Japan Naruhito?

A. Angela Merkel   B. Dmitry Medvedev
C. Vladimir Putin   D. Donald Trump

Q.42 Who has launched the Sahakar Cooptube NCDC Channel in August 2020?
A. Narendra Singh Tomar
B. K. Chandrashekar Rao
C. Amit Shah
D. Piyush Goyal

Q.43 The nation pays homage to first Prime Minister Pandit Jawaharlal Nehru on his __________ death anniversary on 27th May 2020.

A. 56th   B. 54th   C. 57th   D. 55th

Q.44 Which country announced to impose a gradual ban on using wild animals in circuses?
A. Russia
B. United States of America
C. France
D. Germany

Q.45 __________ unveiled the calendar for the "Artemis" program that will return astronauts to the Moon for the first time in half a century, including eight scheduled launches and a mini-station in lunar orbit by 2024.
A. NASA
B. ISRO
C. JAXA
D. European Space Agency

Q.46 The salary and allowances of the Governor are charged to
A. The Consolidated Fund of India
B. The Consolidated Fund of the State
C. The Contingency Fund of India
D. None of the above

Q.47 Can a person act as Governor of more than one state?
A. Yes
B. No
C. Only for a period of six months
D. Only for a period of one year

Q.48 What makes the Judiciary the guardian of the Constitution?
A. Independence   B. Service conditions
C. Salary   D. Judicial Review

Q.49 In the Supreme Court of India, the number of Judges including the Chief Justice is now?

A. 20   B. 21   C. 30   D. 34

Q.50 Sunita Lakra, who announced her retirement recently, is a famous Indian player of which Sports?
A. Tennis   B. Badminton
C. Hockey   D. Cricket

Reasoning

Q.51 Direction: Find out a set of numbers amongst the four sets given in the alternatives, which is the most like the set given in the question.

$$(18,45,63)$$

A. (2,7,8)   B. (2,9,16)
C. (3,21,24)   D. (4,16,18)

Q.52 In the following question, select the related number pair from the given alternatives :

$$8:9:56:?$$

A. 90   B. 73   C. 72   D. 89

Q.53 In a certain code PRUNE is written as 2*#60 and SAINT as ?7=6@, then how is IRATE written in that code ?

A. =*70@   B. =*7@0   C. *=7@0   D. 6*7@ 0

Q.54 What should come in place of question mark (?) in the following number series?

| 132 | 156 | ? | 210 | 240 | 272 |

A. 196   B. 182   C. 199   D. 204

Q.55 If FRISKED is coded as HTKUMGF, then how will SUN be coded as?

A. UWP   B. RGZ   C. KMJ   D. ZBF

Q.56 If the day on 1 June 2001 was Friday then what will be the day on 1 June 2002?

A. Saturday   B. Wednesday
C. Friday   D. Monday

Q.57 Identify the diagram that best represents the relationship between the given classes.

Staff, Manager, Worker

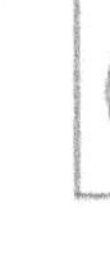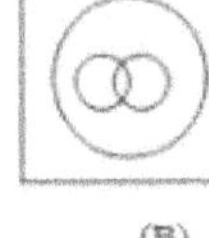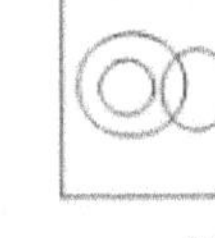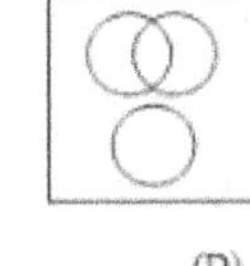

A. A   B. B   C. C   D. D

Q.58 When Anil saw Manish, he recalled "he is the son of the father of my wife". Who is Manish to Anil?
A. Brother-in-law   B. Brother
C. Cousin   D. Uncle

Q.59 Choose proper signs on the place of * to produce the resultant figure-

$$31 * 1 * 2 * 1 = 30$$

A. ×÷×   B. − +÷   C. + −×   D. − ÷ +

Q.60 Arrange the following words as per the order in the dictionary
1. RESIGN
2. REPAIR
3. RESIDUE

4. RESEARCH

5. RESCUE

A. 4, 5, 3, 1, 2   **B.** 2, 5, 4, 3, 1

C. 2, 5, 4, 1, 3   **D.** 5, 4, 3, 1, 2

Q.61 In each of the following letter series, some of the letters are missing which are given in that order as one of the alternatives below it. Choose the correct alternative.

_ acca _ ccca _ acccc _ aaa

A. acca   **B.** ccaa   **C.** caaa   **D.** caac

Q.62 What will come in place of the question mark (?) in the following number series?

$$4, 8, 24, 96, (?)$$

A. 180   **B.** 480   **C.** 280   **D.** 300

Q.63 Direction: In the following question some statements followed by some conclusions based on statements, although they may differ from commonly known facts. Read all the conclusions and then decide which of the given conclusions are rationally based on the given statements.

Statements- I. No key is door.

II. All doors are pens.

III. Some pens are houses.

Conclusions- I. No key is house.

II. Some pens are doors.

A. Only I follows   **B.** Only II follows

C. None follow   **D.** Both I and II follow

Q.64 In the following question, select the related letter pair from the given alternatives.

Z, L, X, J, V, H, T, F, ?,?

A. R, E   **B.** R, D   **C.** S, E   **D.** Q, D

Q.65 Which of the answer figure is exactly the mirror image of the given figure, when the mirror is held on the line AB?

Question Figure:

Answer Figure:

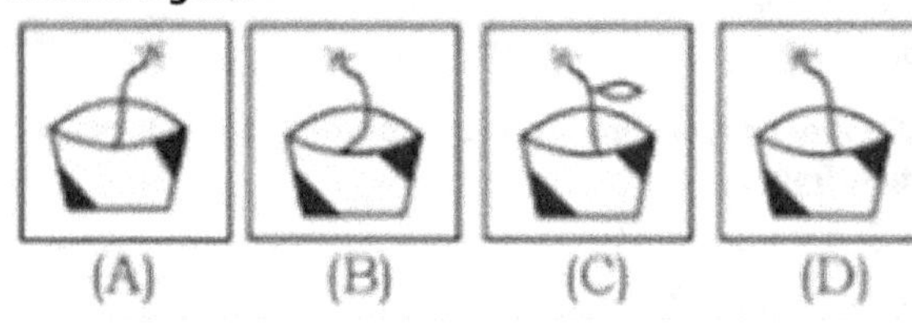

A. A   **B.** B   **C.** C   **D.** D

Q.66 Find out the missing term in the following question?

2	2	2
4	7	7
3	5	4

16	?	32

A. 36   **B.** 37   **C.** 39   **D.** 24

Q.67 From the given answer figures, select the one in which the question figure is hidden/embedded.

Question figure:

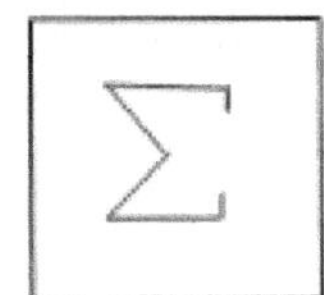

Answer figure:

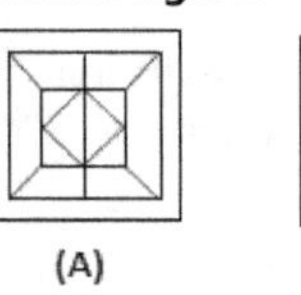 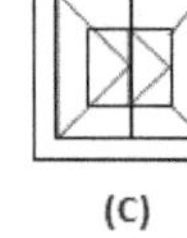 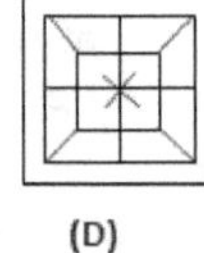

(A)   (B)   (C)   (D)

A. A   **B.** B   **C.** C   **D.** D

Q.68 A piece of paper is folded and cut as shown below in the Question figures from the given answer figures, indicates how it will appear when opened?

Question Figure:

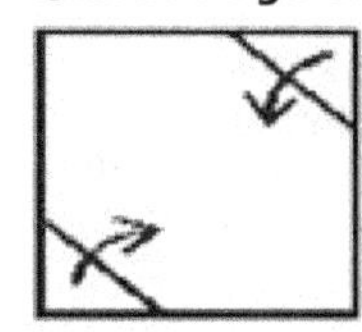 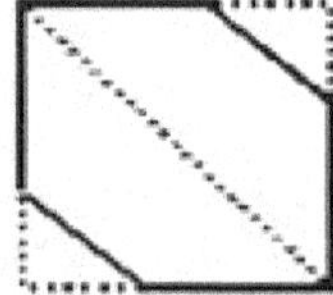 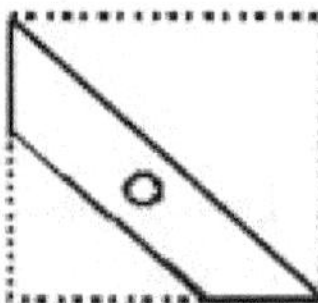

Answer Figure:

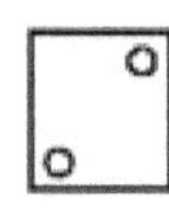 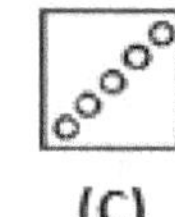 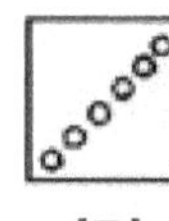

(A)   (B)   (C)   (D)

A. A   **B.** B   **C.** C   **D.** D

Q.69 Which figure will complete the question figure?

Question Figue:

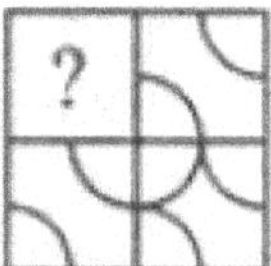

Answer Figure:

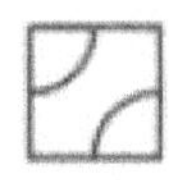  

(A)   (B)   (C)   (D)

A. A   **B.** B   **C.** C   **D.** D

Q.70 If in a code language, COULD is written as BNTKC and MARGIN is written as LZQFHM, how will MOULDING be written in that code

A. CHMFINTK   **B.** LNKTCHMD

C. LNTKCHMF   **D.** NITKHCMF

Q.71 Direction: In the following question two statements are given, which follow by conclusions I, II. You have to take the given statements to be true even if they seem to be at variance from commonly known facts. Read the conclusions and then decide which of the given conclusions logically follows from the given statements disregarding commonly known facts.

Statements:

Some banks are private.

All private are industry.

Conclusions:

I. Some banks are industry.

II. All banks are industry.

A. Only conclusion I follows.

B. Only conclusion II follows.

C. Neither conclusion I nor conclusion II follows.

D. Both conclusions follow.

Q.72 If Vikas finds that he is 16th from the right in the line of boys and 6th from the left, how many boys should be added to the line such that there are 28 boys in the line?

A. 10 **B.** 9 **C.** 8 **D.** 7

Q.73 From the given alternative words, select the word which cannot be formed using the letters of the given word.

SMOTHERS

A. THOSE **B.** METRO **C.** STORE **D.** TEARS

Q.74 In the following question, from the given alternative words, select the word which can be formed using the letters of the given word.

CAPITULATE

A. ABLE **B.** LUPIN

C. PITTY **D.** CAPITAL

Q.75 Which one set of letters when sequentially placed at the gaps in the given letter series shall complete it ?

a_b_a_ _n_bb_abbn

A. abnabb **B.** bnbban **C.** bnbbna **D.** babban

Numerical Ability

Q.76 The mean of 10 observations is 5. If 2 is added to each observation and then multiplied by 3, then what will be the new mean?

A. 5 **B.** 7 **C.** 15 **D.** 21

Q.77 A discount series of $15\%, 20\%,$ and 25% is equal to the single discount of?

A. 48% **B.** 49% **C.** 50% **D.** 51%

Q.78 A number when divided by the sum of 555 and 445 gives two times their difference as quotient and 30 as the remainder. The number is:

A. 220030 **B.** 22030 **C.** 122030 **D.** 125030

Q.79 A bike dealer sold a bike at two successive discounts of 30% and 40%. If the selling price of the bike is $Rs.\,44100$, then what is the marked price?

A. $Rs.\,105000$ **B.** $Rs.\,110000$

C. $Rs.\,108000$ **D.** $Rs.\,100000$

Q.80 In three numbers, the first is twice the second and thrice the third. If the average of these three numbers is 44, then the first number is -

A. 72 **B.** 24 **C.** 36 **D.** 44

Q.81 The Sum of two numbers is 40 and their product is 375. What will be the sum of their reciprocals?

A. $\frac{8}{75}$ **B.** $\frac{1}{40}$ **C.** $\frac{75}{8}$ **D.** $\frac{75}{4}$

Q.82 By what least number should 756 be multiplied to get a perfect cube?

A. 49 **B.** 98 **C.** 7 **D.** 14

Q.83 A, B, and C are three students. A got 18% more marks than B and 12% less than C. If B got 220 marks, then how many marks C has got?

A. 300 **B.** 295 **C.** 230 **D.** 245

Q.84 Shantanu can do a piece of work in 12 days and Manu can do the same work in 10 days. If they work together, in what ratio Shantanu and Manu will receive their wages?

A. $5:6$ **B.** $1:6$ **C.** $3:2$ **D.** $5:7$

Q.85 The ratio of two numbers is $7:11$. If the first number is decreased by 15% and the second number is increased by 30%. Then find the new ratio.

A. $7:11$ **B.** $49:167$

C. $119:286$ **D.** $98:178$

Q.86 Rohit buys two packets of balls. One contains 40 orange colour balls and other contains 60 yellow colour balls. After reaching his home, he finds that 10% of orange colour balls and 20% of yellow colour balls are defective. Find the percentage of balls that are not defective.

A. 64% **B.** 76% **C.** 78% **D.** 84%

Q.87 A boat moves downstream at the rate of 2 km in 12 minutes and upstream at the rate of 1 km in 10 minutes. Find the time taken by boat to covers 3 km in still water.

A. 22.5 minutes **B.** 20 minutes

C. 15 minutes **D.** 18 minutes

Q.88 The length of a train and that of a platform are equal. If with a speed of $135km/hr$ the train crosses the platform in one minute, then the length of the train (in meters) is-

A. 1130 **B.** 1200 **C.** 1125 **D.** 1225

Q.89 The sum of the age of Sonika and her mother is 49 years. Seven years ago, Mother's age was four times the age of Sonika. Find out the age of Sonika?

A. 35 years **B.** 21 years **C.** 12 years **D.** 14 years

Q.90 A table sold for Rs.176 earned double the profit that it would have earned if sold for Rs. 138. Find the CP of the table.

A. Rs.132 **B.** Rs.140 **C.** Rs.120 **D.** Rs.100

Computer Awareness

Q.91 .wpd file is used for-
A. Word Perfect Document
B. Word Passage Document
C. Word Perfect Documentary
D. Word Priority Document

Q.92 Name the database object in MS Access that stores a question about the data in the database?

A. Table **B.** Form **C.** Query **D.** Report

Q.93 Bar charts can be plotted on
A. Multiple data series
B. Only two data series
C. Only one data series
D. None of the above

Q.94 Which of the following is not a transmission medium?

A. Microwave systems **B.** Coaxial cable
C. Telephone lines **D.** Modem

Q.95 V-RAM is used for access to the following-

A. Video & Graphics **B.** Text & Images
C. programs **D.** None of the above

Q.96 The most important system software of a computer is the-

A. Microprocessor
B. Operating system
C. Automation Software
D. Application Software

Q.97 Which of the following can be used to navigate documents?

A. frames **B.** hyperlinks
C. web toolbar **D.** all of the above

Q.98 An excel workbook is a collection of______________.
A. Workbooks
B. Worksheets
C. Charts
D. Worksheets and charts Sheet

Q.99 A set of computer instructions designed to solve a specific problem is referred to as

A. hardware **B.** a device
C. a program **D.** a hardware concept

Q.100 What is a motion path in PowerPoint?
A. A type of animation entrance effect
B. A method of advancing slides
C. A method of moving items on a slide
D. All of the above

// Smart Answer Sheet //

Correct Indicates percentage of students who answered questions correctly.

Skipped Indicates percentage of students who skipped questions.

Q.	Ans.	Correct / Skipped	Q.	Ans.	Correct / Skipped	Q.	Ans.	Correct / Skipped	Q.	Ans.	Correct / Skipped	Q.	Ans.	Correct / Skipped
1	B	57.04 % / 17.99 %	17	A	36.85 % / 24.01 %	33	D	29.48 % / 19.68 %	49	C	27.65 % / 25.74 %	65	D	42.09 % / 29.79 %
2	C	63.15 % / 19.12 %	18	A	26.21 % / 26.62 %	34	D	32.26 % / 19.93 %	50	C	33.27 % / 25.75 %	66	C	35.38 % / 30.29 %
3	A	42.73 % / 22.56 %	19	D	16.55 % / 17.24 %	35	B	23.84 % / 25.12 %	51	C	39.27 % / 23.3 %	67	C	39.64 % / 31.19 %
4	A	56.17 % / 22.45 %	20	D	15.47 % / 14.86 %	36	D	49.67 % / 22.31 %	52	C	46.03 % / 26.57 %	68	B	31.19 % / 31.15 %
5	D	47.72 % / 25.96 %	21	D	23.63 % / 19.69 %	37	D	14.48 % / 24.73 %	53	B	51.99 % / 27.13 %	69	C	44.3 % / 27.88 %
6	D	51.56 % / 24.77 %	22	A	18.85 % / 22.26 %	38	D	28.16 % / 25.4 %	54	B	27.59 % / 30.04 %	70	C	40.18 % / 29.12 %
7	A	30.77 % / 24.56 %	23	D	37.73 % / 20.55 %	39	A	14.37 % / 26.82 %	55	A	52.49 % / 29.49 %	71	A	40.92 % / 29.17 %
8	D	20.82 % / 25.28 %	24	B	26.88 % / 18.15 %	40	D	15.77 % / 27.69 %	56	A	43.17 % / 29.14 %	72	D	42.76 % / 30.68 %
9	A	43.75 % / 25.11 %	25	A	18.05 % / 27.25 %	41	D	15.54 % / 23.5 %	57	B	33.81 % / 29.57 %	73	D	56.01 % / 28.71 %
10	C	62.57 % / 24.92 %	26	B	13.34 % / 27.85 %	42	A	21.51 % / 22.97 %	58	A	56.12 % / 29.21 %	74	D	49.63 % / 30.34 %
11	B	35.76 % / 23.32 %	27	D	22.43 % / 22.27 %	43	A	19.32 % / 24.51 %	59	C	49.78 % / 30.2 %	75	B	33.69 % / 32.03 %
12	A	51.94 % / 22.68 %	28	B	17.58 % / 22.01 %	44	C	20.87 % / 24.46 %	60	B	42.79 % / 29.82 %	76	D	22.5 % / 31.28 %
13	B	38.52 % / 21.64 %	29	C	13.53 % / 24.27 %	45	A	32.26 % / 24.05 %	61	C	30.07 % / 29.62 %	77	B	24.37 % / 30.95 %
14	B	47.97 % / 21.59 %	30	B	18.55 % / 22.28 %	46	B	30.14 % / 21.91 %	62	B	52.29 % / 29.68 %	78	A	20.74 % / 34.03 %
15	C	34.29 % / 24.62 %	31	A	27.98 % / 23.63 %	47	A	37.72 % / 24.46 %	63	B	30.55 % / 28.9 %	79	A	32.92 % / 32.5 %
16	C	38.18 % / 22.05 %	32	C	14.41 % / 24.49 %	48	D	46.04 % / 24.08 %	64	B	49.1 % / 30.01 %	80	A	19.57 % / 35.3 %

Q.	Ans.	Correct / Skipped
81	A	22.15 % / 35.75 %
82	B	14.52 % / 34.91 %
83	B	15.81 % / 36.6 %
84	A	35.74 % / 35.23 %

Q.	Ans.	Correct / Skipped
85	C	23.41 % / 36.91 %
86	D	24.41 % / 35.84 %
87	A	17.23 % / 36.43 %
88	C	22.34 % / 36.93 %

Q.	Ans.	Correct / Skipped
89	D	18.43 % / 34.65 %
90	D	18.15 % / 37.39 %
91	A	33.24 % / 24.36 %
92	C	32.47 % / 25.33 %

Q.	Ans.	Correct / Skipped
93	A	31.17 % / 26.94 %
94	D	20.05 % / 26.21 %
95	A	37.56 % / 26.72 %
96	B	40.8 % / 26.45 %

Q.	Ans.	Correct / Skipped
97	B	18.48 % / 27.2 %
98	D	32.18 % / 27.13 %
99	C	36.64 % / 27.44 %
100	C	11.72 % / 27.8 %

Performance Analysis

Avg. Score (%)	31.0%
Toppers Score (%)	100.0%
Your Score	

//Hints and Solutions//

1. The mitochondria are the powerhouse of the cell where glucose is fructified and chemical energy is produced. This energy conducts the movements of our body and gives us physical force. The energy generated in mitochondria is stored as ATP molecules.

Hence, the correct option is (B).

2. The tortoise has the longest life span among the given options.

Organism	-	Approximate Life Span
Crow	-	12 to 15 years
Parrot	-	90 to 95 years
Crocodile	-	60 to 95 years
Tortoise	-	100 to 150 years

Hence, the correct option is (C).

3. Carbon monoxide poisoning can be cured by exposing the affected person to fresh oxygen. This treatment increases oxygen levels in the blood and helps to remove CO from the blood.

Carbon monoxide is a poisonous gas that has no smell or taste. Breathing it in can make you unwell, and it can kill if you're exposed to high levels.

Hence, the Correct Option is (A).

4. At room temperature, the metal that remains liquid is Mercury. Mercury is a poor conductor of heat, but a fair conductor of electricity. Mercury has a unique electron configuration that strongly resists the removal of an electron, making it behave similarly to noble gas elements. As a result, mercury forms weak bonds and is a liquid at room temperature.

Platinum, zinc, lead are solids at room temperature.

Hence, the correct option is (A).

5. Positron is not present in a matter. A positron is the antimatter partner of an electron. It has exactly the same mass as an electron but has the opposite electric charge. The major difference between electrons is their positive charge. Positrons are formed during the decay of nuclides that have an excess of protons in their nucleus compared to the number of neutrons. When decaying takes place, these radionuclides emit a positron and a neutrino.

Therefore, the positron will not be the form of matter.

Electrons, protons, and neutrons are subatomic particles so they are part of the matter.

Hence, the correct option is (D).

6. An electric motor converts electrical energy to mechanical energy. The working principle of the electric motor mainly depends on the interaction of magnetic and electric fields. The electric motor is mainly classified into two types. The AC motor and the DC motor.

The AC motor takes alternating current as an input, whereas the DC motor takes direct current.

Hence, the correct option is (D).

7. A solid cannot change its shape easily compared to a liquid because of the stronger inter-molecular force.

In solids, the particles are arranged in a regular pattern, touching each other. They attract each other with a strong force (because they are so small and so close). This means that they cannot change places. So solids cannot change their shape.

Hence, the correct option is (A).

8. The father of Geometry is Euclid. Euclid was an ancient Greek mathematician in Alexandria, Egypt. Due to his groundbreaking work in math, he is often referred to as the 'Father of Geometry'. Euclid's most well-known collection of works, called Elements, outlines some of the most fundamental principles of geometry.

Hence, the correct option is (D).

9. The percentage of the earth's surface covered by India is 2.4%. India is the 7th largest country in the world by area. According to the Ministry of Home Affairs, Government of India, the area of India is 3,287,469 square km or 1,269,298 square miles.

Hence, the correct option is (A).

10. Goa is India's smallest state by area and the fourth-smallest by population. Goa has the highest GDP per capita among all Indian states, two and a half times that of the country.

The land area of Goa is 1,429 square miles (3,702 square km).

Hence, the correct option is (C).

11. Ice glacier's melting is a common phenomenon linked to the rise in seawater level. The glaciers are predominantly present in Antarctica. Most of the world's glacial ice is found in Antarctica, but glaciers are found on nearly every continent, even Africa. One of today's prevalent water issues is the rise in sea level.

It is mainly caused by two phenomena: global warming and ozone depletion.

Polar ice caps in Antarctica and other places are melting fast. This has led to an increase in sea level over the years.

Hence, the correct option is (B).

12. Samudra Gupta (335-375 AD) of the Gupta dynasty is known as the Napoleon of India. Historian A V Smith called him so because of his great military conquests known from the 'Prayag Prashati' written by his courtier and poet Harisena, who also describes him as the hero of a hundred battles.

Hence, the correct option (A).

13. Swaraj Party was formed by Motilal Nehru and Chittaranjan Das. Swaraj Party was a political party formed in India in January 1923 after the Gaya annual conference in December 1922 of the National Congress that sought greater self-government and political freedom for the Indian people from the British Raj. It was inspired by the concept of Swaraj. The two most important leaders were Chittaranjan Das, who was its president, and Motilal Nehru, who was its secretary.

Hence, the correct option is (B).

14. The Comptroller and Auditor General (CAG) of India is appointed by the President of India under Article 148 of the constitution. The CAG audits all receipts and expenditures of the union and state government. The CAG also acts as the external auditor for the government-owned companies.

Hence, the correct option is (B).

15. In India, the bicameral legislature is a legislative system that consists of two-tier assemblies, chambers, or houses. It consists of a lower and an upper chamber. Parliament or central legislature of India is a bicameral legislature.

Hence, the correct option is (C).

16. The top five methods for estimating national income:

(i) The census of products method

(ii) The census of income method

(iii) The expenditure method

(iv) Social accounting method

(v) Mixed or combined method

Hence, the correct option is (C).

17. The first Round Table Conference convened by Labour Government Prime Minister Ramsay McDonald from 12 November 1930 to 19 January 1931 in London. The Round Table Conference officially inaugurated by His Majesty George V on November 12, 1930, in the Royal Gallery House of Lords in London.

Hence, the correct option is (A).

18. The Rashtrakutas (755 - 975 AD) were of Kannada origin and the Kannada language was their mother tongue. Rashtrakuta was a royal dynasty ruling large parts of the Indian subcontinent between the sixth and 10th centuries. The earliest known Rashtrakuta inscription is a 7th-century copper plate grant detailing their rule from Manapura, a city in Central or West India.

Hence, the correct option is (A).

19. Buddha born in Lumbini in the Kosala kingdom. Buddh died in Kusinara, in Magadha kingdom. Avanti lay outside the area visited by Buddha and was converted to his teaching by his disciple Mahakaccana. Gandhara is the western part of Pakistan & Afghanistan, where Buddha never went.

Hence, the correct option is (D).

20. In 1852, Elisha Graves Otis invented a safety brake that revolutionized the vertical transport industry. Elevators also have a safety brake that is attached to the underside of the car. This is the innovation that made the passenger elevator possible when it was unveiled at the 1853-54 World's Fair in New York.

Hence, the correct option (D).

21. India ranked 43rd rank in IMD's competitiveness rankings. India continues to remain ranked 43rd on an annual World Competitiveness Index compiled by Institute for Management Development (IMD) with some traditional weaknesses like poor infrastructure and insufficient education investment keeping its ranking low, Singapore has retained its top position on the 63-nation list.

Hence, the correct option is (D).

22. The 44th session of the World Heritage Committee of UNESCO has been postponed due to the impact of the COVID-19 pandemic. The session which will be hosted by the Chinese government was scheduled to be held in Fuzhou of eastern China's Fujian Province from 29th June to 9th July 2020.

Hence, the correct option is (A).

23. Pakistan PM Imran Khan has unveiled a "new political map" of Pakistan that includes Jammu and Kashmir as part of the country's territory for the first time.

Furthermore, the new map also shows Siachen as a part of Pakistan. The Indian government has described it as 'political absurdity' The map also includes parts of Western Gujarat.

Hence, the correct option is (D).

24. The Appointments Committee of the Cabinet recently approved the reappointment of Abhinav Kumar, IPS as the Inspector General (IG) of Border Security Force (BSF) and extended his tenure up to July 2021, following the proposal by the Home affairs ministry. Border Security Force is the national border defence force and also the largest border defence force in the world.

Hence, the correct option is (B).

25. In August 2020, the Defence Ministry signed an MoU with IIT Kanpur and DARPG to develop artificial intelligence and machine learning techniques to conduct a predictive analysis of public grievances. It will develop artificial intelligence and machine learning techniques to conduct predictive analysis of public grievances.

The project is expected to help the Ministry to identify the cause and nature of grievances and bring about systemic changes.

Hence, the correct option is (A).

26. Dr. Dave A Chokshi has been appointed as New York City's new health commissioner by Mayor Bill de Blasio in August 2020.

Chokshi was named Commissioner of the City's Department of Health and Mental Hygiene after serving health commissioner Dr. Oxiris Barbot resigned from her post.

Hence, the correct option is (B).

27. Tata Communications has launched a new platform to help enterprises adopt and rebuild their organizations in a post-COVID-19 world. The 'Secure Connected Digital Experience' (SCDx) will help companies by providing a solution that helps with various aspects like contactless experiences for employees and supply chain partners, shift to digital commerce, and a digital workplace solution.

Hence, the correct option is (D).

28. Lupin Limited has announced the launch of its Favipiravir in India under the brand name Covihalt for the treatment of mild to moderate COVID-19. It is available as 200 mg tablets in the form of a strip of 10 tablets and priced at Rs. 49 per tablet. Favipiravir has received authorization from the Drug Controller General of India (DCGI) for emergency use.

Hence, the correct option is (B).

29. Indian Railways has further revised its Freight Policy during Unlock 3 to promote economic activities. A concession of 40 percent is given for loading in open wagons covered with Tarpaulin.

Hence, the correct option is (C).

30. American computer scientist Fernando Corbato passed away on 21 July 2019. He worked in the 1960s on Computer Time-Sharing System which allowed multiple users in different locations to access a single computer simultaneously through telephone lines which paved the way for the personal computer and the computer passwords. Fernando Corbato was a professor emeritus at the Massachusetts Institute of Technology.

Hence, the correct option is (B).

31.

- In Himachal Pradesh, HRD Minister Ramesh Pokhriyal Nishank, and CM Jai Ram Thakur have laid the foundation stone of IIM at Dhaula Kuan in Sirmour district.

- The first phase of this Institute would be completed by spending an amount of 392.51 crore rupees.

- New courses offered by the institute would open new horizons to the students.

Hence, the correct option is (A).

32. Autistic Pride Day is being observed on 18th June every year. Autistic pride recognizes the importance of pride for autistics and understands it not as a disease but as a difference. Autistic Pride Day was initiated by Aspies For Freedom, a group that raises public awareness about autism rights.

Hence, the correct option is (C).

33. Telangana, the newest state of India, was formed out of Andhra Pradesh in June 2014. It constituted its 1st State Finance Commission (SFC) in December 2017.

Finance Commission is a constitutional body under Article 280 created every five years to recommend the transfer of financial resources from the Centre to the States. The Commission also decides the principles on which grants-in-aid will be given to the States.

Hence, the correct option is (D).

34. Union Minister for 'Information and Broadcasting' Shri Prakash Javadekar launched DD Assam 24×7, a 24-hour dedicated channel for the state, via video conferencing from New Delhi on 4 August 2020.

All northeastern states have state-specific Doordarshan channels that can be viewed anywhere in India.

Hence, the correct option is (D).

35. Ebrahim Alkazi passed away in August 2020. He was related to the theatre fields.

Alkazi, credited for revolutionizing theatre in India, became one of the most prominent theatre artists in Mumbai during the 1940s and 1950s. He later moved to Delhi and served as the director of the National School of Drama (NSD) for the next 15 years (1962 to 1977) the longest tenure ever in the history of the institute.

Hence, the correct option is (B).

36. Since its inception in 1974, World Environment Day is celebrated every year on June 5th in more than 100 countries. The theme for World Environment Day 2020 is, 'Time for Nature,' with a focus on its role in providing the essential infrastructure that supports life on Earth and human development.

Hence, the correct option is (D).

37. India's economy to contract by 3.2 percent in the fiscal year 2020-21. The World Bank revised its January projection on India by a massive negative to contract 3.2% in the current fiscal year, a sharp downgrade from its.

Hence, the correct option is (D).

38. The World Environment Day 2020's theme is 'Celebrate Biodiversity', and it will be hosted in Colombia, in partnership with Germany. The theme is extremely relevant because human beings are part of the ecosystem and cannot continue to survive in isolation.

Hence, the correct option is (D).

39. India's first indigenous 9mm Machine Pistol has been jointly developed by the Indian Army and the Defence Research and Development Organisation (DRDO). This was informed by the Defence Ministry on January 14, 2021.

Hence, the correct option is (A).

40. RBI Releases Report On 'Benchmarking India's Payment Systems'.The report on 'Benchmarking India's Payment Systems' which was released mentions that the country is "strong" in areas like having necessary laws and cash in circulation per capita. The report provides a comparative position of the payment system ecosystem in India relative to comparable payment systems and usage trends in other major countries. The report adds that India needs to make more efforts to decrease the volume of paper clearing and increase acceptance infrastructure to promote digital payments.

Hence, the correct option is (D).

41. US President Donald Trump got the red carpet treatment at Japan's Imperial Palace where he made history, becoming the first world leader to meet with the new emperor of Japan Naruhito.

Angela Merkel, a member of the Christian Democratic Union, is the first female Chancellor of Germany.

Dmitry Medvedev is a Russian politician serving as Deputy Chairman of the Security Council of Russia since 2020. Medvedev served as President of Russia from 2008 to 2012 and Prime Minister to Vladimir Putin from 2012 to 2020.

Vladimir Putin is a Russian politician and a former officer of the KGB who has served as President of Russia since 2012, previously holding the position from 1999 until 2008.

Hence, the correct option is (D).

42. Agriculture Minister Narendra Singh Tomar has launched the Sahakar Cooptube NCDC Channel. It is a new initiative by the National Cooperative Development Corporation.

The Minister also launched guidance videos produced by NCDC on 'Formation and Registration of a Cooperative' for eighteen different states in Hindi and regional languages.

The Channel aims to facilitate the involvement of the youth in the cooperative movement. Cooperatives lend strength to farmers to minimize risks in agriculture and allied sectors and act as a shield against exploitation.

Hence, the correct option is (A).

43. The nation pays homage to first Prime Minister Pandit Jawaharlal Nehru on his 56th death anniversary on 27th May 2020. Jawaharlal Nehru was the first Prime Minister of India. Jawaharlal Nehru emerged as an eminent leader of the Indian independence movement under the tutelage of Mahatma Gandhi.

Nehru was born in Allahabad (now Prayagraj) on November 14, 1889. He died in Delhi on May 27, 1964.

Hence, the correct option is (A).

44. France announced to impose a gradual ban on using wild animals in circuses. The Environment Minister of France has announced that it would impose a gradual ban on using wild animals including bears, tigers, lions, and elephants in circuses.

It also includes the ban on keeping dolphins and killer whales in captivity in marine parks and raising mink on fur farms. However, the ban does not apply to wild animals in other permanent shows and in zoos.

Hence, the correct option is (C).

45. NASA unveiled the calendar for the "Artemis" program that will return astronauts to the Moon for the first time in half a century, including eight scheduled launches and a mini-station in lunar orbit by 2024.

Hence, the correct option is (A).

46. Under Article 266 (1) of the Constitution of India, a Consolidated State Fund is constituted. Salaries and allowances of the Governor of the Indian state are recovered from the Consolidated Fund of the states.

Hence, the correct option is (B).

47. Normally, there is a Governor for each State but the Constitution (7th amendment) Act 1956, makes it possible to appoint the same person as the Governor for two or more States (Article 153).

Hence, the correct option is (A).

48. Judicial Review makes the Judiciary the guardian of the Constitution. The Supreme Court prohibits the House from enacting any law that violates any provision of the Constitution. The Supreme Court is also the protector of our fundamental rights. This power of the Supreme Court is called judicial review. If a law violates any provision of the Constitution, it can declare the related law null and void.

Hence, the correct option is (D).

49. Currently, In the Supreme Court of India, the number of Judges including the Chief Justice is 30 (including the Chief Justice of India) and a maximum probable power of 34. As per the Constitution of India, judges of the Supreme Court retire at age of 65. Justice Sharad Arvind Bobde is the 47th Chief Justice of India.

Hence, the correct option is (C).

50. Former Indian Hockey team captain and the team's defender Sunita Lakra recently announced her retirement from International Hockey citing her knee injuries on 2 January 2020.

In the 2018, Asian Champions Trophy, India bagged second place under her captaincy. She was also a part of the Indian team that participated in the Rio Olympics, 2016. Though she could not participate in the Tokyo Olympics, Sunita will hopefully return to play domestic Hockey after her knee surgery.

Hence, the correct option is (C).

51. In the given question, 18 is the first number and the difference between the third and the second number is equal to the first number. So, in option (C), the same pattern follows i.e., the difference between the third and the second number is 3, which is the first number.

Hence, the correct option is (C).

52. Given sequence $= 8:9:56:?$

The pattern followed is $= n(n-1)$

$$\Rightarrow 8(8-1) = 8 \times 7 = 56$$

Similarly, $9(9-1) = 9 \times 8 = 72$

Hence, the correct option is (C).

53. The common letter in PRUNE and SAINT is N and the common digit is 6 which is below N in both the words. Therefore, every alphabet is assigned the number written below it.

PRUNE $\Rightarrow$ 2*#60

SAINT $\Rightarrow$?7=6@

So, after decoding IRATE become $\Rightarrow$ =*7@0

Hence, the correct option is (B).

54. The given series follows a logic that

11 × 12, 12 × 13, 13 × 14, 14 × 15, 15 × 16,.....

So the missing number is 13 × 14 = 182

Hence, the correct option is (B).

55. In this question, there are the following patterns:

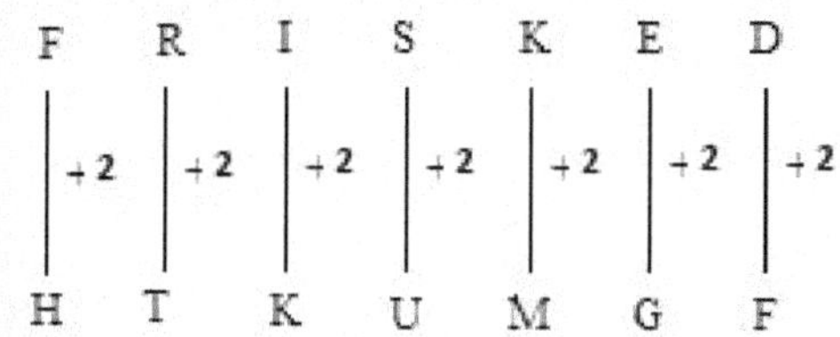

Similarly,

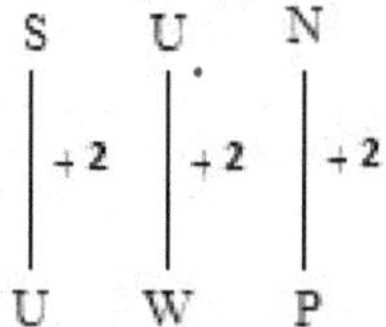

Hence, the correct option is (A).

56. An only 1-year gap is there between given years and it will be called a Normal Year because in both years 29 February will not come.

$\dfrac{364}{7} = 52$, one day is extra, hence on 1st June 2002, it will be Saturday.

Hence, the correct option is (A).

57. Some workers may be managers and vice – versa.

All workers and managers are staff.

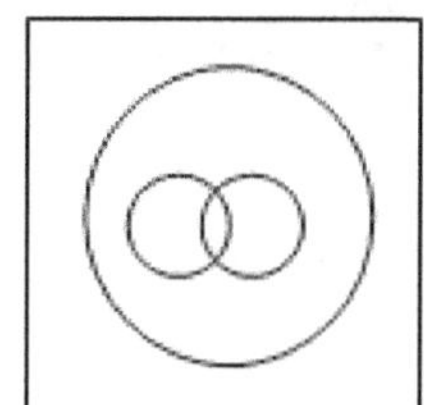

Hence, the correct option is (B).

58. According to the question,

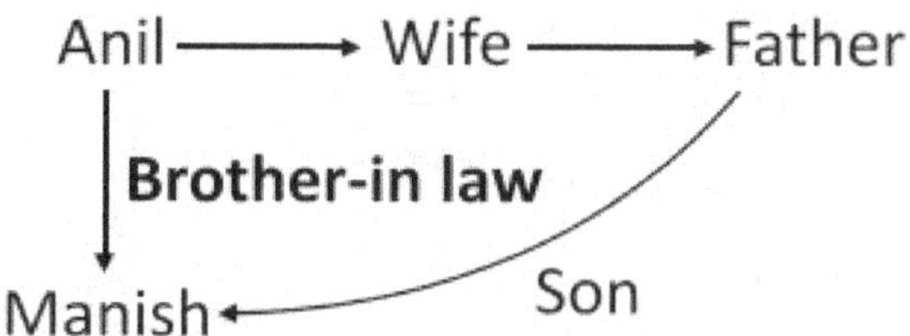

So, Manish is the brother-in-law of Anil.

Hence, the correct option is (A).

59. Given,

$31 * 1 * 2 * 1 = 30$

Solve according to the option, we get:

$31 + 1 - 2 \times 1 = 30$

$31 \times 1 \div 2 \times 1 = 15.5$

$31 - 1 + 2 \div 1 = 32$

$31 - 1 \div 2 + 1 = 31.5$

Hence, the correct option is (C).

60. On arranging words according to dictionary:

REPAIR → RESCUE → RESEARCH → RESIDUE → RESIGN

Hence, the correct option is (B).

61. The series is ca / ccaa / cccaaa / ccccaaaa.

Hence, the correct option is (C).

62. $4,8,24,96,\ldots\ldots$

The pattern is

$4 \times 2 = 8$

$8 \times 3 = 24$

$24 \times 4 = 96$

$96 \times 5 = 480$

Hence, the correct option is (B).

63.

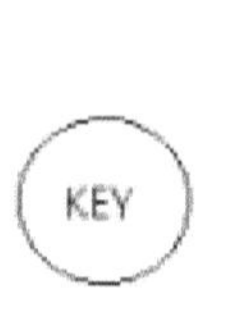
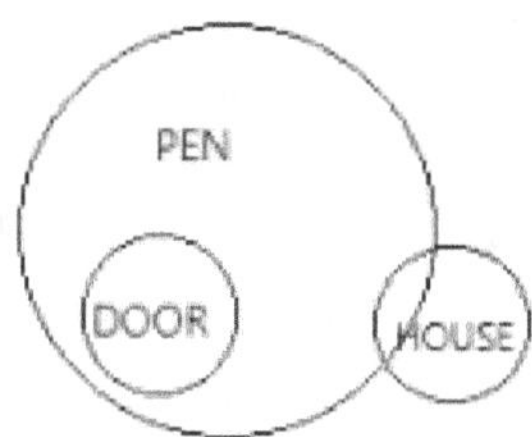

Hence, the correct option is (B).

64. Here is two series

$$Z \xrightarrow{-2} X \xrightarrow{-2} V \xrightarrow{-2} T \xrightarrow{-2} R$$
$$L \xrightarrow{-2} J \xrightarrow{-2} H \xrightarrow{-2} F \xrightarrow{-2} D$$

Hence, the correct option is (B).

65. A mirror image is a reflected duplication of an object that appears almost identical but is reversed in the direction perpendicular to the mirror surface.

When the mirror is placed on the AB line then the mirror image of the given image will be formed:

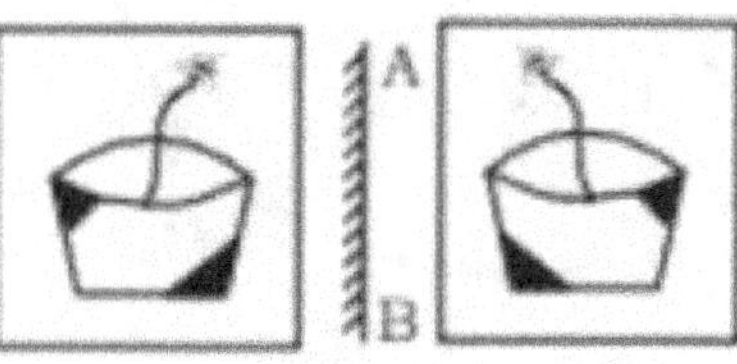

Hence, the correct option is (D).

66. $4 \times 3 = 12 + (2)^2 = 16$

$7 \times 5 = 35 + (2)^2 = 39$

$7 \times 4 = 28 + (2)^2 = 32$

Hence, the correct option is (C).

67. In the following figure, the question figure is embedded.

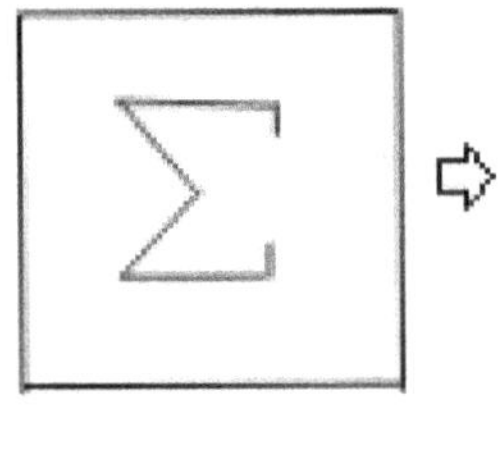

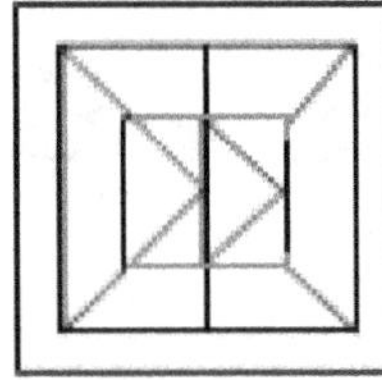

(C)

Hence, the correct option is (C).

68.

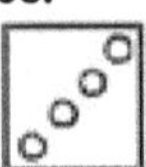

Hence, the correct option is (B).

69. Figure (C) will complete the question figure and would look like this

Hence, the correct option is (C).

70. Each letter in the word is moved one step backward to obtain the corresponding letter of the code.

MOULDING → LNTKCHMF

Hence, The correct option is (C).

71.

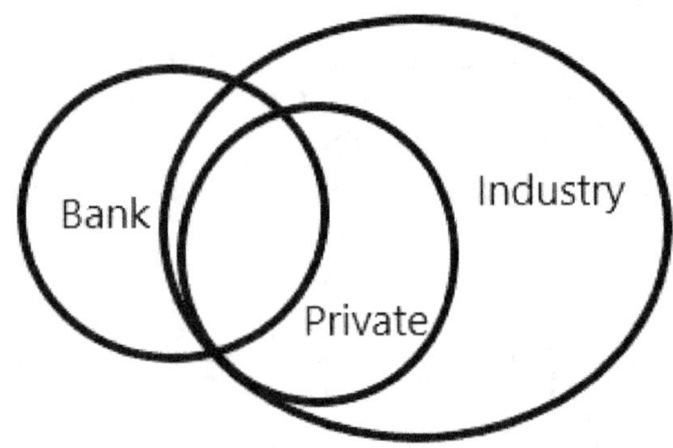

Hence, the correct option is (A).

72.

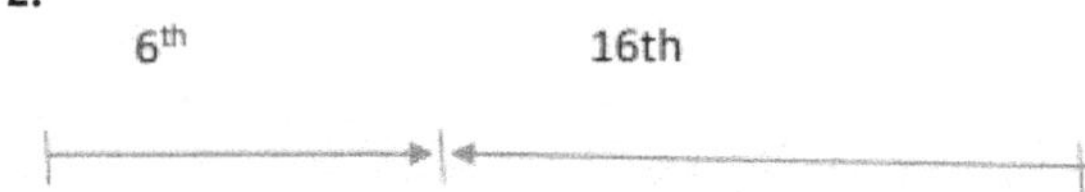

The number of boys in the line = (6 + 16) − 1 = 21

Number of boys to be added to make 28 boys = 28 − 21 = 7

Hence, the correct option is (D).

73. The word 'TEARS' cannot be formed because the letter 'A' is not present in the given word SMOTHERS.

Hence, the correct option is (D).

74. Given,

CAPITULATE

There is no 'B' letter in the given word. Therefore, the word ABLE cannot be formed.

There is no 'N' letter in the given word. Therefore, the word LUPIN cannot be formed.

There is no 'Y' letter in the given word. Therefore, the word PITTY cannot be formed.

Hence, the correct option is (D).

75.

$$a\,\boxed{b}\,b\,\boxed{n}\,/\,a\,\boxed{bb}\,n\,/\,\boxed{a}\,bb\,\boxed{n}\,/\,abbn$$

So the words will be added in the following way,

bnbban

Hence, the correct option is (B).

76. Given:

Mean $= 5$

Number of observations $= 10$

We know that,

$$\text{Mean} = \frac{\text{Sum of observations}}{\text{Number of observations}}$$

$\therefore$ Sum of observations $= 5 \times 10 = 50$

Now 2 added to each observation,

$\therefore$ Sum $= 50 + (10 \times 2) = 70$

Now each observation multiplied by 3,

$\therefore$ New sum $= 70 \times 3 = 210$

$$\text{New mean} = \frac{\text{New sum}}{\text{Number of observations}}$$

$$= \frac{210}{10}$$

$$= 21$$

Hence, the correct option is (D).

77. Equivalent Discount = $A + B - \dfrac{AB}{100}$

where, A = First Discount, B = Second Discount.

Single equivalent discount for 15% and 20%

$= \left(20 + 15 - \dfrac{20 \times 15}{100}\right)\%$

$= (35 - 3)\% = 32\%$

Single equivalent discount for 32% and 25%

$= \left(32 + 25 - \dfrac{32 \times 25}{100}\right)\%$

$= (57 - 8) = 49\%$

Hence, the correct option is (B).

78. Let the number is N,

N is divided by the sum of 555 and 445, the quotient is 2 times difference.

Quotient = 2(555-445) = 220

Remainder = 30 (given)

N = 1000 × 220 + 30 = 220030

Hence, the correct option is (A).

79. Given:

Discounts $= 30\%$ and 40%

$SP = Rs.\,44100$

We know that,

Selling price $= \left[\dfrac{100 - discount\%}{100}\right] \times$ Marked Price

Let the marked price be x.

Selling price $= [(100 - \text{discount }\%)/100] \times$ Marked Price

$44100 = \left[\dfrac{(100-30)}{100}\right] \times \left[\dfrac{(100-40)}{100}\right] \times x$

$\Rightarrow 44100 = \left(\dfrac{7}{10}\right) \times \left(\dfrac{3}{5}\right) \times x$

$\Rightarrow x = 2100 \times 50$

$\Rightarrow x = 105000$

$\therefore$ The marked price of the bike is $Rs.\,105000$.

Hence the correct option is (A).

80. Let, the three numbers be a, b and c

According to question, $a = 2b = 3c$

Therefore, $b = \dfrac{a}{2}$ and $c = \dfrac{a}{3}$

Given, $\dfrac{a+b+c}{3} = 44$

$\Rightarrow \dfrac{a + \frac{a}{2} + \frac{a}{3}}{3} = 44$

$\Rightarrow \dfrac{11a}{18} = 44$

$\Rightarrow a = 72$

Hence, the correct option is (A).

81. Let the numbers be x and y.

According to the question,

$xy = 375$

And,

$x + y = 40$

The sum of reciprocals $= \dfrac{1}{x} + \dfrac{1}{y}$

$= \dfrac{x+y}{xy}$

$= \dfrac{40}{375}$

$= \dfrac{8}{75}$

Hence, the correct option is (A).

82. $756 = 3 \times 3 \times 3 \times 2 \times 2 \times 7$

So to make it a perfect cube we have to multiply 756 by $2 \times 7 \times 7 = 98$

least number should be $= 98$

Hence, the correct option is (B).

83. B's marks $= 220$

A got 18% more marks than B.

$\Rightarrow$ A's marks $= 220 + \left(\dfrac{18}{100} \times 220\right) = 259.6$

Also, A got 12% less marks than C

$\Rightarrow$ C's marks

$= 259.6 \times \dfrac{100}{(100-12)} = 295$

Hence, the correct option is (B).

84. Since, Shantanu and Manu are taking 12 and 10 days respectively for the same work. So,

Shantnu's 1 day work $= \dfrac{1}{12}$

Manu's 1 day work $= \dfrac{1}{10}$

Shantnu's share: Manu's share $= \dfrac{1}{12} : \dfrac{1}{10} = \dfrac{5}{60} : \dfrac{6}{60} = 5:6$

Hence, the correct option is (A).

85. Let the numbers be $7x, 11x$

According to the given condition, the new ratio of two numbers will be,

$$7x - 7x \times \frac{15}{100} : 11x + 11x \times \frac{30}{100} = 119x : 286x$$

Therefore, the ratio of the two numbers is $119 : 286$

Hence, the correct option is (C).

86. Total number of balls bought by Rohit $= 60 + 40 = 100$

Number of defective orange colour balls $= 10\%$ of $40 = 0.1 \times 40 = 4$

Number of defective yellow colour balls $= 20\%$ of $60 = 0.2 \times 60 = 12$

Total number of defective balls $= 12 + 4 = 16$

Total numbers of balls that are not defective $= 100 - 16 = 84$

Therefore, the percentage of fruits those are not defective $= \frac{84}{100} \times 100 = 84\%$

Hence, the correct option is (D).

87. Speed (km/hrs) $= \dfrac{\text{distance in } km}{\text{time in } hrs}$

Downstream speed $= \dfrac{2}{12} \times 60 = 10$ km/hrs

Upstream speed $= \dfrac{1}{10} \times 60 = 6$ km/hrs

Speed of boat in still water $\dfrac{10+6}{2} = 8$ km/hrs

Required times $= \dfrac{3}{8} \times 60 = 22.5$ minutes

Hence, the correct option is (A).

88. Let, length of train $=$ length of platform $= x$ metre

Speed of train $= 135 kmph = 135 \times \dfrac{5}{18} m/sec$

$\therefore$ Speed of train $= \dfrac{\text{Length of train and platform}}{\text{time taken in crossing}}$

$$135 \times \frac{5}{18} = \frac{x+x}{60}$$

$$2x = 225 \times 10 = 2250$$

$$x = \frac{2250}{2} = 1125m$$

length of train $= 1125m$

Hence, the correct option is (C).

89. Sonika's age 7 years ago = x

Then Sonika's mothers age = 4x

According to the question,

(x + 7) + (4x + 7) = 49

x + 7 + 4x + 7 = 49

5x = 49 -14

5x = 35 ⇒ x = 7

Current age of Sonika = 7 + 7 = 14 years.

Hence, the correct option is (D).

90. SP = 176

Let Cp = x

Profit, when sold for 138 = (138 – x)

ATQ,

Profit, when sold for 176 = 2 (138 – x)

(176 – x) = 2 (138 – x)

176 – x = 276 – 2x

x = Rs.100

Hence, the correct option is (D).

91. The .wpd file is used for Word Perfect Document.

A WPD file is a text document created by Corel Word Perfect, a popular word processor. It may contain formatted text, tables, drawn objects, and images.

Hence, the correct option is (A).

92. Databases in Access are composed of four objects i.e. tables, queries, forms, and reports. Together, these objects allow you to enter, store, analyze, and compile your data however you want. Query in the database object in MS Access stores a question about the data in the database.

Hence, the correct option is (C).

93. A bar chart uses bars to show comparisons between categories of data. These bars can be displayed horizontally or vertically. A bar graph will always have two axis. One axis will generally have numerical values, and the other will describe the types of categories being compared.

Thus, bar charts can be plotted on multiple data series.

Hence, the correct option is (A).

94. A modem is not a transmission medium out of the given options.

There are two forms of media of transmission, that is directed and unguided. Cables such as twisted pair cables, coaxial cables, and fiber optic cables are guided transmission devices. Unguided transmission devices include radar, radio waves, and microwaves, are wireless.

In the given options, all are channels of communication but a modem is a tool that transforms analog signals into digital signals or vice-versa. A modem is software allowing a computer, to transmit data over the telephone or cable lines.

Hence, the correct option is (D).

95. V-RAM is also known as video RAM. It is a dual-ported variant of dynamic RAM. V-RAM is basically RAM integrated into a card for using it for storing graphical textures, 3D models temporarily. It is used for video access and graphics.

V-RAM Stands for "Video Random Acess Memory".

Hence, the correct option is (A).

96. The most important system software package for any computer is its operating system. Every computer system runs under the control of an operating system.

Hence, the correct option is (B).

97. Hyperlinks can be used to navigate documents.

Hyperlinks are the primary method used to navigate between pages and Web sites. Links can point to other web pages, web sites, graphics, files, sounds, e-mail addresses, and other locations on the same web page. When text is used as a hyperlink, it is usually underlined and appears as a different color.

Hence, the correct option is (B).

98. A workbook is a collection of worksheets. Worksheets can also display selected data in one of a variety of chart types. When the Excel program is first opened, the user is presented with a workbook that contains three empty worksheets, also called spreadsheets.

Hence, the correct option is (D).

99. A computer program is a collection of instructions that performs a specific task when executed by a computer. Most computer devices require programs to function properly.

Hence, the correct option is (C).

100. A motion path in PowerPoint is a method of moving items on a slide. Motion Path animations determine the route (path) and the direction in which the animated slide object moves across or around on the slide. For example, you can move the slide object up, down, right, or left; on a preset or created motion path.

Hence, the correct option is (C).

General Knowledge/Current Affairs

Q.1 Demand in Economics means _____.
A.   Aggregate demand
B.   Market demand
C.   Individual demand
D.   Demand backed by purchasing power

Q.2 Which of the following is/are required to get more income by the people?
A.   Better price for their produce
B.   Continuous job
C.   Better wages
D.   All options are correct

Q.3 According to which fundamental right 'All persons are equal before law'?
A.   Rights to freedom
B.   Cultural and Educational Rights
C.   Right to Equality
D.   Right against Exploitation

Q.4 Directive principles of state policy are enumerated in which part of Indian Constitution?
A. Part I   B. Part II   C. Part III   D. Part IV

Q.5 In the last years of his reign, Akbar was distracted by the rebellion of Prince Salim, who later became the future emperor _____.
A. Aurangzeb   B. Jahangir
C. Shahjahan   D. Bahadur Shah

Q.6 In 1824 the sepoys refused to go to which place to fight for the East India Company by sea route?
A. United Kingdom   B. Burma
C. France   D. Italy

Q.7 What is the season during summer solstice in the Northern Hemisphere?
A. Winter   B. Summer   C. Spring   D. Autumn

Q.8 Which mountains separate Asia from Europe?
A. Himalayas   B. Andes
C. Ural   D. Rocky

Q.9 Which of the following prevents collapsing of trachea?
A. Diaphragm   B. Ribs
C. Cartilaginous discs   D. Muscles

Q.10 The tricuspid valve occurs between the _____.
A.   Right auricle and right ventricle
B.   Pulmonary aorta
C.   Corotic-systemic aorta and left ventricle
D.   Left ventricle

Q.11 Which category of compound is the most concentrated energy source?
A. Lipid   B. Starch   C. Proteins   D. Vitamins

Q.12 The focal length of a plane mirror is _____.
A. positive   B. negative   C. zero   D. infinity

Q.13 What constitutes the current in a metal wire?
A. Electrons   B. Protons
C. Neutrons   D. None of these

Q.14 What is UBUNTU?
A.   Operating System
B.   Programming Language
C.   Microprocessor
D.   None of these

Q.15 Isotopes of an element do not have _____.
A.   The Same number of electrons
B.   The same physical properties
C.   The same chemical properties
D.   The same number of protons

Q.16 Gold is alloyed with which metal to make it harder?
A. Cu   B. Sn   C. Al   D. C

Q.17 Which Ministry has recently launched the Cyber Security Grand Challenge award?
A.   Ministry of Defence
B.   Ministry of Communications
C.   Ministry of Human Resource Development
D.   Ministry of Electronics and Information Technology

Q.18 Pradhan Mantri Jeevan Jyoti Bima Yojana (PMJJBY) is available to all citizens between the ages of 18 to _____ years.
A. 50   B. 60   C. 75   D. 80

Q.19 Who invented the internet?
A. Steve Jobs   B. Jaap Haartsen
C. Jan Kourn   D. Vint Cerf

Q.20 'Skeet' is associated with which sport?
A. Running   B. Cycling
C. Shooting   D. Swimming

Q.21 Mohiniattam is a classical dance form which state?
A. Kerala   B. Goa
C. Maharashtra   D. Karnataka

Q.22 Shivajirao Patil Nilangekar passed away in August 2020. He was the former CM of which state?
A. Gujarat   B. Maharashtra
C. Punjab   D. Nagaland

Q.23 Who is the author of the book named "Not Just an Accountant"?

A. Raghuram Rajan **B.** Vinod Rai

C. Achal Kumar Jyoti **D.** C. S. Karnan

Q.24 Association of South East Asian Nations (ASEAN) is a group of 10 South Asian nations which came into existence after _____ declaration.

A. Vienna **B.** Kyoto

C. Bangkok **D.** Singapore

Q.25 Which dam is called the Afghan India Friendship Dam?

A. Sawalkot **B.** Barighat

C. Salma **D.** Upper Karnali

Q.26 BrahMos Aerospace is a joint venture company owned by the governments of India and which of the following country?

A. Russia **B.** USA **C.** Iraq **D.** Israel

Q.27 Who unveiled a plaque to mark the laying of the foundation stone and also released a commemorative postal stamp on Shree Ram Janmabhoomi Mandir, in August 2020?

A. Amit Shah **B.** Yogi Adityanath

C. Ram Nath Kovind **D.** Narendra Modi

Q.28 In August 2020, the International Financial Services Centres Authority has constituted a committee of how many members to suggest ways to enhance international retail participation in IFSC?

A. 3 **B.** 5 **C.** 7 **D.** 9

Q.29 In 2020, the Andhra Pradesh government has signed a pact with which of the following companies for marketing and technology support for economic empowerment of women?

A. Hindustan Unilever Ltd

B. ITC

C. Procter and Gamble

D. All of the above

Q.30 A group of researchers from IIT Kharagpur has been conferred the 'Gandhian Young Technological Innovation Awards 2020' for which of the following?

A. Low-cost And Eco-friendly Anti-microbial Nanocomposites

B. Electrical Power Generation from Wet Textiles

C. Electric Vehicle For Disabled And Rural Areas

D. Smart Mirror: The Future Technology

Q.31 Goa CM Pramod Sawant has inaugurated an online building plan approval management system (BPAMS) in which city, in August 2020?

A. Canacona **B.** Mapusa

C. Ponda **D.** Panaji

Q.32 Google will make a $450 million investment in which of the following firms?

A. Vivint **B.** Brink's Inc

C. ADT **D.** Prosegur

Q.33 Which of the following will supply millions of doses of multiple COVID-19 vaccines to the United Kingdom?

A. Wockhardt Ltd

B. Cipla

C. Sun Pharma

D. Glenmark Pharmaceuticals

Q.34 Which is the first Indian state to conduct a household survey at the state and district level to estimate the multidimensional poverty of the state?

A. Kerala **B.** Madhya Pradesh

C. Andhra Pradesh **D.** Maharashtra

Q.35 The one who is known for the establishment of the sovereignty of law in India is_______?

A. Lord William Bentinck

B. Lord Cornwallis

C. Warren Hastings

D. Lord Dalhousie

Q.36 India's largest wind turbine generator has been commissioned in which State?

A. Karnataka **B.** Tamil Nadu

C. Maharashtra **D.** Gujrat

Q.37 Which two organizations have launched the country's first hydrogen fuel cell bus?

A. Maruti Suzuki and Tesla

B. ONGC and Bharat Petroleum

C. Hyundai and Mahindra

D. Indian Oil Corporation Ltd and Tata Motors

Q.38 The Reserve Bank of India (RBI) has scrapped the issuance of _________ for trade credit for imports.

A. Letter of Undertaking

B. Letter of Comfort

C. Letter of Guarantee

D. Both (A) & (B)

Q.39 Who is the author of the best-selling book, "A Brief History of Time"?

A. Ray Bradbury **B.** Isaac Asimov

C. Charles Stross **D.** Stephen Hawkings

Q.40 First "Pi day" was celebrated in which year?

A. 1988 **B.** 1970 **C.** 1990 **D.** 1985

Q.41 Belgaum is in which State?

A. Karnataka **B.** Maharashtra

C. Chattisgarh **D.** Odisha

Q.42 Inflation based on wholesale prices eased to a seven-month low of _____ in February 2020.

A. 2.48% **B.** 3% **C.** 5% **D.** 2%

Q.43 Foreign lawyers/firms in India can _______

A. Open offices in India.

B. Appear in Courts.

C. Give other legal services.

D. Give advice.

Q.44 What is the minimum amount for the transaction to be eligible as an RTGS transfer?

A. Rs 1 lakh   **B.** Rs 2 lakh
C. Rs 4 lakh   **D.** Rs 5 lakh

Q.45 The National Small Industries Corporation Limited (NSIC) was established by the Government of India in:
A. 1965   **B.** 2000   **C.** 1990   **D.** 1955

Q.46 The Geological Survey of India (GSI) was set up in?
A. 1852   **B.** 1851   **C.** 1850   **D.** 1900

Q.47 The airport serving Lakshadweep Island is situated at which of the following island?
A. Kavaratti   **B.** Agatti
C. Minicoy   **D.** Amini

Q.48 The Southern part of Indian mainland from the south of river Krishna till the Southern tip of Mainland India at Cape Comorin is also known as –
A. Konkan Coast   **B.** Gujarat Plains
C. Coromandel coast   **D.** Malabar coast

Q.49 The Indian subcontinent was mainly a part of –
A. Jurassic land   **B.** Angara land
C. Aryavarta   **D.** Gondwanaland

Q.50 Which of the following makes the northern boundary of Deccan Plateau?
A. Aravalli Range
B. Vindhya Range
C. Chota Nagpur Plateau
D. None of these

Reasoning

Q.51 In the following question, select the number which can be placed at the sign of the question mark (?) from the given alternatives.

2	4	3
2	3	2
5	6	4
23	75	?

A. 24   **B.** 27   **C.** 32   **D.** 36

Q.52 How many Triangles are there in the given figure?

A. 4   **B.** 5   **C.** 6   **D.** 3

Q.53 A word is represented by only one set of numbers as given in any one of the alternatives. The sets of numbers given in the alternatives are represented by two classes of alphabets as shown in the given two matrices. The columns and rows of Matrix-I are numbered from 0 to 4 and that of Matrix-II are numbered from 5 to 9. A letter from these matrices can be represented first by its row and next by its column, for example,

'A' can be represented by $21,87$, etc, and 'N' can be represented by $32,78$, etc. Similarly, you have to identify the set of the word $GREAT$.

Matrix - I

	0	1	2	3	4
0	E	G	I	K	M
1	O	Q	S	U	W
2	Y	A	C	F	D
3	J	L	N	P	R
4	T	V	X	Z	B

Matrix - II

	5	6	7	8	9
5	M	O	H	J	A
6	K	D	Q	L	Z
7	I	S	C	N	X
8	G	U	A	P	V
9	E	W	Y	R	T

A. 85,34,00,58,99   **B.** 01,34,95,58,40
C. 01,98,00,21,99   **D.** 85,34,95,20,43

Q.54 From the given figure, select the one in which the question figure is hidden/embedded.

Question Figure:

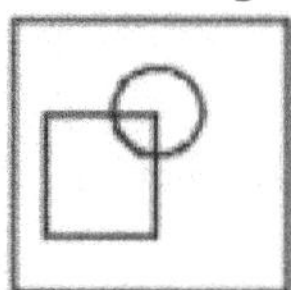

Answer Figure:

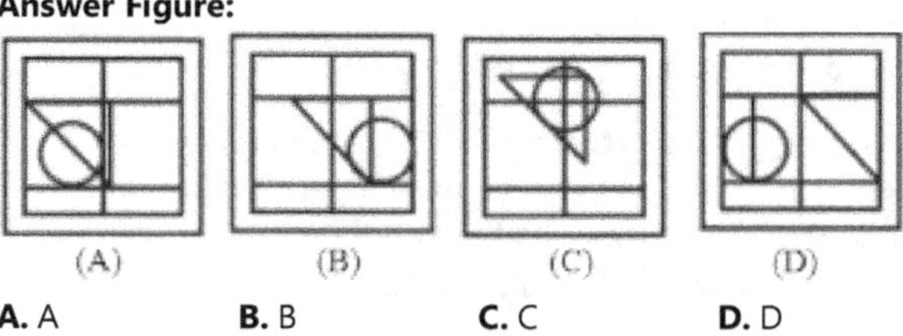

A. A   **B.** B   **C.** C   **D.** D

Q.55 In this series, you will be looking at the letter pattern. Fill the blank in the middle of the series.
SCD, TEF, UGH, ____, WKL
A. CMN   **B.** UJI   **C.** VIJ   **D.** IJT

Q.56 If a mirror is placed on the line AB, then which of the answer figure is the right image of the given figure?

Question Figure:

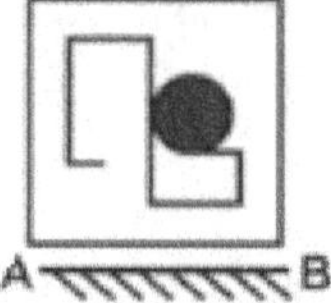

Answer Figure:

 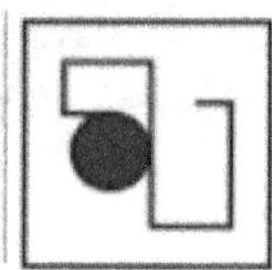  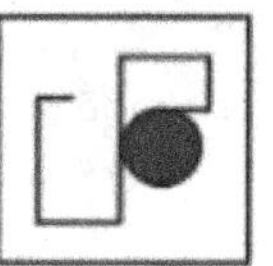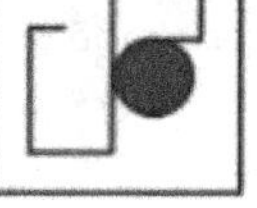

(A)　(B)　(C)　(D)

A. A　**B.** B　**C.** C　**D.** D

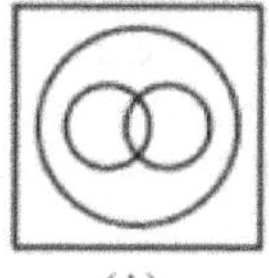 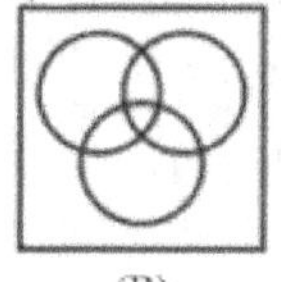  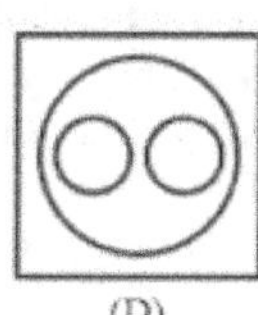

(A)　(B)　(C)　(D)

A. A　**B.** B　**C.** C　**D.** D

Q.57 By interchanging which two signs the equation will be correct?

$$19 + 36 \times 12 \div 4 - 26 = 5$$

A. $\times$ and $\div$　　**B.** $\div$ and $-$

C. $+$ and $-$　　**D.** $+$ and $\times$

Q.58 If ' z ' means ' $+$ ', ' v ' means ' $\div$ ', and ' a ' means ' $\times$ ', then $19\, a\, 4\, z\, 12\, v\, 6 =?$

A. 76　**B.** 78　**C.** 68　**D.** 42

Q.59 If $73 \times 69 \times 43 = 185$ and $41 \times 53 \times 68 = 162$, then $11 \times 31 \times 71 =?$

A. 113　**B.** 123　**C.** 109　**D.** 117

Q.60 Arrange the given words in the sequence in which they occur in the dictionary.

1. Mouse
2. Maiden
3. Mailed
4. Mughal
5. Murder

A. 23145　**B.** 23154　**C.** 21354　**D.** 21345

Q.61 In the following question, select the missing number from the given alternatives.

1053, 351, 117, 39, 13, ?

A. 3.33　**B.** 3.67　**C.** 4.67　**D.** 4.33

Q.62 A series is given with one term missing. Select the correct alternative from the given ones that will complete the series.

SUT, VXW, ?, BDC

A. XZY　**B.** YZA　**C.** YAZ　**D.** XYZ

Q.63 In the following question, select the odd word from the given alternatives.

A. Ice　**B.** Cloud　**C.** Mist　**D.** Fog

Q.64 In the following question, select the odd number pair from the given alternatives.

A. 13 – 167　　**B.** 17 – 291

C. 15 – 223　　**D.** 21 – 439

Q.65 In the following question, select the odd letter from the given alternatives.

A. E　**B.** O　**C.** U　**D.** L

Q.66 Identify the diagram that best represents the relationship between the given classes.

Hospital, Nurse, and Patient

Q.67 Direction: In the following question, select the related words from the given alternatives.

Dog : Kennel : : Horse : ?

A. Stable　　**B.** Shed

C. Farm　　**D.** Aquarium

Q.68 Direction: In the following question, select the related number from the given alternatives.

1648 : 412 : : 2864 : ?

A. 1264　**B.** 1032　**C.** 832　**D.** 716

Q.69 Direction: In the following question, select the related word from the given alternatives.

GOD : FMA : : BAT : ?

A. AXQ　**B.** AYQ　**C.** ZYP　**D.** ZXP

Q.70 In the following question, select the word which cannot be formed using the letters of the given word.

HANGING

A. HANG　**B.** HING　**C.** HAIR　**D.** GANG

Q.71 Ankit remembers his birthday is after 8th August but before 12th August. His mother remembers his birthday is after 5th August but before 10th August. On which day of August is his birthday?

A. 8　**B.** 9　**C.** 7　**D.** 10

Q.72 At 6 o'clock in the evening, Priya was standing facing a tree. The shadow of the tree fell exactly to her right. To which direction was she facing?

A. East　**B.** West　**C.** North　**D.** South

Q.73 Direction: In the following question a statement is given, followed by two conclusions.

Give answer :

Statement: In a one-day cricket match, the total runs made by a team were 200. Out of these 160 runs were made by spinners.

Conclusions:

I. 80% of the team consists of spinners.

II. The opening batsmen were spinners.

A. Only conclusion I follows

B. Only conclusion II follows

C. Either I or II follows

D. Neither I nor II follows

Q.74 In a certain code language, ROUND is written as TQWPF. How is ROBIN written in that code language?

A. TQDKP　**B.** TQEKP　**C.** TREKQ　**D.** TQEPQ

Q.75 Direction: The question given below has a set of three or four statements. Each set of statements is further divided into three segments. Choose the alternative where the third segment in the statement can be logically deduced using both the preceding two, but not just from one of them.

Statement - I. All flower is toy.
II. Some toy is idiot.
III. Some angel is idiot.

Conclusion - I. Some angel is toy.
II. Some idiot is flower.
III. Some flower is angel.

A. Only I follows
B. Only II follows
C. Only III follows
D. None of these

Numerical Ability

Q.76 What is the simplified value of $\dfrac{(5.2)^3-(1.7)^3}{(5.2)^2+5.2\times1.7+(1.7)^2}=?$

A. 3.5   **B.** $\dfrac{1.7}{1.7}$ **C.** 5.2   **D.** 6.9

Q.77 How many two digit numbers are divisible by 11?

A. 8   **B.** 9   **C.** 10   **D.** 1

Q.78 $A,\ B$ and C can complete a work in $5,\ 10$ and 30 days respectively.

In how many days $A,\ B$ and C together can complete the same work?

A. 4   **B.** 2   **C.** 3   **D.** 3.5

Q.79 What is the area (in cm²) of the circle having circumference of 44 cm?

A. 154 cm²   **B.** 226 cm²   **C.** 203 cm²   **D.** 133 cm²

Q.80 An article having marked price of Rs 3900 is sold at a discount of 21%. What is the selling price (in Rs) of the article?

A. 3129   **B.** 3081   **C.** 3243   **D.** 3189

Q.81 If $x:y=3:5$, then what is the value of $(2x+5y):(2y-3x)$?

A. 31:1   **B.** 19:1   **C.** 19:6   **D.** 31:5

Q.82 What is the average of first 8 odd numbers?

A. 7   **B.** 10   **C.** 9   **D.** 8

Q.83 1224 is what percent of 4800?

A. 24.5 %   **B.** 25 %   **C.** 24 %   **D.** 25.5 %

Q.84 If the speed of the boat in still water is 10 km/hr and the speed of the stream is 2 km/hr, then what are the upstream and downstream speeds (in km/hr) of the boat?

A. 12, 16   **B.** 6, 12   **C.** 8, 12   **D.** 6, 14

Q.85 Rs 2200 are invested in a scheme of compound interest. If the rate of interest is 10% per annum, then what is the interest earned (in Rs) in 2 years?

A. 462   **B.** 628   **C.** 576   **D.** 682

Q.86 What is the simplified value of $\dfrac{\sqrt{7}+\sqrt{5}}{\sqrt{7}-\sqrt{5}}=?$

A. $6+\sqrt{35}$ **B.** $6-\sqrt{35}$
C. $12+\sqrt{35}$ **D.** $12-\sqrt{35}$

Q.87 If $A=2^7\times5^2$ and $B=2^3\times5^6$ then what is the value of $A\times B$?

A. $2^{10}\times5^8$ **B.** $2^{21}\times5^{12}$
C. $2^{21}\times5^8$ **D.** $2^{10}\times5^{12}$

Q.88 Which of the following relation(s) is/are true?
I. $\sqrt{5}>\sqrt[3]{9}$
II. $\sqrt[3]{9}>\sqrt{5}$

A. Only I   **B.** Only II
C. Neither I nor II   **D.** Either I or II

Q.89 Direction: Study the following article carefully and answer the following question:

The bar chart given below shows the import of soybean (in quintals) for the year 2011 to 2016.

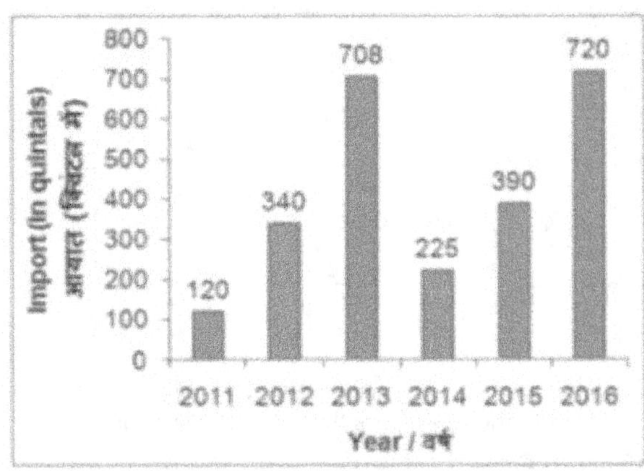

What is the average import (in quintals) of Soybean for the given years?

A. 521.33   **B.** 366.66   **C.** 417.16   **D.** 471.16

Q.90 Direction: Study the following article carefully and answer the following question:

The bar chart given below shows the import of soybean (in quintals) for the year 2011 to 2016.

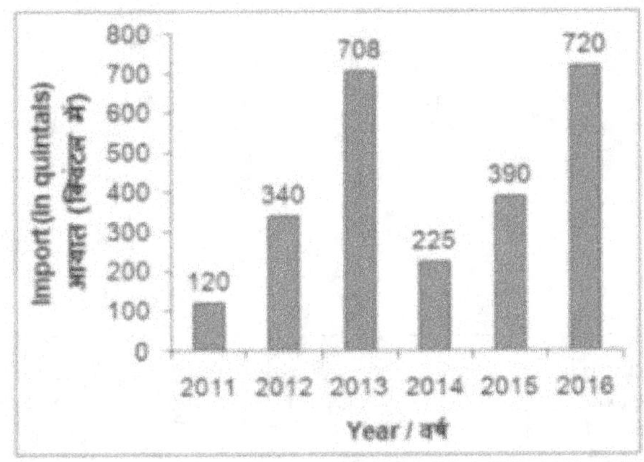

What is the percentage increase in Soybean import in the year **2012** in comparison to year **2011**?

A. 179.66   **B.** 183.33   **C.** 283.33   **D.** 135.29

Computer Awareness

Q.91 What will the function rewind () do?
A. Reposition the file pointer to a character reverse.
B. Reposition the file pointer stream to the end of the file.
C. Reposition the file pointer to the beginning of that line.
D. Reposition the file pointer to the beginning of the file.

Q.92 What we call an intersection of row and column:
A. Line   **B.** column   **C.** Row   **D.** Cell

Q.93 MS-Word is an example of ____
A. An operating system
B. A processing device
C. Application software
D. An input device

Q.94 Which of the following is refers to the main page of a website?
A. Bookmark   **B.** Browser page
C. Home page   **D.** Search page

Q.95 Which of the following is used to write web pages?
A. JAVA   **B.** XML   **C.** HTML   **D.** PAINT

Q.96 What is the meaning of MNG ?
A. Multiple Nano Graphic
B. Multiple Network Graphic
C. Many Network Graphic
D. Multiple New Graphic

Q.97 KYC means:
A. Know your customer
B. Know your character
C. Both of above
D. None of above

Q.98 What is the full form of IP?
A. Internal Protocol   **B.** Internet Protocol
C. Interior Protocol   **D.** None of These

Q.99 Cut, Copy and Paste is in _______ Group in the Home tab.
A. Font   **B.** formatting
C. Clipboard   **D.** Page Setup

Q.100 Business Correspondent means:
A. An agent who provides banking services
B. An agent of business house
C. A type of money lender
D. None of above

// Smart Answer Sheet //

Correct — Indicates percentage of students who answered questions correctly.

Skipped — Indicates percentage of students who skipped questions.

Q.	Ans.	Correct / Skipped	Q.	Ans.	Correct / Skipped	Q.	Ans.	Correct / Skipped	Q.	Ans.	Correct / Skipped	Q.	Ans.	Correct / Skipped
1	D	32.08 % / 14.19 %	17	D	41.68 % / 22.76 %	33	A	19.75 % / 15.0 %	49	D	34.9 % / 23.62 %	65	D	55.41 % / 24.8 %
2	D	57.84 % / 19.89 %	18	A	18.47 % / 21.92 %	34	C	18.29 % / 22.72 %	50	B	20.68 % / 21.83 %	66	D	44.96 % / 24.25 %
3	C	63.19 % / 17.54 %	19	D	27.96 % / 8.88 %	35	B	22.39 % / 20.79 %	51	B	53.92 % / 23.66 %	67	A	58.57 % / 25.21 %
4	D	39.54 % / 22.23 %	20	C	31.02 % / 17.15 %	36	B	22.85 % / 20.02 %	52	B	61.72 % / 23.74 %	68	D	50.93 % / 26.22 %
5	B	36.18 % / 23.38 %	21	A	50.53 % / 15.61 %	37	D	22.74 % / 24.03 %	53	C	42.35 % / 25.63 %	69	B	53.12 % / 25.55 %
6	B	27.24 % / 21.11 %	22	B	33.88 % / 22.02 %	38	D	33.43 % / 22.91 %	54	C	59.18 % / 24.95 %	70	C	65.4 % / 22.31 %
7	B	22.33 % / 23.05 %	23	B	17.74 % / 13.73 %	39	D	34.21 % / 24.28 %	55	C	56.2 % / 26.01 %	71	B	57.17 % / 23.66 %
8	C	23.18 % / 21.43 %	24	C	15.9 % / 22.84 %	40	A	19.31 % / 23.99 %	56	D	40.39 % / 25.35 %	72	C	44.8 % / 25.19 %
9	C	25.13 % / 24.3 %	25	C	17.45 % / 24.35 %	41	A	37.64 % / 17.31 %	57	A	31.82 % / 25.98 %	73	D	22.55 % / 22.16 %
10	A	20.95 % / 22.41 %	26	A	36.04 % / 22.81 %	42	A	29.88 % / 23.5 %	58	B	56.07 % / 26.03 %	74	A	60.36 % / 24.2 %
11	A	25.36 % / 18.75 %	27	D	50.02 % / 15.44 %	43	D	24.25 % / 20.07 %	59	A	45.47 % / 26.76 %	75	D	38.74 % / 26.82 %
12	D	32.71 % / 21.09 %	28	C	18.5 % / 24.59 %	44	B	22.87 % / 23.99 %	60	A	51.12 % / 25.69 %	76	A	33.79 % / 25.89 %
13	A	59.77 % / 17.43 %	29	D	21.93 % / 18.32 %	45	D	13.21 % / 18.93 %	61	D	48.49 % / 25.13 %	77	B	43.36 % / 27.45 %
14	A	24.9 % / 22.04 %	30	B	16.36 % / 21.53 %	46	B	20.58 % / 23.8 %	62	C	48.35 % / 24.84 %	78	C	50.02 % / 27.41 %
15	B	16.72 % / 20.07 %	31	D	28.22 % / 21.22 %	47	B	13.96 % / 20.35 %	63	A	49.4 % / 24.17 %	79	A	36.6 % / 29.71 %
16	A	43.11 % / 18.21 %	32	C	18.8 % / 20.06 %	48	C	28.27 % / 23.37 %	64	B	47.89 % / 24.93 %	80	B	45.13 % / 29.46 %

Q.	Ans.	Correct / Skipped	Q.	Ans.	Correct / Skipped	Q.	Ans.	Correct / Skipped	Q.	Ans.	Correct / Skipped	Q.	Ans.	Correct / Skipped
81	A	45.88 % / 28.32 %	85	A	43.67 % / 29.0 %	89	C	37.0 % / 27.78 %	93	C	35.51 % / 21.93 %	97	A	38.4 % / 21.87 %
82	D	36.15 % / 28.99 %	86	A	25.28 % / 28.8 %	90	B	32.78 % / 28.64 %	94	C	41.45 % / 21.67 %	98	B	49.54 % / 21.96 %
83	D	41.78 % / 28.92 %	87	A	41.22 % / 29.0 %	91	D	14.66 % / 21.64 %	95	C	47.45 % / 22.13 %	99	C	28.01 % / 22.46 %
84	C	34.29 % / 29.98 %	88	A	25.23 % / 27.89 %	92	D	39.47 % / 21.22 %	96	B	37.87 % / 22.74 %	100	A	31.18 % / 22.86 %

Performance Analysis

Avg. Score (%)	36.0%
Toppers Score (%)	100.0%
Your Score	

//Hints and Solutions//

1. Demand in Economics means Demand backed by purchasing power. Demand is an economic term that refers to the number of products or services that consumers want to buy at any price level. Demand expresses the relationship between the price and quantity of the commodity, which must be purchased at that price in a given time.

Hence, the correct option is (D).

2. The people get more income by their regular work. If they work daily, then they automatically get better wages. Farmers do hard work for growing their crops so they should get decent prices for their crops. So better price for their produce, Continuous job, Better wages are responsible factors for generating more income.

Hence, the correct option is (D).

3. Right to Equality - This means that every person living within the territory of India has equal rights before the law. This means that all people standing in the same line are the same. There can be no discrimination on the basis of religion, race, caste, sex, and place of birth. This means that all will be treated equally and there will be no discrimination on the basis of lower or upper class.

Hence, the correct option is (C).

4. The articles of the constitution are divided into the following parts:

Part I - States and Union Territories,

Part II - Citizenship,

Part III - Fundamental Rights,

Part IV - Directive Principles of State Policy.

Directive principles of state policy are mentioned in Part-IV (Articles 36 to 51) of the Indian Constitution.

Hence, the correct option is (D).

5. After the death of Akbar, Salim ascended the throne at Agra on 24th Oct 1605, with the title Jahangir. He was most famous for his Chain of Justice. He was a great patron of arts and under him, the Mughal painting reached its climax. Unfortunately, excessive drinking has affected his health and he died on 28th Oct 1627, on the way from Kashmir. He was buried in Shahdara Bagh in Lahore.

Hence, the correct option is (B).

6. In 1824 the Sepoys were asked to go to Burma by the sea route to fight for the East India Company. The Sepoys refused to do so as they believed that if they crossed the sea they would lose their religion and caste. The Sepoys were severely punished for not obeying the British. In 1856 the Company passed a new law which stated that every new person who took up employment in the company army had to agree to serve overseas if required.

Hence, the correct option is (B).

7. The northern hemisphere has a summer season during the summer solstice.

The solstice occurs because the axis of the Earth's rotation is inclined 23.4 degrees relative to the Earth's orbit around the Sun.

Hence, the correct option is (B).

8. Ural - The Ural Mountains are a mountain range in western Russia that extends from north to south. It geographically separates Asia and Europe. Many rivers originate from it. The major river 'Cama' immerses its water in the Caspian Sea.

This mountain range extends from the Arctic Ocean in the north to the Caspian Sea in the south and separates Europe from the continent of Asia. The rise of this mountain range has taken place in many ages. The ranges extend from north to west and north to east and the highest elevation is found in the southern part. The combined structure of this mountain is clearly reflected by its geological conditions.

Hence, the correct option is (C).

9. C-shaped cartilaginous rings reinforce the anterior and lateral sides of the trachea to protect and maintain the airway open. The cartilaginous rings are incomplete because this allows the trachea to collapse slightly to allow food to pass down the esophagus.

Hence, the correct option is (C).

10. The tricuspid valve or right atrioventricular valve is present on the right dorsal side of the mammalian heart between the right atrium and the right ventricle. The function of the valve is to prevent backflow of blood from the right ventricle into the right atrium.

Hence, the correct option is (A).

11. Lipid is the most concentrated energy source. Animal and vegetable Lipids serve as a concentrated energy source and are the highest energy sources in feedstuffs. Lipids contain 2.25 times the calories per gram than protein or carbohydrates.

Hence, the correct option is (A).

12. The focal length of a plane mirror is infinite because the image can be formed at an infinite distance inside the mirror. Its optical power is zero. Concave and convex mirrors (spherical mirrors) are also capable of creating virtual images similar to plane mirrors. A plane mirror can be identified as a spherical mirror of infinite radius of curvature.

Hence, the correct option is (D).

13. When an electric current flows in a conductor, it flows as a drift of free electrons in the metal. Electricity flows easily through a conductor because the electrons are free to move around in the object. Whenever there is a movement of electrons through a conductor, an electric current is created.

Hence, the correct option is (A).

14. Ubuntu is a free and open-source operating system and Linux distribution based on Debian.

Ubuntu is an open-source, free Linux distribution. It is an operating system for cloud computing, in accordance to support with Open Stack. Ubuntu is developed by the canonical community and it is freely available. Also, Canonical Ltd. is responsible for the funding of Ubuntu.

Hence, the correct option is (A).

15. Isotopes are atoms of the same element with the same number of protons (atomic numbers), but different numbers of neutrons. The same electronic configuration causes similar chemical properties but due to different atomic mass, they have different physical properties.

Hence, the correct option is (B).

16. Pure gold is too soft for everyday wear, so it is alloyed with a mixture of metals like silver(Ag), copper(Cu), platinum(Pt), palladium(Pd), and zinc(Zn) to give it strength and durability.

Hence, the correct option is (A).

17. The Ministry of Electronics & Information Technology (MeitY) and Data Security Council of India (DSCI) have recently launched the Cyber Security Grand Challenge.
It is an initiative to promote innovation and entrepreneurship in the start-up arena of Cyber-Security. Participants will compete in teams at three stages namely Idea, Minimal Viable Product and Final Product Building, to create solutions around six defined areas including Microservices, IoT, Biometrics etc. The award will include a cash prize of Rs.3.2 Crore as the top three teams will be presented with a total cash prize of Rs.2 Crore.

Hence, the correct option is (D).

18. Pradhan Mantri Jeevan Jyoti Bima Yojana (PMJJBY) is a one-year life insurance scheme, renewable from year to year, offering coverage for death. PMJJBY is available to people in the age group of 18 to 50 years (life cover up to age 55) having a savings bank account who give their consent to join and enable auto-debit.

Under the PMJJBY scheme, a life cover of Rs.2 lakhs is available at a premium of Rs.330 per annum per member and is renewable every year.

Hence, the correct option is (A).

19. Vint Cerf - Computer scientists Vinton Cerf and Robert Elliot Kahn are credited with inventing the Internet communication protocols we use today and the system referred to as the Internet.

Hence, the correct option is (D).

20. Skeet shooting is a recreational and competitive activity where participants, using shotguns, attempt to break clay targets mechanically flung into the air from two fixed stations at high speed from a variety of angles.

Hence, the correct option is (C).

21. Kerala - Mohiniyattam is one of the famous classical dances of India that developed and remained popular in the state of Kerala. Kathakali is another classical dance form of Kerala. It is traditionally a solo dance performed by women after extensive training.

Hence, the correct option is (A).

22.

- Former Maharashtra CM Shivajirao Patil Nilangekar passed away in August 2020.
- He had recently tested coronavirus positive but had recovered and was discharged after testing negative.
- Nilangekar, senior Congress leaders from Latur in the Marathwada region, was the state chief minister from June 1985 to March 1986.

Hence, the correct option is (B).

23. Vinod Rai (born 23 May in parsa Gazipur 1948) is a former IAS officer who served as the 11th Comptroller and Auditor General of India. He wrote "Not just an Accountant", which speaks about how the political system was exploited to violate laws in the 2G spectrum case, Krishna-Godavari gas basin contact, Commonwealth Games scam, Indian coal allocation scam, and the controversial purchase of aircraft.

Hence, the correct option is (B).

24. The ASEAN Declaration or Bangkok Declaration is the founding document of the Association of Southeast Asian Nations. The Association of Southeast Asian Nations (ASEAN) is a regional intergovernmental organization comprising ten Southeast Asian countries that promotes intergovernmental cooperation and facilitates economic, political, security, military, educational, and socio-cultural integration amongst its members. It also regularly engages other states in the Asia-Pacific region and beyond. The member countries are Indonesia, Malaysia, Philippines, Singapore, Thailand, Vietnam, Burma, Cambodia, Brunei, and Laos.

Hence, the correct option is (C).

25. Afghan-India Friendship Dam (AIFD), formerly Salma Dam, is a hydroelectric and irrigation dam project located on the Hari River in Chishti Sharif District of Herat Province in western Afghanistan. Since this project is funded and constructed by the Government of India as a part of the Indian aid project, the Afghan cabinet renamed the Salma Dam to the Afghan-India Friendship Dam in a gesture of gratitude to strengthen relations between the two countries.

Hence, the correct option is (C).

26. India has successfully tested the vertical steep dive version of the Brahmos supersonic cruise missile. Made in India 'Brahmos Aerospace' is also ready with a longer (500 km) range version of the Brahmos missile that can be fired from Sukhoi-30 fighter jets. BrahMos Aerospace is a joint venture company owned by the governments of India and Russia and its missiles are produced in India.

Hence, the correct option is (A).

27.

- PM Narendra Modi participated in the Bhumi Poojan function for the construction of Ram Temple in Ayodhya on 5 August 2020.
- He unveiled a plaque to mark the laying of the foundation stone and also released a commemorative postal stamp on Shree Ram Janmabhoomi Mandir.

- 175 guests including 135 Saints belonging to 135 spiritual traditions were invited for the ceremony.

Hence, the correct option is (D).

28.

- The International Financial Services Centres Authority (IFSCA) has constituted a seven-member committee to suggest ways to enhance international retail participation in IFSC.

- The committee will recommend a roadmap for the future growth of international retail business in IFSC.

- The committee is headed by India Fund Advisors Pvt Ltd Chairman Pradip Shah.

Hence, the correct option is (C).

29.

- The Andhra Pradesh government has signed a pact with three companies -- Hindustan Unilever Ltd (HUL), ITC, and Procter and Gamble (P&G).

- It has been signed for marketing and technology support for the economic empowerment of women under two new schemes to be launched soon.

- The companies will give handholding to women under the YSR Cheyutha scheme, to be launched on August 12, 2020.

Hence, the correct option is (D).

30.

- A group of researchers from IIT Kharagpur has been awarded the 'Gandhian Yuva Technological Innovation Award 2020' for their work **"Electrical Power Generation from Wet Textiles"**.

- Another team of the institute was also awarded the same award for solving the problem of energy conservation and thermal management.

Hence, the correct option is (B).

31.

- Goa CM Pramod Sawant has inaugurated an online building plan approval management system (BPAMS) in Panaji.

- It is a step towards the goal of attaining faster and hassle-free clearance for land development and building construction approval in a transparent manner.

- This is also to improve Goa's ranking under Ease of Doing Business by the Department for Promotion of Industry and Internal Trade.

Hence, the correct option is (D).

32.

- Google has announced a partnership with security firm ADT and as a part of this multi-year partnership, it will make a $450 million investment in ADT.

- ADT is a leading US security and home automation, provider.

- Google will combine its Nest devices, services, and technology with ADT's leadership position providing security solutions for millions of homes and small businesses in the US.

Hence, the correct option is (C).

33.

- Indian drugmaker Wockhardt Ltd will supply millions of doses of multiple COVID-19 vaccines to the United Kingdom.

- UK government has entered into an agreement with pharmaceutical and biotechnology major Wockhardt to provide 'fill and finish services'.

- As part of the 18-month agreement, Wockhardt will carry out the crucial 'fill and finish' stage of the manufacturing process.

Hence, the correct option is (A).

34. Andhra Pradesh stands at 51st rank globally in Multidimensional Poverty Index according to a household survey conducted in the state. Andhra Pradesh becomes the first Indian state to conduct a household survey at state and district levels to estimate the multidimensional poverty of the state. The study was conducted by Govt. of Andhra Pradesh in collaboration with the University of Oxford, UK.

Hence, the correct option is (C).

35. Lord Cornwallis - Lord Cornwallis is known for the establishment of the sovereignty of law in India because he established the gradation civil courts for both Hindu and Muslim such as Munsiff Court, Registrar Court, District Court, King-in-Council, and Sadar Diwani Adalat.

Hence, the correct option is (B).

36. Renewable solution provider Suzlon Group announced the installation and commissioning of its new product "S128" claiming it to be the largest wind turbine generator in India. The first prototype of S128 has been commissioned at the Sanganeri site in Tamil Nadu. This has the country's largest single rotor blade measuring 63 meters and a reduced Levelized cost of energy.

Hence, the correct option is (B).

37. Indian Oil Corporation Ltd and Tata Motors have launched the trial demonstration of the country's first hydrogen fuel cell bus. The project is being executed with financial support from the Department of Science & Industrial Research, Ministry of Science & Technology, and the Ministry for New and Renewable Energy. The vehicle will be fuelled at the hydrogen dispensing facility at Indian Oil.

Hence, the correct option is (D).

38. The Reserve Bank of India (RBI) has scrapped the issuance of Letters of Undertaking (LOUs) and Letters of Comfort (LOCs) for trade credit for imports with immediate effect. Banks will continue to issue guarantees and letters of credit for trade purposes which are the international norm. A letter of credit is secure because it has the details of the expiry date and the material purchase.

A letter of comfort is a communication from a party to a contract to the other party that indicates an initial willingness to enter into a contractual obligation absent the elements of a legally enforceable contract.

Hence, the correct option is (D).

39. A Brief History of Time: is a popular-science book on cosmology by English physicist Stephen Hawking.
Stephen Hawking, the British Physicist, and the black hole theorist have died on 14th March. Hawkings redefined cosmology by proposing that black holes emit radiation and later evaporate.

Hence, the correct option is (D).

40. Google has dedicated a doodle to mark 30 years of "Pi Day", a day first recognized by physicist Larry Shaw in 1988 to honor the mathematical constant. Pi is used in every field of science as it's used for calculations involving the volume and surface area of spheres. The first Pi Day was held at a San Francisco Science Museum in 1988.

Hence, the correct option is (A).

41. India's tallest national flag was unfurled in Belagavi (also known as Belgaum) in Karnataka. The flag in Belgaum is much larger than the one at the India-Pakistan border at Attari in Punjab. The flag is reported to be 100m high from the base plate to the top, with a size of 120×80 ft.

Hence, the correct option is (A).

42. Inflation based on wholesale prices eased to a seven-month low of 2.48% in February on cheaper food articles, including vegetables. According to government data released, inflation in food articles slowed to 0.88% in February from 3% in January. Inflation in pulses remained in the negative zone at $(-)24.51\%$ and cereals, wheat and items like egg, fish, and meat were in the negative zone.

Hence, the correct option is (A).

43. The Supreme Court ruled that foreign law firms or foreign lawyers cannot practice law in the country either on the litigation or non-litigation side. This means overseas lawyers or firms cannot open offices in the country, nor appear in courts or before any authority or render other legal services. But overseas lawyers can fly in, fly out for a temporary period to give advice.

Hence, the correct option is (D).

44. The term real-time gross settlement (RTGS) refers to a funds transfer system that allows for the instantaneous transfer of money and/or securities. RGTS is the continuous process of settling payments on an individual order basis without netting debits with credits across the books of a central bank.

The RTGS system is primarily meant for large value transactions. The minimum amount to be remitted through RTGS is Rs 2,00,000/- with no upper or maximum ceiling.

Hence, the correct option is (B).

45. National Small Industries Corporation Limited (NSIC) is a Mini Ratna PSU established by the Government of India in 1955. It falls under the Ministry of Micro, Small & Medium Enterprises of India. It was established to promote and develop micro and small-scale industries and enterprises in the country. It was founded as a Government of India agency later made into a fully owned government corporation.

Hence, the correct option is (D).

46. The Geological Survey of India (GSI) is a scientific agency of India. It was founded in 1851, is a Government of India Ministry of Mines organization, one of the oldest of such organizations in the world and the second oldest survey agency in India, for conducting geological surveys and studies of India. Also, it acts as the prime provider of basic earth science information to the government, industry and the general public, as well as the official participant in steel, coal, metals, cement, power industries and international geoscientific forums.

Hence, the correct option is (B).

47. Agatti Aerodrome is a public airport serving Agatti Island and other islands of Lakshadweep. This is the only airport in Lakshadweep Islands which is located on the southern end of Agatti Island, in the union territory of Lakshadweep in India. It is the sole airstrip in the archipelago, which lies off the west coast of India.

Hence, the correct option is (B).

48. Coromandel coast - Coromandel Coast in the Southern part from the south of river Krishna till the Southern tip of Mainland India at Cape Comorin where it merges with the Western Coastal Plains.

Hence, the correct option is (C).

49. Initially, the earth was a big landmass called Pangea which was surrounded by a large water body called Panthalassa. The big landmass was broken into two pieces known as Angara land and Gondwanaland. India was part of Gondwanaland.

The Indian subcontinent is a southern region and peninsula of Asia, mostly situated on the Indian Plate and projecting southwards into the Indian Ocean from the Himalayas. Geologically, the Indian subcontinent is related to the landmass that rifted from Gondwana and merged with the Eurasian plate nearly 55 million years ago.

Hence, the correct option is (D).

50. Vindhya Range - The term "Vindhyas" was used in a wider sense and included several hills ranges between the Indo-Gangetic plain and the Deccan Plateau. The Deccan Plateau is a plateau situated between two mountain ranges, the Western and Eastern Ghats, in southern and western India. Its northern boundary is formed by the Satpura and Vindhya ranges.

Hence, the correct option is (B).

51. This question follows the following pattern:

$$5 \times 2 \times 2 + 3 = 23$$

$$6 \times 3 \times 4 + 3 = 75$$

So, $3 \times 2 \times 4 + 3 = 27$

Hence, the correct option is (B).

52. In this given figure, there are 5 triangles.

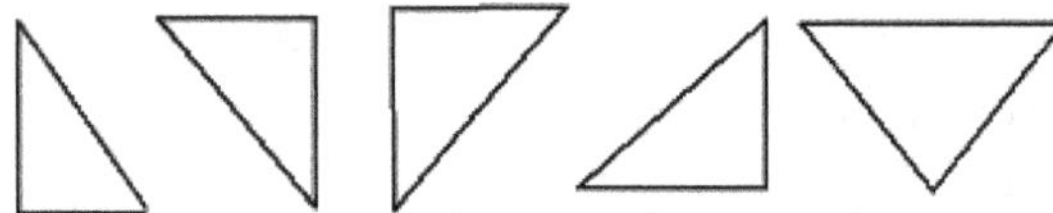

Hence, the correct option is (B).

53. According to the above pattern:

$G - 01,85$

$R - 34,98$

$E - 00,95$

$A - 21,87$

$T - 40,99$

So, $GREAT = 01,98,00,21,99$

Hence, the correct option is (C).

54. On close observation, we find that the question figure is embedded in option (C) as shown below:

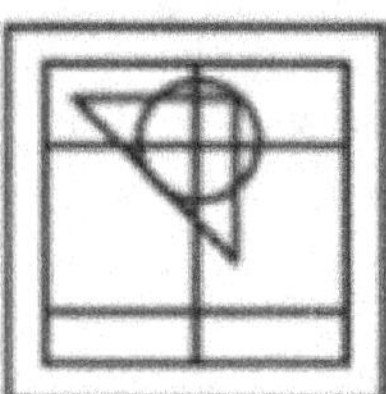

Hence, the correct option is (C).

55. This question follows the following pattern:

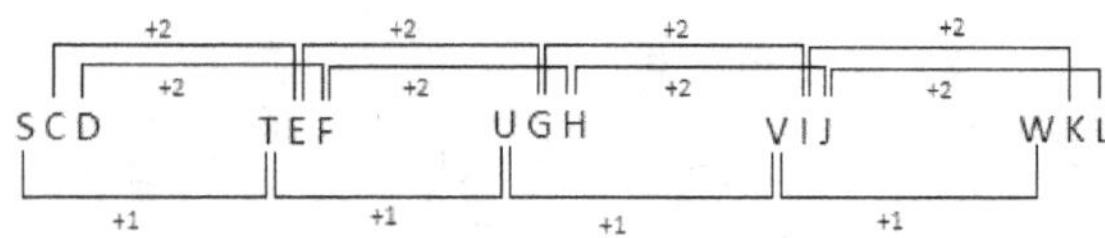

From the above figure, we get the value of the middle of the series is VIJ.

Hence, the correct option is (C).

56. If a mirror is placed on the line AB then the following of the answer figures is the right image of the given figure:

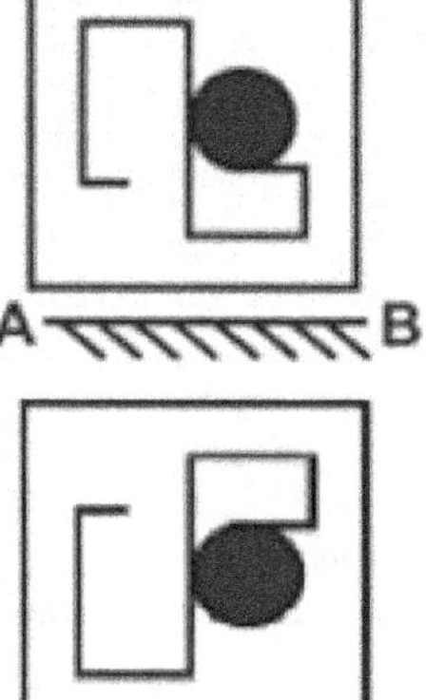

Option (D) is the right image of the given figure.

Hence, the correct option is (D).

57. The correct interchanging of signs is $\times$ and $\div$:

$19 + 36 \div 12 \times 4 - 26 = 5$

$\Rightarrow 19 + 3 \times 4 - 26 = 5$

$\Rightarrow 19 + 12 - 26 = 5$

$\Rightarrow 31 - 26 = 5$

Hence, the correct option is (A).

58. Given: $19\ a\ 4\ z\ 12\ v\ 6$

After replacing the signs:

$19 \times 4 + 12 \div 6$
$76 + 2 = 78$

Hence, the correct option is (B).

59. This question follows the following pattern:

$73 + 69 + 43 = 185$
$41 + 53 + 68 = 162$
$11 + 31 + 71 = 113$

Hence, the correct option is (A).

60. According to the dictionary, The sequence of these words is as follows:

Maiden, Mailed, Mouse, Mughal, Murder.

So, the Correct sequence will be 23145.

Hence, the correct option is (A).

61. The numbers are arranged in Geometric progression with a common ratio of 3.

Alternatively,

$1053 \div 3 = 351$

$351 \div 3 = 117$

$$117 \div 3 = 39$$

$$39 \div 3 = 13$$

$$13 \div 3 = 4.33$$

Hence, the correct option is (D).

62. According to the below pattern, YAZ will complete the series.

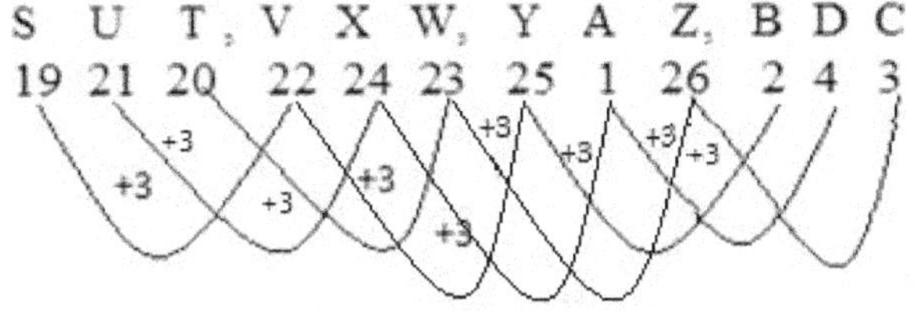

Hence, the correct option is (C).

63. Ice is water frozen into a solid-state.

Cloud, Mist, and Fog are intangible. On the contrary, ice is a tangible object.

Therefore, Ice is the odd word among the given alternatives.

Hence, the correct option is (A).

64. This question follows the following pattern:

$$13^2 - 2 = 167$$
$$17^2 + 2 = 291$$
$$15^2 - 2 = 223$$
$$21^2 - 2 = 439$$

According to the above pattern, the odd pair is $17 - 291$.

Hence, the correct option is (B).

65. Except for the letter 'L', all others are vowels.

The vowels are A, E, I, O, U.

Hence, the correct option is (D).

66. The hospital consists of nurse and patient but nurse and patient are of two different nature.

Therefore, the following diagram represents the three given classes best.

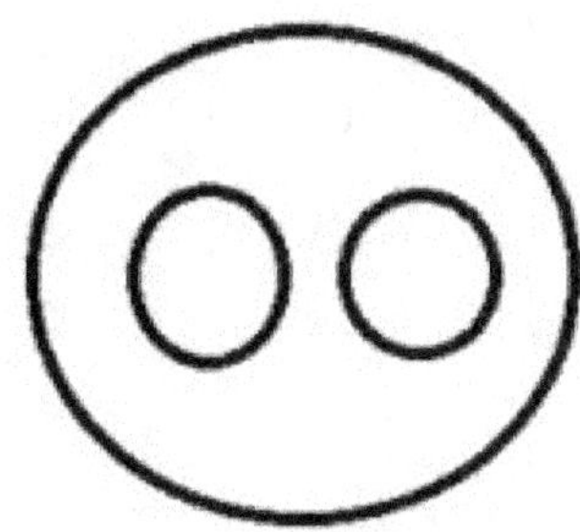

Hence, the correct option is (D).

67. Dog lives in Kennel and Horse live in Stable.

So, Dog : Kennel : : Horse : Stable

Hence, the correct option is (A).

68. The above series is given in the following pattern:

$$1648 \div 4 = 412$$

$$2864 \div 4 = 716$$

Hence, the correct option is (D).

69. The above series is given in the following Pattern:

F + 1 = G

M + 2 = O

A + 3 = D

Same as

A + 1 = B

Y + 2 = A

Q + 3 = T

Hence, the correct option is (B).

70. HAIR cannot be formed because the letter 'R' is not present in the given word.

Hence, the correct option is (C).

71. Ankit remembers his birthday is after 8th August but before 12th August and his mother remembers his birthday is after 5th August but before 10th August.

So, between 8th to 12th August and 5th to 10th August is 9th which August is common.

Hence, the correct option is (B).

72. Given, Priya was standing facing a tree.

The shadow of the tree fell exactly to her right.

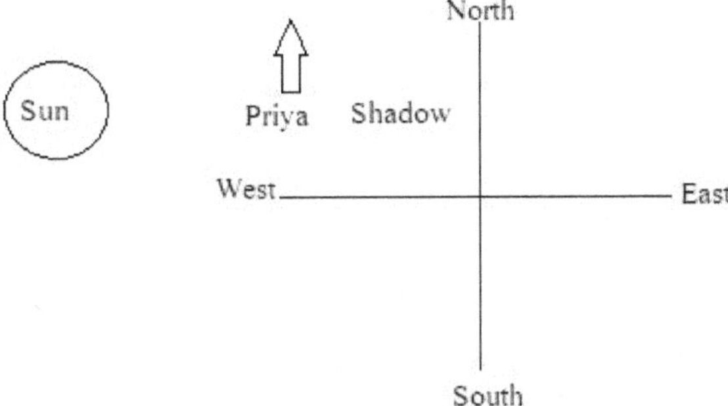

So, According to the question Priya facing north.

Hence, the correct option is (C).

73. According to the statement, 80% of the total runs were made by spinners.

So, the team may consist of the number of spinners more or less than that given in Conclusion I. Hence, the conclusion I do not follow.

Secondly, it is not known from the statement that opening batsmen were spinners. Hence, conclusion II does not follow.

Hence, the correct option is (D).

74. This question follows the following pattern:

R + 2 = T

O + 2 = Q

U + 2 = W

N + 2 = P

D + 2 = F

Same as

R + 2 = T

O + 2 = Q

B + 2 = D

I + 2 = K

N + 2 = P

So, ROBIN is written as TQDKP.

Hence, the correct option is (A).

75. To solve this question, we will make the following diagram as per the statement:

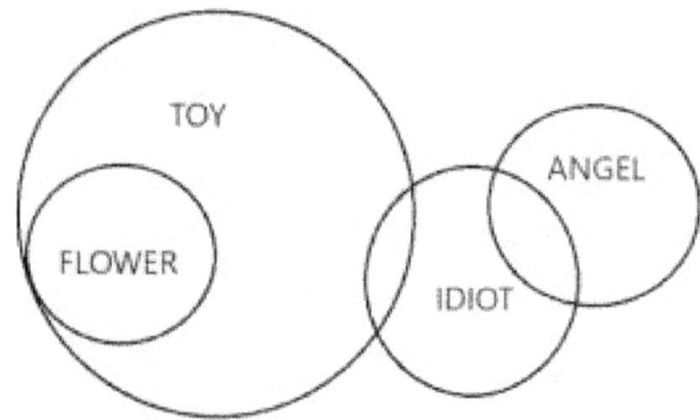

From the above figure, it is clear that none of the conclusions are correct.

Hence, the correct option is (D).

76. Given: $\dfrac{(5.2)^3-(1.7)^3}{(5.2)^2+5.2\times1.7+(1.7)^2}$

We know that,

$$a^3 - b^3 = (a - b)(a^2 + ab + b^2)$$

So, $\dfrac{(5.2)^2-(1.7)^3}{(5.2)^2+5.2\times1.7+(1.7)^2}$

$\Rightarrow \dfrac{(5.2-1.7)\left[(5.2)^2+(5.2\times1.7)+(1.7)^2\right]}{(5.2)^2+5.2\times1.7+(1.7)^2}$

$\Rightarrow 5.2 - 1.7 = 3.5$

Hence, the correct option is (A).

77. First number divisible by 11 is 11.

Last number divisible by $11 = 99$

We know that, $t_n = a + (n - 1)d$

$99 = 11 + (n - 1)11$

$\Rightarrow 99 = 11 + 11n - 11$

$\Rightarrow 99 = 11n$

$\Rightarrow n = 9$

Hence, the correct option is (B).

78. A can complete the work in $= 5$ days

One day work by $A = \dfrac{1}{5}$

B can complete the work in $= 10$ days

One day work by $B = \dfrac{1}{10}$

C can complete the work in $= 30$ days

One day work by $C = \dfrac{1}{30}$

They all together work in one day $= \dfrac{1}{5} + \dfrac{1}{10} + \dfrac{1}{30} = \dfrac{10}{30}$

So, they work all together in $\dfrac{30}{10} = 3$ days

Hence, the correct option is (C).

79. Given: Circumference of a circle $= 44$ cm

We know that, Circumference of circle $= 2\pi r$

$\Rightarrow 2\pi r = 44$ cm

$\Rightarrow 2 \times \dfrac{22}{7} \times r = 44$ cm

$\Rightarrow r = 7$ cm

So, the area of the circle $= \pi r^2 = \dfrac{22}{7} \times 7 \times 7 = 154$ cm²

Hence, the correct option is (A).

80. Let, selling price of an article$= x$

Discount on the marked price $= 3900 \times \dfrac{21}{100} = $ Rs 819

Selling price $=$ marked price $-$ discount

So, the selling price after discount $= 3900 - 819 = $ Rs 3081

Hence, the correct option is (B).

81. Given: $x : y = 3 : 5$

$\Rightarrow \dfrac{x}{y} : \dfrac{3}{5}$

$\Rightarrow x = \dfrac{3}{5}y$

Now, again from the question,

$$(2x + 5y):(2y - 3x) = \frac{(2x+5y)}{(2y-3x)}$$

Now, put the value of $x = \frac{3}{5}y$ in the above equation, we get

$$\frac{2\times\frac{3}{5}y+5y}{2y-3\times\frac{3}{5}y} = \frac{31}{1} = 31:1$$

Hence, the correct option is (A).

82. Given : The first 8 odd numbers $=$
$1, 3, 5, 7, 9, 11, 13$ and 15

The sum of the first 8 odd numbers $= 1 + 3 + 5 + 7 +$
$9 + 11 + 13 + 15 = 64$

$$\therefore Average = \frac{Sum\ of\ observations}{Number\ of\ observations}$$

$$= \frac{64}{8} = 8$$

Thus, 8 is an average of the first 8 natural numbers or positive integers.

Hence, the correct option is (D).

83. Let, 1224 is $x\%$ of 4800
$\Rightarrow 1224 = x\% \times 4800$
$\Rightarrow \frac{1224\times100}{4800} = x$
$\Rightarrow x = \frac{1224\times100}{4800} = 25.5\%$
Hence, the correct option is (D).

84. Given: Speed of boat in still water $(u) = 10$ km/hr

Speed of stream $(v) = 2$ km/hr

Upstream speed of boat $= u - v$

$= 10 - 2$

$= 8$ km/hr

Downstream speed of boat $= u + v$

$= 10 + 2$

$= 12$ km/hr

Hence, the correct option is (C).

85. We know that, Amount $= P\left(1 + \frac{r}{100}\right)^t$

Amount $= 2200\left(1 + \frac{r}{100}\right)^2$

$\Rightarrow$ Amount $= 2200\left(\frac{11}{10}\right)^2 = $ Rs 2262

$\therefore$ Compound interest $=$ Amount $-$ Principal

$= 2662 - 2200 = $ Rs 462

Therefore, compound interest $= $ Rs 462
Hence, the correct option is (A).

86. Given: $\frac{\sqrt{7}+\sqrt{5}}{\sqrt{7}-\sqrt{5}}$

To make it simple, we multiply the numerator and denominator
by $\frac{\sqrt{7}+\sqrt{5}}{\sqrt{7}+\sqrt{5}}$

So, $\frac{\sqrt{7}+\sqrt{5}}{\sqrt{7}-\sqrt{5}} \times \frac{\sqrt{7}+\sqrt{5}}{\sqrt{7}+\sqrt{5}} = \frac{(\sqrt{7}+\sqrt{5})^2}{(\sqrt{7}-\sqrt{5})(\sqrt{7}+\sqrt{5})}$

Using identities, $(a + b)^2 = a^2 + 2ab + b^2$
$(a - b)(a + b) = a^2 - b^2$

Therefore, $\frac{(\sqrt{7}+\sqrt{5})^2}{(\sqrt{7}-\sqrt{5})(\sqrt{7}+\sqrt{5})}$

$\Rightarrow \frac{(\sqrt{7})^2+2\times\sqrt{7}\times\sqrt{5}+(\sqrt{5})^2}{(\sqrt{7})^2-(\sqrt{5})^2}$

$\Rightarrow \frac{7+2\sqrt{35}+5}{7-5}$

$\Rightarrow \frac{12+2\sqrt{35}}{2}$

$\Rightarrow 6 + \sqrt{35}$

Hence, the correct option is (A).

87. Given: $A = 2^7 \times 5^2$

$B = 2^3 \times 5^6$

So, $A \times B = 2^{7+3=10} \times 5^{2+6=8}$ $\left[\because a^m \times a^n = a^{(m+n)}\right]$

$A \times B = 2^{10} \times 5^8$

Hence, the correct option is (A).

88. Given: $5^{\frac{1}{2}}, 9^{\frac{1}{3}}$

$\Rightarrow \left(5^{\frac{1}{2}}\right)^6, \left(9^{\frac{1}{3}}\right)^6$

$\Rightarrow 5^3, 9^2$

$\Rightarrow 125, 81$

So, Only I follows.

Hence, the correct option is (A).

89. From the graph, average soybean imports for 2011 to 2016 (in quintal) $=$
$$\frac{Sum\ of\ soybean\ imports\ for\ each\ year}{Number\ of\ years}$$
$$= \frac{120+340+708+225+390+720}{6} = 417.16$$
Hence, the correct option is (C).

90. From the graph, Import of soybean for year $2011 = 120$

And Import of soybean for year $2012 = 340$

The percentage increase in Soybean import in the year 2012 in comparison to the year 2011,

$$= \frac{Import\ value\ of\ 2012 - Import\ value\ of\ 2011}{Import\ value\ of\ 2011}$$

$$= \frac{340-120}{120} \times 100 = 183.33$$

Hence, the correct option is (B).

91. The rewind() function "rewinds" the position of the file pointer to the beginning of the file. When we are dealing with files then sometimes we need to start with the specified files.

In file handling, we use the rewind() function to move the file position indicator to the start of the specified file stream.

Hence, the correct option is (D).

92. The intersection of a row and column in a worksheet is called a cell. Also called a spreadsheet. The columns are identified by letters (A, B, C), while rows are identified by numbers (1, 2, 3). Each cell has its own name or cell address based on its column and row.

Hence, the correct option is (D).

93. Microsoft Word or MS-Word is an Application software developed by the company Microsoft. It allows users to Type and Save documents. It was first released on October 25, 1983, under the name Multi-Tool Word for Xenix systems.

Hence, the correct option is (C).

94. A home page refers to the main page that appears upon opening a web browser, sometimes called the start page, although the home page of a website can be used as a start page.

Hence, the correct option is (C).

95. HTML is used to write web pages and create electronic documents (called pages) that are displayed on the World Wide Web. Each page contains a series of connections to other pages called hyperlinks. Every web page you see on the Internet is written using one version of HTML code or another.

Hence, the correct option is (C).

96. Multiple Network Graphic is the full form of MNG.

Multiple Network Graphics is a public graphics file format for animated images.

It is a graphics file format, published in 2001, for animated images. Its specification is publicly documented and there are free software reference implementations available.

Hence, the correct option is (B).

97. KYC means "Know Your Customer". It is a process by which banks obtain information about the identity and address of the customers. This process helps to ensure that banks' services are not misused. The KYC procedure is to be completed by the banks while opening accounts and also periodically update the same.

Hence, the correct option is (A).

98. The full form of the IP is Internet Protocol. The Internet Protocol (IP) is the method or protocol by which data is sent from one computer to another on the Internet. Each computer on the Internet has at least one IP address that uniquely identifies it from all other computers on the Internet.

Hence, the correct option is (B).

99. Cut, Copy, and Paste options are located on the Clipboard group of Home Tab.

Cut allows the user to remove the selected text and paste it at a different location. Copy makes a copy of the selected text in the clipboard memory which can then be pasted at another location in the document. Paste allows the cut or copied text to be written at the desired location.

These options are the easiest to locate as they can be found on the Home tab. The clipboard is the first group on the Home tab.

Hence, the correct option is (C).

100. Business correspondents are bank representatives. They help villagers to open bank accounts. The Business Correspondent carries a mobile device and helps villagers in banking transactions. (Deposit money, take money out of savings account, loans, etc.). Thus, business correspondents are agents that provides banking services.

Hence, the correct option is (A).

General Knowledge/Current Affairs

Q.1 The Treaty of Versailles returned Alsace-Lorraine to
________.

A. Italy **B.** Britain **C.** France **D.** Belgium

Q.2 The monk who influenced Ashoka to embrace Buddhism was

A. Vishnugupta **B.** Upagupta
C. Brahmagupta **D.** Brihadratha

Q.3 The common tree species in Nilgiri hills is-

A. Sal **B.** Pine
C. Eucalyptus **D.** Teak

Q.4 Which hill station is called the 'Queen of the Satpura'?

A. Pachmarhi **B.** Nilgiri
C. Mahendragiri **D.** Cardamom

Q.5 Who among the following is the ultimate authority to interpret the Indian Constitution?

A. Parliament
B. Supreme Court of India
C. President
D. Chief Justice of India

Q.6 Who administers the oath of the President of India?

A. Governor General of India
B. Chief Justice of India
C. Prime Minister of India
D. Vice President of India

Q.7 The monetary policy in India is formulated by

A. Central Government
B. Industrial Financial Corporation of India
C. Reserve Bank of India
D. Industrial Development Bank of India

Q.8 The noble gas used for the treatment of cancer is-

A. Helium **B.** Argon **C.** Krypton **D.** Radon

Q.9 Which one of the following is also called the 'power plant' of the cell?

A. Golgi body **B.** Mitochondrion
C. Ribosome **D.** Lysosome

Q.10 Which amongst the following is the largest endocrine gland in the body?

A. Thyroid **B.** Parathyroid
C. Adrenal **D.** Pituitary

Q.11 Which of the following is not a property of heavy water?

A. The Boiling point of heavy water is lower than that of ordinary water.
B. The Density of heavy water is higher than that of ordinary water.
C. The Freezing point of heavy water is higher than that of ordinary water.
D. It produces corrosion.

Q.12 The base used as an antacid is-

A. Calcium hydroxide
B. Barium hydroxide
C. Magnesium hydroxide
D. Silver hydroxide

Q.13 The propagation of sound waves in a gas involve

A. Adiabatic compression and rarefaction
B. Isothermal compression and rarefaction
C. Isochoric compression and rarefaction
D. Isobaric compression and rarefaction

Q.14 The phenomenon of light associated with the appearance of the blue colour of the sky is:

A. Interference **B.** Reflection
C. Refraction **D.** Scattering

Q.15 Blood group was discovered by :

A. Alexander Fleming **B.** William Harvey
C. Landsteiner **D.** Pavlov

Q.16 The most endangered Asiatic top predator on the edge of extinction is

A. Black Bear **B.** Asiatic Lion
C. Siberian Tiger **D.** Dhole

Q.17 First-person who was given Bharat Ratna award posthumously ....?

A. A P J Abdul Kalam **B.** Lal Bahdur Shastri
C. Gulzari Lal Nanda **D.** J R D Tata

Q.18 Who gave the title of 'Dina Bandhu' to C F Andrews?

A. Mahatma Gandhi
B. Madan Mohan Malviya
C. Jawaharlal Nehru
D. Rabindranath Tagore

Q.19 Under Pradhan Mantri Awas Yojana (PMAY) Government of India set a target of building 20 million affordable houses by ________ ?

A. 31 March 2022 **B.** 2 October 2022
C. 15 August 2022 **D.** 26 January 2022

Q.20 The official language of the Delhi Sultanate was?

A. Urdu **B.** Arabic **C.** Persian **D.** Hindi

Q.21 Pitt's India Act of 1784 was a/an :

A. Regulating Act **B.** Ordinance
C. Resolution **D.** White paper

Q.22 The third highest peak in India is -

A. Kanchanjanga
B. Nanda Devi
C. Mount Kamet
D. Anamudi

Q.23 Who is the first Asian swimmer to cross the Catalina Channel of America?

A. Khazan Singh
B. Mihir Sen
C. Satendra Singh Lohia
D. Bula Choudhury

Q.24 The term 'URL' used in Internet technology stands for :

A. Uniform Resource Locater
B. Unique Resource Locater
C. Uniform Remote Locater
D. Unique Remote Locater

Q.25 The Headquarters of the International Atomic Energy Agency is in

A. Geneva
B. Paris
C. Vienna
D. Washington

Q.26 In June 2020, the RBI has approved the extension of tenure for Subramanian Sundar by six months. He is the MD and CEO of which of the following banks?

A. Kotak Mahindra Bank
B. Karnataka Bank
C. South Indian Bank
D. Lakshmi Vilas Bank

Q.27 In June 2020, who among the following has/have nominated for the Arjuna awards by the Boxing Federation of India?

A. Lovlina Borgohain
B. Simranjit Kaur
C. Manish Kaushik
D. All (A), (B) and (C)

Q.28 In June 2020, which of the following has signed Rohit Sharma as its first-ever brand ambassador?

A. Motilal Oswal
B. Angel Broking
C. IIFL Finance
D. 5 Paisa

Q.29 In June 2020, Sibi George has been appointed India's next Ambassador to which of the following countries?

A. Kuwait
B. Saudi Arabia
C. Oman
D. Yemen

Q.30 In June 2020, which bank has announced a special Summer Treats campaign with offers for both merchants and, salaried and self-employed customers?

A. HDFC Bank
B. ICICI Bank
C. PNB
D. SBI

Q.31 Who has been appointed as the new chairman of DLF in June 2020?

A. K.P. Singh
B. Vinay Dubey
C. Rajiv Singh
D. Naresh Goyal

Q.32 Which of the following identity proof is to submit to banks by the customers who receive any benefit or subsidy under Direct Benefit Transfer (DBT) as per Reserve Bank of India(RBI)?

A. Aadhaar Number
B. Permanent Account Number (PAN)
C. Both (A) and (B)
D. Neither (A) nor (B)

Q.33 CPI was in news recently, what does C stands for __________?

A. Currency
B. Consumer
C. Commodity
D. Capital

Q.34 In July 2020, who among the following top executives of Ola has/have resigned?

A. Arun Srinivas
B. Sanjiv Saddy
C. Nilesh Sangoi
D. Both (A) and (B)

Q.35 Amadou Gon Coulibaly passed away in July 2020. He was PM of which of the following countries?

A. Senegal
B. Ivory Coast
C. Ghana
D. Cameroon

Q.36 In July 2020, which bank has announced a reduction in its MCLR (marginal cost of funds-based lending rate) - by 20 basis points across tenors?

A. HDFC Bank
B. ICICI Bank
C. Karnataka Bank
D. Union Bank of India

Q.37 Which state has launched a massive sanitisation drive across the state on 11 July 2020?

A. Uttar Pradesh
B. Bihar
C. Punjab
D. Madhya Pradesh

Q.38 Which of the following has launched Aatamanirbhar Skilled Employee-Employer Mapping (ASEEM) portal in July 2020?

A. NITI Aayog
B. Union Ministry of Skill Development and Entrepreneurship
C. Union Ministry of Human Resource Development
D. DRDO

Q.39 Which of the following has announced the appointment of its new CEO, Karthik Krishnamurthy, in July 2020?

A. Robert Half
B. Kelly Services
C. Aerotek
D. Collabera

Q.40 What is the rank of Joshna Chinappa in the PSA world rankings, released in July 2020?

A. 4th
B. 6th
C. 8th
D. 10th

Q.41 In July 2020, the Mizoram government has launched a mobile application for farmers to give them the latest agriculture-related information. The app will have which of the following features?

A. Information on the cultivation of various crops
B. The maximum requirement for seeds
C. Estimated total production in the first cultivation
D. All (A), (B) and (C)

Q.42 Hockey India named Gyanendro Ningombam as the officiating President at the Emergent Executive Board meeting in July 2020. Whom did he replace?
A. Mushtaque Ahmad
B. Praful Patel
C. Iqbal Mirchi
D. Prithviraj Chavan

Q.43 Where did the Ministry of Tribal Affairs host a Webinar along with Facebook India in July 2020?
A. Pune
B. Mumbai
C. New Delhi
D. Kolkata

Q.44 In July 2020, Who has been appointed as the brand ambassador of SportsAdda?
A. Shane Warne
B. Brett Lee
C. Matthew Hayden
D. Sachin Tendulkar

Q.45 Elyes Fakhfakh handed his resignation to the country's president in July 2020. He was the PM of which country?
A. Algeria
B. Tunisia
C. Libya
D. Lebanon

Q.46 Regarding the Government of India Provisions Act 1935, which of the following statements is not correct?
A. Concurrent Lists
B. A List of Subjects for Princely States
C. Provincial Subjects
D. The Central Subjects

Q.47 Which of the following is not a Fundamental Duty in Part IV A of the Constitution of India?
A. To defend the country and render national service when called upon to do so.
B. To cherish and follow the noble ideals that inspired the national struggle for freedom.
C. pay Income tax fairly.
D. To safeguard public property and to abjure violence.

Q.48 Which of the following was not included originally as the Directive Principle of State Policy in the Constitution of India?
A. Citizen right to an adequate means of livelihood.
B. Free and compulsory education to children under 14 years of age.
C. Free legal aid.
D. Prohibition of slaughter of cows and calves.

Q.49 Right to Property was eliminated from the list of Fundamental Rights during the tenure of one of the following:
A. Indira Gandhi
B. Charan Singh
C. Morarji Desai
D. Rajiv Gandhi

Q.50 Which one of the following does not form a part of the Preamble of the Constitution of India?
A. Liberty of thought
B. Liberty of ideas
C. Liberty of expression
D. Liberty of worship

Reasoning

Q.51 Arrange the following words as per ordering the dictionary:

(1) ASSIGN
(2) ASSOCIATE
(3) ASSIST
(4) ASSISTANT
(5) ASSIGNMENT
A. 1,5,3,4,2
B. 1,3,5,4,2
C. 1,3,5,2,4
D. 1,5,2,4,3

Q.52 January 26, 2007 was Tuesday what day lies on January 26, 2008?
A. Tuesday
B. Wednesday
C. Thursday
D. Saturday

Q.53 For the following question, find the odd word from the given alternatives.
A. Wolf
B. Cat
C. Dog
D. Fox

Q.54 For the following question find the odd letter pair from the given alternatives.
A. BF
B. LR
C. MQ
D. AE

Q.55 For the following question find the odd number pair from the given alternatives.
A. $36 - 72$
B. $17 - 34$
C. $28 - 49$
D. $24 - 48$

Q.56 If E = 5, PEN = 35, then PAGE = ?
A. 27
B. 28
C. 29
D. 30

Q.57 In a certain code CAMEL is written as MFNBD. How shall TIGER be written in that code?
A. SFUJH
B. SFHJU
C. SFJUH
D. SHFJU

Q.58 If $6436 = 14$ and $14416 = 16$, then $324841 = ?$
A. 37
B. 39
C. 47
D. 43

Q.59 A boy runs 20m towards East and turns to the right, runs 10m and turns to the right, runs 9m and again turns to left, runs 5m and turns to left, runs 12m and finally turns to left and runs 6m. Now, which direction is the boy facing?
A. East
B. West
C. North
D. South

Q.60 Which figure represents the relationship among-
Computer skilled, Computer Illiterate, Employees

A.
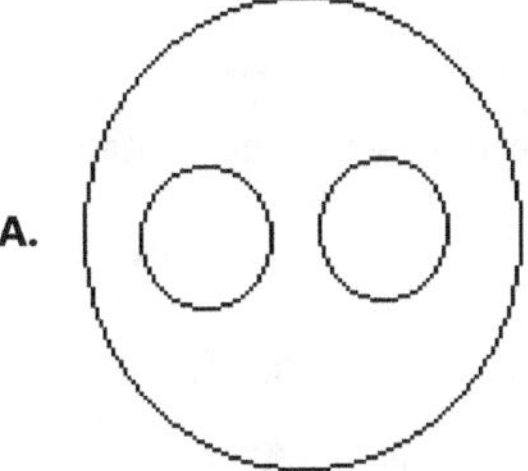

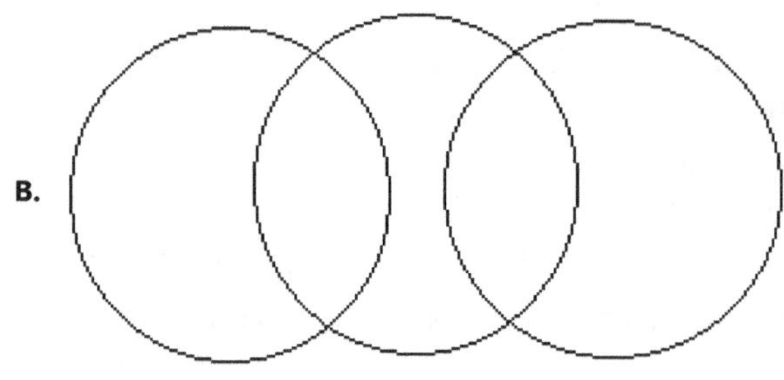

B.

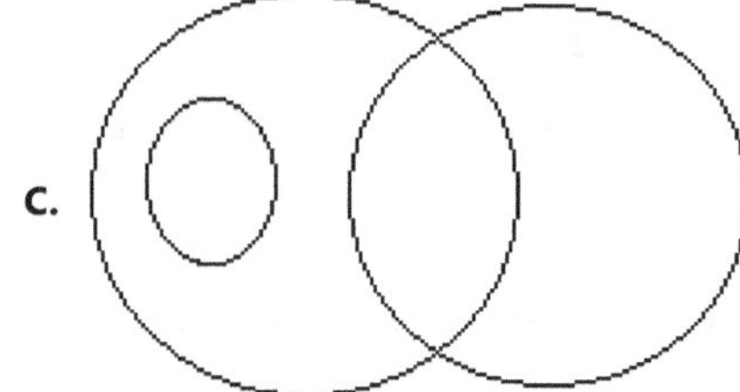

C.

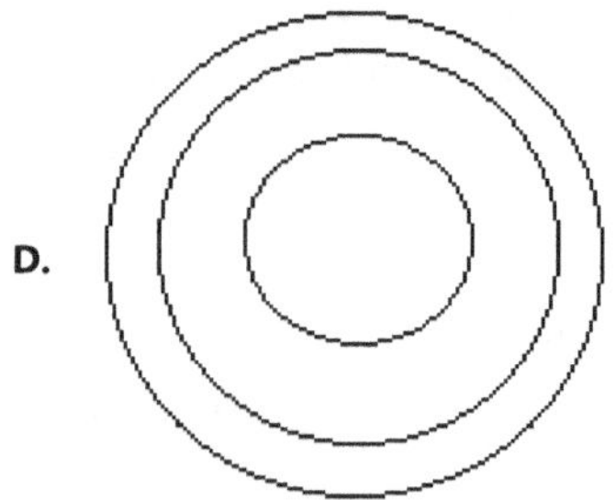

D.

Q.61 If $\times$ stands for $-$, $+$ means $\times$, $\div$ means $+$ and $-$ means $\div$, then what is the value of the given expression?

$$175 - 25 \div 5 + 2 \div 3 + 10 = ?$$

A. 47   **B.** 160   **C.** 240   **D.** 2370

Ques (62-63):Direction: In the following question, select the related letter from the given alternatives.

Q.62 Star : Telescope : : Ship : ?
A. Periscope   **B.** Microscope
C. Deck   **D.** Gyroscope

Q.63 QSUW : TVXZ : : ACEG : ?
A. KMNP   **B.** EGMN   **C.** DFHJ   **D.** FHIL

Q.64 Direction: In the following question, select the related number from the given alternatives.

$$27 : 125 : 64 : ?$$

A. 517   **B.** 162   **C.** 216   **D.** 273

Q.65 In a class, the total number of students are 43. Rohan's position from the top is 23rd and Deepti's position from the bottom is 24. How many students sit between Rohan and Deepti?
A. 3   **B.** 2   **C.** 5   **D.** 6

Q.66 Pointing to the lady in the photograph, Seema said, "Her son's father is the son-in-law of my mother". How is Seema related to the lady?

A. Sister   **B.** Mother   **C.** Cousin   **D.** Aunt

Q.67 A series is given, with one term missing. Choose the correct alternative from the given ones that will complete the series:

$$3, 4, 7, ?, 18, 29, 47$$

A. 8   **B.** 9   **C.** 11   **D.** 12

Q.68 Direction: In this question, statements are given followed by two conclusions I and II. You have to consider both the statements to be true even if they seem to be at variance from commonly known facts. You have to decide which of the given conclusions is/are definitely drawn from the given statements. Select answer as: (A) If only I follows (B) If only II follows (C) If neither I nor II follows (D) If both I and II follow.

Statements:
All coolers are ACs.
No AC is a wall.
Conclusions:
I. Some coolers are walls.
II. No wall is a AC.
A. A   **B.** B   **C.** C   **D.** D

Q.69 Direction: Identify the figure that will complete the pattern.
Question Figure:

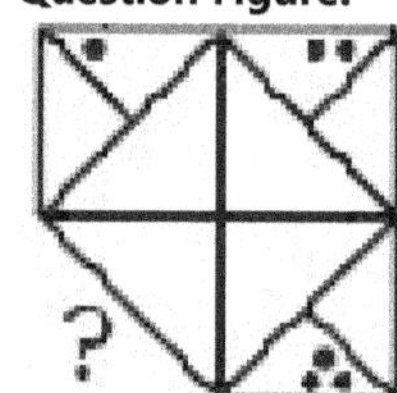

Answer Figures:

 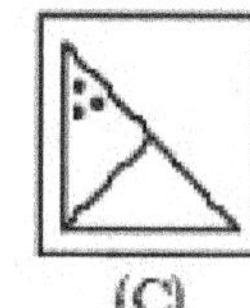 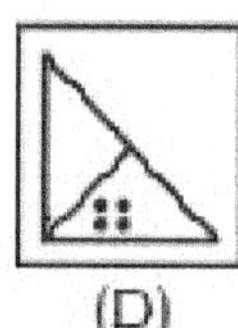

|A| |B| |C| |D|

A. A   **B.** B   **C.** C   **D.** D

Q.70 Direction: Select the alternative in which the question figure can be found.
Question Figure:

Answer Figure:

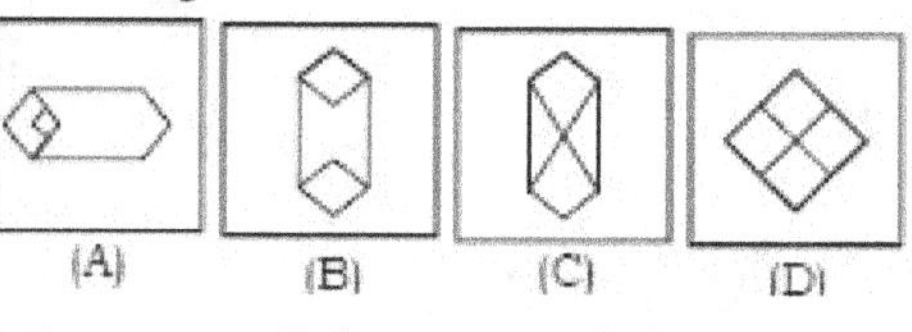

(A)   (B)   (C)   (D)

A. A   **B.** B   **C.** C   **D.** D

Q.71 A word is represented by only one set of numbers as given in any one of the alternatives. The sets of numbers given in the alternatives are represented by two classes of letters as in the two matrices given below. The columns and rows of Matrix-I are numbered from 0 to 4 and that of Matrix-II are numbered from 5 to 9. A letter from these matrices can be represented first by its row and next by its column. E.g., 'A' can be represented by 22,10, etc., 'P' can be represented by 55,67 Similarly, you have to identify the set for the word 'NEAT'.

Matrix - I

	0	1	2	3	4
0	L	N	E	A	C
1	A	C	L	N	E
2	N	E	A	C	L
3	C	L	N	E	A
4	E	A	C	L	N

Matrix - II

	5	6	7	8	9
5	P	T	O	R	S
6	K	S	P	T	O
7	T	O	R	S	P
8	S	P	T	O	R
9	O	R	S	P	T

A. 44,14,34,56

B. 20,33,78,75

C. 13,40,67,99

D. 32,21,41,69

Q.72 If a mirror is placed on the line AB, which of the options figure shows the correct image of the given question figure-

Question figure:

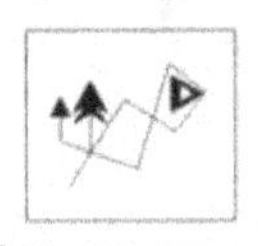

Answer figure:

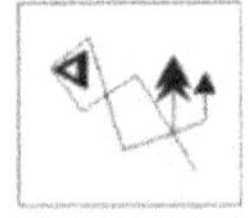 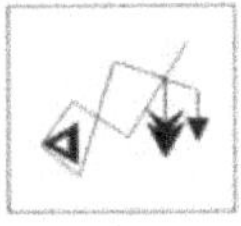 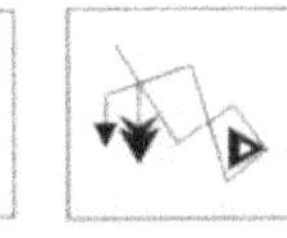 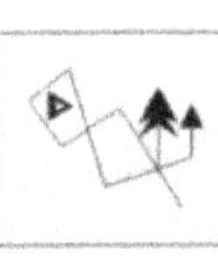

(A) (B) (C) (D)

A. A

B. B

C. C

D. D

Q.73 A piece of paper is folded and cut as shown below in the question figures. From the given answer figures, indicate how it will appear when opened?

Question figures

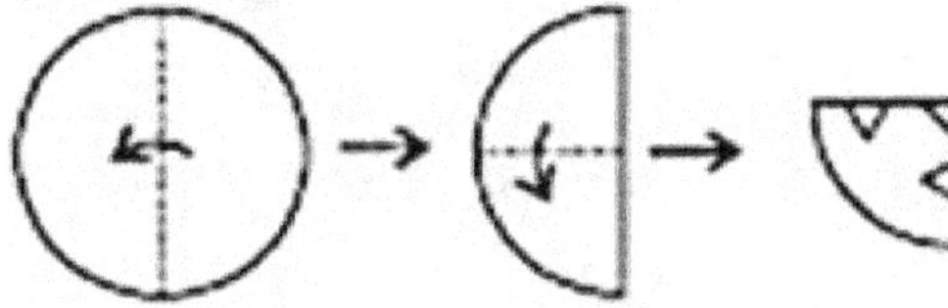

Answer figures

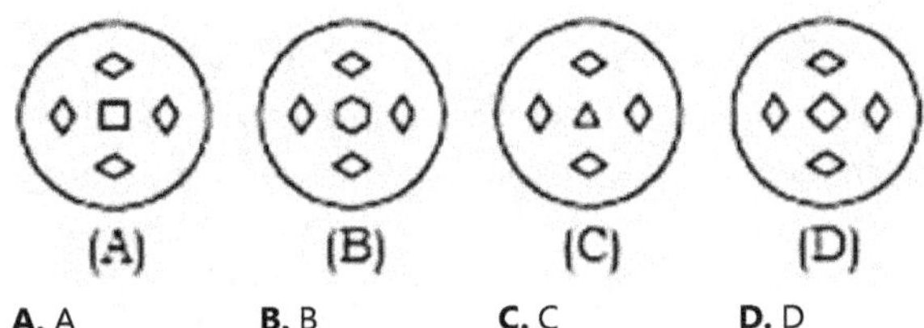

A. A

B. B

C. C

D. D

Q.74 Direction: In the following question, some statements are given followed by some conclusions. You have to take the given statements to be true even if they seem to be at variance with commonly known facts. Read all the conclusions and then decide which of the given conclusions logically follow the given statements, disregarding commonly known facts.

Statements:

All plugs are sockets.

All sockets are cards.

Conclusions:

I. All plugs are cards.

II. All sockets are plugs.

A. If only conclusions I follow

B. If only conclusions II follows

C. If either conclusion I or conclusion II follows

D. If neither conclusion I nor conclusion II follows

Q.75 Suhani is taller than Suman. Suman is neither taller nor Shorter than Brijesh. Brijesh is taller than Priyanka. Piyush is taller than Suhani. Mansi is Shorter than only Suhani. Who is the shortest among them ?

A. Suman

B. Priyanka

C. Mansi

D. Brijesh

Numerical Ability

Q.76 Find the value of $\dfrac{1}{1-x} - \dfrac{1}{1+x} - \dfrac{2x}{1+x^2} - \dfrac{4x^3}{1+x^4} - \dfrac{8x^7}{1+x^8} - \dfrac{16x^{15}}{1-x^{16}}$

A. 0

B. −1

C. 1

D. −2

Q.77 The value of $\sqrt{\dfrac{3+\sqrt{8}}{3-\sqrt{8}}}$

A. $3 - \sqrt{8}$

B. $3 + 2\sqrt{2}$

C. $3 + 2\sqrt{8}$

D. 3

Q.78 Direction: What should come in place of question mark (?) in the following question?

$$\sqrt[4]{\left[\sqrt[4]{\left\{\sqrt[25]{\left(\sqrt[6]{3^{10}}\right)^{12}}\right\}^{10}}\right]^{8}} = ?$$

A. $3^{10/8}$

B. 3^{15}

C. $3^{9/4}$

D. 81

Q.79 Find the value of $x, \dfrac{0.007}{x} = 0.01$

A. 0.77

B. 0.7

C. 0.07

D. 70

Q.80 The number of prime factor is $(8)^{20} \times (15)^{24} \times (7)^{15}$ is-

A. 59   **B.** 98   **C.** 123   **D.** 138

Q.81 How many prime numbers are there between 1 to 100 that even when 18 is subtracted then also it remains a prime number?

A. 11   **B.** 10   **C.** 9   **D.** 12

Q.82 6 men and 8 boys can do a piece of work in 10 days while 26 men and 48 boys finish it in 2 days. 15 men and 20 boys will finish it in.

A. 4 days   **B.** 5 days   **C.** 6 days   **D.** 7 days

Q.83 Machine P can print one lakh books in 8 hours. Machine Q can print the same number of books in 10 hours while machine R can print the same in 12 hours. All the machines started printing at 9 A.M. Machine P is stopped at 11 A.M. and the remaining two machines complete work. Approximately at what time will the printing of one lakh books be completed?

A. 3 PM   **B.** 2 PM   **C.** 1 PM   **D.** 11 AM

Q.84 If a person walks at 15 km/hr instead of 8 km/hr, he would have walked 21 km more. The actual distance traveled by him is:

A. 28 km   **B.** 24 km   **C.** 3 km   **D.** 36 km

Q.85 With a uniform speed, a car covers the distance in 8 hours. If this speed is increased by 4 km/hr, the same distance can be covered in $7\frac{1}{2}$ hours. what is the distance covered?

A. 420 km   **B.** 480 km
C. 640 km   **D.** None of these

Q.86 A sum of Rs. 800 amounts to Rs. 920 is 8 years at simple interest, the interest rate is increased by 8%, it would amount to how much?

A. 992   **B.** 192   **C.** 950   **D.** 882

Q.87 A tree was planted 2 years ago. It increases at the rate of 20% per annum. If at present, the height of the tree 680 cm, what was it when the tree was planted? (Approx)

A. 472 cm   **B.** 380 cm   **C.** 379 cm   **D.** 439 cm

Q.88 A vendor sells 30% of his fruit and throws away 40% of the remaining. The next day he sells 50% of the remaining and throws away the rest. What percentage of the fruit does the vendor throw?

A. 51%   **B.** 49%   **C.** 72%   **D.** 72%

Q.89 Find the cost price of each item. A person sells an article at Rs. 1800 after giving a discount of 15% on labeled price. Had he not given the discount, he would have earned a profit of 10% on the cost price.

A. Rs. 1875.26   **B.** Rs. 1925.13
C. Rs. 1825.75   **D.** Rs. 1935.26

Q.90 If the difference between the selling price with a discount of 30% on the marked price and two successive discounts of 20% and 10% is Rs. 72 then the marked price (in Rs) is:

A. 3600   **B.** 2400   **C.** 2000   **D.** 7200

Computer Awareness

Q.91 What we get when we use the term **FIND**?
A. Format   **B.** Characters
C. Symbol   **D.** All of the above

Q.92 The first graphical browser for the WWW was named
A. Netscape   **B.** Veronica   **C.** Mosaic   **D.** Explorer

Q.93 Which of the following is a chart type present in MS Excel?
A. Bubble   **B.** Satellite   **C.** Both   **D.** None

Q.94 Which is not a data source component?
A. Mail merge toolbar   **B.** Header row
C. Data fields   **D.** Data records

Q.95 The World Wide Web is composed of-
A. 1 Page
B. Only 100 Web pages
C. 500 Web pages
D. Millions of Web pages

Q.96 What type of software is LINUX?
A. Compiler
B. Operating System
C. Utility Software
D. Application Software

Q.97 Each computer connected to the internet must-
A. have a modem connection.
B. be an IBM PC.
C. have a unique IP address.
D. be internet compatible.

Q.98 How many sheets are there in Excel Workbook by default?
A. 2   **B.** 3   **C.** 4   **D.** 5

Q.99 What is the file that is attached to the email and is sent to the recipient?
A. Appendage   **B.** Annexure
C. Attachment   **D.** Add on

Q.100 Which of the following is not related to email?
A. PowerPoint   **B.** Inbox
C. Sender   **D.** Receiver

// Smart Answer Sheet //

Correct — Indicates percentage of students who answered questions correctly.

Skipped — Indicates percentage of students who skipped questions.

Q.	Ans.	Correct / Skipped	Q.	Ans.	Correct / Skipped	Q.	Ans.	Correct / Skipped	Q.	Ans.	Correct / Skipped	Q.	Ans.	Correct / Skipped
1	C	17.68 % / 16.73 %	17	B	35.74 % / 34.98 %	33	B	31.18 % / 34.03 %	49	C	24.9 % / 36.89 %	65	B	28.52 % / 41.25 %
2	B	22.81 % / 34.6 %	18	A	23.19 % / 36.7 %	34	D	19.2 % / 37.26 %	50	B	21.1 % / 36.31 %	66	A	37.07 % / 40.12 %
3	C	24.14 % / 35.94 %	19	A	27.57 % / 33.08 %	35	B	29.85 % / 39.73 %	51	A	39.16 % / 38.41 %	67	C	38.59 % / 42.59 %
4	A	22.81 % / 34.98 %	20	C	41.63 % / 30.42 %	36	D	10.46 % / 40.3 %	52	B	42.21 % / 40.87 %	68	B	41.06 % / 41.26 %
5	B	38.4 % / 36.7 %	21	A	36.12 % / 34.03 %	37	A	29.85 % / 35.55 %	53	B	27.76 % / 39.35 %	69	D	51.33 % / 36.69 %
6	B	53.04 % / 35.55 %	22	A	12.93 % / 34.6 %	38	B	31.18 % / 37.83 %	54	B	50.0 % / 41.06 %	70	B	45.82 % / 39.92 %
7	C	45.44 % / 35.74 %	23	C	25.29 % / 38.78 %	39	D	15.78 % / 40.3 %	55	C	52.09 % / 42.02 %	71	A	42.97 % / 40.11 %
8	D	37.83 % / 36.31 %	24	A	39.16 % / 32.7 %	40	D	7.79 % / 42.4 %	56	C	50.19 % / 40.87 %	72	C	29.28 % / 42.2 %
9	B	46.58 % / 35.74 %	25	C	25.48 % / 36.69 %	41	D	30.61 % / 35.93 %	57	B	49.81 % / 43.35 %	73	D	48.67 % / 37.64 %
10	A	29.85 % / 35.55 %	26	D	14.64 % / 38.21 %	42	A	32.7 % / 38.4 %	58	C	25.48 % / 45.62 %	74	A	36.31 % / 41.64 %
11	A	19.2 % / 37.07 %	27	D	29.09 % / 38.02 %	43	C	29.28 % / 37.45 %	59	C	36.5 % / 41.83 %	75	B	41.63 % / 41.83 %
12	C	20.15 % / 38.79 %	28	C	21.1 % / 37.07 %	44	B	20.34 % / 36.31 %	60	B	23.76 % / 41.26 %	76	A	15.59 % / 45.82 %
13	A	11.6 % / 40.11 %	29	A	38.02 % / 36.5 %	45	B	17.3 % / 39.73 %	61	A	49.43 % / 40.11 %	77	B	23.0 % / 45.25 %
14	D	40.3 % / 34.6 %	30	A	12.17 % / 39.16 %	46	B	20.91 % / 36.5 %	62	A	14.64 % / 41.25 %	78	D	19.58 % / 47.34 %
15	C	36.69 % / 34.98 %	31	C	12.93 % / 39.73 %	47	C	28.9 % / 37.45 %	63	C	55.13 % / 41.07 %	79	B	33.46 % / 44.68 %
16	D	9.89 % / 36.31 %	32	A	10.08 % / 35.55 %	48	C	11.98 % / 36.31 %	64	C	47.91 % / 41.44 %	80	C	14.83 % / 51.71 %

Q.	Ans.	Correct
		Skipped
81	D	8.94 %
		49.62 %
82	A	20.53 %
		49.05 %
83	C	19.58 %
		48.86 %
84	B	24.9 %
		47.91 %

Q.	Ans.	Correct
		Skipped
85	B	25.67 %
		47.52 %
86	A	20.72 %
		47.15 %
87	A	21.1 %
		46.96 %
88	B	30.99 %
		43.53 %

Q.	Ans.	Correct
		Skipped
89	B	16.54 %
		49.05 %
90	A	21.1 %
		46.77 %
91	D	48.48 %
		38.59 %
92	C	13.69 %
		40.49 %

Q.	Ans.	Correct
		Skipped
93	A	7.22 %
		39.74 %
94	A	19.2 %
		40.31 %
95	D	42.97 %
		39.54 %
96	B	38.02 %
		39.55 %

Q.	Ans.	Correct
		Skipped
97	C	31.18 %
		40.3 %
98	B	18.25 %
		42.59 %
99	C	43.73 %
		40.11 %
100	A	50.38 %
		39.16 %

Performance Analysis

Avg. Score (%)	33.0%
Toppers Score (%)	97.0%
Your Score	

//Hints and Solutions//

1. The Treaty of Versailles returned Alsace-Lorraine to France.

The Treaty of Versailles was the most important of the peace treaties that brought World War I to an end. The Treaty ended the state of war between Germany and the Allied Powers. It was signed on 28 June 1919 in Versailles, exactly five years after the assassination of Archduke Franz Ferdinand, which had directly led to the war. The signing of the Treaty of Versailles after World War I restored Alsace and Lorraine to France. After approximately 200 years of French rule, Alsace and the German-speaking part of Lorraine were ceded to Germany in 1871 under the Treaty of Frankfurt. In 1919, both regions were returned to France.

Hence, the correct option is (C).

2. The monk who influenced Ashoka to embrace Buddhism was Upagupta.

Upagupta (3rd Century BC) was a Buddhist monk. According to some stories in the Sanskrit text Ashokavadana, he was the spiritual teacher of the Mauryan emperor Ashoka. Upagupta's teacher was Sanavasi who was a disciple of Ānanda, the Buddha's attendant.

Hence, the correct option is (B).

3. Eucalyptus (Eucalyptus) is the common tree species found in the Nilgiri Hills. Nilgiri is defined as a category of mountains. The border lies at the junction of the South Indian states namely Karnataka and Kerala. It is a part of the Western Ghats, called its original range in western TN. This range of mountains is also known as 'N Nilgiri Hills' or 'The Queen of Hills' or 'Blue Mountains'.

Hence, the correct option is (C).

4. Pachmarhi hill is known as Satpura ki Rani ("Queen of Satpura").

Pachmarhi is a hill station in the Hoshangabad district of Madhya Pradesh state of central India. It has been the location of a cantonment (Pachmarhi Cantonment) since British Raj. It is widely known as Satpura ki Rani ("Queen of Satpura"), situated at a height of 1067 m in a valley of the Satpura Range in Hoshangabad district. Dhupgarh, the highest point (1,352 m) in Madhya Pradesh and the Satpura range is located here. It is a part of Satpura Biosphere Reserve. Pachmarhi is a hill station in central India. It is also famous for Satpura Tiger Reserve, Satpura National Park, Lord Shiva, Pandavas of Mahabharata.

Hence, the correct option is (A).

5. Supreme Court of India is the ultimate authority to interpret the Indian Constitution.

As per Article 141, the law declared by the Supreme Court of India is to be binding on each court within the Indian territory as it's the apex court of the nation. It also has the final judicial authority of interpreting the constitution as well as for deciding questions on national law and local bylaws. The implementation of rule of law is vested in the Supreme Court.

Hence, the correct option is (B).

6. The Chief Justice of India administers the oath of the President of India.

The oath of the President is taken in the presence of the Chief Justice of India, and in his absence, by the most senior judge of the Supreme Court of India.

Hence, the correct option is (B).

7. The monetary policy in India is formulated by the Reserve Bank of India.

Monetary policy refers to the policy of the central bank with regard to the use of monetary instruments under its control to achieve the goals specified in the Act, 1934. The Reserve Bank of India (RBI) is vested with the responsibility of conducting monetary policy.

Hence, the correct option is (C).

8. The noble gas used for the treatment of cancer is Radon. Radon is a colorless, inert, and radioactive gas. Small doses of radon radiation are used in radon therapy for cancer treatment.

Hence, the correct option is (D).

9. The Mitochondrion is also called the 'power plant' of the cell.

Mitochondria are described as "cellular power plants," because they generate most of the cell's supply of ATP, used as a source of chemical energy.

In addition to supplying cellular energy, mitochondria are involved in other functions such as signaling, cell differentiation, cell death, as well as control of the cell cycle and cell growth.

Hence, the correct option is (B).

10. The thyroid gland is the largest purely endocrine gland.

The thyroid, or thyroid gland, is an endocrine gland in the neck consisting of two connected lobes. The lower two-thirds of the lobes are connected by a thin band of tissue called the thyroid isthmus. The thyroid is located at the front of the neck, below Adam's apple.

Hence, the correct option is (A).

11. The boiling point of heavy water is lower than that of ordinary water is not a property of heavy water.

The density of heavy water (1.1056 g/mL) is higher than that of ordinary water (1.054 g/mL). The freezing point of heavy water (3.82°C) is higher than that of ordinary water (0°C). The boiling point of heavy water is about 101.4°C and the boiling point of normal water is 100ºC. Heavy water is corrosive in nature due to the presence of heavy isotopes of hydrogen (deuterium).

Hence, the correct option is (A).

12. The base used as an antacid is Magnesium hydroxide.

Milk of magnesia (Magnesium hydroxide) is an alkaline suspension, meaning that it will cause neutralization when it encounters anything acidic. This is why it makes an excellent antacid, as it neutralizes excess stomach acid (hydrochloric acid) when swallowed.

Hence, the correct option is (C).

13. The propagation of sound waves in a gas involves adiabatic compression and rarefaction.

An adiabatic process is one that occurs without the transfer of heat or matter between a thermodynamic system and its surroundings. In an adiabatic process, energy is transferred only as work. Compressions are regions of high pressure due to particles being close together. Rarefactions are regions of low pressure due to particles being spread further apart.

Hence, the correct option is (A).

14. The phenomenon of light associated with the appearance of the blue colour of the sky is Scattering.

The scattering of colour depends on its wavelength. The color of which the wavelength of light is the least, that colour has the highest scattering, and the colour of which the wavelength of light is the highest, that colour has the least scattering. An example of this is the colour of the sky, which appears blue due to the scattering of sunlight.

Hence, the correct option is (D).

15. A Blood group was discovered by Landsteiner.

The blood group was discovered by Landsteiner. When Karl Landsteiner at the University of Vienna discovered some blood transfusions were successful, while others proved fatal. Landsteiner discovered the ABO blood group system by mixing the red cells and serum of each of his staff. He reported that some people's serum-stimulated the red cells of others. From these early experiments, he identified three types, called A, B, and O.

Hence, the correct option is (C).

16. The most endangered Asiatic top predator on the edge of extinction is Dhole.

Dhole is a member of the canine family found in Central, South, and Southeast Asia. This Asiatic wild dog is extremely endangered, with the IUCN estimating a declining population of fewer than 2,500 dholes are left in the world.

Hence, the correct option is (D).

17. First-person who was given Bharat Ratna award posthumously was Lal Bahdur Shastri.

In 1966, Shri Lal Bahadur Shastri was the first to receive the Bharat Ratna posthumously. As per the Government of India, Bharat Ratna is given for exceptional service/ performance of the highest order in any field of human endeavour. The prime minister gives the recommendations for the Bharat Ratna to the president.

Hence, the correct option is (B).

18. Mahatma Gandhi gave the title of 'Dina Bandhu' to C F Andrews.

Charles Freer Andrews (12 February 1871- 5 April 1940) was a priest of the England Church. A Christian missionary, educator, and social reformer in India, he became a close friend of Mahatma Gandhi and identified with the cause of India's independence.

Hence, the correct option is (A).

19. Under Pradhan Mantri Awas Yojana (PMAY) Government of India set a target of building 20 million affordable houses by 31 March 2022.

Pradhan Mantri Awas Yojana (PMAY) is an initiative by the Government of India in which affordable housing will be provided to the urban poor with a target of building 20 million affordable houses by 31 March 2022. It has two components: Pradhan Mantri Awas Yojana (Urban) (PMAY-U) for the urban poor and Pradhan Mantri Awaas Yojana (Gramin) (PMAY-G and also PMAY-R) for the rural poor.

Hence, the correct option is (A).

20. The official language of the Delhi Sultanate was Persian.

The Delhi Sultanate literature began with the rise of Persian speaking people to the throne of the Sultanate of Delhi. Soon literary works in Persian began to appear and it was declared the official language.

Hence, the correct option is (C).

21. Pitt's India Act of 1784 was a Regulating Act.

The East India Company Act (EIC Act 1784), also known as Pitt's India Act, was an Act of the Parliament of Great Britain intended to address the shortcomings of the Regulating Act of 1773 by bringing the East India Company's rule in India under the control of the British Government.

Hence, the correct option is (A).

22. The third highest peak in India is Kanchenjunga.

Kanchenjunga is the third highest Himalayan peak in the world that lies partly in Nepal and partly in Sikkim, India. Mount Everest is the highest peak in the world Sikkim is a small state located in the North East of India. It is surrounded by Nepal to the West, Bhutan to the East, China to the North, and State West Bengal to the South.

Hence, the correct option is (A).

23. Satendra Singh Lohia, Para-swimmer from Madhya Pradesh, has become the first Asian swimmer to cross the Catalina Channel of America. Gwalior born Satendra led the Indian Para Relay team along with five teammates and crossed the Catalina Channel in 11 hours 34 minutes. At that time, the water temperature was around 13 degrees Celsius. Satendra holds the Asian record of crossing both the English and Catalina channels.

Hence, the correct option is (B).

24. The term 'URL' used in Internet technology stands for Uniform Resource Locator.

The abbreviation form URL is known as the Uniform Resource Locator. Generally, this is known as a web address. The URL is a reference to the web resource, which specifies its location on the computer and retrieves it for the system.

Hence, the correct option is (A).

25. The Headquarters of the International Atomic Energy Agency is in Vienna, Austria.

The International Atomic Energy Agency (IAEA) is an international organization that seeks to promote the peaceful use of nuclear energy and to inhibit its use for any military purpose, including nuclear weapons. The IAEA has its headquarters in Vienna, Austria.

Hence, the correct option is (C).

26. In June 2020, the RBI has approved the extension of tenure for Subramanian Sundar by six months. He is the MD and CEO of Lakshmi Vilas Bank.

The RBI has approved the extension of tenure for Lakshmi Vilas Bank's MD and CEO, Subramanian Sundar by six months. This is the second extension given to Mr. Sundar who was the MD & CEO (interim) from January 1 to April 30, 2020. On 1 June 2020, the board extended his tenure till November 30 or till the appointment of the new CEO, whichever is earlier.

Hence, the correct option is (D).

27. The BFI has nominated the trio of Lovlina Borgohain, Simranjit Kaur and Manish Kaushik for the Arjuna awards.

Lovlina Borgohain: Lovlina Borgohain (born 2 October 1997) is an Indian amateur woman boxer who won a bronze medal at the 2018 AIBA Women's World Boxing Championships and the 2019 AIBA Women's World Boxing Championships.

Simranjit Kaur: Simranjit Kaur Baatth is an Indian amateur boxer from Punjab. She has represented India internationally since 2011. Kaur won a bronze medal for India at the 2018 AIBA Women's World Boxing Championships.

Manish Kaushik: Subedar Manish Kaushik (born 11 January 1996) is an Indian boxer who won a silver medal in the 2018 Commonwealth Games, in the lightweight division, Kaushik won a gold medal at the 2017 National Boxing Games in the same weight category. He hails from the village of Devsar in the Bhiwani district of Haryana.

Hence, the correct option is (D).

28. Rohit Sharma has signed with IIFL Finance as its first-ever brand ambassador.

Besides being the vice-captain of the Indian cricket team in the limited-overs format, Rohit also holds the record for the highest individual score in one-day internationals (ODI).

He is also the only player to hit three double centuries in ODIs, and 1-5 winning captain of the Indian Premier League (IPL).

Hence, the correct option is (C).

29. Sibi George, an Indian Foreign Service officer of 1993 batch, has been appointed India's next Ambassador to Kuwait. He is at present India's Ambassador in Switzerland. K Jeevasagar, the present Indian Ambassador to Kuwait, retired in the last week of May 2020.

Hence, the correct option is (A).

30. In June 2020, HDFC Bank has announced a special Summer Treats campaign with offers for both merchants and, salaried and self-employed customers. As part of the campaign, the bank will offer no-cost EMI and no down payment for large appliances, discounts and cashback on select brands, and 50 percent extra reward points on online spend using credit cards.

HDFC Bank: Headquarters - Mumbai.

Hence, the correct option is (A).

31. Rajiv Singh has been appointed as the new chairman of DLF in June 2020.

DLF on June 4, 2020, appointed vice-chairman Rajiv Singh as the new chairman of the company, replacing K.P. Singh. The latter will continue in a non-executive role as Chairman Emeritus.

Hence, the correct option is (C).

32. Aadhaar number is to submit to banks by the customers who receive any benefit or subsidy under Direct Benefit Transfer (DBT) as per Reserve Bank of India (RBI).

The Reserve Bank of India (RBI) has permitted banks to accept Aadhaar number (Offline verification) to Know Your Customer (KYC) verification with the consent of the customers. RBI has added the 'Proof of possession of Aadhaar number' to the list of Officially Valid Documents (OVD). This was notified by the RBI in its amended Master Direction on KYC. RBI's Master Direction is a rule book that the regulated entities need to follow. The bank should obtain the Aadhaar number from the customers who receive any benefit or subsidy under Direct Benefit Transfer (DBT). For Non-DBT beneficiary customers, the Regulated Entities (RES) should obtain a certified copy of any OVD describing the details of the customer's identity and address along with 1 recent photograph.

Hence, the correct option is (A).

33. C stands for Consumer. The full form of CPI is (Consumer Price Index). Consumer Price Index or CPI as it is commonly called is an index measuring retail inflation in the economy by collecting the change in prices of most common goods and services used by consumers.

Hence, the correct option is (B).

34. In July 2020, Arun Srinivas, and Sanjiv Saddy top executives of Ola has resigned.

Arun Srinivas, chief sales and marketing officer, and Sanjiv Saddy, senior vice-president, corporate affairs, have resigned.

Srinivas, who was appointed as Ola CMO in July 2019, managed marketing, category management, sales and supply management for the cab-hailing platform both in India and abroad.

Hence, the correct option is (D).

35. Amadou Gon Coulibaly passed away in July 2020. He was PM of Ivory Coast.
Amadou Gon Coulibaly (10 February 1959 – 8 July 2020) was an Ivorian politician who served as Prime Minister of Ivory Coast from January 2017 until his death in July 2020.
Ivory Coast (Republic of Ivory Coast) - is a country located on the south coast of West Africa. Ivory Coast's political capital is

Yamoussoukro in the centre of the country, while its economic capital and largest city is the port city of Abidjan.

Hence, the correct option is (B).

36. Union Bank of India has announced a reduction in its marginal cost of funds-based lending rate - MCLR by 20 basis points across tenors.

The new rates were applicable from 11 July 2020. The revised one-year MCLR stands at 7.40 percent as against 7.60 percent earlier. The three-month and six-month MCLRs have been cut to 7.10 percent and 7.25 percent, respectively.

Hence, the correct option is (D).

37. Uttar Pradesh government launched a massive sanitisation drive across the state on 11 July 2020.
Chief Minister of Uttar Pradesh Mr. Yogi Adityanath monitored the drive aimed at containing COVID-19 in the state. UP was under a series of restrictions for a period of 55 hours since 10 July 2020. The restrictions, which started at 10 PM on 10 July 2020, was continued till 5 AM on 13 July 2020.

Hence, the correct option is (A).

38. Union Ministry of Skill Development and Entrepreneurship has launched Aatamanirbhar Skilled Employee-Employer Mapping (ASEEM) portal.

It will help skilled people find sustainable livelihood opportunities.

The portal will map details of workers based on regions and local industry demands and will bridge the demand-supply gap of skilled workforce across sectors.

Hence, the correct option is (B).

39. Collabera, a global technology talent solutions provider, has announced the appointment of its new CEO, Karthik Krishnamurthy.

Previously, Karthik was SVP and Global Markets Leader at Cognizant and a member of their Executive Leadership team. He was instrumental in driving multi-million dollar growth for a slew of businesses that included Artificial Intelligence (AI) & Analytics, IoT, etc.

Hence, the correct option is (D).

40. Joshna Chinappa is the 10th ranker in the PSA world.

India's squash star Joshna Chinappa has broken back into the top-10 of the PSA world rankings following the retirement of Egyptian world number one Raneem El Welily. Joshna, who has not played since March 2020 due to the COVID-19 pandemic, moved up a spot to be in 10th position.

Tarek Momen is the 4th ranker in the PSA world.

Diego Elias is the 6th ranker in the PSA world.

Simon Rosner is the 8th ranker in the PSA world.

Hence, the correct option is (D).

41. In July 2020, the Mizoram government has launched a mobile application for farmers to give them the latest agriculture-related information. The app features:

- **Information on the cultivation of various crops.**
- **The maximum requirement for seeds.**
- **Estimated total production in the first cultivation.**
- **protection of crops from pest infestation.**

The state government has been making massive efforts to alleviate the difficulties faced by farmers, who have been affected by the lockdown.

Hence, the correct option is (D).

42. Hockey India named Gyanendro Ningombam as the officiating President at the Emergent Executive Board meeting after Mushtaque Ahmad tendered his resignation.
Mushtaque Ahmad had been in his role as President of the national sports body since 2018. Sports Ministry had asked Mushtaque Ahmad to step down having declared that his 2018 election was a violation of the National Sports Code's tenure guidelines.

Hence, the correct option is (A).

43. Ministry of Tribal Affairs on 10 July 2020 hosted a Webinar along with Facebook India in New Delhi.

It was for sensitization of Members of Parliament from Scheduled Tribe (ST) Constituencies on Going Online As Leaders (GOAL) Project.

Union Minister for Tribal Affairs Arjun Munda and Minister of State for Tribal Affairs Renuka Singh Saruta also participated in the Webinar.

Hence, the correct option is (C).

44. In July 2020, Brett Lee has been appointed as the brand ambassador of SportsAdda.

SportsAdda, an Indian news and information website for cricket, football, and kabaddi, has signed former Australian cricket legend Brett Lee, as its brand ambassador. As an ambassador, Lee will be conducting a host of fun activities including contests, quizzes, Q&As, bowling master classes, and giveaways that will feature exclusively on the SportsAdda app, website, and social handles. Lee has taken over 700 wickets in his international career across all three formats.

Hence, the correct option is (B).

45. Elyes Fakhfakh handed his resignation to the country's president in July 2020. He was the PM of Tunisia.

Tunisia's Prime Minister Elyes Fakhfakh handed his resignation to the country's president on 15 July 2020, amid a brewing political crisis. Fakhfakh was appointed Prime Minister by President Kais Saied in January 2020. Fakhfakh was accused of conflict of interest by owning shares in companies that had received state contracts.

Hence, the correct option is (B).

46. A List of Subjects for the Princely States doesn't come under Regarding Government of India Provisions Act 1935. So, it is not a correct statement.

A princely state, also called native state, feudatory state or Indian state (for those states on the subcontinent), was a vassal state under a local or indigenous or regional ruler in a subsidiary alliance with the British Raj.

Government of India Provisions Act 1935 was the last constitution of British India, before the division of the country, in 1947 and worked till the Indian Constitution was framed. It has consisted of 321 sections and 10 schedules. Some of its features were:

- Introduced provincial autonomy and dyarchy at centre.
- It provided for the establishment of a federal court.
- It gave a measure to form a federal form of government and an all India Federation.
- The act divided the powers between the Centre and provinces in terms of three list-Federal List (for Centre, with 59 items), Provincial List (for Provinces, with 54 items), and Concurrent list (for both, with 36 items). Residuary powers were given to the Viceroy.

Hence, the correct option is (B).

47. Pay income tax fairly is a part of civic duty, not fundamental duty.

The followings are the Fundamental Duty in Part IV A of the Constitution of India:

To defend the country and render national service when called upon to do so.

To cherish and follow the noble ideals that inspired the national struggle for freedom.

The Fundamental Duties were added to the Constitution in 1976 on the recommendation of the Sardar Swaran Singh Committee. Initially, there were 10 Fundamental Duties but one more was added in 2002.

To safeguard public property and to abjure violence.

Hence, the correct option is (C).

48. Free legal aid was not included originally as the Directive Principle of State Policy in the Constitution of India.

Article 39A of the Constitution of India provides for free legal aid to the poor and weaker sections of the society, to promote justice on the basis of equal opportunity.

The following was included originally as the Directive Principle of State Policy in the Constitution of India:

- Citizen right to an adequate means of livelihood.
- Free and compulsory education to children under 14 years of age.
- Equal justice and free legal Article 39A was added in the Indian Constitution by the 42nd Constitutional Amendment Act, 1976.
- Prohibition of slaughter of cows and calves.

Hence, the correct option is (C).

49. Right to Property was eliminated from the list of Fundamental Rights during the tenure of Morarji Desai.

The Morarji Desai government eventually scrapped the fundamental right to property with the forty-fourth amendment in 1978. In its place came Article 300-A that makes it possible for a citizen to be dispossessed without compensation through an act of legislation. Successive governments chipped away at the right to property by arguing that it was an obstacle in the way of pursuing the social justice agenda embedded in the directive principles of state policy.

Hence, the correct option is (C).

50. Liberty of ideas is not a part of the Preamble of the Constitution of India.

The preamble of the constitution of India professes to secure the liberty of belief, thought, expression, faith, and worship which are essential to the development of the individuals and the nation. Liberty or freedom signifies the absence of external impediments of motion.

The Preamble declares:

- "WE, THE PEOPLE OF INDIA, having solemnly resolved to constitute India into a SOVEREIGN SOCIALIST SECULAR DEMOCRATIC REPUBLIC and to secure to all its citizens:
- JUSTICE, social, economic and political;
- LIBERTY, of thought, expression, belief, faith and worship;
- EQUALITY of status and of opportunity; and to promote among them all.
- FRATERNITY assuring the dignity of the individual and the unity and integrity of the Nation;
- In our constituent assembly this twenty-sixth day of November 1949, do hereby adopt, enact and give to ourselves this constitution."

Hence, the correct option is (B).

51. According to dictionary order-

The Sequence will be as follows : 1,5,3,4,2

(1) ASSIGN

(5) ASSIGNMENT

(3) ASSIST

(4) ASSISTANT

(2) ASSOCIATE

Hence, the correct option is (A).

52. Year 2007 is an ordinary year

So, number of odd days = 1

Hence, day on 26 January, 2008 = Tuesday + 1 = Wednesday

Hence, the correct option is (B).

53. All of the above animals i.e., WOLF, FOX & DOG are belonging to the dog species, except the cat.

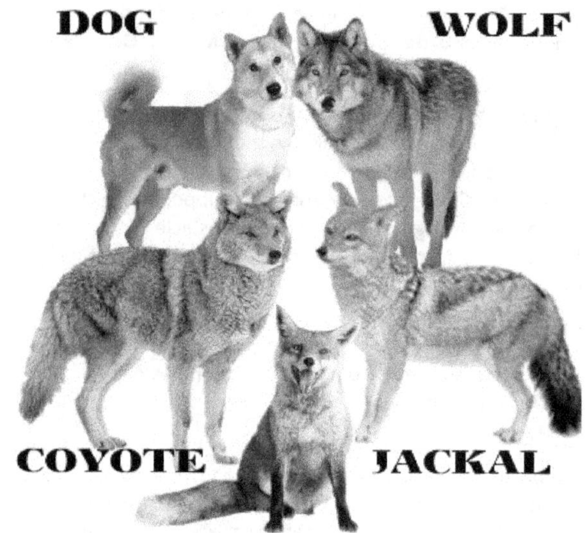

Hence, the correct option is (B).

54. According to the alphabetical sequence, there is 6 letter difference between L, R, Whereas the difference between the other three is 4.

BCDE**F**

LMNOPQ**R**

MNOPQ

ABCD**E**

Hence, the correct option is (B).

55. Given alternatives,

$$36 \times 2 = 72$$
$$17 \times 2 = 34$$
$$24 \times 2 = 48$$

All of the above are multiple of 2,

But in $28 - 49$, the second number is not double the first number.

Hence, the correct option is (C).

56. It is given that E is coded as 5.

We can also see that its rank from letters is also 5.

Similarly in PEN,

P ⇒ 16

E ⇒ 5

N ⇒ 14

Now, we should add this,

16+5+14 = 35

We are getting like 35, therefore it following the question.

Now in PAGE,

P ⇒ 16

A ⇒ 1

G ⇒ 7

E ⇒ 5

Now add these,

16+1+7+5 = 29

∴ The required answer for this Question is 29.

Hence, the correct option is (C).

57. Alphabet+1 is working in reversed order.

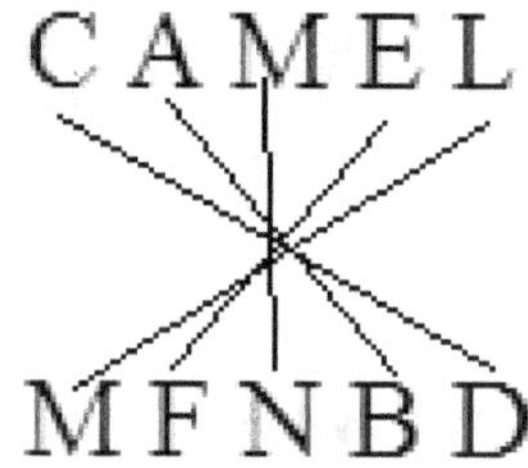

Hence, the correct option is (B).

58. Given, $6436 = 14$

$$\Rightarrow 8^2 + 6^2 = 8 + 6 = 14$$

and $14416 = 16$

$$\Rightarrow 12^2 + 4^2 = 12 + 4 = 16$$

Similarly,

$$324841 = ?$$
$$\Rightarrow 18^2 + 29^2 = 18 + 29 = 47$$

Hence, the correct option is (C).

59.

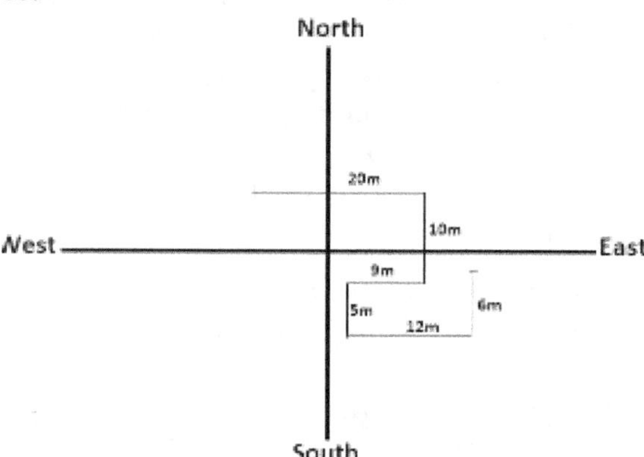

A boy runs 20m towards East and turns to the right, runs 10m and turns to the right, runs 9m and again turns to left, runs 5m and turns to left, runs 12m and finally turns to left and runs 6m. Now, The boy facing to the North direction.

Hence, the correct option is (C).

60. Only option B represents the correct relation as:

As we can see the figure it represents that all the employees can be skilled or illiterate too, so when we observe the above figure which clearly shows that some employees can be computer skilled and some can be computer illiterate.

Hence, the correct option is (B).

61. According to the question

$$175 - 25 \div 5 + 2 \div 3 + 10 = ?$$

After converting:

$$175 \div 25 + 5 \times 2 + 3 \times 10 = ?$$

$$7 + 10 + 30 = ?$$

$$= 47$$

Hence, the correct option is (A).

62. As the telescope is used to gaze at the stars the same way a periscope is used to see ships.

Hence, the correct option is (A).

63. Each letter of the first group is moved three steps forward to obtain the corresponding letter of the second group.

Q + 3 ⇒ T

S + 3 ⇒ V

U + 3 ⇒ X

W + 3 ⇒ Z

Similarly, we can have the corresponding letter for ACEG :

A + 3 ⇒ D

C + 3 ⇒ F

E + 3 ⇒ H

G + 3 ⇒ J

Hence, the correct option is (C).

64.
$$27 : \quad 125 : \quad 64 : \quad 216$$
$$\downarrow \qquad \downarrow \qquad \downarrow \qquad \downarrow$$
$$(3)^3 \quad (5)^3 \quad (4)^3 \quad (6)^3$$

As we can see that the given values are the cube (x^3) of their corresponding number.

Hence, the correct option is (C).

65.

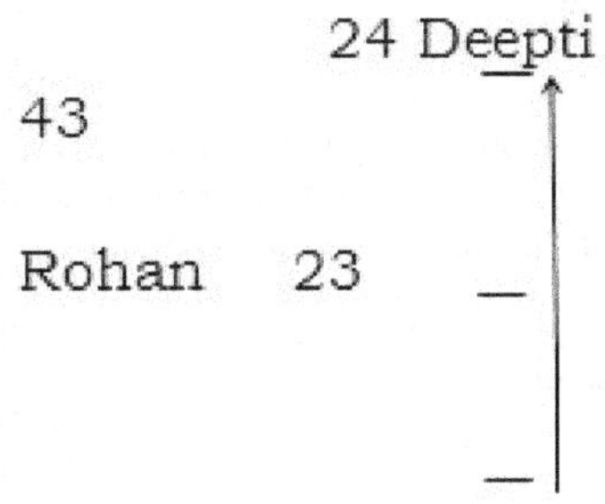

If Rohan's position from the Top is 23 then,

Deepti's position from the Top = 43-24+1 = 20

So, total students sit between them = 23-20-1 = 2

Hence, the correct option is (B).

66.

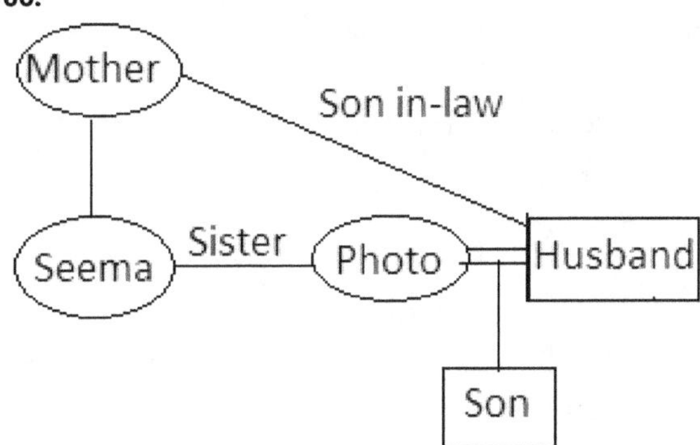

Seema was pointing to a photo in which a boy who was the son of his father (husband of lady) who was the son in law of Seema's Mother that clears out the lady was Seema's sister.

Hence, the correct option is (A).

67. $3,4 \xrightarrow{3+4} 7 \xrightarrow{4+7} 11 \xrightarrow{7+11} 18 \xrightarrow{11+18} 29 \xrightarrow{18+29} 47$

Hence, the correct option is (C).

68.

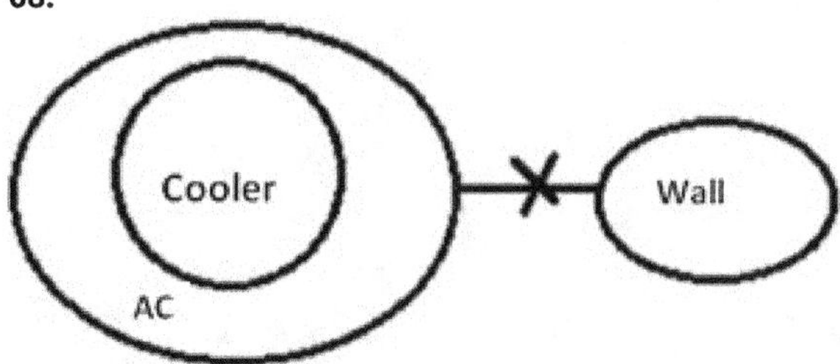

As we can see in the above figure all the ACs are coolers but none of them is a wall. So we can say that option (B) is the correct conclusion for the question.

Only (II) conclusion follows.

Hence, the correct option is (B).

69.

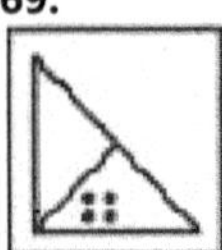

One dot is increasing in each part on moving in the clockwise direction from the top left. Triangles having dots are touching each other in the upper part of the image same will be followed in the lowest part also.

Clearly, answer figure (D) completes the pattern.

Hence, the correct option is (D).

70.

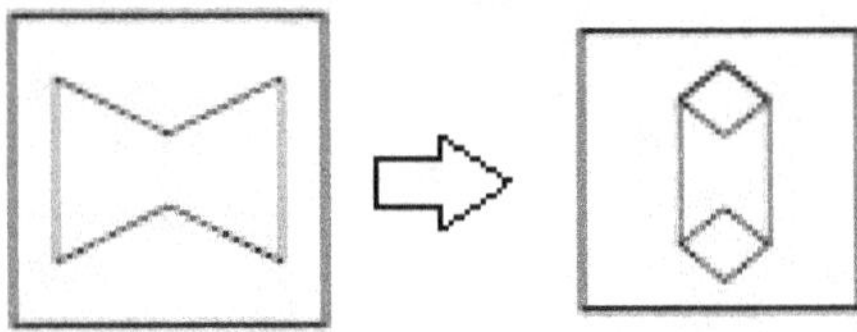

On the rotating structure given in question at 90°, we can see that it is the same structure given in option (B).

Hence, the correct option is (B).

71. NEAT → 44, 14, 34, 56

N - 01, 13, 20, 32, **44**

E - 02, **14**, 21, 33, 40

A - 03, 10, 22, **34**, 41

T - **56**, 68, 75, 87, 99

So the code for **NEAT** is **44, 14, 34, 56**

Hence, the correct option is (A).

72. If a mirror is placed on the line AB, the option (C) figure shows the correct mirror image of the given figure in the question.

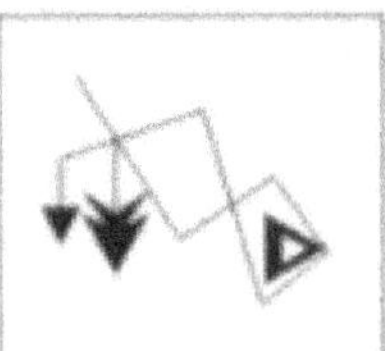

Hence, the correct option is (C).

73. A piece of paper is folded and cut then it will appear like option (D) when opened.

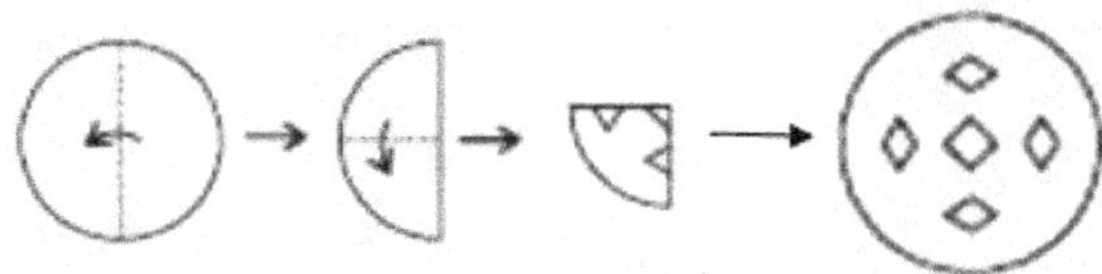

Hence, the correct option is (D).

74.

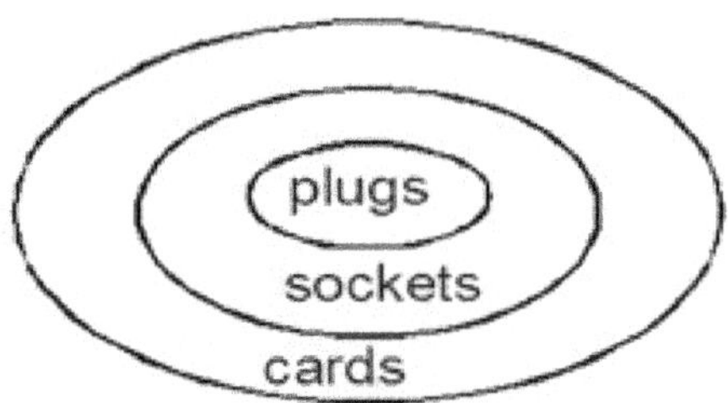

As we can see in the above figure which clearly describes the above question as all the plugs are sockets and all sockets are cards. So, only conclusions I follow.

Hence, the correct option is (A).

75. Piyush > Suhani > Suman = Brijesh > Priyanka ..... (i)

Piyush > Suhani > Mansi ......(ii)

From the above two equations -

Priyanka is the shortest among them.

Hence, the correct option is (B).

76. Given,

$$\frac{1}{1-x} - \frac{1}{1+x} - \frac{2x}{1+x^2} - \frac{4x^3}{1+x^4} - \frac{8x^7}{1+x^8} - \frac{16x^{15}}{1-x^{16}}$$

So,

$$= \frac{1+x-1+x}{1-x^2} - \frac{2x}{1+x^2} - \frac{4x^3}{1+x^2} - \frac{8x^7}{1+x^8} - \frac{16x^{15}}{1-x^{16}}$$

$$= \frac{2x}{1-x^2} - \frac{2x}{1+x^2} - \frac{4x^3}{1+x^4} - \frac{8x^7}{1+x^8} - \frac{16x^{15}}{1-x^{16}}$$

$$= \frac{4x^3}{1-x^4} - \frac{4x^3}{1+x^4} - \frac{8x^7}{1+x^8} - \frac{16x^{15}}{1-x^{16}}$$

$$= \frac{16x^{15}}{1-x^{16}} - \frac{16x^{15}}{1-x^{16}} = 0$$

Hence, the correct option is (A).

77. Given,

$$\sqrt{\frac{3+\sqrt{8}}{3-\sqrt{8}}} = \sqrt{\frac{3+\sqrt{8}}{3-\sqrt{8}} \times \frac{3+\sqrt{8}}{3+\sqrt{8}}}$$

$$= \sqrt{\frac{\left(3+\sqrt{8}\right)^2}{9-8}}$$

$$= 3 + \sqrt{8} = 3 + 2\sqrt{2}$$

Hence, the correct option is (B).

78. Given,

$$\sqrt[4]{\left[\sqrt[4]{\left\{\sqrt[25]{\left(\sqrt[6]{3^{10}}\right)^{12}}\right\}^{10}}\right]^{8}}$$

So,

$$= 3^{\frac{10\times12\times10\times8}{6\times25\times4\times4}} = 3^4 = 81$$

Hence, the correct option is (D).

79. Given,

$$\frac{0.007}{x} = 0.01$$

So,

$$\frac{0.007}{0.01} = x$$

$$x = 0.7$$

Hence, the correct option is (B).

80. Here, $8^{20} = 2^{60}$

So, there are 60 $2's$

Next one, ie

$$15^{24} = (3 \times 5)^{24}$$

So here there are 24 $3's$, 24 $5's$

next,

$$7^{15}$$

Here there are 15 $7's$

as, $2,3,5,7$ are primes.

So,

$$= 2^{60} \times 3^{24} \times 5^{24} \times 7^{15}$$

Total number of prime factors $= 60 + 24 + 24 + 15 = 123$

Hence, the correct option is (C).

81. $11,19,29,43,61,79$ these prime numbers are there between 1 to 100 that even when 18 is subtracted then also it remains a prime number.

$$23 - 18 = 5, 29 - 18 = 11$$
$$31 - 18 = 13, 37 - 18 = 19$$
$$41 - 18 = 23, 47 - 18 = 29$$
$$59 - 18 = 41, 61 - 18 = 43$$
$$71 - 18 = 53, 79 - 18 = 61$$
$$89 - 18 = 71, 97 - 18 = 79$$

Hence, the correct option is (D).

82. 6 men and 8 boys can do a piece of work in 10 days

$$6n + 8y = \frac{1}{10} \quad .....(i)$$

while 26 men and 48 boys finish it in 2 days

$$26n + 48y = \frac{1}{2} \quad .....(ii)$$

Now multiplying equation (i) by 6 subtracting from equation (ii) we get

$$10n = \frac{1}{10}; n = \frac{1}{100}$$

$$\therefore y = \frac{1}{200}$$

15 men and 20 boys will finish it in-

$$\frac{1}{100} \times 15 + \frac{1}{200} \times 20 = \frac{1}{4} \Rightarrow 4 \text{ days}$$

Hence, the correct option is (A).

83. Work done by P in 1 hour $= \frac{1}{8}$

Work done by Q in 1 hour $= \frac{1}{10}$

Work done by R in 1 hour $= \frac{1}{12}$

Work done by P, Q and R in 1 hour

$$= \frac{1}{8} + \frac{1}{10} + \frac{1}{12} = \frac{37}{120}$$

Work done by Q and R in 1 hour

$$= \frac{1}{10} + \frac{1}{12} = \frac{22}{120} = \frac{11}{60}$$

From 9 am to 11 am, all the machines were operating, they all operated for 2 hours and work completed $= 2 \times \left(\frac{37}{120}\right) = \frac{37}{60}$

Pending work $= 1 - \frac{37}{60} = \frac{23}{60}$

Hours taken by Q an R to complete the pending work

$$= \frac{\frac{23}{60}}{\frac{11}{60}} = \frac{23}{11} = 2$$

Which is approximately equal to 2. Hence the work will be completed approximately 2 hours after 11 am i.e. around 1 pm.

Hence, the correct option is (C).

84. Assume that the person would have covered x km if travelled at 8 km/hr speed $= \frac{x}{8} \quad .....(i)$

Give that the person would have covered $(x21)$ km if travelled at 15 km/hr speed $= \frac{x+21}{15} \quad .....(ii)$

From equation (i) and (ii)

$$\frac{x}{8} = \frac{(x+21)}{15}$$

$$\Rightarrow 15x = 8x + 168$$

$$x = 24 \text{ km}$$

Hence, the correct option is (B).

85. Let the speed of car be x km/hr

Distance $=$ Speed $\times$ Time

Distance $= 8$ km

According to the question,

$\Rightarrow (x + 4) \times 7.5 = 8x$

$\Rightarrow 7.5x + 30 = 8x$

$\Rightarrow 8x - 7.5x = 30$

$\Rightarrow 0.5x = 30$

$\Rightarrow x = \dfrac{30}{0.5} = 60$ km/hr

Required distance :

$= 8 \times 60$

$= 480$ km

Hence, the correct option is (B).

86. S.I. $=$ Rs. $(920 - 800) =$ Rs. $120; p =$ Rs. $800, T = 3$ yrs.

$R = \left(\dfrac{(100 \times 120)}{800 \times 3}\right) \% = 5\%.$

New rate $= (5 + 3)\% = 8\%$

New S.I. $=$ Rs. $\dfrac{(800 \times 8 \times 3)}{100}\% =$ Rs. 192

New amount $= Rs.(800 + 192) =$ Rs. 992

Hence, the correct option is (A).

87. A tree was planted 2 years ago. Increase in 2 years $=$

$\left(20 + 20 + \dfrac{20 \times 20}{100}\right) = 44\%$

If at present, the height of the tree is

$144\% \rightarrow 680$

$100\% \rightarrow \dfrac{680}{144} \times 100 = 472$ cm

it's height was 472 cm when it was planted.

Hence, the correct option is (A).

88.

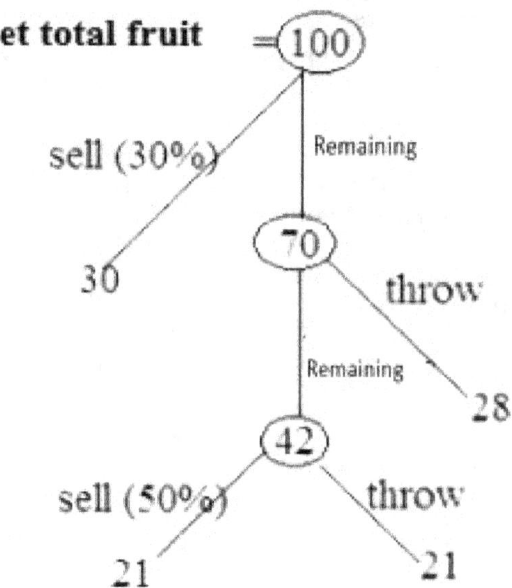

A vendor sells 30% of his fruit and throws away 40% of the remaining. The next day he sells 50% of the remaining and throws away the rest.

Fruits vendor throws $\% = \dfrac{(28 + 21)}{100} \times 100 = 49\%$

Hence, the correct option is (B).

89. SP $=$ Rs. 1800

Discount $= 15\%$

MP $= \dfrac{1800 \times 100}{15} = 2117.64$

If there was no discount, S.P. = Rs. 2117.64, Profit $\% = 10$

$\dfrac{2117.64 \times 100}{110} = 1925.12$

Hence, the correct option is (B).

90. Let the marked price = Rs. x

The discount equivalent to successive

Discounts 20% and $10\% = \left(r_1 + r_2 - \dfrac{r_1 r_2}{100}\right)\%$

where, $r_1 = 20$ and $r_2 = 10$

Then, $30 - 2 = 28\%$

According to the question,

$\dfrac{(100 - 28)x}{100} - \dfrac{(100 - 30)x}{100} = 72$

$\therefore$ SP $= \dfrac{72x}{100}$

$\therefore \dfrac{72x}{100} - \dfrac{70x}{100} = 72$

$$\Rightarrow \frac{2x}{100} = 72$$

$$\therefore \ x \ = \ \frac{72 \times 100}{2} = \text{Rs.} \ 3600$$

Hence, the correct option is (A).

91. FIND (ctrl+F) in Microsoft excel sheet is used to find any type of data existing in that excel. Data can be in any form of alphabets, numbers, format, symbol, characters, etc.

Hence, the correct option is (D).

92. The first graphical browser for the WWW was named Mosaic.

Mosaic is one of the first web browsers. It was instrumental in popularizing the World Wide Web and the general Internet by integrating multimedia such as text and graphics. Microsoft licensed Mosaic to create Internet Explorer in 1995.

Hence, the correct option is (C).

93. Available chart types in Excel are Column chart, Line chart, Bar chart, bubble chart, etc.

A Bubble chart is like a Scatter chart with an additional third column to specify the size of the bubbles it shows to represent the data points in the data series.

A Bubble chart has the following sub-types –

- Bubble
- Bubble with 3-D effect

Hence, the correct option is (A).

94. Mail merge toolbar is not a data source component.

The Mail Merge Toolbar contains commands for the final steps of the mail merge process.

A data source is defined as the device or small place where data comes from. If you have ever retrieved data from another computer or another device, then this probably came from a data source.

Data source components are header row, data fields, and data records.

Hence, the correct option is (A).

95. The World Wide Web is made from millions of interlinked webpages.

There are three main ingredients that make up the World Wide Web. URL (uniform resource locator), which is the addressing scheme to find a document; HTTP (hypertext transfer protocol), which connects computers together; and HTML (hypertext markup language), which formats pages containing hypertext links.

Hence, the correct option is (D).

96. Linux is an open-source operating system (OS). An operating system is software that directly manages a system's hardware and resources, like CPU, memory, and storage.

The primary difference between Linux and many other popular contemporary operating systems is that the Linux kernel and other components are free and open-source software. Linux is not the only such operating system, although it is by far the most widely used.

Hence, the correct option is (B).

97. Every computer connected to the network should have a unique address, and this address is known as an IP address.

Every web-capable device needs an IP (Internet Protocol) address to enable it to access the Internet. Without an IP address, computers wouldn't be able to communicate with each other. Every internet-capable device, from your computer to your smartphone, has its own unique identifying IP address.

Hence, the correct option is (C).

98. When you open an Excel workbook, there are three worksheets by default. The default names on the worksheet tabs are Sheet1, Sheet2, and Sheet3.

Hence, the correct option is (B).

99. Attachment is the file that is attached to the email and is sent to the recipient.

Email attachment: One or more files can be attached to any email message, and be sent along with it to the recipient. This is typically used as a simple method to share documents and images. A paper clip icon is the standard indicator for an attachment in an email client. Thus, the file that is attached to the email and is sent to the recipient is called an attachment.

Hence, the correct option is (C).

100. PowerPoint is not related to email. Microsoft PowerPoint is a presentation program, created by Robert Gaskins and Dennis Austin at a software company named Forethought, Inc. It was released on April 20, 1987, initially for Macintosh System Operating system based computers only.

Hence, the correct option is (A).

General Knowledge/Current Affairs

Q.1 In August 2020, the Ministry of Tribal Affairs (MoTA) has received the SKOCH Gold Award for which of its project?

A. Grant in Aid to Voluntary Organizations working for the welfare of STs

B. Vocational Training Centres in Tribal Areas

C. Strengthening education among ST Girls in low literacy Districts

D. Empowerment of Tribals through IT-enabled Scholarship Schemes

Q.2 In August 2020, Which state has rolled out mobile COVID-19 testing centers in containment zones and low-income group residential areas across the state?

A. Telangana **B.** Gujarat

C. Maharashtra **D.** Rajasthan

Q.3 Which of the following has signed a dollar 200 million financing deal with the Reliance Bangladesh LNG and Power Limited (RBLPL) in August 2020?

A. NDB **B.** World Bank

C. ADB **D.** AIIB

Q.4 People living in coastal areas suffer less from goiter. This is because of :

A. They eat sea food

B. They drink sea water

C. They bathe in sea water

D. All of the above

Q.5 Which one of the following is a non- biodegradable substance :

A. DDT **B.** Manure

C. paper **D.** Cotton cloth

Q.6 Pickles, jam, jellies have a low risk of spoilage as they cause:

A. Citation **B.** Diffusion

C. Plasmolysis **D.** Imbibition

Q.7 Monazite is an ore of

A. Thorium **B.** Zirconium

C. Iron **D.** Titanium

Q.8 Which of the following is used to make bristles of toothbrush?

A. Viscose **B.** Rayon **C.** Nylon **D.** Lexan

Q.9 The average miles per gallon rating of U.S. vehicles has

________.

A. Doubled in the past two decades

B. Slightly decreased in the past two decades

C. Now matched the 45 mpg rating mandated by the European union

D. Been the target of several bills now pending in Congress

Q.10 Which type of Economic system is controlled by the federal government?

A. Traditional economic system

B. Command economic system

C. Market economic system

D. Mixed economic system

Q.11 Uranus was discovered by:

A. Clyde Tombaugh **B.** William Herschel

C. Halley **D.** U. J. Leverrier

Q.12 Biodiversity hot spots are:

A. Areas where a large number of different species are found

B. Hot Areas where a large number of different species are found

C. Areas which became hot due to a large number of different species

D. Areas where a large spot has been created due to the death of a number of species

Q.13 In India, there are many coal fields found in :

A. Cauvery Valley **B.** Krishna Valley

C. Ganga Valley **D.** Damodar Valley

Q.14 What is the capital of Saudi Arabia?

A. Riyadh **B.** Santiago

C. Pyongyang **D.** Lisbon

Q.15 Which of the following is not the essential element of the State?

A. Government **B.** Sovereignty

C. Population **D.** Institutions

Q.16 Articles 23 and 24 of the Indian Constitution are related to -

A. Right against Exploitation

B. Right to Freedom

C. Right to Freedom of Religion

D. Right to Education

Q.17 Which among the following rulers of the Chola Empire conquered the Maldives during his regime?

A. Kulothunga Chola I **B.** Rajendra Chola

C. Raja Chola I **D.** Vikrama Chola

Q.18 The classical Dance of Andhra Pradesh is –

A. Kathakali **B.** Kuchipudi

C. Bharatanatyam **D.** Odissi

Q.19 Debenture holders of a company are its:

A. shareholders **B.** creditors

C. debtors **D.** directors

Q.20 In which Five Year Plan, "Heavy Industry" was given priority —

A. Second   **B.** First   **C.** Seventh   **D.** Fourth

Q.21 Paris St Germain lifted the French League Cup in August 2020 after defeating which of the following Football Clubs?

A. Olympique Lyonnais
B. Real Madrid
C. Liverpool
D. Barcelona

Q.22 Plantation drive carried out by UP's forest department in how many districts have now entered Guinness World Record for most species planted simultaneously in 240 locations within an hour in August 2020?

A. 4   **B.** 6   **C.** 8   **D.** 10

Q.23 Who has won the Prem Bhatia Award for political reporting for his work on issues related to the COVID-19?

A. Anuj Gupta   **B.** Pankaj Singh
C. Sourabh Mishra   **D.** Dipankar Ghose

Q.24 As per the FutureBrand Index, what is the rank of Mukesh Ambani's oil-to-telecom conglomerate in terms of biggest brand?

A. 1   **B.** 2   **C.** 3   **D.** 4

Q.25 The Five Permanent Members of the UN Security Council Are :

A. Germany, Italy, France, India, China
B. UK, US, China, Australia, New Zealand
C. China, France, Russia, UK, US
D. India, China, France, Russia, UK

Q.26 Which one of the following categories of emergency has not been declared so far?

A. National emergency
B. Emergency due to break down of constitutional machinery
C. Financial emergency
D. None of the above

Q.27 'Education' which was initially a state subject was transferred to the Concurrent List by the :

A. 24th Amendment   **B.** 25th Amendment
C. 42nd Amendment   **D.** 44th, Amendment

Q.28 How many fundamental Rights are mentioned in Indian constitution?

A. Five   **B.** Six   **C.** Seven   **D.** Eight

Q.29 In which year was Nationalist Congress Party (NCP) founded?

A. 1949   **B.** 1999   **C.** 1972   **D.** 1997

Q.30 Which of the following is not included in the Directive Principles of State Policy?

A. Prohibition of Liquor
B. Right to Work
C. Equal Wage for Equal Work
D. Right to Information

Q.31 What is the literal meaning of the term "Quo-Warranto"?

A. We command
B. To forbid
C. By what authority (or) warrant
D. None of these

Q.32 Which of the following has published the book titled "Amazing Ayodhya"?

A. Oxford University Press
B. Bloomsbury
C. Penguin Books
D. Random House

Q.33 Which country has marked its national day on July 14th, which is also known as Bastille Day?

A. Germany   **B.** France
C. Russia   **D.** England

Q.34 Mukund Lath passed away in August 2020. In which year was awarded India's 4th highest civilian honour, **The Padma Shri**?

A. 2004   **B.** 2006   **C.** 2008   **D.** 2010

Q.35 Sadia Dehlvi passed away in August 2020. She was related to which of the following fields?

A. Acting   **B.** Writing   **C.** Politics   **D.** Chess

Q.36 Who among the following has co-chaired the 17th ASEAN-India Economic Ministers' consultations along with Vietnam's Tran Tuan Anh?

A. Prakash Javadekar
B. Piyush Goyal
C. Ramesh Pokhriyal Nishank
D. S. Jaishankar

Q.37 Which organization has decided to invest 650 million euros into Kanpur city metro rail line?

A. European Investment Bank
B. Asian Development Bank
C. International Monetary fund
D. Asian Infrastructure Investment Bank

Q.38 Which of the following institute has developed World's Largest Solar Tree?

A. CSIR-AMPRI   **B.** CSIR-CBRI
C. CSIR-CCMB   **D.** CSIR-CMERI

Q.39 Hitler party which came into power in 1933 is known as

A. Labour Party   **B.** Nazi Party
C. Ku-Klux-Klan   **D.** Democratic Party

Q.40 Which state Government has launched 'I Rakhwali' app to make citizens "Greenery Saviours" to ensure greenery and to protect the environment?

A. Uttar Pradesh   **B.** Karnataka
C. Madhya Pradesh   **D.** Punjab

Q.41 The website of the Lokpal has been launched. What is the URL of the website?

A. www.lokpal.gov.in

B. www.lokpal.gov.com
C. www.lokpal.gov
D. www.lokpal.com

Q.42 Name the free mobile application launched by Union Minister of Education developed by the English and Foreign Languages University, Hyderabad.

A. Languages Plus
B. English Pro
C. En Language
D. Angrezi Plus

Q.43 Which country has now the world's 2nd largest road network?

A. Russia
B. Japan
C. India
D. UK

Q.44 Who among the following has attended the 5th BRICS Culture Ministers Meet from India?

A. Rao Inderjit Singh
B. Ravi Shankar Prasad
C. Dharmendra Pradhan
D. Prahlad Singh Patel

Q.45 Which state government has relaunched "SVAYEM" scheme to provide self-employment to youths of state?

A. Andhra Pradesh
B. Meghalaya
C. Mizoram
D. Assam

Q.46 Who among the following has released 'The State of Young Child in India' report prepared by the Mobile Creches?

A. M Venkaiah Naidu
B. Om Birla
C. Ram Nath Kovind
D. Narendra Modi

Q.47 Which company has partnered with Cyber Peace Foundation to drive cyber safety awareness?

A. Twitter
B. Facebook
C. Amazon
D. WhatsApp

Q.48 Which company has acquired product design firm Kaleidoscope Innovation for $42 million?

A. IBM
B. Google
C. Microsoft
D. Infosys

Q.49 For which of the following disciplines is Nobel Prize awarded?

A. Physics and Chemistry
B. Physiology or Medicine
C. Literature, Peace and Economics
D. All of the above

Q.50 Which State Government has launched "GARIMA" welfare scheme for sanitation workers?

A. Bihar
B. Uttar Pradesh
C. Odisha
D. Madhya Pradesh

Reasoning

Q.51 Directions: Read the following information carefully and answer the question given below-

Seven persons A, B, C, D, E, F, and G are standing in a straight line and are all facing towards the north direction. D is to the right of G. C is between A and B. E is between F and D. There are three persons between G and B. Who is on the extreme left?

A. A
B. B
C. D
D. G

Q.52 How many circles are there in the following figure?

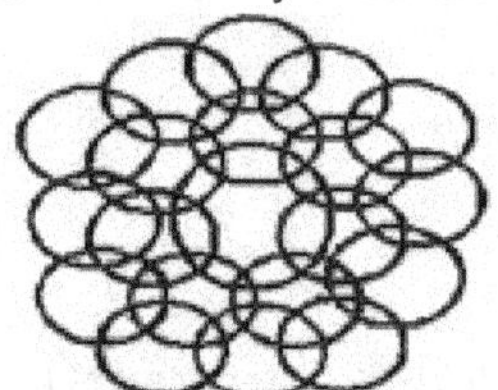

A. 19
B. 21
C. 20
D. 22

Q.53 Mohan walks 50 meters towards the west, then turns to the right and walks 50 meters. He again turns towards the right and stops after walking 25 meters. Mohan is in which direction from his initial point?

A. East
B. North-West
C. North-East
D. South-west

Q.54 A word is represented by only one set of numbers as given in any one of the alternatives. The sets of numbers given in the alternatives are represented by two classes of letters as in the two matrices given below. The columns and rows of Matrix-I are numbered from 0 to 3 and that of Matrix- II are numbered from 4 to 7. A letter from these matrices can be represented first by its row and next by its column. You have to identify the set for the word 'TALE'.

Matrix - I

	0	1	2	3
0	A	D	G	H
1	P	S	V	Z
2	C	F	I	M
3	T	L	E	Q

Matrix - II

	4	5	6	7
4	R	U	B	O
5	N	W	J	X
6	T	K	S	G
7	I	H	A	F

A. 64,00,31,32
B. 64,13,00,23
C. 00,31,64,32
D. 30,76,23,32

Q.55 Which answer figure will complete the pattern in the question figure?

Question Figure:

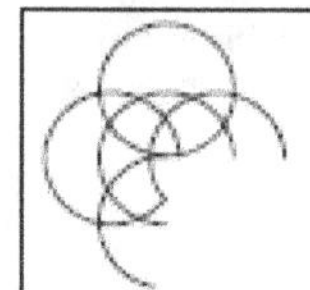

Answer Figure:

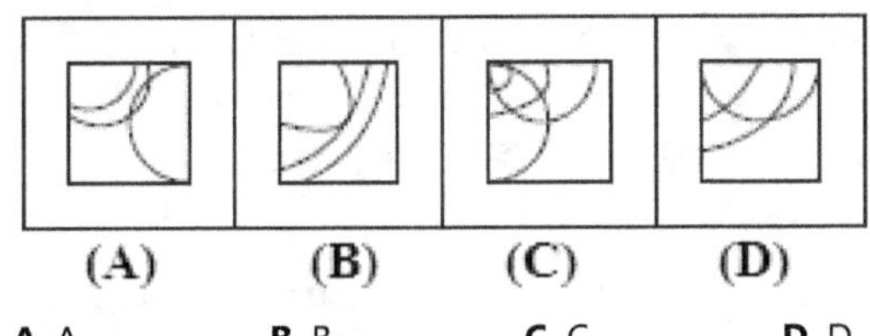

(A)   (B)   (C)   (D)

A. A   **B.** B   **C.** C   **D.** D

Q.56 In the following questions, if a mirror is placed on the line PQ, then which of the answer figures is the correct image of the given figure?

Question Figure:

Answer Figure:

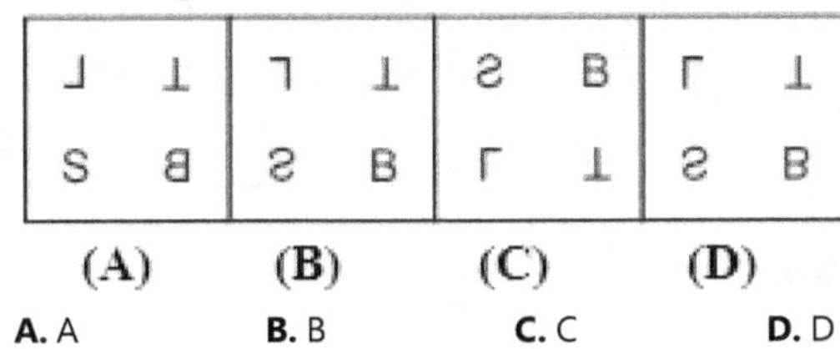

(A)   (B)   (C)   (D)

A. A   **B.** B   **C.** C   **D.** D

Q.57 Choose from the four answer figures, the figure that will be formed when the question figure is folded into a box.

Question Figure:

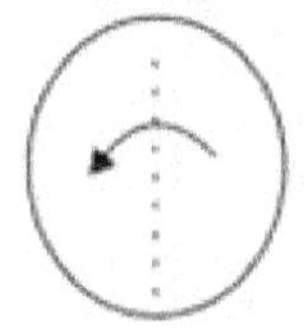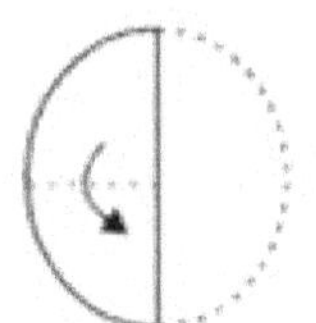

Answer Figure:

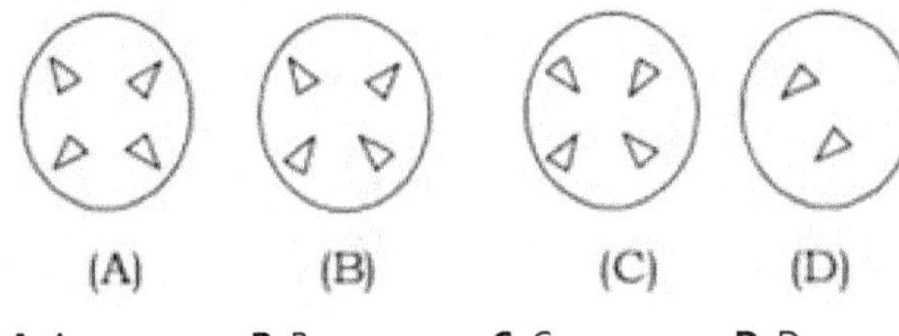

(A)   (B)   (C)   (D)

A. A   **B.** B   **C.** C   **D.** D

Q.58 Complete the third equation on the basis of a certain system followed in the first two equations.

If 4 + 2 = 8, 10 + 5 = 8 then 9 + 3 = ?

A. 12   **B.** 9   **C.** 5   **D.** 14

Q.59 Choose from the given options, which cannot be made using the letters of the given word.

MUSICAL

A. SLIM   **B.** CALCIUM
C. LASIUM   **D.** CLAIM

Q.60 Which one set of letters when sequentially placed at the gaps in the given letter series shall complete?

a_cbc_ca_ab_bca_ab

A. b a b c c   **B.** b c a b b
C. a b c b c   **D.** b c a b c

Q.61 There are five friends –Sachin, Kamal, Mohan, Arun and Ram. Sachin is shorter than Kamal, but taller than Ram. Mohan is the tallest. Arun is a little shorter than Kamal and a little taller than Sachin. Who is the second tallest?

A. Ram   **B.** Sachin   **C.** Kamal   **D.** Arun

Q.62 Directions: In each of the following questions, select the one which is different from the others.

(A) 5329   (B) 2439
(C) 1438   (D) 3238

A. A   **B.** B   **C.** C   **D.** D

Q.63 Directions: In each of the following questions, select the one which is different from the others.

(A) Calf   (B) Puppy
(C) Lamb   (D) Tiger

A. A   **B.** B   **C.** C   **D.** D

Q.64 Directions: In each of the following questions, select the one which is different from the others.

(A) 9, 10   (B) 24, 25
(C) 2, 3   (D) 20, 21

A. A   **B.** B   **C.** C   **D.** D

Q.65 The diagram below represents the students who play cricket , football and kabaddi.

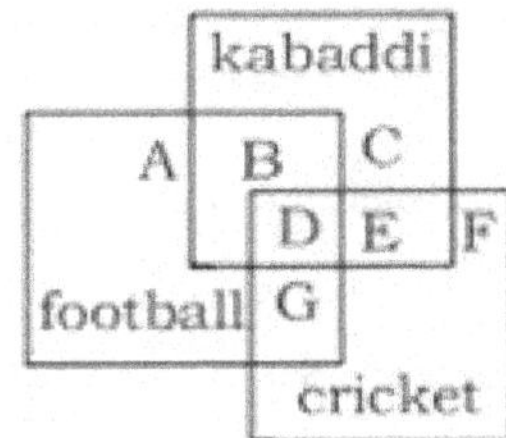

Seeing the indicate the students who play all the 3 game ?

A. A+B+C   **B.** B+ G +E   **C.** D+C+G   **D.** D

Q.66 What should come in place of the blank?

70.4, 88, 88, ____, 33, 8.25

A. 66   **B.** 69   **C.** 76   **D.** 79

Q.67 Directions: In the following questions, select the related word/letters/number from the given alternatives.

China: Beijing:: Kazakhstan:?

A. Japan   **B.** Egypt
C. Nur-Sultan   **D.** Dublin

Q.68 Directions: What will come in place of the question mark (?) in the following number series?

5, 8, 14, 23, ?, 50

A. 34   **B.** 35   **C.** 36   **D.** 37

Q.69 Arrange the following in ascending order :

1. Centimeter

2. Kilometre

3. Decimeter

4. Metre

A. 3, 1, 2, 4 **B.** 4, 2, 1, 3 **C.** 1, 3, 4, 2 **D.** 2, 4, 3, 1

Q.70 The day before the day before yesterday is three days after Saturday. What day is it today?

A. Thursday **B.** Friday

C. Tuesday **D.** Wednesday

Q.71 Directions: In these questions, statements are given followed by two conclusions I and II. You have to consider both the statements to be true even if they seem to be at variance from commonly known facts. You have to decide which of the given conclusions is/are definitely drawn from the given statements. Select answer as: (A) If only I follows (B) If only II follows (C) If neither I nor II follows (D) If both I and II follow.

Statements:

All tables are books.

All pens are books

Conclusions:

I. All tables are pens.

II. All pens are tables.

A. A **B.** C **C.** B **D.** D

Q.72 If O = 16, FOR = 42, then what is FRONT equal to?

A. 61 **B.** 65 **C.** 73 **D.** 78

Q.73 If "JOSEPH" is coded as "FKOALD", then "GEORGE" will be coded as:

A. CAKNIJ **B.** CAKNCA

C. JAKINS **D.** CADMNO

Q.74 If the word PRINCIPAL is written as LAPICNIRP, how ADOLESCENCE can be written in that code?

A. ECNCESELODA **B.** ECNECSLEODA

C. ECNSCEELODA **D.** ECNECSELODA

Q.75 In the following letter series, how many times do PQR occur in such a way that Q is in the middle of P and R?

Q M P N P Q R R O P Q N O P P Q R P M Q R O P Q R P P R R P Q R P

A. 5 **B.** 6 **C.** 4 **D.** 3

Numerical Ability

Q.76 A sack contains two types of rice A and B grades in the ratio of $5:3$. In another sack, there are two types of rice A and C grades in the ratio of $8:5$. The grocery store owner mixes these two mixtures in equal quantities. What is the quantity of the rice of grade C in 1 kg of the new mixture?

A. $\frac{500}{13}g$ **B.** $\frac{1800}{13}g$ **C.** $400g$ **D.** $\frac{2500}{13}g$

Q.77 Three persons walk from place A to place B.Their speeds are in the ratio $4:3:5$. The ratio of the times taken by them to reach B will be :

A. 15 : 20 : 12 **B.** 12 : 15 : 20

C. 12 : 20 : 15 **D.** 15 : 12 : 20

Q.78 The radius of a hemispherical balloon increases from 6 cm to 12 cm as air is being pumped into it. The ratios of the surface areas of the balloon in the two cases are-

A. $1:4$ **B.** $4:1$ **C.** $2:1$ **D.** $1:2$

Q.79 A man bought a watch at 25% discount on the original price. He got Rs. 40 more than the original price by selling it at 140% of the price at which he bought. The price of buying the watch was:

A. Rs. 900 **B.** Rs. 600 **C.** Rs. 800 **D.** Rs. 700

Q.80 A merchant marked his goods 20% above the cost price and sold the goods at a profit of 8%. The rate percent of the discount is-

A. 12 **B.** 10 **C.** 15 **D.** 8

Q.81 Growing up, you lived in a tiny country village. When you left for college, the population was 840. You recently heard that the population has grown by 5%. What is the present population?

A. 899 **B.** 844 **C.** 811 **D.** 882

Q.82 40% of 70% of a number is 336. What is $\frac{1}{3}$ of that number?

A. 475 **B.** 450

C. 420 **D.** None of these

Q.83 Two men, A and B, start from a place x walking at $4\frac{1}{2}$km/hr and $5\frac{3}{4}$km/hr respectively. How many km apart they will be at the end of $3\frac{1}{2}$ hours if they are walking in the same direction?

A. $4\frac{1}{2}km$ **B.** $5\frac{3}{4}km$ **C.** $4\frac{3}{8}km$ **D.** $35\frac{7}{8}km$

Q.84 If a ship moves from one side to another side in a flowing river, it will be found in the middle of the river after some time in the direction of -

A. The point exactly opposite to the port

B. Diagonally in the flow of the stream.

C. The point opposite to the flow of the stream

D. None of these

Q.85 Some amount out of Rs. 7000 was lent at 6% per annum and the remaining at 4% per annum. If the total simple interest from both the fractions in 5 yrs was Rs. 1600, find the sum lent at 6% per annum.

A. 2000 **B.** 16000 **C.** 5400 **D.** 3200

Ques (86-88):Directions: Read the following graph carefully and answer the question given below.

Numbers of trees planted by three different NGOs in five different states

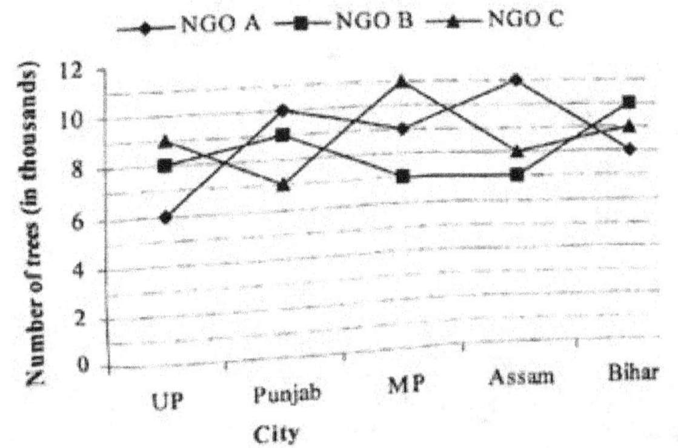

Q.86 What was the ratio of the number of trees planted by NGO B in Assam and the number of trees planted by NGO C in Punjab together to the number of trees planted by NGO A in UP and MP together?

A. $11:13$ **B.** $6:7$ **C.** $14:15$ **D.** $9:11$

Q.87 What was the approximate average number of trees planted in UP by all the NGOs together?

A. 5895 **B.** 6832 **C.** 7667 **D.** 9478

Q.88 What was the difference between the number of trees planted by NGO A in Punjab and the number of trees planted by NGO C in Assam?

A. 1800 **B.** 2400 **C.** 1200 **D.** 2000

Q.89 A well has to be dug out that is to be 22.5 m deep and of diameter 7 m. Find the cost of plastering the inner curved surface at Rs. 3 per sq. meter.

A. Rs. 1465 **B.** Rs. 1485 **C.** Rs. 1475 **D.** Rs. 1495

Q.90 $1^2 + 2^2 + 3^2 \dots 10^2 =?$

A. 330 **B.** 345 **C.** 365 **D.** 385

Computer Awareness

Q.91 Google Chrome, Mozilla Firefox, Internet Explorer, Netscape Navigator are examples of

A. Web server **B.** Internet
C. Web browser **D.** World Wide Web

Q.92 What is the Software on a computer?

A. Enhances the capabilities of the hardware machine.
B. Increases the speed of the central processing unit.
C. Both (a) and (b)
D. None of the above

Q.93 What is the short cut key to open Font dialog box?

A. Ctrl + Shift + C **B.** Alt + Ctrl + C
C. Ctrl + D **D.** Ctrl + Shift + D

Q.94 Who is the father of Computer?

A. Allen Turing **B.** Charles Babbage
C. Simur Cray **D.** Augusta Adaming

Q.95 The hard disk is coated on both sides with

A. Magnetic metallic oxide
B. Optical metallic oxide
C. Carbon layer
D. All of the above

Q.96 Which of the following is a communication device ?

A. Printer **B.** Monitor
C. Keyboard **D.** Modem

Q.97 Which of this not a input device?

A. Joystick **B.** Keyboard
C. Printer **D.** Mouse

Q.98 What term refers to a specific set of values saved with the workbook?

A. Range **B.** Scenario
C. Trend line **D.** What-if analysis

Q.99

Input/output function prototypes and macros are defined in which header file?

A. conio.h **B.** stdlib.h **C.** stdio.h **D.** dos.h

Q.100 Which standard library function will you use to find the last occurance of a character in a string in C?

A. strnchar() **B.** strchar()
C. strrchar() **D.** strrchr()

// Smart Answer Sheet //

Correct   Indicates percentage of students who answered questions correctly.

Skipped   Indicates percentage of students who skipped questions.

Q.	Ans.	Correct / Skipped
1	D	27.99 % / 16.99 %
2	A	38.52 % / 30.14 %
3	C	23.92 % / 32.3 %
4	A	20.1 % / 27.99 %
5	A	36.12 % / 30.39 %
6	C	29.19 % / 33.49 %
7	A	29.67 % / 31.33 %
8	C	32.54 % / 32.77 %
9	B	12.2 % / 37.08 %
10	B	14.83 % / 34.93 %
11	B	39.71 % / 32.78 %
12	A	39.71 % / 29.67 %
13	D	38.52 % / 29.9 %
14	A	61.48 % / 27.75 %
15	D	13.88 % / 31.1 %
16	A	41.39 % / 28.47 %

Q.	Ans.	Correct / Skipped
17	C	29.43 % / 30.62 %
18	B	56.94 % / 29.66 %
19	B	18.9 % / 25.84 %
20	A	37.8 % / 26.79 %
21	A	15.31 % / 32.3 %
22	C	31.1 % / 31.82 %
23	D	24.4 % / 30.15 %
24	B	26.56 % / 28.7 %
25	C	49.76 % / 29.91 %
26	C	43.06 % / 31.1 %
27	C	39.71 % / 28.71 %
28	B	53.11 % / 27.99 %
29	B	15.07 % / 31.1 %
30	D	19.38 % / 28.47 %
31	C	41.87 % / 30.86 %
32	B	17.22 % / 32.06 %

Q.	Ans.	Correct / Skipped
33	B	23.21 % / 31.81 %
34	D	18.42 % / 33.25 %
35	B	31.58 % / 35.17 %
36	B	21.77 % / 33.73 %
37	A	9.57 % / 33.73 %
38	D	28.47 % / 34.69 %
39	B	21.53 % / 32.54 %
40	D	18.42 % / 32.78 %
41	A	49.76 % / 28.71 %
42	B	19.38 % / 32.77 %
43	C	25.36 % / 32.3 %
44	D	19.14 % / 30.86 %
45	D	17.22 % / 34.69 %
46	A	23.44 % / 31.34 %
47	D	17.22 % / 33.26 %
48	D	30.14 % / 32.06 %

Q.	Ans.	Correct / Skipped
49	D	30.86 % / 31.1 %
50	C	13.64 % / 32.29 %
51	D	29.19 % / 35.64 %
52	C	53.59 % / 33.25 %
53	B	50.72 % / 33.73 %
54	A	53.35 % / 35.41 %
55	C	49.76 % / 34.69 %
56	D	42.82 % / 34.45 %
57	A	59.57 % / 34.69 %
58	B	14.35 % / 38.52 %
59	B	61.24 % / 34.69 %
60	A	47.61 % / 36.12 %
61	C	51.91 % / 34.69 %
62	A	42.58 % / 34.21 %
63	D	43.54 % / 32.78 %
64	A	13.88 % / 33.97 %

Q.	Ans.	Correct / Skipped
65	D	62.44 % / 33.25 %
66	A	27.51 % / 39.24 %
67	C	52.63 % / 33.97 %
68	B	56.7 % / 34.45 %
69	C	52.63 % / 30.62 %
70	B	8.13 % / 33.02 %
71	B	35.17 % / 33.25 %
72	D	49.04 % / 35.17 %
73	B	62.44 % / 32.78 %
74	D	53.59 % / 34.45 %
75	C	55.02 % / 34.45 %
76	D	7.89 % / 40.44 %
77	A	39.0 % / 37.79 %
78	A	23.21 % / 37.56 %
79	B	29.43 % / 39.95 %
80	B	28.47 % / 41.15 %

Q.	Ans.	Correct	Skipped
81	D	50.0 %	38.28 %
82	D	40.43 %	39.95 %
83	C	25.36 %	42.1 %
84	B	27.27 %	41.39 %

Q.	Ans.	Correct	Skipped
85	A	25.36 %	41.63 %
86	C	34.45 %	40.67 %
87	C	34.69 %	39.47 %
88	D	34.21 %	42.11 %

Q.	Ans.	Correct	Skipped
89	B	20.1 %	44.01 %
90	D	45.69 %	38.04 %
91	C	49.76 %	29.43 %
92	D	6.94 %	29.66 %

Q.	Ans.	Correct	Skipped
93	C	14.11 %	31.34 %
94	B	65.79 %	29.43 %
95	A	22.73 %	31.58 %
96	D	44.98 %	30.86 %

Q.	Ans.	Correct	Skipped
97	C	46.41 %	29.67 %
98	B	19.86 %	35.64 %
99	C	35.65 %	32.53 %
100	D	39.95 %	32.78 %

Performance Analysis

Avg. Score (%)	35.0%
Toppers Score (%)	100.0%
Your Score	

//Hints and Solutions//

1. In August 2020, the Ministry of Tribal Affairs (MoTA) has received the SKOCH Gold Award for **Empowerment of Tribals through IT-enabled Scholarship Schemes** of its project. The project aimed to achieve Digital India and bringing transparency and ease in the delivery of services.

The project is implemented by IIPA. It would help in understanding the aspirations of tribal youth and help in realizing their cherished dream to develop as entrepreneurs, researchers and flag-bearers of schemes of the Government of India meant for welfare for STs.

Hence, the correct option is (D).

2. In August 2020, Telangana state has rolled out mobile COVID-19 testing centres in containment zones and low-income group residential areas across the state.

• Each bus has 10 sample collection counters and antigen test results will be notified to the individuals within a few minutes.

• The buses are built with 'Intelligent Monitoring Analysis Services Quarantine' (iMASQ) technology.

Hence, the correct option is (A).

3. ADB (Asian Development Bank) has signed a dollar 200 million financing deal with Reliance Bangladesh LNG and Power Limited (RBLPL) in August 2020 to build and operate a 718MW gas-fired power plant in Bangladesh.

The Asian Development Bank is a regional development bank established on 19 December 1966, which is headquartered in the Ortigas Center located in the city of Mandaluyong, Metro Manila, Philippines. The company also maintains 31 field offices around the world to promote social and economic development in Asia.

Hence, the correct option is (C).

4. People living in coastal areas suffer less from goitre this is because goitre disease is caused by iodine deficiency in the diet and people living in coastal areas mainly eat seafood that contains a sufficient amount of iodine. Therefore, they do not usually suffer from goitre disease.

Hence, the correct option is (A).

5. DDT(dichloro-diphenyl-trichloroethane) is a non-biodegradable substance because it cannot be decomposed by micro-organisms and is capable of exerting its harmful effects on the environment. This is because to date there is no such enzyme has been found in any microbes that can degrade DDT.

Biodegradable substance - Biodegradable waste can be found in municipal solid waste (sometimes called biodegradable municipal waste, or as green waste, food waste, **paper** waste, and biodegradable plastics).

Hence, the correct option is (A).

6. Pickles, jam, jellies have a low risk of spoilage as they cause Plasmolysis. In the process of making pickles, jams, and jellies addition of more concentration of salt and sugar takes place. Because of the hypertonic nature of these items, the food spoiling organisms such as yeast, moulds cannot grow on them. When a cell placed in a hypertonic solution, it undergoes plasmolysis. In the same manner, due to the high concentration of salt and sugar, they preserve for a long time.

Hence, the correct option is (C).

7. Monazite is an important ore for thorium, lanthanum, and cerium. It is often found in placer deposits. India, Madagascar, and South Africa have large deposits of monazite sands. The deposits in India are particularly rich in monazite.

Hence, the correct option is (A).

8. Nylon is used to make bristles of the toothbrush. It is durable and flexible. It is non-toxic and does not harm our teeth that's the reason why nylon is used to make toothbrush bristles.

Hence, the correct option is (C).

9. The average miles per gallon rating of U.S. vehicles have slightly decreased in the past two decades. The average fuel-economy rating for new vehicles sold in the United States in December 2017 was 25.0 miles per gallon, down from the revised average of 25.2 mpg.

Hence, the correct option is (B).

10. Command economic system is controlled by the federal government. The command economic system is the next step up from the traditional economy. The most important feature of this system is that a large part of the economic system is controlled by centralized power, often, a federal government.

Hence, the correct option is (B).

11. Uranus was discovered by **William Herschel**. Like the classical planets, Uranus is visible to the naked eye, but it was never recognized as a planet by ancient observers because of its dimness and slow orbit. **Sir William Herschel** announced its discovery on 13 March 1781, expanding the known boundaries of the Solar System for the first time in history and making Uranus the first planet discovered with a telescope.

Hence, the correct option is (B).

12. To qualify as a biodiversity hotspot Myers 2000 edition of the hotspot-map, a region must meet two strict criteria: it must contain at least 0.5% or 1,500 species of vascular plants as endemics, and it has to have lost at least 70% of its primary vegetation. Around the world, 36 areas qualify under this definition. These sites support nearly 60% of the world's plant, bird, mammal, reptile, and amphibian species, with a very high share of those species as endemics.

Hence, the correct option is (A).

13. The Damodar valley along the Bihar–West Bengal border includes India's most important coal and mica-mining fields. The major coalfields (Jharia, Raniganj, and Giridih) are mostly open-pit and are easily mined. Damodar River is a river flowing across the Indian states of Jharkhand and West Bengal. Rich in mineral resources, the valley is home to large-scale mining and industrial activity.

Hence, the correct option is (D).

14. Riyadh is the capital and largest city of Saudi Arabia. It is also the capital of Riyadh Province and belongs to the historical regions of Najd and Al-Yamama. The Kingdom of Saudi Arabia is the largest country in the Arabian Peninsula. It occupies an area about the size of the United States east of the Mississippi River.

Hence, the correct option is (A).

15. Institutions are not the essential element of the State because the state has four essential elements. These are (1) population, (2) territory, (3) government, (4) sovereignty (or independence). The first two elements constitute the physical or material basis of the state while the last two form its political and spiritual basis.

Hence, the correct option is (D).

16. Articles 23 and 24 of the Indian Constitution are related to the Right against Exploitation. The Right against exploitation enshrined in Article 23 and 24 of the Indian Constitution guarantees human dignity and protect people from any such exploitation. Thus, upholding the principles of human dignity and liberty upon which the Indian Constitution is based.

Hence, the correct option is (A).

17. Raja Chola I, is one of the greatest emperors of the Tamil Chola Empire of India who ruled between 985 and 1014 CE. By conquering several small kingdoms in South India, he expanded the Chola Empire as far as Sri Lanka in the south and Kalinga (Orissa) in the northeast. One of the last conquests of Raja was the naval conquest of the 'old islands of the sea numbering 12,000', the Maldives.

Hence, the correct option is (C).

18. The classical Dance of Andhra Pradesh is Kuchipudi. Kuchipudi is the name of a village in the Divi Taluka of Krishna District. An orphan named Siddhendra Yogi is considered to be the founder of Kuchipudi dance.

Hence, the correct option is (B).

19. Companies issue debentures instead of shares to extend their business. These debentures are issue to borrow loan from the general public; interest is paid on the borrowed money to the debenture holders. So, a debenture holder is essentially a creditor who simply gives loan to the company.

Hence, the correct option is (B).

20. "Heavy Industry" was given priority in the IInd Five Year Plan. The IInd plan was particularly for the development of the public sector. The plan followed the Mahalanobis model, an economic development model developed by the Indian statistician Prashant Chandra Mahalanobis in 1953.

Hence, the correct option is (A).

21. Paris St Germain lifted the French League Cup in August 2020 after defeating Olympique Lyonnais Football Clubs.

- Paris St Germain completed a domestic treble as they beat Olympique Lyonnais 6-5 on penalties to lift the French League Cup.
- The match ended in a 0-0 stalemate after regular and extra time.

Hence, the correct option is (A).

22. Plantation drive carried out by UP's forest department in 8 districts has now entered Guinness World Record for most species planted simultaneously in 240 locations within an hour on July 28, 2020.

- The state has been made greener by planting 25 crore trees in a massive plantation drive.
- The drive started by planting more than 150 species of trees at two or three sites in Lucknow division.

Hence, the correct option is (C).

23. The Indian Express Special Correspondent **Dipankar Ghose** has won the Prem Bhatia Award for political reporting for his work on issues related to the COVID-19. The award for reporting on environmental and development issues was given to the People's Archive of Rural India (PARI), a journalism website dedicated to reporting on rural India.

Hence, the correct option is (D).

24. Mukesh Ambani's oil-to-telecom conglomerate Reliance Industries has been ranked **second** biggest brand after Apple on the FutureBrand Index 2020. The FutureBrand Index is a global perception study that reorders PwC's Global Top 100 Companies by Market Cap on perception strength rather than financial strength. The 2020 list is topped by Apple, while Samsung is ranked third.

Hence, the correct option is (B).

25. The permanent members of the UN Security Council also known as the Permanent Five, Big Five, or P5, include the following five governments – China, France, Russia, The United Kingdom, and The United States. These countries can veto any substantive resolution. There has been a growing demand to increase the number of permanent members to reflect the contemporary global reality.

Hence, the correct option is (C).

26. Article 360 empowers the president to proclaim a FinancialEmergency if he is satisfied that a situation has arisen due to which thefinancial stability or credit of India or any part of its territory isthreatened. It has never been declared.

Hence, the correct option is (C).

27. The 42nd Amendment Act of 1976 five subjects were transferred from the State to the concurrent list. They are:

1. Education
2. Forests
3. Weights & Measures
4. Protection of Wild Animals and Birds
5. Administration of Justice

Hence, the correct option is (C).

28. The Constitution guarantees six fundamental rights to Indian citizens as follows:

(i) Right to equality,

(ii) Right to freedom,

(iii) Right against exploitation,

(iv) Right to freedom of religion,

(v) Cultural and Educational rights, and

(vi) Right to constitutional remedies.

Hence, the correct option is (B).

29. The NCP (Nationalist Congress Party) was formed on 25 May 1999, by Sharad Pawar, P. A. Sangma, and Tariq Anwar after they were expelled from the Indian National Congress (INC) on 20 May 1999, for disputing the right of Italian-born Sonia Gandhi to lead the party. At the time of formation of the NCP, the Indian Congress (Socialist) party merged with the new party.

Hence, the correct option is (B).

30. Right To Information (RTI) is not included in the Directive Principles of State Policy (DPSP). India borrowed the DPSP from the Irish Constitution of 1937, the directive principles place an ideal before the legislator of India which shows that light while they frame the policies & laws. They are basically a code of conduct for the legislature and administrators of the country, Prohibition of Liquor, Right to Work, Equal Wage for Equal Work are some examples of the directive principle.

Hence, the correct option is (D).

31. The word Quo-Warranto literally means "by what warrants?" or "what is your authority"? It is a write issued with a view to restrain a person from holding a public office to which he is not entitled. The write requires the concerned person to explain to the Court by what authority he holds the office.

Hence, the correct option is (C).

32. Coinciding with the Ram temple 'Bhoomi pujan', publishing house Bloomsbury announced their latest book that will shed light on the history of Ayodhya. Titled "Amazing Ayodhya", the book by Neena Rai promises to offer "authentic information" about the city.

It will not only help understand the life and times of ancient Hindus but also the revered figures of Rama and Sita.

Hence, the correct option is (B).

33. The **France government** marked the national day on July 14th. The day is also known as "Bastille Day". This is the 230th anniversary of the storming of the Bastille prison which took place in Paris on 14 July 1789.

Hence, the correct option is (B).

34. Mukund Lath, a prominent cultural historian, scholar, passed away in August 2020. He was awarded India's 4th highest civilian honour, **The Padma Shri**, in 2010 for his trailblazing contributions to the field of arts and cultural history.

Hence, the correct option is (D).

35. Noted writer and activist Sadia Dehlvi passed away in August 2020. Sadia, who hailed from the royal 'Shama' family, edited "Bano, an Urdu women's journal". A well-known food connoisseur, she wrote a book on Delhi's culinary history in 2017, titled Jasmine & Jinns: Memories and Recipes of My Delhi.

She also produced and scripted documentaries and television programmes, including "Amma and Family".

Hence, the correct option is (B).

36. Minister of Commerce and Industry & Railways Piyush Goyal and Minister of Industry and Trade of Vietnam Tran Tuan Anh co-chaired the 17th ASEAN-India Economic Ministers Consultations held virtually on 29th August. The Ministers reaffirmed their commitment to take collective action to mitigate the economic impact of the epidemic and vowed to ensure the unaffected flow of essential goods and medicines, particularly economic and flexible supply chain connectivity in the region in compliance with WTO regulations.

Hence, the correct option is (B).

37. The European Investment Bank (EIB) has decided to invest 650 million euros into the construction of Kanpur's first city metro line. The agreement to this effect was signed in the virtual presence of Ambassador of the European Union to India Ugo Astuto.

The project aims at enabling some 3 million people in the city to benefit from green, safe, fast, and affordable public transport.

Hence, the correct option is (A).

38. The CSIR's Central Mechanical Engineering Research Institute (CMERI) has claimed to have developed the world's largest 'solar tree' which is installed at its residential complex in Durgapur in West Bengal and created a model that can be customized for use in agricultural activities. "The installed capacity of the Solar Tree is above 11.5 kilowatts peak (kWp). It has the annual capacity to generate 12,000-14,000 units of Clean and Green Power".

Hence, the correct option is (D).

39. Hitler's party came into power in 1933 is known as Nazi government soon came to control every aspect of German life. Under Nazi rule, all other political parties were banned. Adolf Hitler's rise to power began in Germany in September 1919 when Hitler joined the political party, then known as the Deutsche Arbeiterpartei – DAP (German Workers' Party). The name was changed in 1920 to the NSDAP (National Socialist German Workers' Party, commonly known as the Nazi party). It was anti-Marxist and opposed to the democratic post-war government.

Hence, the correct option is (B).

40. Punjab State Forest Department on 3rd September launched 'I Rakhwali' application to help citizens to become 'Greenery Saviours'. To further strengthen its drive to preserve and maintain the environment in Punjab. Launching the application, Punjab Forest Minister Sadhu Singh Dharamsot said that the application has been developed to ensure greenery and to protect the environment in Punjab, and its main aim is to inspire people to plant more trees.

Hence, the correct option is (D).

41. The website of the Lokpal has been launched. The website, www.lokpal.gov.in, was inaugurated by Chairperson Justice Pinaki Chandra Ghose in presence of all the Members of Lokpal in New Delhi. It provides basic information about the working and functioning of the anti-corruption ombudsman.

The Lokpal is the first institution of its kind in India established under the Lokpal and Lokayuktas Act, 2013 to inquire and investigate into allegations of the corruption against public functionaries.

Hence, the correct option is (A).

42. Union Minister of Education has launched a free mobile app named as "English Pro". The mobile application has been developed by the English and Foreign Languages University, Hyderabad under University Social Responsibility (USR).

This app will be a useful digital tool and will act as an educational resource for the teachers, students and for the people from varied backgrounds.

Hence, the correct option is (B).

43. India has now the 2ⁿᵈ largest road network in the world being fuelled by the tremendous growth in the construction of expressways and highways. Road, Transport and Highways Minister Nitin Gadkari said this while addressing the 60th annual convention of SIAM through video conference on 4th September. He informed that the current rate of road building per day has averaged to 30 Kilometres a day, with the highest being 40 Kilometre per day of highways.

Hence, the correct option is (C).

44. Prahlad Singh Patel has attended the 5th BRICS Culture Ministers Meet from India. It was held under the chairmanship of the Russian Federation. The Declaration of the meeting was agreed upon and was signed by all the representatives of BRICS Nations at the end of the meeting.

Hence, the correct option is (D).

45. Assam state government has relaunched the "SVAYEM" scheme to provide self-employment to youths state employment to around 2 lakh youths of the state known as Swami Vivekananda Assam Youth Empowerment (SVAYEM), it would provide 50 thousand rupees each as seed money to selected youths to start business ventures.

Assam Government is launching the redesigned SVAYEM with a budget of 1,000 crore rupees which will be spent in the next three months without any banking linkage.

Hence, the correct option is (D).

46. M Venkaiah Naidu has released "The State of Young Child in India" report prepared by a policy advocacy organization, Mobile Creches. The report measured Health and Nutrition in the country.

The top five high performing states according to Environment Index are Kerala, Goa, Punjab, Sikkim, and Himachal Pradesh.

There are eight states in the country that have scores less than the country's average in child development. They are Assam, Rajasthan, Meghalaya, Madhya Pradesh, Chhattisgarh, Jharkhand, Bihar, and Uttar Pradesh.

Hence, the correct option is (A).

47. Facebook-owned WhatsApp has partnered with Cyber Peace Foundation (CPF) to create awareness on cyber safety among students. The partners aim to reach about 15,000 students in five Indian states, including Delhi, Madhya Pradesh, Bihar, Jharkhand, and Maharashtra by the end of this year, under the first phase of a pan-India programme.

Hence, the correct option is (D).

48. Infosys company has acquired product design firm Kaleidoscope Innovation for $42 million. Global software major Infosys 3ʳᵈ September announced it has acquired U.S. based product design firm Kaleidoscope Innovation for $42 million to expand its engineering service offerings in medical devices, consumer and industrial markets across America.

Hence, the correct option is (D).

49. The Nobel Prize is awarded to 'those who, during the preceding year, shall have conferred the greatest benefit on mankind'. Prizes in **physics, chemistry, physiology or medicine, literature, and peace** have been awarded since 1901 – and economic sciences since 1968.

Hence, the correct option is (D).

50. Odisha State Government has Launched "GARIMA" Welfare Scheme For Sanitation Workers. Chief Minister Naveen Patnaik on 12th September launched "GARIMA" a new scheme to ensure the safety and dignity of core sanitation workers of the state. Under this scheme, about 20,000 core sanitation workers and their families covering one lakh population are likely to be benefitted.

Aims: The scheme aims to identify through statewide survey and register core sanitation workers, mandates registration of sanitation service providers, ensures the provision of necessary machines and appropriate PPEs to ensure safe working conditions.

Hence, the correct option is (C).

51. We can draw a figure in which D is to the right of G.

C is between A and B.

E is between F and D.

There are three persons between G and B.

As shown in figure G is on the extreme left.

Standing arrangement:

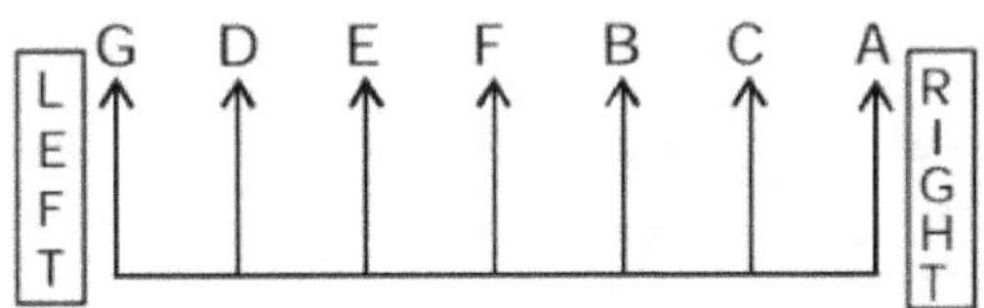

Hence, the correct option is (D).

52. No. of outermost circles = 12

No. of inner circles = 7

Innermost circle = 1

Total = 20

Hence, the correct option is (C).

53. According to Question,

Mohan walks 50 meters towards the west.

Then turns to the right and walks 50 meters.

He again turns towards the right and stops after walking 25 meters.

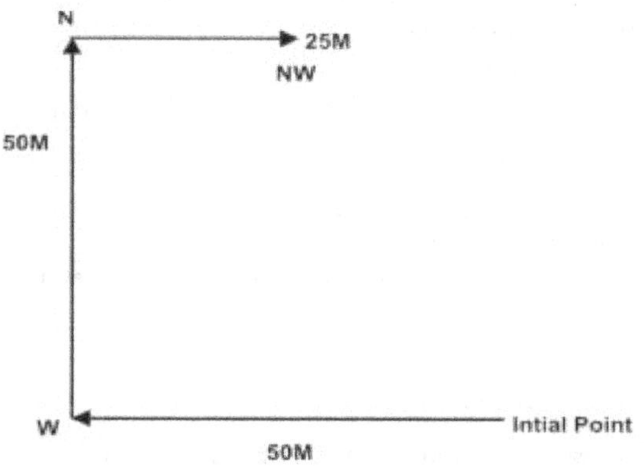

From the figure, it is clear Mohan is walking now in a North-West direction.

Hence, the correct option is (B).

54. According to the matrix:

T = 64

A = 00

L = 31

E = 32

TALE = 64,00,31,32

Hence, the correct option is (A).

55. Figure (C) will complete the pattern in the question figure.

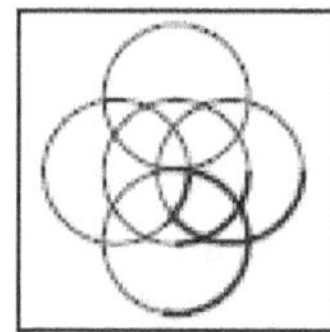

Missing parts are highlighted with bold lines.

Hence, the correct option is (C).

56. The answer figure (D) is the correct image of the question figure.

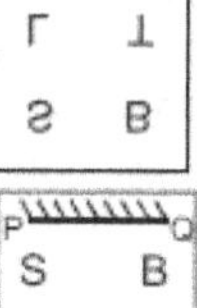

Hence, the correct option is (D).

57. Given image is

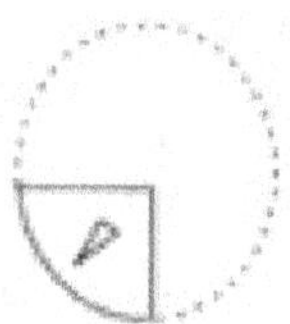

The first time when we unfold the image we will get

and finally, when we fully unfold the image we will get

Hence, the correct option is (A).

58. Given,

4 + 2 = 8, 10 + 5 = 8

So,

4 + 2 ⇒ 4 ÷ 2 + 6 = 2 + 6 = 8

10 + 5 ⇒ 10 ÷ 5 + 6 = 2 + 6 = 8

According to the above equation

9 + 3 ⇒ 9 ÷ 3 + 6 = 3 + 6 = 9

Hence, the correct option is (B).

59. CALCIUM cannot be formed using MUSICAL because in **Cal**c**i**um have two 'C' whereas there are no two C in MUSI**C**AL.

Hence, the correct option is (B).

60. When b a b c c is added to a_cbc_ca_ab_bca_ab,

we get,

abcbcacababcbcacab

Hence, the correct option is (A).

61. According to the question,

Sachin is shorter than Kamal, but taller than Ram

So,

Mohan > Kamal > Sachin > Ram ...(i)

Arun is a little shorter than Kamal and a little taller than Sachin

Kamal >Arun > Sachin ...(ii)

So, from Eqs. (i) and (ii),

Mohan > Kamal > Arun > Sachin > Ram ...(iii)

It becomes clear from equation (iii), clearly, the Kamal is the second-longest.

Hence, the correct option is (C).

62. (A) 5 + 3 + 2 = 10

(B) 2 + 4 + 3 = 9

(C) 1 + 4 + 3 = 8

(D) 3 + 2 + 3 = 8

Except in the number 5329, in all the others, the sum of the first three numbers is equal to the fourth number.

Hence, the correct option is (A).

63. All except 'Tiger' are young ones of animals. The Tiger's young one is known as 'cub'.

Hence, the correct option is (D).

64. In all four pairs, the serial numbers are given. Except for number pairs 9–10, in all others, the first number is even and the second number is odd.

Hence, the correct option is (A).

65. D plays all the 3 games cricket, football, and kabaddi.

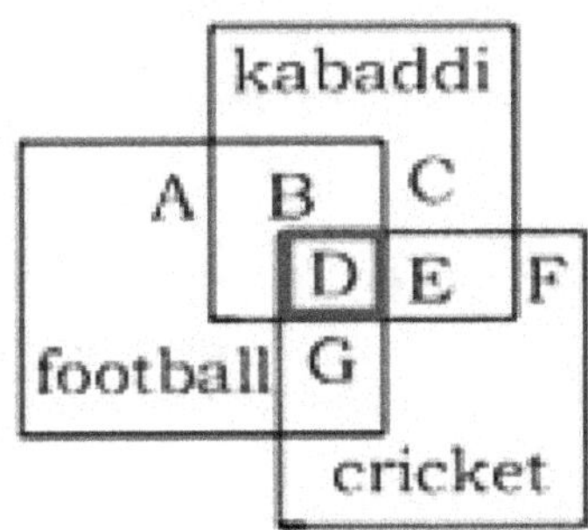

Hence, the correct option is (D).

66. In the given series, the first term is multiplied by 1.25, the second term is multiplied by 1, the third term is multiplied by 0.75, and so on.

So, the fourth term in the series is,

88 × 0.75 = 66

Hence, the correct option is (A).

67. In the given analogy, China is related to Beijing because Beijing is the capital of China.

Similarly, Nur-Sultan is the capital of Kazakhstan.

Hence, the correct option is (C).

68.

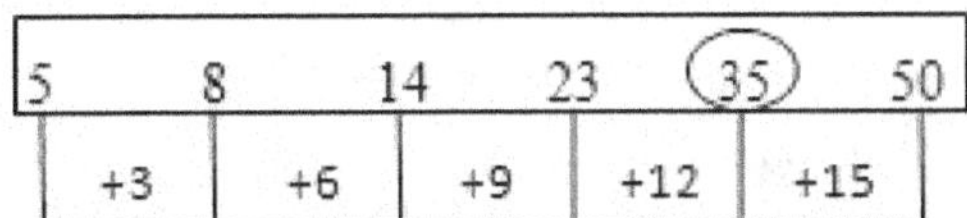

According to the given pattern in the figure, the value will come in place of the question mark (?) is 35.

Hence, the correct option is (B).

69. 1 kilometer = 1000000 mm.

1 meter = 1000 mm.

1 Decimeter = 100 mm.

1 centimeter = 10 mm.

Words in ascending order are as follows-

Centimeter → Decimeter → Meter → Kilometer

Hence, the correct option is (C).

70. ⇒ The day before yesterday = Three days after Saturday

⇒ Three days after Saturday is = Tuesday. ---(1)

⇒ So, "The day before the day before yesterday" = Tuesday (From Equation (1))

Now breaking the sentence even further,

The day before yesterday will be = Wednesday

Yesterday will be = Thursday

Today will be = Friday

Hence, the correct option is (B).

71.

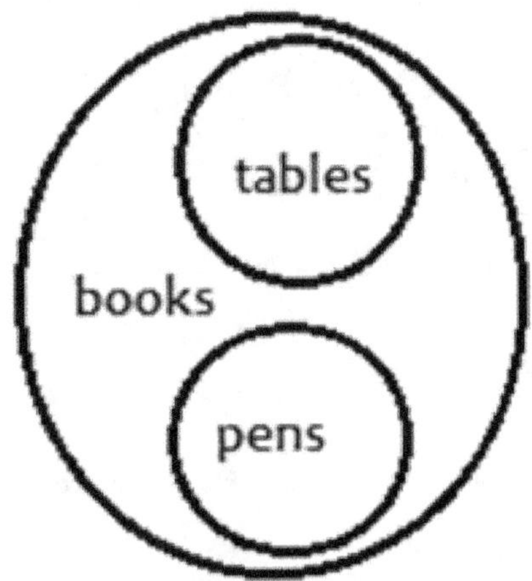

None of the conclusions is a definite case So neither I nor II follows.

Hence, the correct option is (B).

72. Given,

O = 16, FOR = 42

We have A = 2, B = 3, ..., Z = 27. Then.

FOR = F + O + R = 7 + 16 + 19 = 42.

FRONT = F + R + O + N + T = 7 + 19 + 16 + 15 + 21 = 78.

Hence, the correct option is (D).

73.

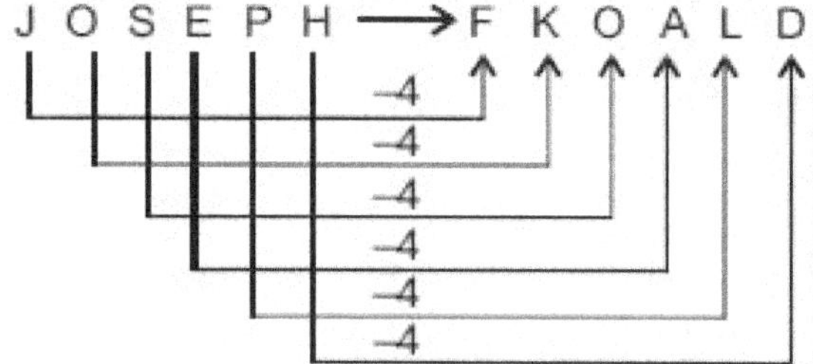

Therefore,

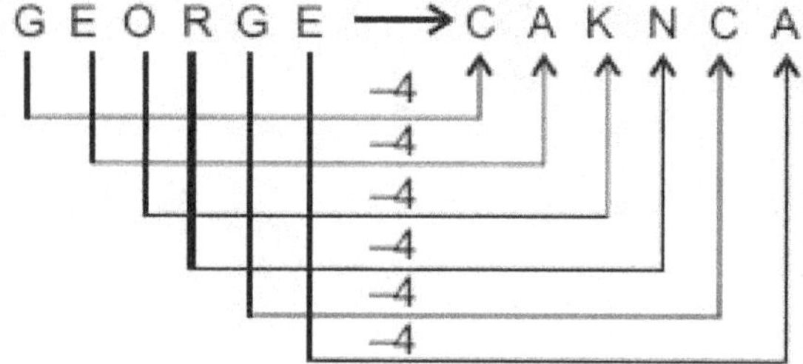

Hence, the correct option is (B).

74. P R I N C I P A L $\rightarrow$ L A P I C N I R P

Reverse order of letters.

Therefore,

A D O L E S C E N C E $\rightarrow$ E C N E C S E L O D A

Hence, the correct option is (D).

75.

QMPN	PQR	ROPQNOP	PQR

PMQRO	PQR	PPRR	PQR	P

So 4 times do PQR occur in such a way that Q is in the middle of P and R

Hence, the correct option is (C).

76. Given,

A sack contains two types of rice A and B grades in the ratio of $5:3$.

In another sack, there are two types of rice A and C grades in the ratio of $8:5$.

Both the mixtures (of two sacks) have been mixed in equal quantities (note this fact).

So, 1 kg of the new mixture will have 500 grams of mixtures from each sack.

The quantity of rice of C grade in 500 grams of second Sack's

mixture $= \dfrac{5}{8+5} \times 500 = \dfrac{5 \times 500}{13} = \dfrac{2500}{13} g$

So, In 1 kg of the new mixture; the amount of rice of Grade $= \dfrac{2500}{13} g$.

Hence, the correct option is (D).

77. Given,

Three persons walk from place A to place B.

Their speeds are in the ratio $4:3:5.$

Time taken is inversely proportional to relevant speeds.

$\therefore$ Required ratio $= \dfrac{1}{4} : \dfrac{1}{3} : \dfrac{1}{5}$

$= \dfrac{1}{4} \times 60 : \dfrac{1}{3} \times 60 : \dfrac{1}{5} \times 60$

$= 15 : 20 : 12$

Hence, the correct option is (A).

78. Total surface area of a Hemisphere $= 2\pi r^2 + \pi r^2 = 3\pi r^2$

Where,

$R = 6,$ Surface area $= 3\pi(6)^2$

$R = 12,$ Surface area $= 3\pi(12)^2$

Required ratio $= \dfrac{3\pi(6)^2}{3\pi(12)^2} = \dfrac{36}{144} = \dfrac{1}{4}$

Ratio $= 1:4$

Hence, the correct option is (A).

79. Let original price be Rs. x

$C.P. = Rs. 0.75x$

According to question

$0.75x \times \dfrac{140}{100} = x + 40$

$\Rightarrow 1.05x = x + 40$

$\Rightarrow x = 800$

The price of buying the watch $= 800 \times 0.75$

$= Rs. 600$

Hence, the correct option is (B).

80. Let C.P = Rs. 100

Then,

M.P = Rs. 120

S.P = Rs. 108

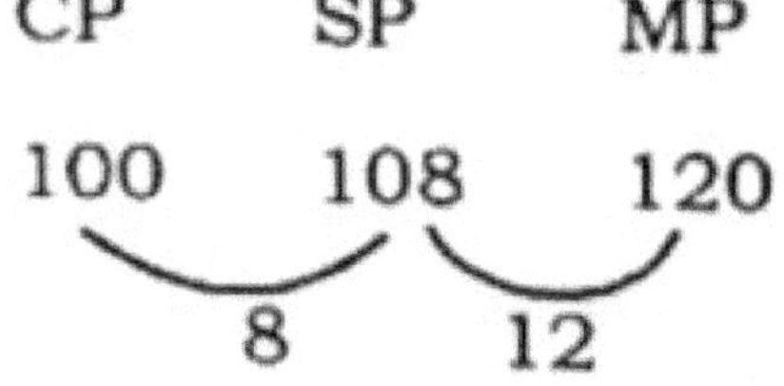

Discount Rate $= \dfrac{Discount}{Marked\ Price} = \dfrac{12}{120} \times 100 = 10$

Hence, the correct option is (B).

81. Previous population of the village $= 840$

% increase $= 5\%$ of $840 = \dfrac{5}{100} \times 840 = 42$

New population $= 840 + 42 = 882$

Hence, the correct option is (D).

82. Let the number be x

According to the question, 40% of 70% of the number is 336.

$\Rightarrow x \times \dfrac{40}{100} \times \dfrac{70}{100} = 336$

$\Rightarrow x \times 0.4 \times 0.7 = 336$

$\Rightarrow 0.28x = 336$

$\Rightarrow x = \dfrac{336}{0.28} = 1200$

$\dfrac{1}{3}$rd of this number will be $\dfrac{1200}{3} = 400$

Hence, the correct option is (D).

83. The relative speed of A and B = $5\dfrac{3}{4} - 4\dfrac{1}{2} = 1\dfrac{1}{4}$

Distance between A and B in $3\dfrac{1}{2}$ hrs = speed × time

$= 1\dfrac{1}{4} \times 3\dfrac{1}{2} = \dfrac{5}{4} \times \dfrac{7}{2} = 4\dfrac{3}{8} km$

Hence, the correct option is (C).

84. The ship will move in a direction along a diagonal, as shown here

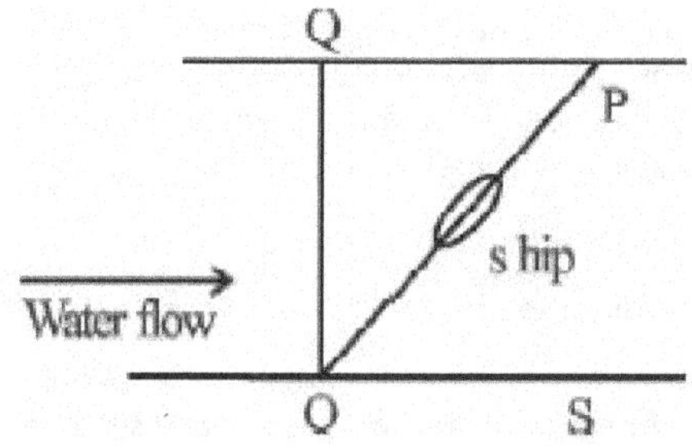

If river waters are still, the ship moves along OQ. (Directly opposite from starting point)

If the waters are moving, the ship moves along OP. (Diagonally in the flow of water)

Hence, the correct option is (B).

85. Total simple interest received, $I =$ Rs 1600

Principal, $p = 7000$

period, $n = 5$ years

Rate of interest, $r =?$

Simple Interest, $I = \dfrac{pnr}{100}$

$\Rightarrow 1600 = \dfrac{7000 \times 5 \times r}{100}$

$\Rightarrow r = \dfrac{1600 \times 100}{7000 \times 5} = \dfrac{160}{35} = \dfrac{32}{7}\%$

By rule of alligation,

$$\begin{array}{cc}
\text{Rate of interest \%} & \text{Rate of interest \%} \\
\text{from part}_1 & \text{from part}_2 \\
6 & 4
\end{array}$$

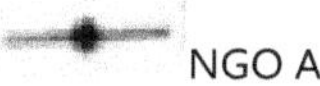

Net rate of interest %

$$\dfrac{32}{7}$$

$$\dfrac{32}{7} - 4 = \dfrac{4}{7} \qquad 6 - \dfrac{32}{7} = \dfrac{10}{7}$$

$\Rightarrow$ Part 1: part $2 = \dfrac{4}{7} : \dfrac{10}{7} = 4 : 10 = 2 : 5$

Given that total amount is Rs. 7000. Therefore, the amount lent at 6% per annum (part 1 amount) $= 7000 \times \dfrac{2}{7} = $ Rs. 2000

Hence, the correct option is (A).

86. According to Question,

NGO A

NGO B

NGO C

The total number of trees planted by NGO B in Assam and NGO C in Punjab = $(7 + 7) \times 1000 = 14000$

The total number of trees planted by NGO A in UP and MP together = $(6 + 9) \times 1000 = 15000$

Therefore, the ratio of the number of trees planted by NGO B in Assam and the number of trees planted by NGO B in Punjab together to the number of trees planted by NGO A in UP and MP together is,

Required ratio $= \dfrac{14000}{15000} = \dfrac{14}{15} = 14 : 15$

Hence, the correct option is (C).

87. According to Question,

NGO A

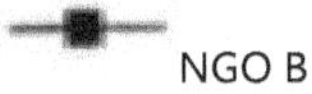
NGO B

NGO C

Required average $= \dfrac{(6+8+9)\times 1000}{3}$

$= \dfrac{23000}{3} \approx 7667$

Hence, the correct option is (C).

88. According to Question,

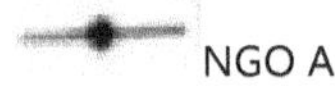
NGO A

NGO B

NGO C

Number of trees planted by NGO A in Punjab $= 10000$

Number of trees planted by NGO C in Assam $= 8000$

$\therefore$ Required difference $= 10000 - 8000 = 2000$

Hence, the correct option is (D).

89. Given,

$h = 22.5\ m$

diameter $(d) = 7\ m$

Therefore, $r = \dfrac{7}{2}\ m$

area of the inner curved surface $= 2\pi rh$

$= 2 \times \dfrac{22}{7} \times \dfrac{7}{2} \times 22.5\ m^2$

$= 495\ m^2$

Total cost = Surface area $\times$ Rate

$= 2\pi rh \times 3$

$= 495 \times 3 =$ Rs. 1485

Hence, the correct option is (B).

90. We know that-

$1^2 + 2^2 + 3^2 \ldots n^2 = \dfrac{n(n+1)(2n+1)}{6}$

So, $1^2 + 2^2 + 3^2 \ldots 10^2 = \dfrac{10(11)(21)}{6} =$

$5 \times 11 \times 7 = 385$

Hence, the correct option is (D).

91. Google Chrome, Mozilla Firefox, Internet Explorer, Netscape Navigator are examples of Web browsers.

A web browser is a software application for accessing the information on the World Wide Web.

Web - Browser Types:

- Internet Explorer: Internet Explorer (IE) is a product from software giant Microsoft.

- Google Chrome: This web browser is developed by Google and its beta version was first released on September 2, 2008, for Microsoft Windows.

- Mozilla Firefox: Firefox is a new browser derived from Mozilla.

- Netscape: The first commonly available web browser with a graphical user interface was Erwise.

Hence, the correct option is (C).

92. The system software is a collection of programs designed to operate, control, and extend the processing capabilities of the computer itself. The system software is generally prepared by computer manufacturers. These software products comprise of programs written in low-level languages, which interact with the hardware at a very basic level. System software serves as the interface between the hardware and the end-users.

Hence, the correct option is (D).

93. Ctrl + D is the shortcut key to open the Font dialog box.

Key-Action

- Ctrl + Shift + C $\Rightarrow$ Copy the formatting of the selected text.

- Alt + Ctrl + C $\Rightarrow$ Inserts a copyright symbol (©).

- Ctrl + D $\Rightarrow$ Opens the Font dialog box with the focus at the Font combo box.

- Ctrl+Shift + D $\Rightarrow$ Toggles double underlining.

Hence, the correct option is (C).

94. Charles Babbage was considered to be the **father of the computer,** and later he gave the invention of the Analytical Engine in 1837. The Analytical Engine contained an ALU (arithmetic logic unit), basic flow control, and integrated memory.

Hence, the correct option is (B).

95. The hard disk is coated with **magnetic metallic oxide** on both sides. It consists of rotating disks (circular round object, disc) that are coated with magnetic material. The data storage device keeps the data safe even when there is no electricity.

Hence, the correct option is (A).

96. Modem is a communication device.

The modem is an abbreviation for modulator-demodulator. It is a device that modulates numeric (digital) information and sends it in analog format and de-modulates the signal in the analog format and receives it digitally. It is an essential component for establishing communication between a transmission medium and a numeric machine (such as a computer).

Hence, the correct option is (D).

97. The printer is not an input device.

Examples of Input Devices of Computer-

- Mouse, Light Pen.

- Optical/magnetic Scanner, Touch Screen.

- Microphone for voice as input, TrackBall.

- Joystick, Camera.

- Webcam (PC video camera).

- Keyboard: A keyboard is the most common input device.

- Mouse: A mouse is an electro-mechanical, handheld device.

Hence, the correct option is (C).

98. A special set of values saved with the workbook is called **Scenario**. MS Excel gives you the facility of Scenario where more than one version of any data can also be saved and kept.

Hence, the correct option is (B).

99. Input/output function prototypes and macros are defined in the **stdio.h** header file. stdio means Standard Input and Output. In this file (stdio.h), all those functions are defined which are used to take input/output. printf output is used to print while scanf input is used.

Hence, the correct option is (C).

100. strrchr() returns a pointer to the last occurrence of the character in a string.

Example:

#include <stdio.h>#include <string.h>int main(){ char str[30] = " 12345678910111213"; printf("The last position of '2' is %d.\n", strrchr(str, '2') - str); return 0;}

Output: The last position of '2' is 14.

Hence, the correct option is (D).

General Knowledge/Current Affairs

Q.1 Identify the proper food chain:
A. Grass → frog → insect → snake
B. Grass → insect → frog → snake
C. Insect → frog → grass → snake
D. Grass → frog → snake → insect

Q.2 The direction of impulse in a typical neuron is -
A. Axon to dendron
B. Dendron to axon
C. Both A and B are correct
D. Both A and B are wrong

Q.3 Transpiration takes place from ________.
A. Leaves
B. Stem
C. Flowers
D. All the above

Q.4 Secondary extraction of petroleum ______.
A. occurs immediately after enhanced recovery.
B. is less expensive than primary extraction.
C. uses solvents, water, or steam.
D. allows the oil to be extracted to the last drop.

Q.5 The main constituents of pearls are:
A. calcium oxide and ammonium chloride
B. aragonite and conchiolin
C. only calcium carbonate
D. calcium carbonate and magnesium carbonate

Q.6 730 watts = _____ hp
A. 0.97
B. 2
C. 746
D. 6

Q.7 Crescograph was invented by
A. S.N. Bose
B. P.C. Roy
C. J.C. Bose
D. P.C. Mahalanobis

Q.8 What does the term 'Lithosphere' refer to?
A. Plants and animals
B. Interior of the earth
C. Crust of the earth
D. None of the above

Q.9 Gandhi Sagar Reservoir is of the river ?
A. Chambal
B. Narmada
C. Rihand
D. Sutlej

Q.10 Where is Asiatic Wild ass found ?
A. Rann of Kutch
B. Kaziranga
C. Sariska
D. Ranthambore

Q.11 Match the following.

A.	Vikram Era.	1.	248 CE
B.	Saka Era.	2.	318-319 CE
C.	Kalachuri Era.	3.	57 CE
D.	Gupta Era.	4.	78 CE

A. A-1, B-2, C-3, D-4
B. A-3, B-4, C-1, D-2
C. A-4, B-3, C-2, D-1
D. A-2, B-1, C-4, D-3

Q.12 The first Governor-General of Bengal was
A. Lord Clive
B. Lord Warren Hastings
C. Lord John Shore
D. Lord Cornwallis

Q.13 The Environment (Protection) Bill was passed by the Parliament of India in —
A. 1984
B. 1986
C. 1981
D. 1972

Q.14 The legislature in a democratic country can influence public opinion by—
A. Granting rights
B. Enacting non-controversial laws
C. Defining the duties of the citizens
D. Focusing attention on public issues

Q.15 A tax is said to be regressive when its burden falls :
A. More heavily on the poor than on the rich.
B. Less heavily on the poor than on the rich.
C. Equally on the poor as on the rich.
D. None of the above

Q.16 The Novel 'Two' has been written by whom?
A. Chetan Bhagat
B. Gulzar
C. Salil S Prakash
D. William Dalrymple

Q.17 Which among the following organization has developed first indigenous bulletproof vest?
A. Indira Gandhi Centre for Atomic Research
B. Bhabha Atomic Research Centre
C. Global Centre for Nuclear Energy Partnership
D. None of the above

Q.18 In parts of which state, scientists have identified a new species of frog called Fejervarya goemchi?
A. Maharashtra
B. Punjab
C. Goa
D. Kerala

Q.19 Which new project has been launched in India to address Vitamin D Deficiencies among youngsters?
A. Project Sooraj
B. Project Sun
C. Project Dhoop
D. Project Sunlight

Q.20 Which one of the following industries is the biggest consumer of water in India?
A. Engineering
B. Paper and pulp
C. Taxtiles
D. Thermal power

Q.21 Where was the first conference of SAARC (South Asian Association for Regional Cooperation) held ?

A. Dhaka
C. Colombo
B. New Delhi
D. Kathmandu

Q.22 How many Indian- origin kids were among the 8 who won the 92nd Scripps National Spelling Bee Contest held in Maryland, US ?
A. 6   **B.** 5   **C.** 4   **D.** 7

Q.23 Who sworn in as the Prime Minister of India for the second consecutive term ?
A. Priyanka Gandhi Vadra
B. Narendra Damodardas Modi
C. Rahul Gandhi
D. Amit Shah

Q.24 Which international organization has visited India as the chief guest of PM Modi's Swearing-in Ceremony ?
A. South Asian Association for Regional Cooperation (SAARC) Countries
B. Association of Southeast Asian Nations(ASEAN)
C. BRICS Countries
D. Bay of Bengal Initiative for Multi Sectoral Technical and Economic Cooperation (BIMSTEC)

Q.25 Which satellite would be launched on January 17, 2020 as the first satellite of the year 2020?
A. GSAT-30
C. GSAT-17
B. GSAT-29
D. GSAT-11

Q.26 Name the new ministry, which is formed by merging Ministries of Water Resources and Drinking Water and Sanitation .
A. Ministry of Water and Sanitation
B. Ministry of Jal Shakti
C. Ministry of Jal and Sanitation
D. Ministry of Drinking Water

Q.27 Who has become the youngest council of ministers in second term of Modi government ?
A. Giriraj Singh
C. Smriti Irani
B. Piyush Goyal
D. Harsh Vardhan

Q.28 Which city is hosts the 107th edition of the Indian Science Congress (ISC)?
A. New Delhi
C. Kolkatta
B. Lucknow
D. Bengaluru

Q.29 After Indore at first rank, which cities ranked second and third (in first quarter) in Swachh Survekshan League, 2020, released recently?
A. Ahmedabad and Jaipur
B. Gurugram and Bengaluru
C. Pune and Bhubaneswar
D. Bhopal and Surat

Q.30 Which Airport has won the CII-GBC 'National Energy Leader' and 'Excellent Energy Efficient Unit' award at the 21st National Awards for 'Excellence in Energy Management'?
A. Chhatrapati Shivaji International Airport, Mumbai
B. Rajiv Gandhi International Airport, Hyderabad

C. Indira Gandhi International Airport, New Delhi
D. Kempegowda International Airport, Bengaluru

Q.31 Where was the 107th International Science Congress for the year 2020 with the theme "Science and Technology: Rural Development" inaugurated ?
A. Kochi, Kerala
B. Bengaluru, Karnataka
C. Guwahati, Assam
D. Kolkata, West Bengal

Q.32 Which E-commerce firm has revamped seller financing program 'Growth Capital' to empower MSMEs ?
A. Snapdeal   **B.** Flipkart   **C.** Amazon   **D.** Myntra

Q.33 At what rate, sellers at Flipkart avail loan upto Rs.3 crore from 10 Non-Banking Financial Companies (NBFCs) and banks under seller financing program 'Growth Capital' ?
A. 6.5 percent
C. 7.5 percent
B. 8.5 percent
D. 9.5 percent

Q.34 What is the full form of CAR, which is in news recently?
A. CAR – Capital Adequacy Ratio
B. CAR – Capital Asset Ratio
C. CAR – Capital Account Ratio
D. CAR – Capital Averse Ratio

Q.35 What is the Capital Adequacy Ratio(CAR) for Housing Finance Companies (HFCs) in March 2020?
A. 14%   **B.** 15%   **C.** 13%   **D.** 12%

Q.36 Which city topped in the 5th edition of Swachh Survekshan League 2020 (Quarter 1 and Quarter 2) having more than 10 lakh population?
A. Nashik, Maharashtra
B. Surat, Gujarat
C. Bhopal, Madhya Pradesh
D. Indore, Madhya Pradesh

Q.37 How much percent of India's Gross Domestic Product (GDP) was forecasted for the fiscal year 2020 by DBS Bank ?
A. 6.9%   **B.** 6.4%   **C.** 6.5%   **D.** 6.8%

Q.38 Name the organization, which has formed a working group to review the current framework of margins in the futures and options segment .
A. Small Industries Development Bank of India(SIDBI)
B. Insurance Regulatory and Development Authority(IRDA)
C. Securities and Exchange Board of India (SEBI)
D. Reserve Bank of India(RBI)

Q.39 Which organization heads the working group formed by Securities and Exchange Board of India (SEBI) to review the current framework of margins in the futures and options segment ?
A. NSE Clearing Ltd.
B. Metropolitan Clearing Corporation of India Ltd.
C. National Commodity Clearing Ltd.
D. Indian Clearing Corporation Ltd.

Q.40 Name the world famous handcrafted footwear, which gets a Geographic Indication (GI) tag from the Controller General of Patents, Designs and Trade Mark .

A. Dharwadi chappal   **B.** Kolhapuri chappal

C. Solapuri chappal   **D.** Satari chappal

Q.41 Team of scientists from which university have developed a chemical process that turns 'dirty' coal into biomedical 'Carbon Quantum Dots (CQDs)',that helps in detection of cancer cells ?

A. Indian Institute of Integrative Medicine

B. Tata Institute of Fundamental Research

C. Central Glass and Ceramic Research Institute

D. CSIR - North East Institute of Science and Technology

Q.42 Which one of the following founded the 'Atmiya Sabha'?

A. Raja Ram Mohan Roy

B. Devendranath Tagore

C. Swami Vivekanand

D. Akshay Kumar Dutt

Q.43 John Elliot Drinkwater Bethune was closely associated with

A. Abolition of Pardah system

B. Women education

C. Widow remarriage

D. Abolition of slavery

Q.44 Dev Samaj was founded by-

A. Shiv Narayan Agnihotri

B. Devendranath Tagore

C. Vivekanand

D. None of Above

Q.45 Dronacharya award is given for excellence in which of the following fields?

A. Sports   **B.** Gallantry

C. Coaching in sports   **D.** Social work

Q.46 Article 36 to Article 51 of Indian Constitutional mainly deals with Directive Principles of State Policy, given in _____ of Indian Constitution.

A. Part II   **B.** Part III   **C.** Part IV   **D.** Part V

Q.47 Prohibition of discrimination on grounds of religion, race, caste, sex or place of birth comes under which category of Fundamental Rights in Indian Constitution?

A. Right to Freedom

B. Right to Constitutional Remedies

C. Right to Equality

D. Right to Freedom of Religion

Q.48 According to Article 75 of the Indian Constitution, the ministers are collectively responsible to the Parliament in general and to the _____ in particular.

A. People   **B.** Lok Sabha

C. Rajya Sabha   **D.** President

Q.49 Which of the following is NOT correctly matched?

A. Loktak Lake – Manipur

B. Sambhar Lake – Rajasthan

C. Lonar Lake – Maharashtra

D. Hussain Sagar – Karnataka

Q.50 Kapildhara Falls is situated on which river?

A. Tapi   **B.** Sharavati

C. Narmada   **D.** Indravati

Reasoning

Q.51 Directions: Read the following information carefully and answer the question given below-

All the opposite faces of a big cube are colored with red, black, and green colors. After that is cut into 64 small equal cubes.

How many small cubes are there with only one face coloured?

A. 32   **B.** 8   **C.** 16   **D.** 24

Q.52 From the given alternative words select the one which cannot be formed using the letters of the given word.

JERUSALEM

A. EASE   **B.** SALE   **C.** MAIL   **D.** RULE

Q.53 If **DELHI** is coded as 73541 and **CALCUTTA** as 82589662, then how would **CALICUT** be coded in that code?

A. 5978213   **B.** 8251896   **C.** 8543691   **D.** 5279431

Q.54 In a code language, the following alphabets are coded in a particular way:

A B C D E F G H I P R S T O

? ! ; : . > < Δ □ ◉ ⊕ ★ ω +

Which word can be decoded as:

? ◉ ◉ ⊕ + ? : Δ

A. ABOLISH   **B.** APPROVAL

C. ACCOMPLISH   **D.** APPROADH

Q.55 In a certain code language DRAMA is written as IWZZN. How is TOWER written in that code language?

A. LGDIV   **B.** GLDIV   **C.** LGDVI   **D.** GLDVI

Q.56 Meena correctly remembers that her father's birthday is after 18 May but before 22 May. Her brother correctly remembers that their father's birthday is before 24 May but after 20 May. On which date in May was definitely their father's birthday?

A. 20   **B.** 19

C. 18   **D.** None of these

Q.57 Which figure best represents the relationship among **Sun, Moon, Molecule ?**

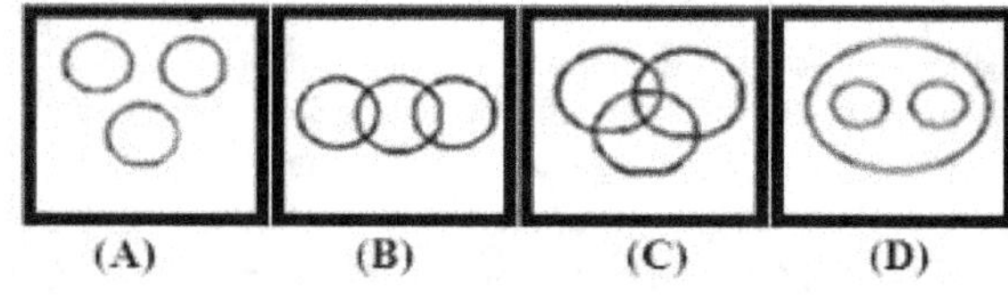

A. A   **B.** B   **C.** C   **D.** D

Q.58 If X + Y means X is the daughter of Y; X - Y means X is the brother of Y; X % Y means X is the father of Y and X × Y means X is the sister of Y. Which of the following means I is the niece of J?

A. J - N % C × I

B. I × C - N % J

C. J + M × C % I

D. I × C + N - J

Q.59 If '+' stands for division, '×' stands for addition, '−' stands for multiplication, '÷' stands for substraction , which of the following is correct ?

A. $15 + 5 - 2 + 6 \times 3 = 3$

B. $15 \times 5 + 2 - 6 + 3 = 56.5$

C. $15 \div 5 \times 2 - 6 + 3 = 28$

D. $15 - 5 + 2 \times 6 \div 3 = 41$

Q.60 If you are 11th in a queue starting either end, how many are there in the queue?

A. 11 **B.** 12 **C.** 21 **D.** 22

Ques (61-62):Directions: In each of the following questions, select the related word/letters/number from the given alternatives.

Q.61 ACAZX : DFDWU : : GIGTR : __

A. JKJQO **B.** JLJQO **C.** JKJOQ **D.** JLJOP

Q.62 64 : ? :: 72 : 53

A. 44 **B.** 54 **C.** 52 **D.** 70

Q.63 Directions: In each of the following questions, a series is given with one/two-term(s) missing. Choose the correct alternatives from the given ones that will complete the series.

975, 864, 753, 642, ?

A. 431 **B.** 314 **C.** 531 **D.** 532

Q.64 Direction: In the following question, select the related word from the given alternatives.

Maharashtra : India :: Texas : ?

A. Canada **B.** Mexico **C.** Brazil **D.** USA

Q.65 Directions: What will come in place of the question mark (?) in the following number series?

```
  9      3     7
 12      2     9
 13      5     ?
1404    30    504
```

A. 5 **B.** 8 **C.** 15 **D.** 56

Q.66 Identify the alternative which resembles the mirror-image of the given word.

DL9Q3574

A. 

B. 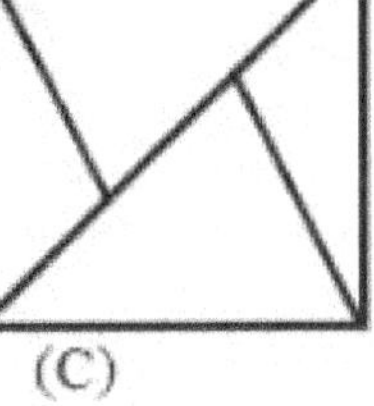

C. 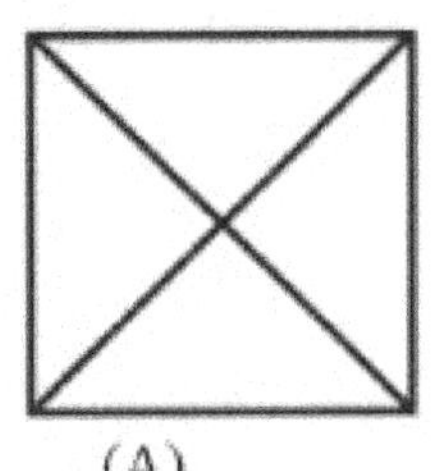

D. 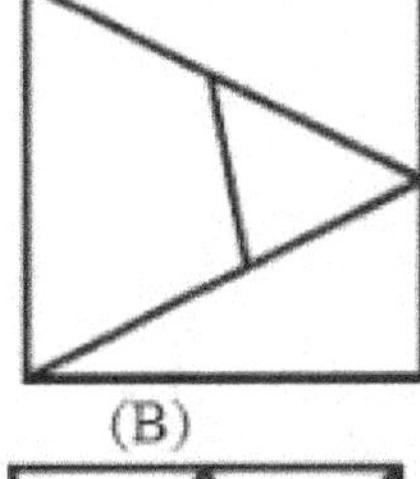

Q.67 From the given answer figures, select the one in which the question figure is hidden/embedded.

Question Figure:

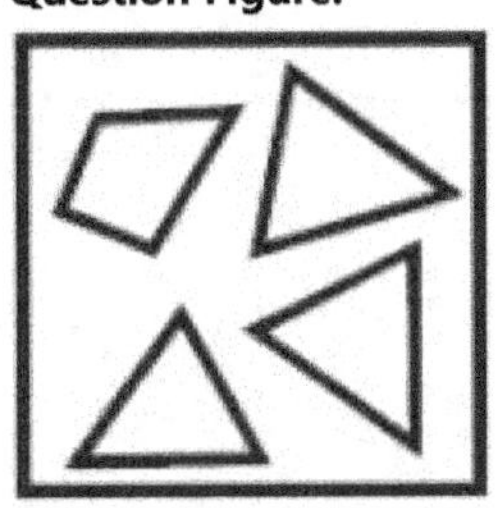

Answer Figure:

(A) (B) (C) (D)

A. A **B.** B **C.** C **D.** D

Q.68 In the following questions, a piece of paper is folded and cut as shown below in the question figures. From the given answer figures, indicate how it will appear when opened.

Questin Figure:

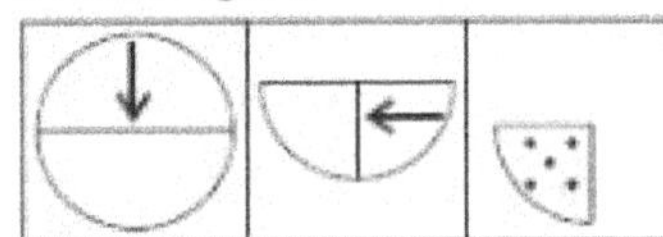

Answer Figure:

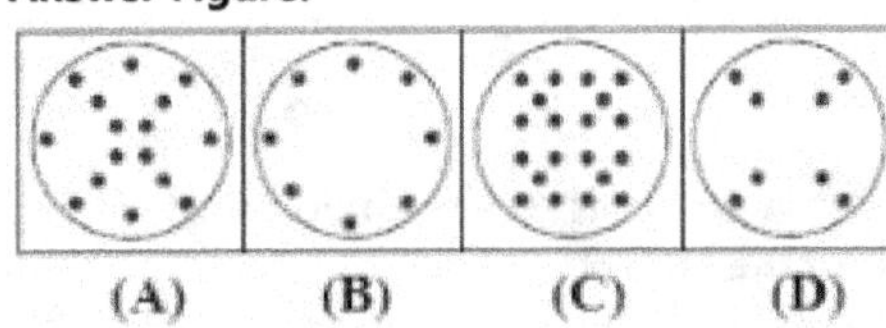

(A) (B) (C) (D)

A. A **B.** B **C.** C **D.** D

Q.69 In the question, one part of the problem figure is subtracted. Select the option that shows the correct shape after subtraction.

Question Figure:

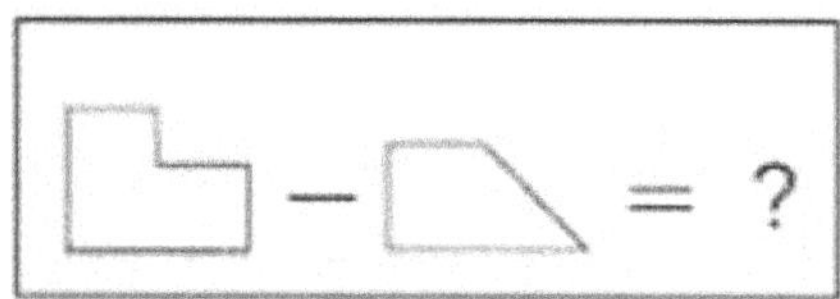

Answer Figure:

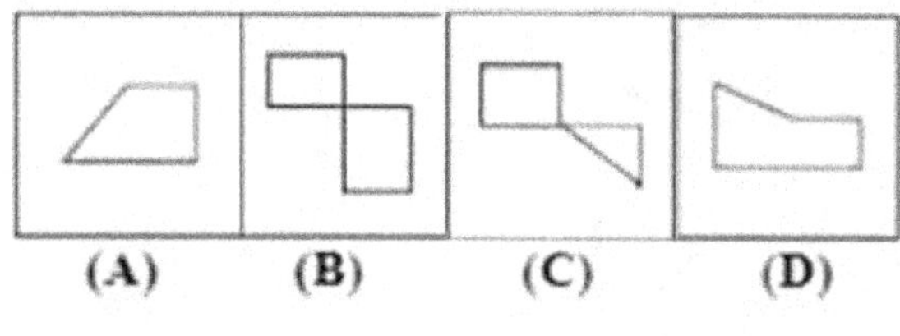

(A)   (B)   (C)   (D)

A. A   **B.** B   **C.** C   **D.** D

Q.70 How many triangles are there is the given figure?

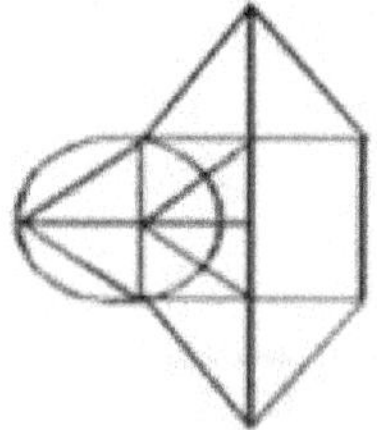

A. 10   **B.** 12   **C.** 14   **D.** 16

Q.71 Directions In these questions, statements are given followed by two conclusions I and II. You have to consider both the statements to be true even if they seem to be at variance from commonly known facts. You have to decide which of the given conclusions is/are definitely drawn from the given statements. Select answer as: (A) If only I follows (B) If only II follows (C) If neither I nor II follows (D) If both I and II follows

Statements:

All squares are triangles.

No circle is a triangle.

Conclusions:

I. No square is a circle.

II. All triangles are squares.

A. A   **B.** B   **C.** C   **D.** D

Q.72 In a row of boys, Srinath is 7th from the left and Venkat is 12th from the right. If they interchange their positions, Srinath becomes 22nd from the left. How many boys are there in the row?

A. 19   **B.** 31   **C.** 33   **D.** 34

Q.73 Which one of the given responses would be a meaningful order of the following?

1. Large intestine 2. Rectum

3. Small intestine 4. Mouth

5. Stomach 6. Oesophagus

A. 5, 4, 2, 3, 6, 1   **B.** 6, 4, 2, 1, 3, 5

C. 4, 6, 3, 2, 5, 1   **D.** 4, 6, 5, 3, 1, 2

Q.74 Arrange the following words as per order in the English dictionary—

1. Activity 2. Attention 3. Arise 4. Absent

A. 2, 3, 4, 1   **B.** 3, 2, 1, 4   **C.** 4, 1, 3, 2   **D.** 4, 3, 2, 1

Q.75 Which one of the given responses would be a meaningful order of the following ?

I. Absorption

II. Digestion

III. Nutrition

IV. Excretion

A. III, I, II, IV   **B.** II, I, III, IV

C. III, IV, II, I   **D.** III, II, I, IV

Numerical Ability

Q.76 A cricketer scored 180 runs in the first test and 258 runs in the second. How many runs should he score in the third test so that his average score in the three tests would be 230 runs?

A. 210   **B.** 245   **C.** 270   **D.** 252

Q.77 10% discount and then 20% discount in successive is equivalent to the total discount of—

A. 15%   **B.** 30%   **C.** 24%   **D.** 28%

Q.78 If $a + \dfrac{1}{b} = 1$ and $b + \dfrac{1}{c} = 1$, then $c + \dfrac{1}{a} = ?$

A. 2   **B.** -1 **C.** 1   **D.** 0

Q.79 If $a + b = 3$ and $a - b = 1$, then the value of ab is -

A. 1   **B.** 2   **C.** 3   **D.** 4

Q.80 If $x + y = 2$ and $x^2 + y^2 = 4$ then the value of $x^3 + y^3$ is-

A. 8   **B.** 14   **C.** -16 **D.** 40

Q.81 Find the remainder when $1! + 2! + 3! + 4! + \cdots \ldots + 100!$ is divided by 5.

A. 0   **B.** 1   **C.** 2   **D.** 3

Q.82 The greatest number, which when subtracted from 5834, gives a number exactly divisible by each of $20, 28, 32$ and 35, is:

A. 1120   **B.** 4714   **C.** 5200   **D.** 5600

Q.83 The population of a town is 50000. If the number of male increase by 5% and females by 10%, the population becomes 53500, the number of males and females are -

A. 30000 Males, 25000 females

B. 25000 Males, 25000 females

C. 30000 Males, 20000 females

D. 15000 Males, 35000 females

Q.84 'A' can do a piece of work in 7 days. 'A' and 'B' can do the same work in 3 days. In how many days can 'B' do the same work?

A. $5\frac{1}{4}$ days   **B.** $6\frac{1}{4}$ days   **C.** $8\frac{1}{4}$ days   **D.** $9\frac{1}{4}$ days

Q.85 If 5 women or 8 girls can do work in 84 days. In how many days can 10 women and 5 girls can do the same work?

A. 14   **B.** 32   **C.** 20   **D.** 24

Ques (86-89):Directions : Read the following graph carefully and answer the question given below.

The bar-graph given below shows the percentage distribution of the total production of a car manufacturing company into various models over two years.

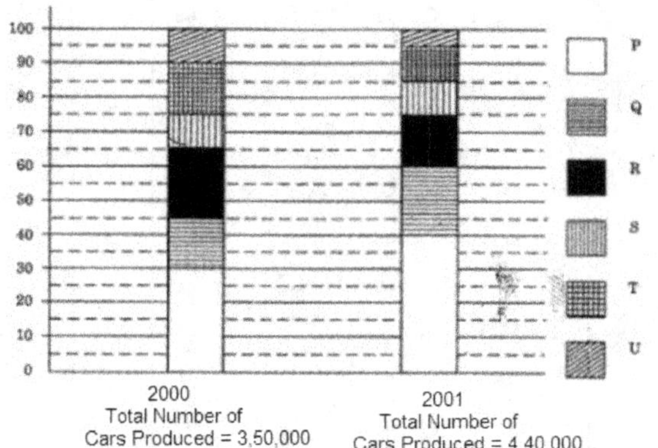

Q.86 If 85% of the S type cars produced in each year were sold by the Company how many S type cars remained unsold?

A. 7650   **B.** 9350   **C.** 11,850   **D.** 12,250

Q.87 If the percentage production of P-type cars in 2001 was the same as that in 2000, then the number of P-type cars produced in 2001 would have been:

A. 1,40,000   **B.** 1,32,000
C. 1,17,000   **D.** 1,05,000

Q.88 What was the difference in the number of Q type cars produced in 2000 and that produced in 2001?

A. 35,500   **B.** 22,500   **C.** 17,500   **D.** 27,000

Q.89 For which model the percentage rise/fall in production from 2000 to 2001 was minimum?

A. Q   **B.** R   **C.** S   **D.** T

Q.90 A shopkeeper's price is 50% above the cost price. If he allows his customer a discount of 30% what profit does he make?

A. 5%   **B.** 10%   **C.** 15%   **D.** 20%

Computer Awareness

Q.91 In which menu can you find features like Slide Design, Slide Layout, etc.?
A. Insert Menu   **B.** Format Menu
C. Tools Menu   **D.** Slide Show Menu

Q.92 Which operation is not performed by the computer?
A. Inputting   **B.** Outputting
C. Controlling   **D.** Understanding

Q.93 Which of the following types of memory loses data when power is switched off?
A. Magnetic tape
B. Static Random Access Memory
C. Magnetic disk
D. CD-ROM

Q.94 A keyboard is this kind of device
A. Black   **B.** Output
C. Input   **D.** Word processing

Q.95 Which of the following terms is just the connection of networks that can be joined together?
A. Internet
B. Virtual private network
C. Intranet
D. Extranet

Q.96 MODEM word is made from:
A. Modulator, Demodulator
B. Modulation, Rough Modulation
C. Modulation, Defination
D. None of these

Q.97 What are the columns in a Microsoft Access table called?
A. Rows   **B.** Fields   **C.** Records   **D.** Columns

Q.98 Which of the following is the second step in creating a macro?
A. Using your mouse or keyboard, perform the task you want to automate
B. Give the macro a name
C. Assign a keyboard shortcut to the macro
D. Start recording

Q.99 In TDM-
A. Several signals are sent in a time-slotted mode on a channel
B. Several signals are sent on separate channels at a time
C. One signal is sent to several users
D. None of these

Q.100 If a computer on the network shares, resources for others to use, it is called ....
A. Server   **B.** Client
C. Mainframe   **D.** None of these

// Smart Answer Sheet //

Correct Indicates percentage of students who answered questions correctly.

Skipped Indicates percentage of students who skipped questions.

Q.	Ans.	Correct / Skipped	Q.	Ans.	Correct / Skipped	Q.	Ans.	Correct / Skipped	Q.	Ans.	Correct / Skipped	Q.	Ans.	Correct / Skipped
1	B	58.87 % / 12.6 %	17	B	29.82 % / 36.76 %	33	D	4.37 % / 40.87 %	49	D	42.42 % / 35.73 %	65	B	57.58 % / 38.56 %
2	B	7.97 % / 36.5 %	18	C	16.2 % / 38.81 %	34	A	21.34 % / 33.67 %	50	C	18.51 % / 38.05 %	66	D	43.96 % / 38.82 %
3	D	14.91 % / 34.96 %	19	C	17.22 % / 33.68 %	35	C	10.28 % / 42.16 %	51	D	11.57 % / 40.62 %	67	B	38.05 % / 39.84 %
4	C	10.03 % / 39.33 %	20	D	47.56 % / 29.05 %	36	D	34.96 % / 35.48 %	52	C	58.87 % / 38.3 %	68	C	54.76 % / 38.81 %
5	D	11.31 % / 38.56 %	21	A	22.11 % / 34.19 %	37	D	9.0 % / 38.56 %	53	B	59.13 % / 38.56 %	69	C	34.7 % / 36.25 %
6	A	33.16 % / 37.79 %	22	D	11.05 % / 38.56 %	38	C	19.28 % / 40.1 %	54	D	50.9 % / 39.07 %	70	C	37.28 % / 38.04 %
7	C	23.91 % / 37.79 %	23	B	62.47 % / 33.67 %	39	A	8.23 % / 40.1 %	55	A	19.54 % / 43.44 %	71	A	33.42 % / 37.79 %
8	C	29.56 % / 36.25 %	24	D	15.17 % / 33.42 %	40	B	38.05 % / 38.3 %	56	D	48.33 % / 39.33 %	72	C	42.67 % / 39.85 %
9	A	25.45 % / 36.5 %	25	A	47.3 % / 35.73 %	41	D	17.22 % / 39.85 %	57	D	21.34 % / 39.07 %	73	D	51.41 % / 37.28 %
10	A	34.7 % / 37.28 %	26	B	41.39 % / 35.47 %	42	A	34.96 % / 33.68 %	58	D	14.65 % / 42.93 %	74	C	50.9 % / 38.82 %
11	B	32.39 % / 35.73 %	27	C	23.91 % / 34.7 %	43	B	14.65 % / 41.65 %	59	A	48.33 % / 40.62 %	75	D	24.94 % / 38.56 %
12	B	42.93 % / 34.19 %	28	D	35.73 % / 32.91 %	44	A	33.68 % / 35.47 %	60	C	46.79 % / 38.56 %	76	D	44.47 % / 41.39 %
13	B	21.08 % / 37.02 %	29	D	48.59 % / 35.21 %	45	C	50.9 % / 35.22 %	61	B	51.41 % / 38.82 %	77	D	46.02 % / 39.58 %
14	D	20.82 % / 37.28 %	30	B	42.42 % / 33.93 %	46	C	51.16 % / 33.93 %	62	B	20.57 % / 40.61 %	78	C	30.33 % / 40.88 %
15	A	27.51 % / 35.99 %	31	B	35.99 % / 35.48 %	47	C	44.47 % / 34.96 %	63	C	58.61 % / 38.31 %	79	B	49.61 % / 39.85 %
16	B	9.51 % / 39.08 %	32	B	27.25 % / 37.02 %	48	B	38.82 % / 35.47 %	64	D	27.51 % / 40.1 %	80	A	34.7 % / 42.42 %

Q.	Ans.	Correct		Q.	Ans.	Correct		Q.	Ans.	Correct		Q.	Ans.	Correct		Q.	Ans.	Correct
		Skipped				Skipped				Skipped				Skipped				Skipped
81	D	3.6 % 42.93 %		85	B	31.36 % 44.48 %		89	B	9.51 % 43.45 %		93	B	47.3 % 34.71 %		97	B	22.62 % 35.22 %
82	B	28.28 % 41.64 %		86	C	13.62 % 47.56 %		90	A	39.07 % 41.39 %		94	C	50.9 % 33.93 %		98	C	14.4 % 38.56 %
83	C	25.71 % 43.44 %		87	B	12.08 % 46.27 %		91	B	19.02 % 35.22 %		95	A	32.65 % 35.22 %		99	A	12.85 % 36.76 %
84	A	43.7 % 40.62 %		88	A	13.37 % 48.33 %		92	D	43.7 % 33.93 %		96	A	9.0 % 36.5 %		100	A	23.91 % 37.27 %

Performance Analysis

Avg. Score (%)	**35.0%**
Toppers Score (%)	**98.0%**
Your Score	

//Hints and Solutions//

1. A food chain is a linear network of links in a food web starting from producer organisms (such as grass or trees which use radiation from the Sun to make their food) and ending at apex predator species (like grizzly bears or killer whales), detritivores (like earthworms or woodlice), or decomposer species (such as fungi or bacteria).

The proper food chain consists of grass, which is the food of insects, insects are the food of frogs, and frogs are eaten by snakes.

So, the food chain is as follow:

Grass→Insects→Frog→Snake

Hence, the correct option is (B).

2. Neurons are cells within the nervous system that transmit information to other nerve cells, muscle, or gland cells. Most neurons have a cell body, an axon, and dendrites.

The direction of impulse in a typical neuron is one direction that is from dendrites/dendron to the axon. The dendrons receive the nerve impulses from other neurons and the axons transmit the impulse to another neuron.

Hence, the correct option is (B).

3. Transpiration is the process of water movement through a plant and its evaporation from aerial parts, such as leaves, stems and flowers. Water is necessary for plants but only a small amount of water taken up by the roots is used for growth and metabolism. The remaining 97–99.5% is lost by transpiration and guttation.

Hence, the correct option is (D).

4. Secondary extraction of petroleum uses solvents, water, or steam.

Secondary recovery techniques increase the reservoir's pressure by water injection, natural gas reinjection, and gas lift, which injects air, carbon dioxide, or some other gas into the bottom of an active well, reducing the overall density of the fluid in the wellbore.

Hence, the correct option is (C).

5. A pearl is a hard, glistening object produced within the soft tissue (specifically the mantle) of a living shelled mollusca or another animal, such as fossil conulariids. A pearl is composed of calcium carbonate (mainly aragonite or a mixture of aragonite and calcite) and magnesium carbonate.

Hence, the correct option is (D).

6. Given,

$$P_{(W)} = 730\,watts$$

One electrical horsepower is equal to 746 watts:

$$1hp(E) = 746\ W$$

So, the power conversion of watts to horsepower is given by:

$$P_{(hp)} = P_{(W)}/746$$

Substituting the value of $P(W)$ in above equation, we get

$$P_{(hp)} = 730/746$$

$$P_{(hp)} = 0.97hp$$

Hence, the correct option is (A).

7. A crescograph is a device for measuring the growth in plants. It was invented in the early 20th century by Sir Jagadish Chandra Bose. The Bose crescograph uses a series of clockwork gears and a smoked glass plate to record the movement of the tip of a plant (or its roots). It was able to record at magnifications of up to 10,000 times through the use of two different levers.

Hence, the correct option is (C).

8. Lithosphere, rigid, rocky outer layer of the Earth, consisting of the crust and the solid outermost layer of the upper mantle. It extends to a depth of about 60 miles (100 km).

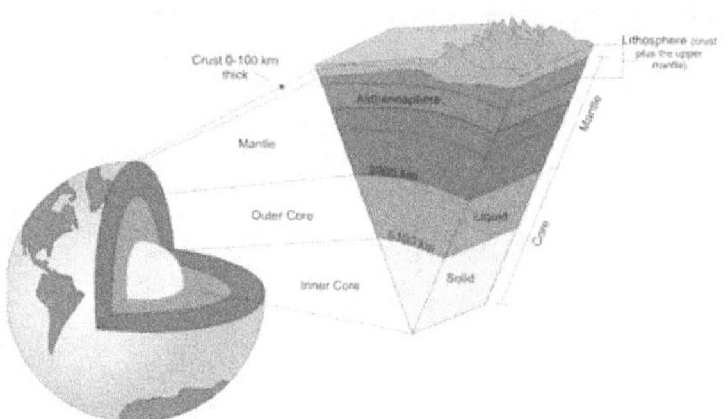

Hence, the correct option is (C).

9. The Gandhi Sagar Dam is one of the four major dams built on India's Chambal River. The dam is located in the Mandsaur district of the state of Madhya Pradesh. It is a masonry gravity dam, standing 62.17 meters (204.0 ft) high, with a gross storage capacity of 7.322 billion cubic meters from a catchment area of 22,584 km² (8,720 sq mi). The dam's foundation stone was led by Prime Minister of India, Pandit Jawaharlal Nehru on 7 March 1954, and construction of the main dam was completed in 1960. Additional dam structures were completed downstream in the 1970s.

Hence, the correct option is (A).

10. Asiatic wild Ass is found in Indian Wild Ass Sanctuary also known as the Wild Ass Wildlife Sanctuary which is located in the Little Rann of Kutch in the Gujarat state of India. It is spread over an area of 4954 km².

Hence, the correct option is (A).

11. (A-3, B-4, C-1, D-2)

The Vikram era or Vikram samvat is an Indian (Hindustani) calendar starting in 57 CE. The Vikram Samvat calendar starts half a century before the Gregorian calendar and works on an Indian calendar cycle. The calendar starts in the month of Vaisakha, which usually falls in the Gregorian month of April.

Saka Era of 78 CE, or simply Saka Era, a system that is common in epigraphic evidence from southern India. A parallel northern India system is the Vikrama Era, which is used by the Vikrami calendar linked to Vikramaditya. The beginning of the Shaka era is now widely equated to the ascension of king Chashtana in 78 CE.

The Kalachuri Era or the Chedi era was a Hindu system of year numbering started by the Abhira King Isvarasena, in which the year numbering started at some time from 248-250 CE. Origin

The Gupta era is a historical calendar era that begins from 318–319 CE. It was used by the Gupta emperors, as well as their vassals and their successors in present-day northern India and Nepal. It is identical to the Vallabhi era (or Valabhi era), which was used in the Saurashtra region of western India, although regional differences lead to a slightly different calculation for the conversion of Vallabhi era years to Common Era (CE).

Hence, the correct option is (B).

12. Lord Warren Hastings was the first Governor of Bengal and first Governor-General Of India with tenure of office from 1772-1785.

Hence, the correct option is (B).

13. The government of India enacted the Environment Protection Act of 1986 under Article 253 of the Constitution. Passed in March 1986, it came into force on 19 November 1986. It has 26 sections and 4 chapters. The purpose of the Act is to implement the decisions of the United Nations Conference on the Human Environment. They relate to the protection and improvement of the human environment and the prevention of hazards to human beings, other living creatures, plants, and property. The Act is an "umbrella" legislation designed to provide a framework for central government coordination of the activities of various central and state authorities established under previous laws, such as the Water Act and the Air Act.

Hence, the correct option is (B).

14. The legislature is a deliberative body of persons, usually elective, who are empowered to make, change, or repeal the laws of a country or state; the branch of government having the power to make laws.

Public opinion consists of the desires, wants, and thinking of the majority of the people. It is the collective opinion of the people of a society or state on an issue or problem.

Legislature in a democratic country can influence public opinion by focusing attention on public issues by making a certain decision that will be in favor of the public.

Hence, the correct option is (D).

15. A regressive tax is a tax imposed in such a manner that the average tax rate decreases as the amount subject to taxation increases. "Regressive" describes a distribution effect on income or expenditure, referring to the way the rate progresses from high to low, where the average tax rate exceeds the marginal tax rate. In terms of individual income and wealth, a regressive tax imposes a greater burden (relative to resources) on the poor than on the rich.

Hence, the correct option is (A).

16. Gulzar's debut novel was "two" which was released in English. It examines the status of refugees after partition. "Two" was originally written in Urdu.

Hence, the correct answer is (B).

17. The Bhabha Atomic Research Centre (BARC) has first developed an indigenous bulletproof vest, bulletproof jacket for the Indian armed forces, which is not only cheaper but also much lighter. It was named Bhabha Kavach, named after nuclear physicist Dr. Homi J. Bhabha, the jacket was developed at BARC's Trombay center.

Hence, the correct option is (B).

18. In the highland plateaus of the Western Ghats parts of Goa, scientists have identified a new species of frog called Fejervarya goemchi. The new species is named after the historical name of the state of Goa where the species is discovered.

Fejervarya goemchi are large-sized terrestrial frogs. They sit next to water bodies making calls to attract females for mating and breeding. Though most of these frogs are terrestrial, they need water bodies to survive.

Hence, the correct option is (C).

19. The Food Safety and Standards Authority of India has launched a unique initiative 'Project Dhoop' to encourage schools to shift their morning assembly to around noontime, mainly between 11 am to 1 pm, to ensure maximum absorption of vitamin D in students through natural sunlight.

Hence, the correct option is (C).

20. Water is essential for living things, industries, and other household works. Industries use a hell of a lot of water in plants and they discharge it in downgraded or polluted form. Thermal Power Plants consume maximum industrial water in India.

Industrial Water Use in India: (2004 data)

Industry	Annual Consumption (Million Cubic Meters)	Use Percentage
Thermal Power Plants	35157	87.8%
Engineering	2019	5.05%
Pulp and Paper	905.8	2.26%
Textiles	830	2.07%
Steel	516.6	1.29%
Sugar	194.9	0.49%
Fertiliser	73.5	0.18%
Total	40012M cubic meters	

Hence, the correct option is (D).

21. The first SAARC summit was held in Dhaka, Bangladesh on 7–8 December 1985 and was attended by the Government representative and president of Bangladesh, Maldives, Pakistan, and Sri Lanka, the kings of Bhutan and Nepal, and the Prime Minister of India.

Hence, the correct option is (A).

22. For the first time in 92 years, 7 Indian-origin kids were among the 8 who won the 92nd Scripps National Spelling Bee Contest. They were awarded the cash of $50,000 and prizes. The competition, broadcasted on ESPN, was held at Gaylord National Resort in National Harbor, Maryland, US.

Hence, the correct option is (D).

23. National Democratic Alliance (NDA) leader Narendra Damodardas Modi had taken oath as Prime Minister for the second consecutive term. Along with Narendra Modi, a total of 57 ministers had taken the oath of Office and Secrecy which is administered by President Ram Nath Kovind. Out of a total of 57 councils of ministers, 24 cabinet ministers had taken oath.

Hence, the correct option is (B).

24. India has invited the leaders of The Bay of Bengal Initiative for Multi-Sectoral Technical and Economic Cooperation (BIMSTEC) to the Member States for the swearing-in ceremony of Prime Minister Narendra Modi on 30 May 2019. This invitation is in line with the Government's focus on its 'Neighbourhood First' policy.

Hence, the correct option is (D).

25. GSAT-30: The Indian Space Research Organisation (ISRO) has successfully launched 'GSAT-30' from French Guiana on January 17, 2020. The launch of the high power communication satellite is ISRO's first satellite launch of the year 2020.

Hence, the correct option is (A).

26. Ministry of Jal Shakti is a ministry under the Government of India which was formed in May 2019 under the second Modi ministry. This was formed by merging of two ministries; "Ministry of Water Resources, River Development & Ganga Rejuvenation" and the "Ministry of Drinking Water and Sanitation". The formation of this ministry reflects India's seriousness towards the mounting water challenges the country has been facing over the past few decades.

Hence, the correct option is (B).

27. BJP leader Smriti Irani (43) became the youngest council of ministers in the second term of the Modi government. She scripted a massive victory in the Amethi seat in the Lok Sabha Elections.

Hence, the correct option is (C).

28. Bengaluru, India's tech city, has hosted the 107th Indian Science Congress (ISC 2020) for 5 days starting from January 3, 2020, to January 7, 2020. Prime Minister Narendra Modi has inaugurated the mega summit at a huge makeshift hall. This was the third time Bengaluru is hosting the science congress after 2002 and 1987.

Hence, the correct option is (D).

29. The result of Swachh Survekshan League 2020 was released by the Minister for Housing and Urban Affairs, Hardeep Singh Puri for the first and second quarters of this year. Under the category of cities with 10 lakh plus population, Indore topped in both the first and second quarters. The famous city of Madhya Pradesh, Indore was also the topper of the league in the previous year. Bhopal and Surat were ranked second and third in the first quarter respectively and Rajkot and Navi Mumbai in the second quarter.

Hence, the correct option is (D).

30. On August 28, 2020, The GMR led Rajiv Gandhi International Airport (Hyderabad International Airport) won the 'National Energy Leader' and 'Excellent Energy Efficient Unit' awards at the 21st National Awards for 'Excellence in Energy Management'. It was organized by the Confederation of Indian Industry (CII) and Godrej Green Business Centre (GBC).

Hence, the correct option is (B).

31. Prime Minister was inaugurating the 107th Indian Science Congress (ISC) at the University of Agricultural Sciences (UAS) in Bengaluru, Karnataka. The theme of ISC for the year 2020 was "Science and Technology: Rural Development". The 5-day ISC event will have 15,000 participants.

Hence, the correct option is (B).

32. E-commerce firm Flipkart has revamped its Micro, Small, and Medium Enterprises (MSME) seller financing program 'Growth Capital' in order to empower MSMEs across the country. The program enables financial inclusion and independence for MSMEs who operate online.

According to the company, It will allow the platform's 1 lakh-plus sellers to avail credit at competitive interest rates from 10 NBFCs and banks, with an approval time of one day and with disbursal into the sellers' bank accounts occurring within 48 hours.

Hence, the correct option is (B).

33. E-commerce firm Flipkart has revamped its Micro, Small, and Medium Enterprises (MSME) seller financing program 'Growth Capital' in order to empower MSMEs across the country. The average loan size is Rs 7 lakh. But sellers can take loans up to Rs 3 crore with interest rates at 9.5%. The tenure on the term loan and credit line options is 1 year.

Hence, the correct option is (D).

34. Capital Adequacy Ratio (CAR) is also known as Capital to Risk (Weighted) Assets Ratio (CRAR), is the ratio of a bank's capital to its risk. National regulators track a bank's CAR to ensure that it can absorb a reasonable amount of loss and complies with statutory Capital requirements. It is a measure of a bank's capital. It is expressed as a percentage of a bank's risk-weighted credit exposures.

Hence, the correct option is (A).

35. The capital adequacy ratio (CAR) for HFCs is increased to 13% by March 2020, 14% by March 2021, and 15% by March 2022. Tier I capital should not be less than 10% (6% at present).

Hence, the correct option is (C).

36. The union minister of State (MoS- Independent Charge) Housing and Urban Affairs(MoHUA) Shri Hardeep Singh Puri, has announced the results of Swachh Survekshan League 2020 (Quarter 1 and Quarter 2) at an event in New Delhi. During the event, the 5th edition of the Swachh Survekshan 2020 (urban cleanliness survey), which is to commence from 4 January 2020 by MoHUA was also rolled out. > 10lakh population: Among the cities with more than 10 lakh population category, Indore ranked 1st in both quarter 1 and quarter 2.

Hence, the correct option is (D).

37. DBS Bank in its report on the Indian economy revised India's Gross Domestic Product (GDP) forecast for the fiscal year 2020 to 6.8% year-on-year (YoY) from 7% due to headwinds for exports amidst a challenging trade outlook. The inflation rate was estimated at 3.8% for FY20 against 3.4% for FY19.

Hence, the correct option is (D).

38. Securities and Exchange Board of India (SEBI):

It is the regulator of the securities and commodity market in India owned by the Government of India. It framed a working group to review the current framework of margins in the futures and options segment. It will submit its recommendations to the Secondary Market Advisory Committee. The existing derivatives segment is increasing the costs of trading and it does not manage risk in an efficient manner. In order to look into these details, the panel was formed.

Hence, the correct option is (C).

39. The Securities and Exchange Board of India (SEBI) framed a working group headed by NSE Clearing Ltd. to review the current framework of margins in the futures and options segment. It will submit its recommendations to the Secondary Market Advisory Committee. The existing derivatives segment is increasing the costs of trading and it does not manage risk in an efficient manner. In order to look into these details, the panel was formed.

Hence, the correct option is (A).

40. World-famous handcrafted footwear, Kolhapuri chappal gets a Geographic Indication (GI) tag from The Controller General of Patents, Designs, and Trade Mark. The tag was given to the states of Maharashtra and Karnataka, covering four districts each. Tagging will help artisans in Kolhapur make & market their products domestically and internationally.

Hence, the correct option is (B).

41. A team of scientists from CSIR-NEIST (North East Institute of Science and Technology) in Assam has developed a chemical process that turns 'dirty' coal into a biomedical 'dot' to help detect cancer cells.

Carbon Quantum Dots (CQDs) are carbon-based nanomaterials whose size is less than 10 nm, or nanometre. They are used as diagnostic tools for bio-imaging, especially in detecting cancer cells, chemical sensing, and optoelectronics.

Hence, the correct option is (D).

42. Atmiya Sabha was a philosophical discussion circle in India. The association was started by Raja Ram Mohan Roy in 1815 in Kolkata. They used to conduct debate and discussion sessions on philosophical topics and also used to promote free and collective thinking and social reform. The main activity of the Sabha was to conduct discussion and debate sessions on monotheistic Hindu Vedantism and similar subjects.

Hence, the correct option is (A).

43. John Elliot Drinkwater Bethune (1801 – 1851), a barrister and law member of the Governor-General's Council, was an Anglo-Indian lawyer and a pioneer in promoting women's education in 19th-century India. In 1849, Bethune founded an institution for women's education in Calcutta (now Kolkata), then the capital of British India. The institute later bore his name and became famous as Bethune College. Bethune was closely associated with the Calcutta Public Library and translation activities into Bengali. He published a treatise on women's education by Pandit Gour Mohan Vidyalankar and distributed it at his own cost.

Hence, the correct option is (B).

44. The Dev Samaj is a Religious Society mainly devoted to the cause of serving humanity along with social, educational, moral, and higher life-building lines, irrespective of caste, creed, colour, or country. It was founded on 16th February 1887 by the most worshipful Shiv Narayan Agnihotri.

Hence, the correct option is (A).

45. The **Dronacharya Award**, officially known as Dronacharya Award **for Outstanding Coaches in Sports and Games**, is sports coaching honor of the Republic of India. The award is named after Drona, often referred to as "Dronacharya".

It is awarded annually by the Ministry of Youth Affairs and Sports.

Hence, the correct option is (C).

46. Articles 36-51 under Part-IV of the Indian Constitution deal with Directive Principles of State Policy (DPSP). They are borrowed from the Constitution of Ireland, which had copied it from the Spanish Constitution. This article will solely discuss the Directive Principles of State Policy, its importance in the Indian Constitution, and the history of its conflict with Fundamental Rights.

Hence, the correct option is (C).

47. Prohibition of discrimination on grounds of religion, race, caste, sex, or place of birth comes the Right to equality of Fundamental Rights in the Indian Constitution. Fundamental Rights are the rights and Charter of Rights as enshrined in Part III (Articles 12 to 35) of the Constitution of India. It guarantees the citizen independence such that all Indians can lead their lives in peace and harmony as citizens of India.

Hence, the correct option is (C).

48. Article 75 (3) provides that the council of the minister shall be collectively responsible to the Lok Sabha.

According to Article 75, the President first appoints the Prime Minister as the head of the Council of Ministers. The Prime Minister appoints the highly talented leaders of his party as ministers through the President. In practice, when the new elections are over, the President invites the person to the post of Prime Minister who has majority support in the Lok Sabha.

Hence, the correct option is (B).

49. Hussain Sagar is an artificial lake in Telangana, India, in Hyderabad. It was built in 1572 on a tributary of the Musi River. In 1992, a large monolithic statue of Gautama Buddha was erected on an island in the middle of the lake. It separates Hyderabad from its twin city of Sikandarabad.

Hence, the correct option is (D).

50. Kapildhara waterfall is located in the Amarkantak district of the central Indian state of Madhya Pradesh. It lies at a distance of 6 kilometers from the Narmada Kund. The holy waters of the River Narmada plunge from a height of about 100 feet, from the ground level. This cascade gets its name from the famous sage Kapil, who had resided at this place and performed severe religious austerities.

Hence, the correct option is (C).

51. Number of small cubes having only one face colored $= 4$ from each face $= 4 \times 6 = 24$

Hence, the correct option is (D).

52. The word given is JERUSALEM

Alternative words which can be formed from Jerusalem is as follow:

Ease, Sale and rule.

The above words are formed by the alphabets present in the parent word Jerusalem.

The word Mail cannot be formed from Jerusalem, as the alphabet 'I' is not present in Jerusalem.

Hence, the correct option is (C).

53. The alphabets are coded as follows:

D	E	L	H	I
↓	↓	↓	↓	↓
7	3	5	4	1

C	A	L	C	U	T	T	A
↓	↓	↓	↓	↓	↓	↓	↓
8	2	5	8	9	6	6	2

So,

C	A	L	I	C	U	T
↓	↓	↓	↓	↓	↓	↓
8	2	5	1	8	9	6

Hence, the correct option is (B).

54. Alphabets are coded using a particular symbol which is given below:

A B C D E F G H I P R S T O

? ! ; : . > < Δ □ ⦿ ⊕ ★ ω +

By decoding the symbols given below

? ⦿ ⦿ ⊕ + ? : Δ

We get the word APPROADH

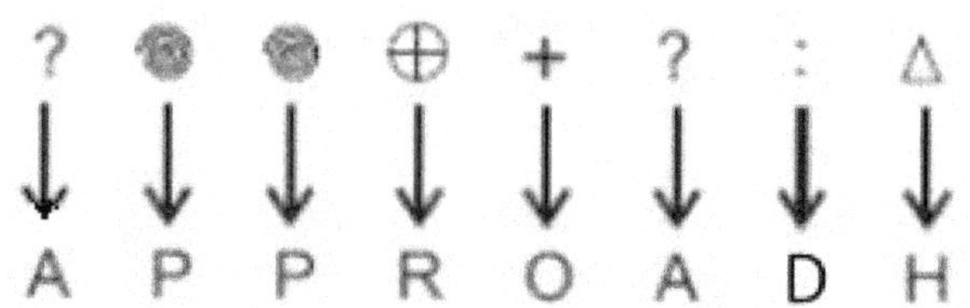

Hence, the correct option is (D).

55.

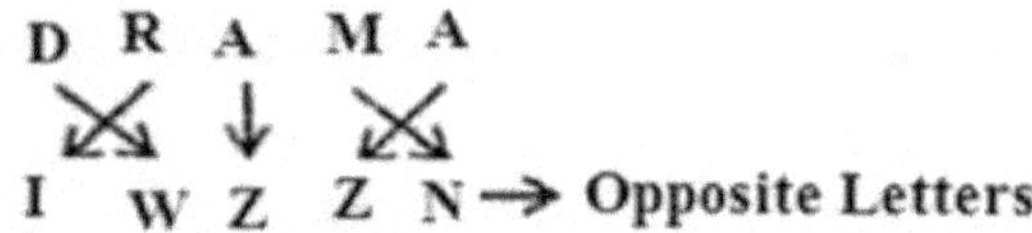

Similarly,

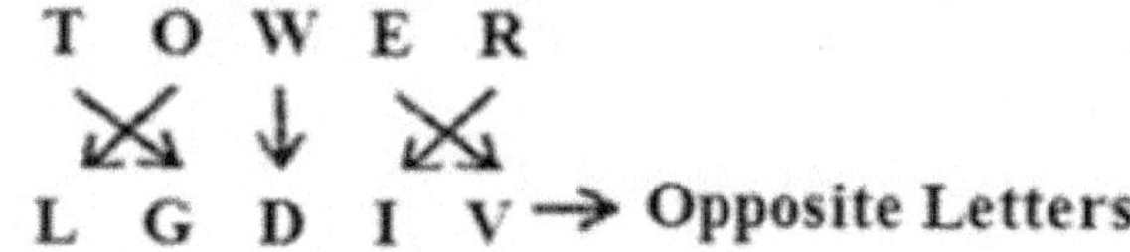

Hence, the correct option is (A).

56. According to Meena, her father's birthday can be on the following dates:

19 May, 20 May, and 21 May

According to her brother, his father's birthday can be on the following dates:

21 May, 22 May, 23 May

So, by combining both the fact, it is clear that her father's birthday is on 21 May.

Hence, the correct option is (D).

57. As we know,

Everything is composed of molecules. Sun is different from Moon. So, Sun and Moon comprise molecules but they are separate entities.

In option (D), two circles are part of a bigger circle and they are separate individuals, and this exactly matches the given information.

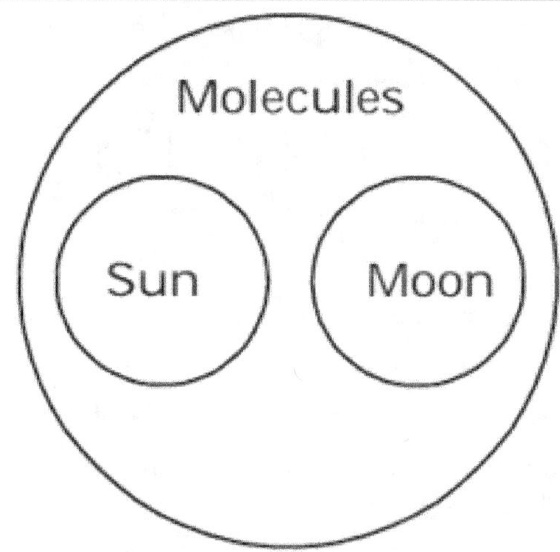

Hence, the correct option is (D).

58. Given,

X + Y means X is the daughter of Y

X - Y means X is the brother of Y

X % Y means X is the father of Y

X × Y means X is the sister of Y

So, from the above facts, it is concluded that,

+ means 'daughter of'

- means 'brother of'

% means 'father of'

× means 'sister of'

In the option (D), 'I × C + N – J' means ' I is the sister of C, C is the daughter of N and N is the brother of J'. So, I is the niece of J.

Hence, the correct option is (D).

59. Given,

'+' stands for division

'×' stands for addition

'–' stands for multiplication

'÷' stands for subtraction

(A)

$$15 + 5 - 2 \div 6 \times 3$$

According to the given condition above expression will change into

$$15 \div 5 \times 2 - 6 + 3$$

Solving the above case, we get

$$3 \times 2 - 6 + 3 = 6 - 6 + 3 = 3$$

(B)

$$15 \times 5 + 2 - 6 \div 3$$

According to the given condition above expression will change into

$$15 + 5 \div 2 \times 6 - 3$$

Solving above case, we get

$$15 + 5 \div 2 \times 6 - 3 = 27$$

(C)

$$15 \div 5 \times 2 - 6 + 3$$

According to the given condition above expression will change into

$$15 - 5 + 2 \times 6 \div 3$$

Solving above case, we get

$$15 - 5 + 2 \times 6 \div 3 = 14$$

(D)

$$15 - 5 + 2 \times 6 \div 3$$

According to the given condition above expression will change into

$$15 \times 5 \div 2 + 6 - 3$$

Solving above case, we get

$$15 \times 5 \div 2 + 6 - 3 = 40.5$$

Hence, the correct option is (A).

60. According to the given condition, the person is standing in 11th position from either end, these convey us that 10 other persons are standing on both the end of the given person.

So, the total person in the queue = 10 + 1 + 10 = 21

Pictorial representation of the above case is shown below:

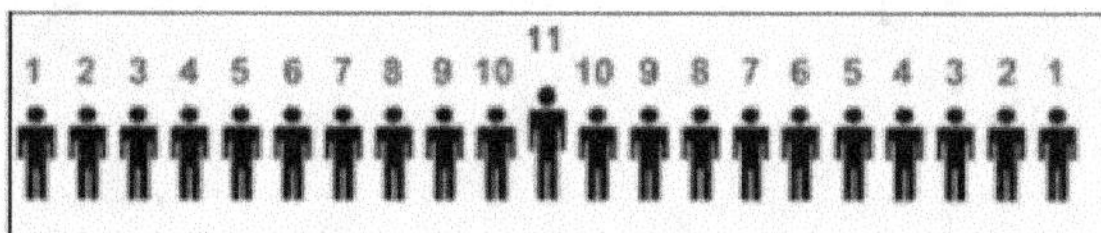

Hence, the correct answer is (C).

61. According to the given information,

ACAZX is decoded as DFDWU.

From the above words, it is clear that when we move three alphabets forward from A it is D and similarly in the case of C, Z, and X, on moving the three alphabets forward, we will get F, W, and U.

Similarly, GIGTR can be decode as JLJQO.

Pictorial representation is as follow:

ACAZX is decoded as DFDWU.

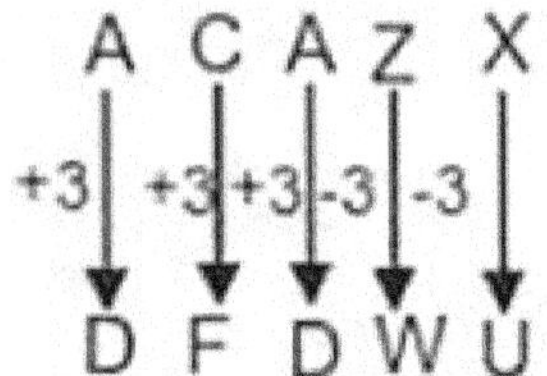

Similarly, GIGTR can be decode as JLJQO.

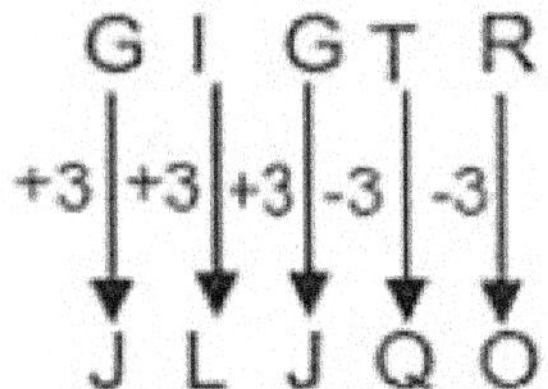

Hence, the correct option is (B).

62. According to the given information

72 is related to 53

It can be done in the following way:

$7 + 2 = 9; 5 + 3 = 8$

$9 - 8 = 1$

Option (A)

$6 + 4 = 10; 4 + 4 = 8$

And $10 - 8 = 2$

Option (B)

$6 + 4 = 10; 5 + 4 = 9$

And $10 - 9 = 1$

Option (C)

$6 + 4 = 10; 5 + 2 = 7$

And $10 - 7 = 3$

Option (D)

$6 + 4 = 10; 7 + 0 = 7$

And $10 - 7 = 3$

Hence, the correct option is (B).

63. In the given series When we subtract 111 from the first number it will give us the successive number.

For Example $975 - 111 = 874$

$874 - 111 = 753$

$753 - 111 = 642$

$642 - 111 = 531$

So, after 642 will be followed by 531 in the series

Pictorial representation of the above case:

Hence, the correct option is (C).

64. According to the given condition;

Maharashtra is related to India as Maharashtra is a state of India.

Similarly, Texas can be belong to the USA because it is a state in the South Central region of the USA.

Hence, the correct option is (D).

65. In the given series.

In the first column.

When we multiply the first three number, we will get the fourth number in the column.

$9 \times 12 \times 13 = 1404$

Similarly

In the second column

$3 \times 2 \times 5 = 30$

Let us consider the number in the third column be 'p'

So, $7 \times 9 \times p = 504$

$\Rightarrow p = 8$

Hence, the correct option is (B).

66. As per the given above question figure,

Figure (D) of the answer figures is exactly the mirror image of the given original image. Thus, the given image will become the opposite in a mirror across the given line.

DI9E35T4

Hence, the correct option is (D).

67.

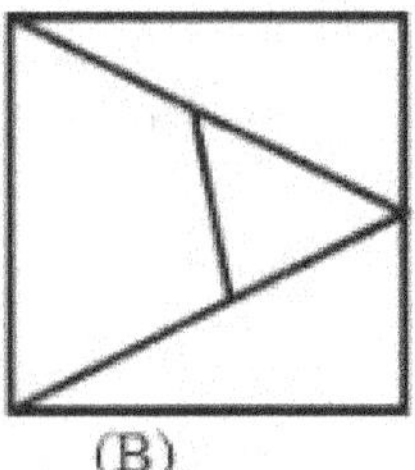

(B)

Hence, the correct option is (B).

68.

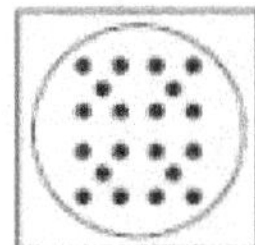

When the third part in the above figure is unfolded, the right side will be the mirror image and it will also have five dots, similar to the left part.

Now, when the lower part is unfolded, the upper part will be the mirror image of the lower part and will contain 10 dots in the same position as it is present in the lower part.

So, matching to the above condition, we will get

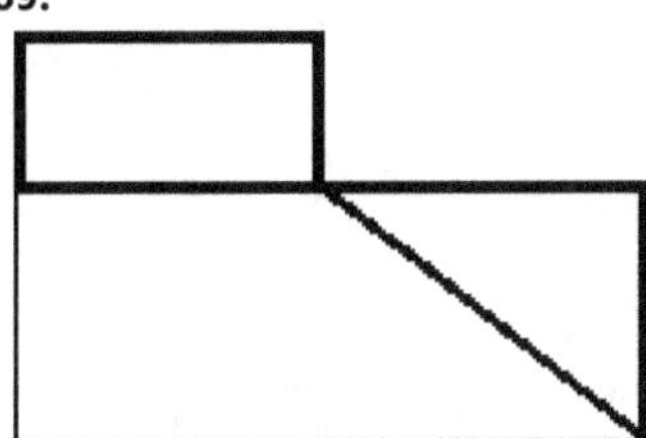

Hence, the correct option is (C).

69.

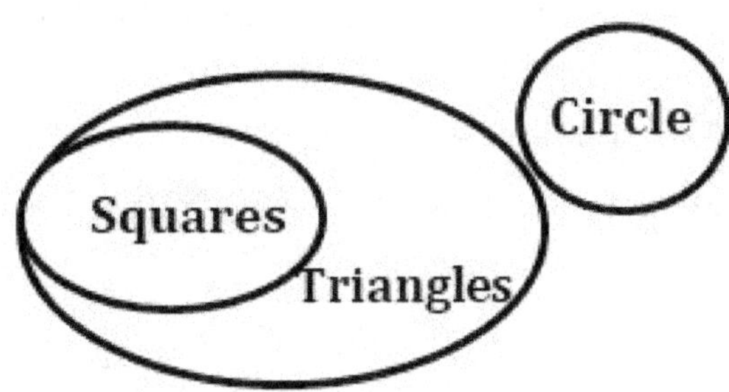

Hence, the correct option is (C).

70. Total Single triangle = 10

Triangle made by two sub triangles = 4

Therefore, the total number of triangles = 14

Hence, the correct option is (C).

71. According to the given statement, below is the Venn diagram.

So, it can be concluded that all squares can be a triangle but reversed cannot be true and there is no relation exists between circle and square.

Hence, the correct option is (A).

72. Srinath is 7th from the left and Venkat is 12th from the right.

Now, If they interchange their positions, Srinath becomes 22nd from the left.

So, Srinath is 22 from the left and 12 from the right.

So, he has 21 boys before him and 11 boys after him.

So, the total number of boys = number of boys before him + Number of boys after him + Srinath

= 21 + 11 + 1

= 33

Hence there are 33 boys.

Hence, the correct option is (C).

73. Meaningful order of words :

4. Mouth

6. Oesophagus

5. Stomach

3. Small Intestine

1. Large Intestine

2. Rectum

Hence, the correct option is (D).

74. The following words are as per correct order in the English dictionary:

4. Absent   1. Activity   3. Arise   2. Attention

Hence, the correct option is (C).

75. Meaningful order of the words:

(III) Nutrition (II) Digestion (I) Absorption (IV) Excretion

Hence, the correct option is (D).

76. Given,

Run score in the first test, $x_1 = 180$

Run score in the second test, $x_2 = 258$

Average runs in three matches, $x = 230$

Let us suppose the run score in the third match is x_3

$\Rightarrow$ Average run, $x = \dfrac{x_1 + x_2 + x_3}{3}$

Substituting the value, we get

$\Rightarrow 230 = \dfrac{180 + 258 + x_3}{3}$

$\Rightarrow 690 = 438 + x_3$

$\Rightarrow x_3 = 690 - 438 = 252$

Therefore,

The cricketer scored 252 runs in the third match.

Hence, the correct option is (D).

77. Successive Discount: It means a discount on the discount. (Analogous to Compound Interest rate which signifies interest on interest).

As the successive discount is 10% and 20%

Total discount $= \left(x + y - \dfrac{xy}{100}\right)\%$

$x = 10\%$ and $y = 20\%$

Substituting the value, we get

$\Rightarrow$ Total discount

$= \left[10 + 20 - \dfrac{(10 \times 20)}{100}\right]\% = \left(30 - \dfrac{200}{100}\right) = 28\%$

Hence, the correct option is (D).

78. Given,

$\Rightarrow a + \dfrac{1}{b} = 1 \quad .....(i)$

$\Rightarrow b + \dfrac{1}{c} = 1 \quad .....(ii)$

From equation (i), we get

$\Rightarrow a = 1 - \dfrac{1}{b} = \dfrac{b-1}{b}$

Taking reciprocal

$\Rightarrow \dfrac{1}{a} = \dfrac{b}{b-1} \quad .....(iii)$

From equation (ii), we get

$\Rightarrow \dfrac{1}{c} = 1 - b \quad .....(iv)$

Taking reciprocal

$\Rightarrow c = \dfrac{1}{1-b} \quad .....(v)$

Adding equation (iii) and (v) we get

$\Rightarrow \dfrac{1}{a} + c = \dfrac{b}{b-1} + \dfrac{1}{1-b} = \dfrac{b}{b-1} - \dfrac{1}{b-1} = 1$

Therefore, $c + \dfrac{1}{a} = 1$

Hence, the correct option is (C).

79. Given,

$a + b = 3 \quad .....(i)$

$a - b = 1 \quad .....(ii)$

As we know,

$(a + b)^2 = a^2 + b^2 + 2ab \quad .....(iii)$

$(a - b)^2 = a^2 + b^2 - 2ab \quad .....(iv)$

On subtracting equation (iv) from equation (iii), we get

$(a + b)^2 - (a - b)^2 = 4ab$

$ab = \dfrac{(a+b)^2 - (a-b)^2}{4} \quad .....(v)$

On substituting the value in equation(v) from (i) and (ii), we get

$\Rightarrow ab = \dfrac{(3)^2 - (1)^2}{4} = \dfrac{9-1}{4} = \dfrac{8}{4} = 2$

$\therefore ab = 2$

Hence, the correct option is (B).

80. Given,

$x + y = 2 \quad .....(i)$

$x^2 + y^2 = 4 \quad .....(ii)$

As we know that,

$(x + y)^2 = x^2 + y^2 + 2xy$

Substituting the value, we get

$\Rightarrow (2)^2 = 4 + 2xy$

$\Rightarrow 2xy = 4 - 4 = 0$

$xy = 0$

As we know

$x^3 + y^3 = (x + y)(x^2 - xy + y^2)$

Substituting the value, we get

$\Rightarrow x^3 + y^3 = (2)(4 - 0) = 8$

$\therefore x^3 + y^3 = 8$

Hence, the correct option is (A).

81. $1! + 2! + 3! + \cdots + 100! = 1! + 2! + 3! + 4! + k \quad ....(i)$

Where k is integers divisible by 5.

Notice that from $5!$ onwards all the numbers up till $100!$ are multiples of 5, i.e., they have at least one factor of 5.

As: $5! = 120, 6! = 720$ and so on.

So we basically have to find the remainder of $1! + 2! + 3! + 4!$

If, $1! = 1$

$2! = 2$
$3! = 6$
$4! = 24$

Substituting the value in equation (i), we get

$1 + 2 + 6 + 24 + k = 33 + k$

So when $1! + 2! + 3! + \cdots + 100$ is divided by 5, the remainder is the same as when 33 is divided by 5.

Therefore we will get 3 as the remainder when 33 is divided by 5.

Hence, the correct option is (D).

82. Firstly, we find LCM of $20, 28, 32, 35$

$20 = 2 \times 2 \times 5$

$28 = 2 \times 2 \times 7$

$32 = 2 \times 2 \times 2 \times 2 \times 2$

$35 = 5 \times 7$

LCM = $2 \times 2 \times 2 \times 2 \times 2 \times 5 \times 7 = 1120$

Required greatest number which subtracts from 5834 is divide by $20, 28, 32$ and 35

$= 5834 - 1120$

$= 4714$

Hence, the correct option is (B).

83. The population of the town = 50000

Let no. of males be M and no. of females be F.

Thus,

$M + F = 50,000$

$\Rightarrow F = 50000 - M$ .....(i)

Now, M increases by 5%, and F increases by 10%, and the population after the increase becomes 53500. Thus, we can write

$1.05M + 1.10F = 53500$ .....(ii)

From equation (i) and equation (ii), we get

$\Rightarrow 1.05M + 1.10(50000 - M) = 53500$

$\Rightarrow 1.05M + 55000 - 1.10M = 53500$

$\Rightarrow 0.05M = 1500$

$\Rightarrow M = \frac{1500}{0.05} = 30000$

Now, substituting the value of M in equation (i) we get

$F = 50000 - 30000 = 20000$

Hence, the number of males and females in the town is 30000 and 20000 respectively.

Hence, the correct option is (C).

84. According to the question,

'A' can do a piece of work in 7 days. So, in one day 'A' can do work equal to $\frac{1}{7}$.

'A' and 'B' can do the same work in 3 days,

So in one day, 'A' and 'B' can do work equal to $\frac{1}{3}$.

So, 'B' one day work is,

$= \frac{1}{3} - \frac{1}{7}$

$= \frac{(7-3)}{21}$

$= \frac{4}{21}$

Therefore, B can do the same work in $\frac{21}{4} = 5\frac{1}{4}$ days

Hence, the correct option is (A).

85. Given:

5 Women or 8 girls can complete a task in 84 days, So 5 women are equal to 8 girls to complete a work.

So, 10 women = 16 girls.

Therefore,

10 women $+ 5$ girls = 16 girls $+ 5$ girls = 21 girls.

8 girls can do work in 84 days

So, One girl can do work in 84×8 days

Then, 21 girls can do work in $\frac{8 \times 84}{21} = 8 \times 4 = 32$ days.

$\therefore 10$ women and 5 girls can do work in 32 days.

Hence, the correct option is (B).

86. Number of S type cars which remained unsold in $2000 = 15\%$ of 10% of $3,50,000$

And the number of S type cars which remained unsold in $2001 = 15\%$ of 10% of $4,40,000$

So, the total number of S type cars which remained unsold

$= 15\%$ of $(35,000 + 44,000) = 15\%$ of $79,000 = 11,850$

Hence, the correct option is (C).

87. If the percentage production of P type cars in $2001 =$ percentage production of P type cars in $2000 = 30\%$

So,

Number of P type cars produced in $2001 = 30\%$ of $4,40,000 = 1,32,000$

Hence, the correct option is (B).

88. Required difference = 20% of $4,40,000 - 15\%$ of $3,50,000$

$= 88,000 - 52,500 = 35,500$

Hence, the correct option is (A).

89. Using the above calculation, the percentage change (rise/fall) in production from 2000 to 2001 for various models is:

For P = $\left[\dfrac{(176000-105000)}{105000} \times 100\right] \% = 67.62\%$, rise.

For Q = $\left[\dfrac{(88000-52500)}{52500} \times 100\right] \% = 67.62\%$, rise.

For R = $\left[\dfrac{(70000-66000)}{70000} \times 100\right] \% = 5.71\%$, fall.

For S = $\left[\dfrac{(44000-35000)}{35000} \times 100\right] \% = 25.71\%$, rise.

For T = $\left[\dfrac{(52500-44000)}{52500} \times 100\right] \% = 16.19\%$, fall.

For U = $\left[\dfrac{(35000-22000)}{35000} \times 100\right] \% = 37.14\%$, fall.

So,

The minimum percentage rise/fall in production is in the case of model R.

Hence, the correct option is (B).

90. Let us consider that the cost price is Rs 100

So, according to the given condition marked price will be 50% above the cost price.

Marked Price, M.P. $= 100 + 50 \times \left(\dfrac{100}{100}\right)$ = Rs 150

Now, if shopkeeper gives 30% discount

The selling price (SP) will be 70% of the market price

SP = 70% of $150 = 70 \times \left(\dfrac{150}{100}\right) = 105$

% Profit $= \dfrac{(SP-CP)}{CP} \times 100 = \dfrac{(105-100)}{100} \times 100 = 5\%$

Hence, the correct option is (A).

91. In 'Format Menu' we can find features like Slide Design, Slide Layout, etc, in Powerpoint 2003 and earlier versions.

Hence, the correct option is (B).

92. Five basic operations of a computer-

Inputting: The process of entering data and instructions into the computer system.

Storing: Saving data and instructions to make them readily available for initial or additional processing whenever required.

Processing: Performing arithmetic operations (add, subtract, multiply, divide, etc.) or logical operations (comparisons like equal to, less than, greater than, etc.) on data to convert them into useful information.

Outputting: The process of producing useful information or results for the user such as a printed report or visual display.

Controlling: Directing the manner and sequence in which all of the above operations are performed.

Thus, the understanding operation is not performed by the computer.

Hence, the correct option is (D).

93. A computer's main memory made up of dynamic RAM or static RAM chips.

SRAM (Static RAM) is random access memory (RAM) that retains data bits in its memory as long as power is being supplied. Unlike dynamic RAM (DRAM), which stores bits in cells consisting of a capacitor and a transistor, SRAM does not have to be periodically refreshed.

Hence, the correct option is (B).

94. In a computer, an input device is a piece of computer hardware equipment used to provide data and control signals to an information processing system such as a computer or information appliance. Examples of input devices include keyboards, mouse, scanners, digital cameras, joysticks, and microphones.

Hence, the correct option is (C).

95. The internet is a globally connected network system that uses TCP/IP to transmit data via various types of media. The internet is a network of global exchanges – including private, public, business, academic, and government networks – connected by guided, wireless, and fiber-optic technologies. It is a connection of connections.

Hence, the correct option is (A).

96. The modem is short for "Modulator - Demodulator" that allows a computer or other devices, such as a router or switch, to connect to the Internet. It converts or "modulates" an analog signal from a telephone or cable wire to a digital signal that a computer can recognize. Similarly, it converts outgoing digital data from a computer or other device to an analog signal.

Hence, the correct option is (A).

97. In Access, rows and columns are referred to as records and fields. A field is a way of organizing information by type. A record is one unit of information. Every cell on a given row is part of that row's record.

Hence, the correct option is (B).

98. On the Tools menu, click Macro. Click Macros from the submenu; you can also use the Alt + F8 shortcut key to access the Macros dialog box. In the dropdown menu beside the Macros in the label, select Word Commands. An alphabetical list of the command names will appear.

Hence, the correct option is (C).

99. Time-division multiplexing (TDM) is a method of transmitting and receiving independent signals over a common signal path by means of synchronized switches at each end of the transmission line so that each signal appears on the line, only a fraction of time in an alternating pattern.

Hence, the correct option is (A).

100. A server is a computer program or a device that provides functionality for other programs or devices, called "clients". This architecture is called the client-server model, and a single overall computation is distributed across multiple processes or devices.

Hence, the correct option is (B).

General Awareness/Current Affairs

Q.1 India's rank in Human Development Index, 2018 is:

[Super TET Paper - I, 2019]

A. 128th **B.** 129th **C.** 130th **D.** 131st

Q.2 In January 2022, which country took over the G7 Presidency?

A. Netherlands **B.** Germany
C. Austria **D.** France

Q.3 Who among the followings has been elected as the 15 th President of India in July 2022 ?

A. Nirmala Sitharaman **B.** Swati Piramal
C. Hima Kohli **D.** Droupadi Murmu

Q.4 Which city has been chosen by the Union of European Football Associations (UEFA) as a replacement of St Petersburg for the Champions League 2022 ?

[Delhi Forest Guard, 2021]

A. Paris **B.** Brussels **C.** London **D.** Munich

Q.5 Who among the following has won the Mexican open 2022 held in Acapulco, Mexico?

A. Rafael Nadal **B.** Novak Djokovic
C. Roger Federer **D.** Alexander Zverev

Q.6 Which country has signed a $ 2.25 billion deal with a Russian state-run nuclear energy company 'ASE' in August 2022?

[RBI Assistant, 2020], [UPSSSC Rajasva Lekhpal, 2015]

A. India **B.** China
C. Japan **D.** South Korea

Q.7 Which institution launched the 'India Digital Summit 2022'?

A. Internet and Mobile Association of India (IAMAI)
B. Confederation of Indian Industries (CII)
C. Ministry of Electronics and IT
D. NITI Aayog

Q.8 Which of the following launched a report titled 'India's Booming Gig and Platform Economy'?

A. NITI Aayog **B.** RBI
C. FICCI **D.** NASSCOM

Q.9 In which of the following countries did Prime Minister Narendra Modi start 'Ramayana Circuit' on May 11, 2018?

[Super TET Paper - I, 2019]

A. Nepal **B.** Indonesia
C. Sri Lanka **D.** Myanmar

Q.10 How many hi-tech libraries will be built in the villages of Haryana?

A. 500 **B.** 700 **C.** 900 **D.** 1000

Q.11 What is the contribution of India to the UN Women Core budget in 2022?

[HSSC Canal Patwari, 2021], [Delhi Forest Guard, 2021]

A. USD 10,000 **B.** USD 50,000
C. USD 100,000 **D.** USD 500,000

Q.12 Who among the following was a poet of the fourteenth century?

[Rajasthan Police Constable, 2020]

A. Sarala Dasa **B.** Amir Khusro
C. Dhurjati **D.** Pitambar Dvija

Q.13 With which is Yamini Krishnamurti related?

[Rajasthan Police Constable, 2020]

A. Tennis **B.** Singing
C. Kuchipudi Dance **D.** Writing

Q.14 What was the real name of freedom fighter Vijay Singh Pathik?

[Rajasthan Police Constable, 2020]

A. Roop Singh **B.** Bhup Singh
C. Hamir Singh **D.** Anup Singh

Q.15 In August 1858, the British parliament passed an act that set an end to the rule of the company, It was called _______ .
A. Government of India Act
B. Indian Trusts Act
C. Kazis Act
D. Fort William Act

Q.16 The sale or liquidation of assets by the government, usually Central and State public sector enterprises, projects, or other fixed assets is called _____.
A. Devaluation **B.** Capitalisation
C. Disinvestment **D.** Privatisation

Q.17 In modern Industrialized society the status of women in industry
A. Has considerately gone down
B. Has gradually risen
C. Has remained unchanged
D. Has not been defined

Q.18 Who is of the view that incest taboo enables a relationship with wider society?
A. Claude Levi Strauss **B.** H. Spencer
C. K. Gough **D.** E. Westermarck

Q.19 The transformation of time in, modern society in the form of timelessness was emphasized by which scholar?

[UGC NET Sociology, 2020]

A. Marshall McLuhan   **B.** David Harvey
C. Manuel Castells   **D.** Anthony Giddens

Q.20 Which of the following statement is true about the tropical convergence?
1. It is called ITCZ in short
2. It is a low-pressure zone between tropic of Cancer and tropic of Capricorn
3. Seasonal changes in position are found

A. 1, 2 and 3   **B.** 1 and 2
C. 2 and 3   **D.** 1 and 3

Q.21 'Amphan' made landfall in a part of West Bengal and Orissa in May 2020. It is an example of:
A. Tropical cyclone
B. Temperate cyclone
C. Extra-tropical cyclone
D. Anticyclone

Q.22 Arrange the layer of the atmosphere from top to bottom.
A. Troposphere - Stratosphere - Mesosphere - Ionosphere
B. Ionosphere - Troposphere - Stratosphere - Mesosphere
C. Ionosphere - Mesosphere - Stratosphere - Troposphere
D. Troposphere - Stratosphere - Ionosphere - Mesosphere

Q.23 Who is the writer of "Humayun-Nama"?
[Uttarakhand Public Service Commission (UKPSC), 2011]

A. Zebunnisa   **B.** Jahanara
C. Gulbadan Begum   **D.** Roshanara

Q.24 Leelawati, a treatise on Mathematics, was written by:
[Uttarakhand Public Service Commission (UKPSC), 2011]

A. Ramanuj   **B.** Kautilya
C. Amartya Sen   **D.** Bhaskaracharya

Q.25 Who wrote the book "A Passage to India"?
[Uttarakhand Public Service Commission (UKPSC), 2011]

A. Jawaharlal Nehru   **B.** Minoo Masani
C. E.M. Forster   **D.** None of them

Q.26 Which of the following statements is correct regarding Kalamkari?
1. It is an ancient style of hand painting done on cotton or silk fabric with a tamarind pen.
2. It uses both natural and artificial colours.
3. It constitutes two styles, Srikalahasti style and Machilipatnam style.

A. 1 and 2 only   **B.** 2 and 3 only
C. 1 and 3 only   **D.** 1, 2 and 3

Q.27 Which of the following is not correctly matched?
1. Madhubani Painting: Bihar
2. Thanjavur Painting: Tamil Nadu
3. Bani Thani: Rajasthan
4. Warli Painting: Odisha

A. 1 and 3 only   **B.** 2 and 4 only
C. 2 only   **D.** 4 only

Q.28 Which of the following statements is/are incorrect about Tholu Bommalata?
1. It is a shadow puppet from Karnataka which has a rich and strong tradition.
2. The theme of the puppet plays is drawn from the Ramayana, Mahabharata, and Puranas.
3. The screen for the shadow puppet show is a bamboo box-like stage erected in the open air.

A. 1 only   **B.** 2 only
C. 1 and 2 only   **D.** 2 and 3 only

Q.29 Which of the following city is popularly known as Silicon Valley of India?
[Rajasthan Police Constable, 2020]

A. Bangalore   **B.** Lucknow
C. Chandigarh   **D.** New Delhi

Q.30 In which state/UT is the Chaukhandi Stupa located?
[Rajasthan Police Constable, 2020]

A. Ladakh   **B.** Himachal Pradesh
C. Karnataka   **D.** Uttar Pradesh

Q.31 In which of the following cities the observatory was not built by the King of Jaipur?
[Rajasthan Police Constable, 2020]

A. Varanasi   **B.** Ujjain   **C.** Delhi   **D.** Udaipur

Q.32 What are 'the camel', 'the mongoose', 'kaboom' and 'aluminum' that have been in news recently?
A. Cricket bats   **B.** Military codes
C. Squadrons   **D.** Chess moves

Q.33 Which country is to play host to the ICC Under -19 World Cup 2020 tournament?
A. England   **B.** New Zealand
C. South Africa   **D.** Zimbabwe

Q.34 Which badminton player recently clinched the 'Indonesia Masters title'?
A. Carolina Marin   **B.** Ratchanok Intanon
C. P V Sindhu   **D.** Nozomi Okuhara

Q.35 Which of the following system is established on the basis of the direct election ?
[HSSC Canal Patwari, 2021]

A. Gram Panchayat   **B.** Block Committee
C. Zila Parishad   **D.** Both (B) and (C)

Q.36 The 'Swadeshi' and 'Boycott' were adopted as methods of struggle in Bengal at the same time Vande Mataram Movement was in which place?
A. Tamil Nadu   **B.** Punjab
C. Andhra Pradesh   **D.** Poona

Q.37 Which of the following was an outcome of Alexander's invasion of India?

1. Development of important geographical accounts of India.

2. The decrement in trade facilities with Greece.

3. Expansion of the Mauryan empire.

Select the correct answer using the codes:

A. 1, 2 and 3 only
B. 1 and 2 only
C. 2 and 3 only
D. 1 and 3 only

Q.38 With reference to Ashokan inscriptions, consider the following statements:

1. Rummindei pillar edict mentioned about the tax exemption of Lumbini.

2. Kandhar inscription was carved in Aramaic language.

3. The second rock edict mentioned names of the Kerelaputras.

Which of the statement given above is/are correct?

A. 1,2 and 3
B. 3 only
C. 1 and 2 only
D. 1 and 3 only

Q.39 Bronze is an alloy of copper and:

[UPSC Central Armed Police Forces AC, 2017]

A. Nickel
B. Iron
C. Tin
D. Aluminium

Q.40 Which one of the following instruments is used for measuring moisture content of air?

[UPSC Central Armed Police Forces AC, 2017]

A. Hydrometer
B. Hygrometer
C. Hypometer
D. Pycnometer

Q.41 Which one of the following is NOT correct about organic farming?

[UPSC Central Armed Police Forces AC, 2017]

A. It does not use genetically modified seeds
B. Synthetic pesticides or fertilizers are not used
C. It uses minimal crop rotation
D. It uses ecologically protective practices

Q.42 In 2019, Nobel Prize in Chemistry is given for which development?

A. For the development of Lithium-ion batteries
B. To develop protein
C. For developing cryoelectron microscopy
D. None of the above

Q.43 Which of the following statement is correct regarding bipolar disorder?

A. It is a mental health condition
B. Patients with this disorder undergo intense mood shifts
C. Patients with this disorder face difficulties in planning and decision making
D. All of the above

Q.44 From which among the following place Nepal has launched its first Satellite NepaliSat-1?

A. USA
B. India
C. China
D. EU

Q.45 Which of the following SAARC member has the highest population?

A. Bangladesh
B. Pakistan
C. Nepal
D. Afghanistan

Q.46 Where is the headquarters of the SAARC?

A. Manila
B. Kathmandu
C. New Delhi
D. Jakarta

Q.47 The headquarter of the International Atomic Energy Agency (IAEA) are situated at-

A. Paris
B. Geneva
C. Rome
D. Vienna

Q.48 Which among the following entities/organizations has received the Asia Environmental Enforcement Award-2020?

A. Central Zoo Authority
B. National Tiger Conservation
C. PETA India
D. Wildlife Crime Control Bureau

Q.49 Which Indian writer won the regional award for Asia of the Commonwealth Short Story Prize, 2020?

A. Kritika Pandey
B. Madhuri Vijay
C. Aravind Adiga
D. Vikram Seth

Q.50 Who among the following sports person from Para-Athletics given Arjuna award 2017?

A. Ms. Vinesh
B. Shri Amit Kumar
C. Shri Sandeep Singh Mann
D. Varun Singh Bhati

Reasoning

Ques (51-52):Directions: In the following question, select the related word/letters/numbers from the given alternatives.

Q.51 86 : 62 : : 49 : ?

A. 29
B. 49
C. 35
D. 42

Q.52 62 : 155 : : 58 : ?

A. 131
B. 148
C. 145
D. 256

Q.53 Optical glass used in the construction of spectacles is made by:

A. Flint glass
B. Crookes glass
C. Quartz glass
D. Hard glass

Q.54 What should be the position of the object when a concave mirror is used as a shaving mirror?

A. Between the focus and the center of curvature
B. Between the pole and the focus
C. At the focus
D. Beyond the center of curvature

Q.55 A series of figures are given with one figure missing. Select the correct alternative from the given ones that will complete the series.

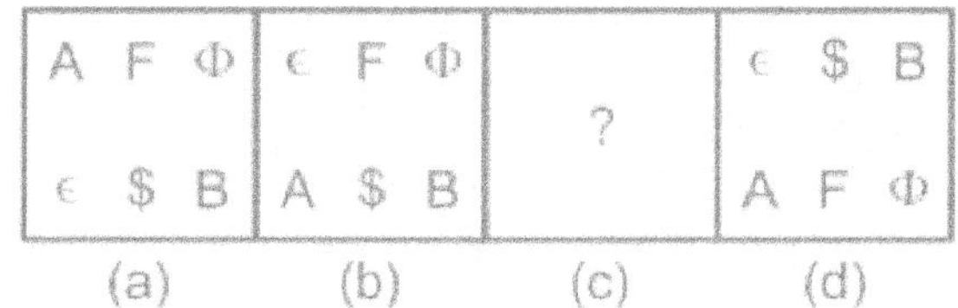

| (a) | (b) | (c) | (d) |

A. 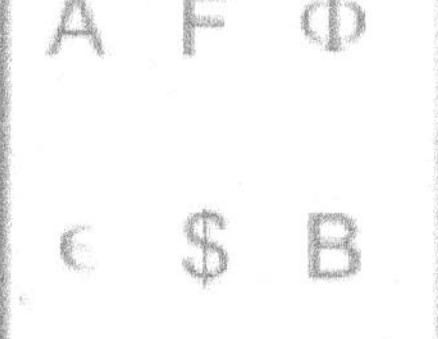

B.

C.

D.

C.   **D.**

Q.57 Direction: In the question, three elements are given below followed by four different Venn diagrams in the options. Select the appropriate Venn diagram as the answer which depicts the relation between the elements.

Tie, Shirt, Shoe

A. 

B. 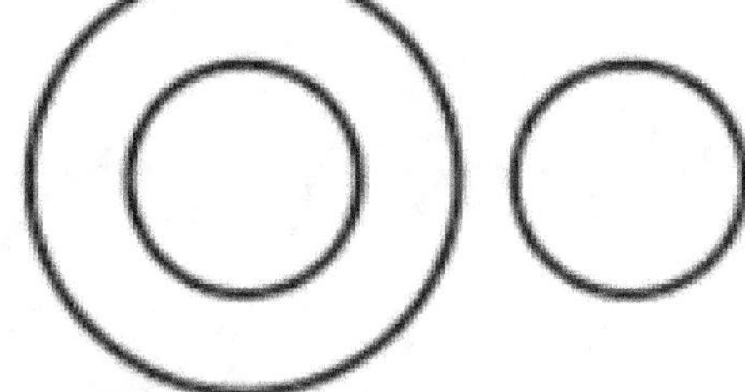

C. 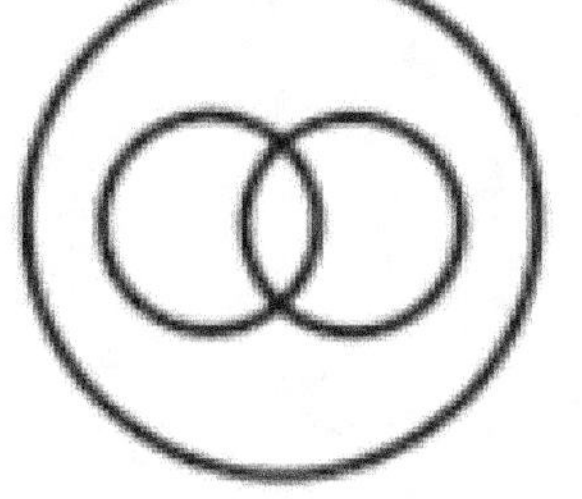

D. 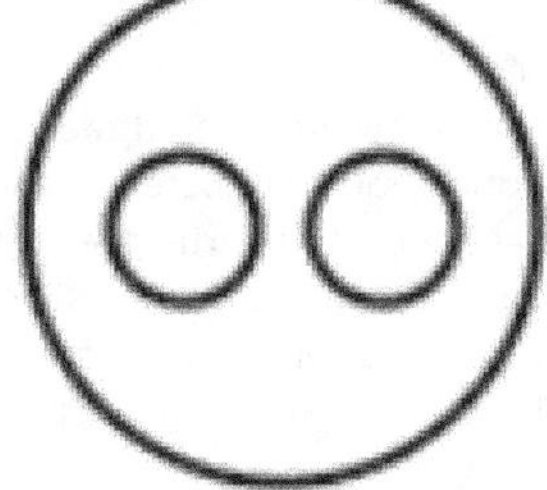

Q.56 A series is given with one figure missing. Select the correct alternative from the given ones that will complete the series.

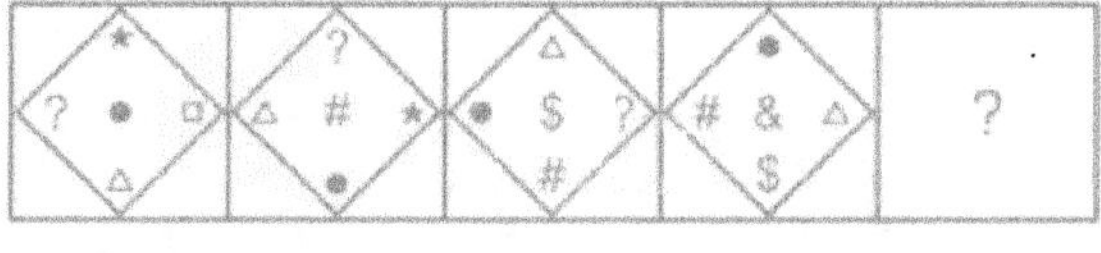

A.    **B.** 

Q.58 Direction: In the question, three elements are given below followed by four different Venn diagrams in the options. Select the appropriate Venn diagram as the answer which depicts the relation between the elements.

Dictionary, Book, Printer

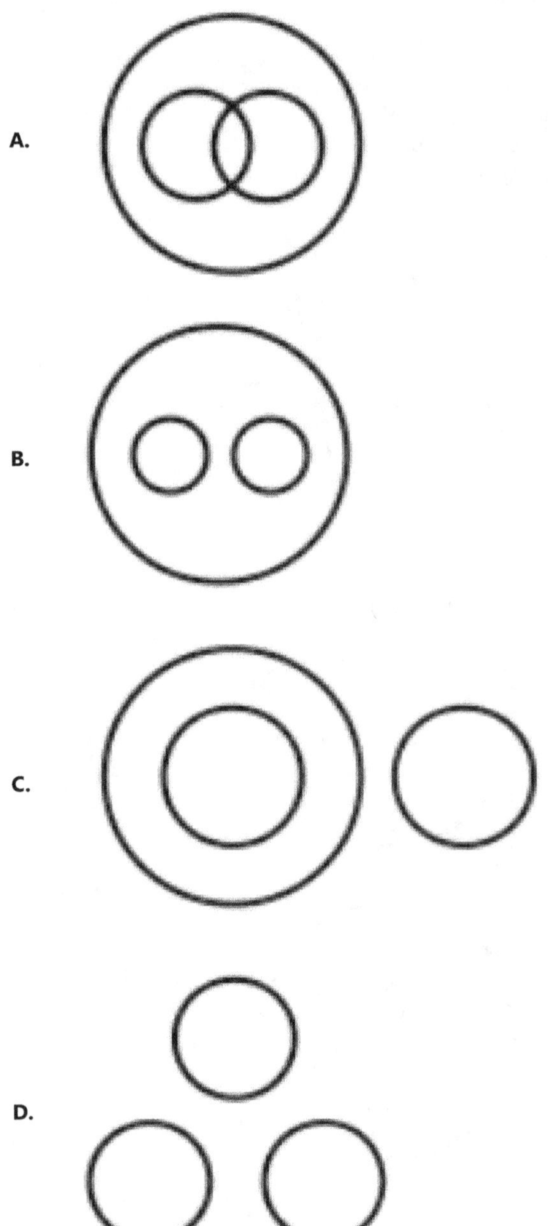

A.

B.

C.

D.

Q.59 Direction: In the question below are given three statements followed by two conclusions numbered (i) and (ii). You have to take the given statements to be true even if they seem to be at variance with commonly known facts. Read all the conclusions and then decide which of the given conclusions logically follows from the given statements disregarding commonly known facts.

Statements:

Only A are B.

Only C are D.

Some A are C.

Conclusions:

(i) Some B can be C.

(ii) Some D are A.

A. Only (i) follows

B. Only (ii) follows

C. Either (i) and (ii) follows

D. None follows

Q.60 Direction: In the question below are given two statements followed by two conclusions I and II. You have to take the given statements to be true even if they seem to be at variance from commonly known facts. Read all the conclusions and then decide which of the given conclusions logically follows from the given statements disregarding commonly known facts.

Statements:

Some electricians are plumbers.

Only a few plumbers are mechanics.

Conclusions:

I. At least some mechanics are not plumbers is a possibility.

II. All electricians are mechanics is a possibility.

A. Only II follows

B. Only I follows

C. Both I and II follow

D. Either I or II follows

Q.61 What is the next number of the following sequence?

$$3.4, 9.3, 4, 9.8, 4.6, 10.3, 5.2, 10.8, \ldots$$

A. 5.8   B. 12.5   C. 13.5   D. 5.5

Q.62 What should come in place of question mark in the following Number Series?

$$121, 102, 84, 71, 59, 52, ?$$

A. 42   B. 48   C. 43   D. 46

Q.63 How many triangles are there in the given figure?

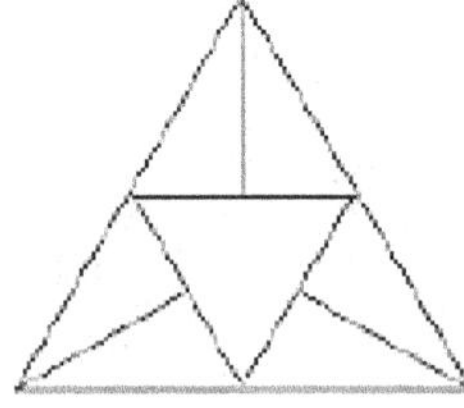

[SSC CGL, 2021]

A. 10   B. 11   C. 12   D. 14

Q.64 Which of the answer figure is embedded in the question figure?

Question Figure:

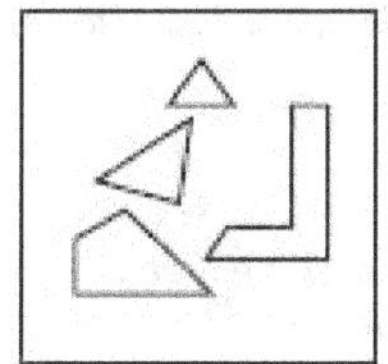

Answer Figures:

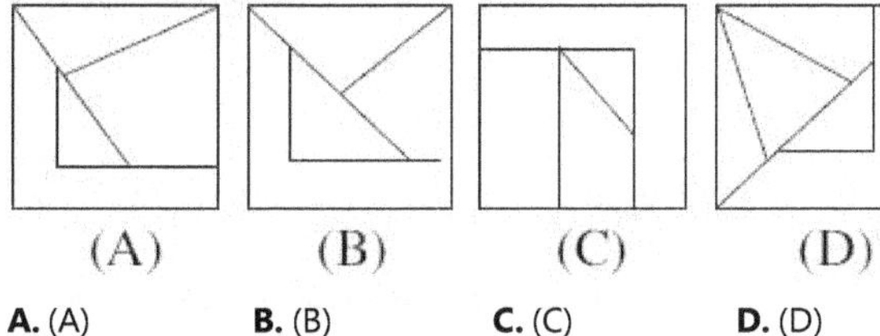

(A)   (B)   (C)   (D)

A. (A)   **B.** (B)   **C.** (C)   **D.** (D)

Q.65 What day of the week was 20th June 1837?
A. Monday   **B.** Tuesday
C. Wednesday **D.** Thursday

Q.66 Direction: A piece of paper is folded and punched as shown below in the question figures. From the given answer figures, indicate how it will appear when opened?

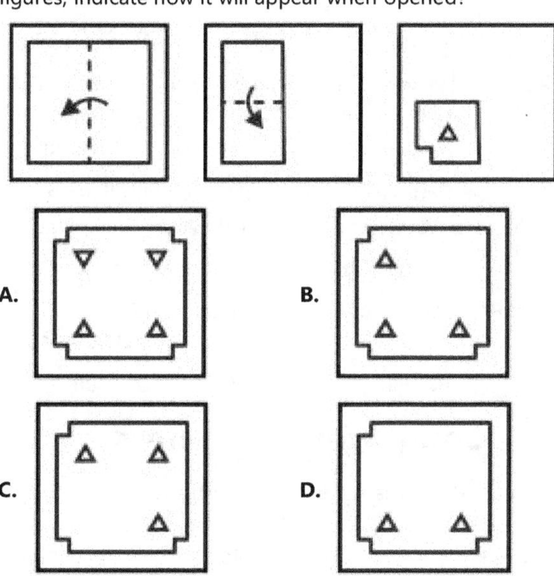

Q.67 The sequence of folding a piece of paper and the manner in which the folded paper has been cut in shown in the question figure. Select the figure from the answer figures that would most closely resemble the unfolded paper.

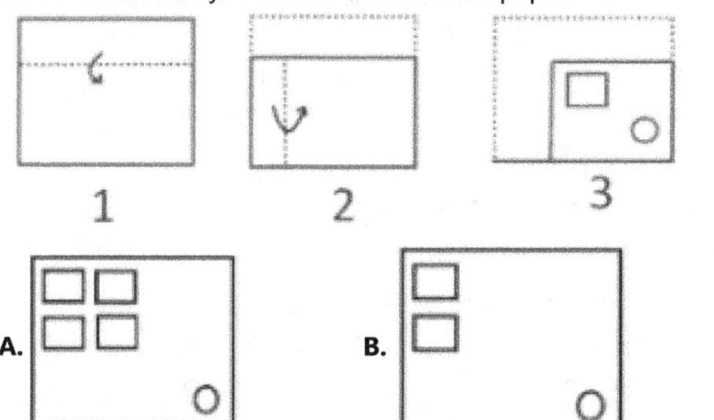

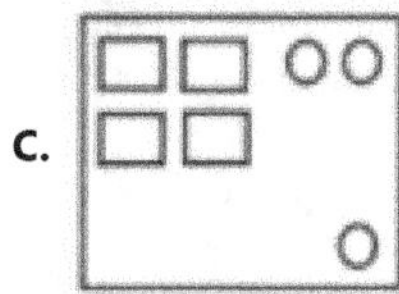

C.

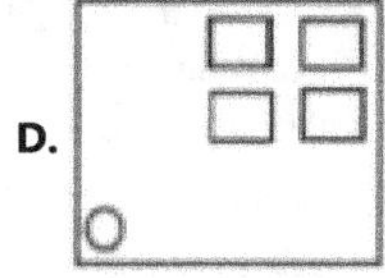

D.

Q.68 In a code language, SKILLS is written as HPROOH. How will PLACES be written in that language?

[SSC Selection Post Phase IX, 2020]

A. KOZXVH   **B.** KOBXVG
C. LOZXVI   **D.** KPZXUH

Q.69 In a code language, if SECRETE is written as 1922318222022 and SOUND is written as 19126144 , then how will NOISE be written in the same language?

[SSC Selection Post Phase IX, 2020]

A. 1312181920   **B.** 141514195
C. 1412181922   **D.** 1415182922

Ques (70-71):Direction: Arrange the given words as per dictionary order and select the right option.

Q.70 1. Truth
2. Troll
3. Terrific
4. Trauma
5. Trouble
A. 3, 4, 5, 2, 1   **B.** 2, 4, 3, 5, 1
C. 3, 4, 2, 5, 1   **D.** 4, 2, 3, 5, 1

Q.71 1. Grecian
2. Greater
3. Greasepaint
4. Grebe
5. Greasy
A. 3, 1, 4, 5, 2   **B.** 5, 1, 2, 4, 3
C. 1, 5, 3, 2, 4   **D.** 3, 5, 2, 4, 1

Q.72 Devraj is the brother of Ronit, who is the son of Radhika, who is the sister of Areem. How is Devraj related to Radhika?
A. Son   **B.** Brother   **C.** Nephew   **D.** Father

Q.73 Shashank saw Vimal, he recalled "He is the son of the father of my daughter's mother". Who is Vimal?
A. Brother   **B.** Brother-in-law
C. Father-in-law   **D.** Father

Q.74 Find the odd word from the given alternative.
A. Cheetah
B. Lion
C. Bear
D. Tiger

Q.75 In the following question, select the odd letters from the given alternatives.
A. DZVR   **B.** GCYU   **C.** QMIF   **D.** RNJF

Numerical Ability

Q.76 An article is listed at Rs. 7,600 and the discount offered for the unit is 10%. What additional discount must be given to bring the net selling price to Rs. 5,814?

A. 15%   **B.** 12%   **C.** 8%   **D.** 10%

Q.77 The average age of A, B, C, D and E is 40 years. The average age of A and B is 35 years and the average age of C and D is 42 years. The age of E is?

A. 46   **B.** 48
C. 32   **D.** None of these

Ques (78-82):Direction: Read the information carefully and answer the following question.

For a country, CO_2 emission (million metric tons) from various sectors are given in the following table.

CO₂ emissions (million metric tons)					
Sector	Power	Industry	Commercial	Agriculture	Domestic
2005	500	200	150	80	100
2006	600	300	200	90	110
2007	650	320	250	100	120
2008	700	400	300	150	150
2009	800	450	320	200	180

Q.78 What is the percentage $(\%)$ growth of CO_2 emissions from the power sector from 2005 to 2009?

A. 60   **B.** 50   **C.** 40   **D.** 80

Q.79 Which sector has recorded maximum growth in CO_2 emissions from 2005 to 2009?

A. Power   **B.** Industry
C. Commercial   **D.** Agriculture

Q.80 By what percentage $(\%)$, the total emissions of CO_2 have increased from 2005 to 2009?

A. 89.32%   **B.** 57.62%
C. 40.32%   **D.** 113.12%

Q.81 What is the average annual growth rate of power has increased from 2005 to 2009?

A. 12.57%   **B.** 16.87%   **C.** 30.81%   **D.** 50.25%

Q.82 What is the percentage contribution of the power sector to total CO₂ emissions in the year 2008?

A. 30.82%   **B.** 41.18%   **C.** 51.38%   **D.** 60.25%

Q.83 Ganesh and Bhima can complete a work in 6 days. If Ganesh alone can finish it in 10days, in how many days Bhima can complete the work?

A. 18   **B.** 14   **C.** 12   **D.** 15

Q.84 If $\frac{1}{5}$ of $\frac{3}{4}$ of $\frac{1}{3}$ of the number is 24. then 20% of that number is:

[Haryana Primary Teacher (PRT), 2021]

A. 66   **B.** 72   **C.** 96   **D.** 48

Q.85 If Mahesh's is older than Suresh by 6 years and the ratio of their age is 9:7, then find the age of Mahesh.

[MP Police (Constable), 2017]

A. 21   **B.** 28   **C.** 27   **D.** 30

Q.86 If base and hypotenuse of a right triangle are $(u^2 - v^2)$ and $(u^2 + v^2)$ respectively and the area of the triangle is 2016 square units, then the perimeter of triangle may be:

[Indian Military Academy (IMA), 2018]

A. 224 units   **B.** 288 units
C. 448 units   **D.** 576 units

Q.87 If a is the predecessor of b, then the value of $(a - b)$ and $(b - a)$ are:

[Jawahar Navodaya Entrance Class VI, 2018]

A. -1 and 1 **B.** 1 and -1
C. 0 and 1 **D.** 1 and 0

Q.88 Rishu saves $x\%$ of her income. If her income increases by 26% and the expenditure increases by 20%, then her savings increase by 50%. What is the value of x?

[SSC CGL, 2020]

A. 30   **B.** 10   **C.** 20   **D.** 25

Q.89 A person crosses a road of length 1200 m in 10 minutes. What is the speed of the person?

A. 3 km/h   **B.** 5 km/h   **C.** 8.5 km/h   **D.** 7.2 km/h

Q.90 A person divides a certain amount among his three sons in the ratio of $3:4:5$. If he had divided this amount in the ratio of $\frac{1}{3}, \frac{1}{4}, \frac{1}{5}$ his son, who had got the lowest share earlier, would get Rs. 1188 more. Find the amount (in Rs).

[SSC CGL, 2020]

A. 5640   **B.** 6840   **C.** 6768   **D.** 7008

Computer Awareness

Q.91 How are data organized in a spreadsheet?
A. Lines and spaces   **B.** Layers and planes
C. Rows and columns   **D.** Height and width

Q.92 How many columns can you insert in a word document in maximum?
A. 35   **B.** 63   **C.** 55   **D.** 65

Q.93 Statistical calculations and preparation of tables and graphs can be done using:
A. Adobe Photoshop   **B.** Excel
C. Notepad   **D.** Power Point

Q.94 The process of arrenging the items of a column in some sequence or order is known as:
A. Arrengin   **B.** Autofill   **C.** Sorting   **D.** Filtering

Q.95 What do you use to create a chart?
A. Pie Wizard   **B.** Excel Wizard
C. Data Wizard   **D.** Chart Wizard

Q.96 What is the maximum font size you can apply for any character?

A. 163   **B.** 1638   **C.** 1639   **D.** 1634

Q.97 The science of examining raw data with the purpose of drawing conclusions about that information.

A. Data Analytics
B. Descriptive Analytics
C. In-memory Analytics
D. Predictive Analytics

Q.98 What is the first webpage of the website called?

A. First page   **B.** Main page
C. Home page   **D.** None of these

Q.99 Why is the tower model of CPU most appropriate and used widely?

A. Components can be installed in it with ease
B. Cheap
C. The tower occupies less space
D. All of these

Q.100 _______ is the full form of Wi-Fi.

A. Wireless focus   **B.** Wireless fidelity
C. Wired Fidelity   **D.** Wired focus

// **Smart Answer Sheet** //

Correct   Indicates percentage of students who answered questions correctly.

Skipped   Indicates percentage of students who skipped questions.

Q.	Ans.	Correct / Skipped	Q.	Ans.	Correct / Skipped	Q.	Ans.	Correct / Skipped	Q.	Ans.	Correct / Skipped	Q.	Ans.	Correct / Skipped
1	C	43.85 % / 53.85 %	17	B	63.86 % / 32.64 %	33	C	66.19 % / 33.18 %	49	A	48.67 % / 46.77 %	65	B	85.5 % / 12.72 %
2	B	55.54 % / 36.48 %	18	A	57.75 % / 38.76 %	34	B	48.18 % / 43.31 %	50	D	56.31 % / 32.32 %	66	A	44.69 % / 54.51 %
3	D	76.82 % / 21.04 %	19	C	66.05 % / 30.05 %	35	A	50.9 % / 46.57 %	51	B	54.95 % / 33.9 %	67	A	83.98 % / 13.39 %
4	A	58.87 % / 34.38 %	20	A	48.75 % / 32.63 %	36	C	61.09 % / 37.82 %	52	C	22.4 % / 76.26 %	68	A	56.9 % / 41.35 %
5	A	59.7 % / 38.84 %	21	A	46.57 % / 47.76 %	37	D	10.82 % / 73.33 %	53	A	82.49 % / 16.47 %	69	C	14.56 % / 84.58 %
6	D	83.35 % / 11.54 %	22	C	89.74 % / 10.09 %	38	A	29.53 % / 69.38 %	54	B	58.02 % / 41.57 %	70	C	85.88 % / 13.15 %
7	A	41.18 % / 46.1 %	23	C	52.44 % / 39.65 %	39	C	81.14 % / 15.76 %	55	B	11.46 % / 70.87 %	71	D	80.23 % / 14.05 %
8	A	64.59 % / 31.23 %	24	D	64.1 % / 32.36 %	40	B	76.05 % / 14.95 %	56	D	49.96 % / 44.4 %	72	A	45.17 % / 35.4 %
9	A	61.74 % / 32.74 %	25	C	26.11 % / 67.46 %	41	C	40.79 % / 54.55 %	57	A	76.62 % / 18.29 %	73	B	30.34 % / 67.18 %
10	D	44.46 % / 34.87 %	26	C	69.26 % / 30.45 %	42	A	66.61 % / 30.23 %	58	C	83.65 % / 14.35 %	74	C	63.09 % / 32.34 %
11	D	79.1 % / 13.69 %	27	D	81.43 % / 14.41 %	43	D	61.9 % / 31.3 %	59	D	87.14 % / 12.22 %	75	C	41.74 % / 41.87 %
12	B	51.79 % / 34.45 %	28	A	56.18 % / 33.4 %	44	A	61.75 % / 38.04 %	60	C	42.8 % / 44.82 %	76	A	56.2 % / 32.17 %
13	C	89.24 % / 10.12 %	29	A	89.95 % / 10.0 %	45	B	66.54 % / 32.31 %	61	A	67.77 % / 31.97 %	77	A	86.79 % / 12.83 %
14	B	66.16 % / 33.55 %	30	D	40.51 % / 34.19 %	46	B	51.83 % / 30.94 %	62	D	78.89 % / 18.35 %	78	A	47.42 % / 36.24 %
15	A	64.79 % / 31.62 %	31	D	76.02 % / 20.87 %	47	D	51.98 % / 42.02 %	63	B	48.3 % / 40.63 %	79	D	69.55 % / 30.06 %
16	C	47.84 % / 37.01 %	32	A	65.11 % / 31.91 %	48	D	56.99 % / 40.09 %	64	A	50.21 % / 30.51 %	80	A	52.21 % / 40.59 %

Q.	Ans.	Correct / Skipped
81	A	58.38 %
		34.35 %
82	B	66.21 %
		33.37 %
83	D	89.49 %
		10.09 %
84	C	88.81 %
		10.17 %

Q.	Ans.	Correct / Skipped
85	C	63.97 %
		34.3 %
86	B	10.42 %
		77.02 %
87	B	76.57 %
		13.11 %
88	C	65.01 %
		30.24 %

Q.	Ans.	Correct / Skipped
89	D	78.24 %
		20.65 %
90	C	51.2 %
		31.51 %
91	C	87.59 %
		11.65 %
92	B	85.82 %
		11.62 %

Q.	Ans.	Correct / Skipped
93	B	43.31 %
		42.53 %
94	C	62.86 %
		30.6 %
95	D	82.26 %
		12.23 %
96	B	65.7 %
		30.5 %

Q.	Ans.	Correct / Skipped
97	A	60.68 %
		35.14 %
98	C	77.4 %
		15.26 %
99	C	51.95 %
		30.67 %
100	B	65.81 %
		31.15 %

Performance Analysis

Avg. Score (%)	52.0%
Toppers Score (%)	68.0%
Your Score	

//Hints and Solutions//

1. India's rank in Human Development Index, 2018 is 130th.

India has been positioned at 131 out of 189 countries and territories, according to the report. India had ranked 130 in 2018 in the index.

The United Nations Development Programme(UNDP) is the United Nations' global development network. UNDP works in about 170 countries and territories, helping to eradicate poverty, reduce inequalities and exclusion, and build resilience so countries can sustain progress. As the UN's development agency, UNDP plays a critical role in helping countries achieve Sustainable Development Goals.

Hence, the correct option is (C).

2. In January 2022, Germany took over the G7 Presidency.

On 1 January, Germany takes over the G7 Presidency. The G7, or "Group of Seven," consists of the US, Canada, Japan, France, the UK, Italy, and Germany. In June 2021 Summit, the G7 leaders agreed to distribute 2.3 billion vaccine doses. Germany is the second-largest donor in the COVAX vaccination alliance.

Hence, the correct option is (B).

3. Former Jharkhand Governor and National Democratic Alliance candidate Droupadi Murmu has been elected as the 15th President of India on 21 July 2022.

She is the first tribal woman to be elected to the position & the youngest as well.

She defeated opposition candidate Yashwant Sinha by bagging 64.03% of the electoral college votes.

Hence, the correct option is (D).

4. Russia was stripped of hosting the Champions League final by UEFA on 25 Feb 2022 with St. Petersburg replaced by Paris after Russia's invasion of Ukraine. France last hosted the Champions League final 16 years ago, when Barcelona beat Arsenal in the 2006 final.

Hence, the correct option is (A).

5. Rafael Nadal has won the Mexican Open 2022 held in Acapulco, Mexico. Nadal, who first won the title in 2005 and took it again in 2013 and 2020, stormed through the Acapulco draw without dropping a set, to claim his third straight title of 2022.

Hence, the correct option is (A).

6. South Korea has signed a $ 2.25 billion deal with a Russian state-run nuclear energy company 'ASE'in August 2022.

- It has been signed to provide components for Egypt's first nuclear power plant.
- ASE is a subsidiary of Rosatom, a state-owned Russian nuclear conglomerate.
- South Korea has also signed a $ 20 billion contract to build nuclear power reactors in the UAE.

Hence, the correct option is (D).

7. The 16th edition of 'India Digital Summit 2022' was organized by the Internet and Mobile Association of India (IAMAI). The report. titled 'Creating 10 million Digitally Enabled Micro-entrepreneurs' was also released during the summit. The report noted that micro-entrepreneurs are a crucial part of the Indian economy, both for job creation and contribution to GDP.

Hence, the correct option is (A).

8. NITI Aayog launched a report titled 'India's Booming Gig and Platform Economy', on 27 June 2022.

It is a first-of-its-kind study that presents comprehensive perspectives and recommendations on the gig–platform economy in India.

The report provides a scientific methodological approach to estimate the current size and job-generation potential of the sector.

Hence, the correct option is (A).

9. On May 11, 2018, Prime Minister Narendra Modi and Nepalese Prime Minister KP Sharma Oli jointly flagged-off a direct bus service between the two sacred cities Janakpur and Ayodhya, as part of the Ramayana Circuit.

The bus service seeks to promote religious tourism and built a strong foundation for people-to-people contact between the two countries. As per the mythological story 'Ramayana', Ayodhya is Lord Rama's birthplace, while, Janakpur is the birthplace of goddess Sita.

Hence, the correct option is (A).

10. Haryana Development and Panchayat Minister Devendra Singh Babli said that one thousand hi-tech libraries would be built in the villages as a pilot project in the state. Addressing a public meeting during the 'Madhur Milan Program' organized at Kheri Raiwali village of Kaithal district, the ministers said that the youth of rural areas will be able to make their future bright by taking education according to the present requirement from these libraries. Along with this, work is also going on to build 1000 gyms in villages to encourage youth towards sports and keep them away from drugs.

Hence, the correct option is (D).

11. India has contributed USD 500,000 to the UN Women, the United Nations agency for gender equality and women empowerment for their core budget.

India's Permanent Representative to the United Nations T.S.Tirumurti announced that India reaffirmed its partnership of women-led development and gender parity. UN Women Executive Director, Sima Bahous thanked India for its contribution.

Hence, the correct option is (D).

12. Amir Khusro was a poet of the fourteenth century.

Amir Khusro (1253 AD-1325 AD) was a Persian associated with royal courts of more than seven rulers of the Delhi Sultanate. He innovated Khayal (a style of singing). In his book Tarikh-i-Alai, he gave an account of the conquest of Alauddin Khilji. He also lived in the court of Ghiyasuddin Tughlaq and wrote Tughlaqnamah. Amir Khusro is also known as Tuti-i-Hind or 'Parrot of India'. Its introduced many Persian Arabic ragas. He also invented the Sitar.

Hence, the correct option is (B).

13. Yamini Krishnamurti is related to Kuchipudi Dance. Yamini Krishnamurti is a Kuchipudi dancer. She also knows Bharatnatyam. 'A Passion For Dance' is her autobiography.

Kuchipudi is the classical dance of Andhra Pradesh. Kuchipudi derives its name from the Kuchipudi village of Andhra Pradesh. Kuchipudi exhibits scenes from the Hindu Epics, legends and mythological tales through a combination of music, dance and acting. There are now two forms of Kuchipudi:

- The traditional musical dance drama
- The solo dance

Hence, the correct option is (C).

14. Bhup Singh was the real name of freedom fighter Vijay Singh Pathik.

Vijay Singh Pathik, popularly known as Rashtriya Pathik, was an Indian revolutionary. He was among the first Indian revolutionaries who lit the torch of the freedom movement against British rule. Much before Mohandas K. Gandhi initiated the Satyagrah movement, Pathik experimented during the Bijolia's Kisan agitation.

Hence, the correct option is (B).

15. The Company's rule in India was abolished by the 'Government of India Act' 1858.

By this act, the control of the rule of India was handed over to the 'British Emperor'.

Now the entire responsibility of the Indian government was on the 'Secretary of India'.

A minister of the British government was called the 'Secretary of India'.

Indian Trusts Act, 1882 is relating to private trusts and trustees.

Hence, the correct option is (A).

16. The sale or liquidation of assets by the government, usually Central and State public sector enterprises, projects, or other fixed assets is called Disinvestment.

Disinvestment:

- The government undertakes disinvestment to reduce the fiscal burden on the exchequer, or to raise money for meeting specific needs, such as to bridge the revenue shortfall from other regular sources.
- Strategic disinvestment is the transfer of the ownership and control of a public sector entity to some other entity (mostly to a private sector entity).
- Unlike simple disinvestment, strategic sale implies a kind of privatization.

- The disinvestment commission defines strategic sale as the sale of a substantial portion of the Government shareholding of a central public sector enterprise (CPSE) of up to 50%, or such a higher percentage as the competent authority may determine, along with transfer of management control.
- The Department of Investment and Public Asset Management (DIPAM) under the Ministry of Finance is the nodal department for the strategic stake sale in the Public Sector Undertakings (PSUs).

Hence, the correct option is (C).

17. In modern industrialized society, as a result of increased opportunities given to women in the labour market, it has indeed translated better outcome for women and her family income. Unlike the pre-industrial era, women are now participating in the economic process and she has more independence and freedom. Thus, the status of women has gradually risen.

Hence, the correct option is (B).

18. Claude Levi Strauss has given emphasis in his study on Alliance theory which discusses alliances or the relation between two families. The two families include the wife givers and the wife takes. Here he says that an incest taboo will determine who will be the wife giver and who will be the wive taker.

Hence, the correct option is (A).

19. The concept of timeless time or timelessness is a character of digitalization given by Manual Castells. Here he refers to the digital networks that allow us to have real-time communication with others in the form of a video conferencing or a chat and also an asynchronous communication such as a post in a social media which a person comes across and may read or take a reference in the future.

Hence, the correct option is (C).

20. The southeast trade winds in the southern hemisphere and the northeast trade winds in the northern hemisphere meet each other near the equator. The meeting place of these winds is known as the Inter-Tropical Convergence Zone (ITCZ).

Characteristics features related to ITCZ:

- The Intertropical Convergence Zone (ITCZ) lies in the equatorial trough.
- It is a permanent low-pressure feature where surface trade winds, laden with heat and moisture, converge to form a zone of increased convection, cloudiness, and precipitation.
- It is a low-pressure zone between tropic of Cancer and tropic of Capricorn
- This is the region of ascending air, maximum clouds, and heavy rainfall.
- The location of ITCZ shifts north and south of the equator with the change of season.
- In the summer season, the sun shines vertically over the Tropic of Cancer, and the ITCZ shifts northwards.

Therefore, all the statements are correct about ITCZ or tropical convergence zone.

Hence, the correct option is (A).

21. 'Amphan' made landfall in a part of West Bengal and Orissa in May 2020. It is an example of a Tropical cyclone.

A tropical cyclone is a rapidly rotating storm system characterized by a low-pressure center, a closed low-level atmospheric circulation, strong winds, and a spiral arrangement of thunderstorms that produce heavy rain and/or squalls.

It caused widespread damage in Eastern India, specifically West Bengal, Odisha, and in Bangladesh in May 2020.

Hence, the correct option is (A).

22. The order of the layers of the atmosphere from top to bottom: Ionosphere - Mesosphere - Stratosphere - Troposphere

The space in which the air surrounds the earth is called the atmosphere.

The lower part of the atmosphere (which usually extends from four to eight miles) is called the troposphere, the upper part of it is called the stratosphere, and the part above it is called the mesosphere and the upper part from the mesosphere is called the ionosphere.

Hence, the correct option is (C).

23. Gulbadan Begum is the writer of "Humayun-Nama".

Gulbadan Begum was a Mughal princess and the daughter of Emperor Babur, the founder of the Mughal Empire. She is best known as the author of Humayun-Nama, the account of the life of her half-brother, Emperor Humayun, which she wrote on the request of her nephew, Emperor Akbar.

Hence, the correct option is (C).

24. Leelawati, a treatise on Mathematics, was written by Bhaskaracharya.

Leelawati is Indian mathematician Bhaskaracharya's treatise on mathematics, written in 1150, it is the first volume of his main work. He has been called the greatest mathematician of medieval India. His main work Siddhanta-Siromani, is divided into four parts called Leelawati , Bijaganita, Grahaganita and Goladhyaya. These four sections deal with arithmetic, algebra, mathematics of the planets, and spheres respectively.

Bhaskara II also known as Bhaskaracharya, was an Indian mathematician and astronomer. His book on arithmetic is the source of interesting legends that assert that it was written for his daughter, Leelawati.

Hence, the correct option is (D).

25. E.M. Forster wrote the book "A Passage to India".

Edward Morgan Forster (E.M. Forster) was an English fiction writer, essayist and librettist. Many of his novels examine class difference and hypocrisy, including A Room with a View, Howards End and A Passage to India. The last brought him his greatest success.

This is the first edition of E M Forster's A Passage to India, which was published in 1924. It is widely considered to be Forster's finest work and it became his last novel, despite the fact that he remained active as a writer and critic for more than four decades after its publication.

Hence, the correct option is (C).

26. Kalamkari is an ancient style of hand painting done on cotton or silk fabric with a tamarind pen, using natural dyes. So, Statement 1 is correct. The word Kalamkari is derived from a Persian word where 'kalam' meaning pen and 'Kari' meaning craftsmanship. This art involves 23 tedious steps of dyeing, bleaching, hand painting, block-printing, searching, and cleaning. Motifs of flowers, peacocks, divine characters of Hindu epics like Mahabharata and Ramayana are drawn. Prime colours: indigo, mustard, rust, black, and green. Natural dyes are used to paint colours in Kalamkari art, extracted from natural sources with no use of chemicals and artificial ingredients. So, Statement 2 is incorrect. There are two styles of Kalamkari art in India: the Srikalahasti style and the Machilipatnam style. So, Statement 3 is correct. In the Machilipatnam style of Kalamkari, motifs are essentially printed with hand-carved traditional blocks with intricate detailing painted by hands. The Srikalahasti style of painting draws inspiration from the Hindu mythology describing scenes from the epics and folklore. It has its origin in the temples. The quality of the water, air, and sunshine are all-important in the process of art-making of this nature.

Hence, the correct option is (C).

27. Warli tribals of Thane district in Maharashtra decorate their house walls with paintings depicting their lives: planting saplings, carrying grain, dancing, travelling to the market, and other routine activities of their daily lives. So, pair 4 is not correct. Symbols of the sun, moon, and stars along with plants, animals, insects, and birds show their belief in the integration of all forms of life. On ritual and ceremonial occasions, Warli home walls are plastered with dung. Rice paste is used with red ochre powder to tell stories and to invoke the blessings of their goddess of fertility, Palaghata. The paintings bear a close resemblance to the Bimbhetka paintings.

Hence, the correct option is (D).

28. Tholu Bommalata is a shadow puppet from Andhra Pradesh which has a rich and strong tradition. So, Statement 1 is incorrect. The puppets are large in size to cast a shadow. They have a jointed waist, shoulders, elbows, and knees. They are colored on both sides and throw colored shadows on the screen. The classical music of the region is used. The theme of the puppet plays is drawn from the Ramayana, Mahabharata, and Puranas. So, Statement 2 is correct. The skin of wild animals (Goats) is used to make the puppet. The skin is treated with herbs and oils and then beaten till it becomes translucent. The different parts of the puppetís body are separately cut out of this skin. Gods and heroes are made the largest in size, because of their importance. The angle of the head has significance: a downward glance suggests modesty, a high chin indicates arrogance. Colors too have meaning: giant bullies and their kind have red faces, while white stands for a fiery nature. The pieces are then joined together with a thick knotted string, which facilitates easy movement. A split-bamboo or palm leaf stem is used for the main central support of the puppet. The legs are loosely attached from below the knees, and the manipulator can jerk the puppet to produce the swaying movement of the legs. The screen for the shadow puppet show is a bamboo box-like stage erected in the open air. So, Statement 3 is correct. In the rural areas, very often, oil lamps made of split coconut shells are used for lighting. The flickering light keeps the puppets in constant movement, and lends an air of magic to the show.

Hence, the correct option is (A).

29. Bangalore is popularly known as the Silicon Valley of India.

Bangalore is considered the center of India's high-tech industry. ISRO, Infosys, Wipro, HAL and other Indian technological organizations have their headquarters in this city. Don Hoefler a journalist for the publication had titled a three-part series examining the history of the semiconductor "Silicon Valley U.S.A." The term rapidly became associated with technology. Additionally, Silicon Valley is a region in Northern California that serves as a global center for high technology and innovation. It is located in the southern part of the San Francisco Bay Area.

Hence, the correct option is (A).

30. Chaukhandi Stupa is located in Sarnath, Uttar Pradesh. It was built in the period of the 4th and 5th century A.D during the Gupta period. It is believed that Buddha first time met his five disciples here. It was built to mark the site where Lord Buddha and his first disciples met while traveling from Bodh Gaya to Sarnath. It is declared as a 'protected area of national importance' in 2019. The Archaeological Survey of India declared Chaukhandi Stupa as a monument of national importance in June 2019.

Hence, the correct option is (D).

31. In Udaipur, the observatory was not built by the King of Jaipur.

Jai Singh noticed that the Zij, which was used for determining the position of celestial objects, did not match the positions calculated on the table. He constructed five new observatories in different cities(Varanasi, Ujjain, Mathura, Delhi, and Jaipur) in order to create a more accurate Zij. The astronomical tables Jai Singh created, known as the Zij-i Muhammad Shahi, were continuously used in India for a century. Also, it was used to measure time.

Hence, the correct option is (D).

32. These terms were mentioned in the news recently to indicate the different the cricket bats used. "The Camel" bat was recently used by Afghanistan's Rashid Khan. Mangoose, Kaboom and Aluminium are some of the other names used to describe different cricket bats.

Hence, the correct option is (A).

33. The ICC Under-19 World Cup 2020 tournament will be hosted by South Africa. Indian U-19 Cricket Team is led by Priyam Garg. India is the defending champion of the U-19 World cup and winner of the championship for four times.

Many IPL 2020-fame players are to play for India, including Yashasvi Jaiswal and Ravi Bishnoi. India's first match is against Sri Lanka on January 19. India is placed in Group A with Sri Lanka, Japan and New Zealand. Recently the India U-19 team has won the U-19 Asia Cup and a Tri-Nations Tournament with Bangladesh and England.

Hence, the correct option is (C).

34. Ratchanok Intanon, the Badminton player of Thailand, defeated Spain's Carolina Marin in the women's singles final match of the Indonesia Masters tournament in Jakarta, held recently. This is her second win in the Indonesian Masters event after her triumph in 2010.

Ratchanok Intanon became world champion in women's singles in 2013 and became the first Thai player to become No.1 in women's singles. Carolina Marin is the present Olympic Champion and three-time World Champion.

Hence, the correct option is (B).

35. The Gram Panchayat is established on the basis of direct election.

Gram Panchayat is a basic village governing institute in Indian villages.

The panchayat is chaired by the president of the village, known as a Sarpanch.

Hence, the correct option is (A).

36. The 'Swadeshi' and 'Boycott' were adopted as methods of struggle in Bengal at the same time the Vande Matram Movement was in Andhra Pradesh.

This was the most important movement in Bengal and was known as Vande Mataram movement in Andhra Pradesh. This movement ended in 1911. The government made the decision of partition of Bengal in December 1903.

Hence, the correct option is (C).

37. The Greek invasion paved the way for the expansion of the Mauryan empire in North-west India as the petty local states were destroyed by the Greeks.

These historical creations provide us with valuable information about the socio-economic conditions of that time. So, Statement 1 is correct.

Chandragupta Maurya also acquired knowledge about the working of Alexander's military tactics which helped him in destroying the power of the Nandas. So, Statement 3 is correct.

Invasion paved the way for Greek merchants and craftsmen to trade with India and increase the trade facilities. So, Statement 2 is incorrect.

Hence, the correct option is (D).

38. Kandhar Inscription deals with Ashoka's policies.

- The inscription was carved in Aramaic & Greek language.
- It is bilingual and specifies that fisherman and hunters gave up hunting. So, statement 2 is correct.

Minor Pillar inscriptions:

- Rummindei Pillar Inscription: It mentioned the exemption of Lumbini (the birth place of Buddha) from tax.
- Ashoka visited Lumbini in the 29th year of his coronation.
- It is the only inscription which makes a precise reference to taxation. So, statement 1 is correct.

Hence, the correct option is (A).

39. Bronze is an alloy of copper but consists 12-12.5% tin in that.

So, it is an alloy of both copper and tin.
Hence, the correct option is (C).

40. Hygrometer is the instrument which is used to measure the humidity. This instrument is also known as psychrometer.
Hence, the correct option is (B).

41. In organic farming we use genetically modified seeds and in that no insecticide and pesticides are used for farming and in that method of farming we use crop rotation because due to crop rotation soil organic matter does degrade as quickly.
Hence, the correct option is (C).

42. The Nobel Prize in Chemistry 2019 rewards the development of the lithium-ion battery. This lightweight, rechargeable and powerful battery are now used in everything from mobile phones to laptops and electric vehicles. It can also store significant amounts of energy from solar and wind power, making possible a fossil fuel-free society.

Hence, the correct option is (A).

43. Bipolar Disorder is a mental health condition in which patients undergo intense mood shifts that oscillate between depression and elevated moods. After researching, scientists found that such patients carry some residual impairment in terms of processing of information even in their 'normal' phases. The study has been done by jointly researchers from the National Institute of Mental Health and Neuroscience (Nimhans), Bengaluru and All India Institute of Medical Sciences, New Delhi.

Hence, the correct option is (D).

44. NepaliSat-1 satellite was launched by Nepal successfully from Virginia in the United States on 18 April 2019. Its aim is to gather detailed geographical information of the Himalayan nation.

Hence, the correct option is (A).

45. India is the most populous country among the SAARC nations but as per the options given in the question, Pakistan is the most populous country which has population of 200,813,818 in 2018.

Hence, the correct option is (B).

46. SAARC was founded in Dhaka on 8 December 1985. Its secretariat is based in Kathmandu (Nepal). The SAARC Secretariat was established in Kathmandu on 16 January 1987 and was inaugurated by Late King Birendra Bir Bikram Shah of Nepal.

Hence, the correct option is (B).

47. The headquarter of the International Atomic Energy Agency (IAEA) are situated at Vienna. The IAEA has its headquarters in Vienna, Austria. The IAEA has two "Regional Safeguards Offices" which are located in Toronto, Canada, and in Tokyo, Japan. The IAEA also has two liaison offices which are located in New York City, United States, and in Geneva, Switzerland.

Hence, the correct option is (D).

48. Wildlife Crime Control Bureau (WCCB) has received the Asia Environmental Enforcement Award-2020.

United Nations Environment Programme has given this award.

The WCCB received this award in the 'Innovation category', in a virtual ceremony held on 17th Feb 2021.

This is the second time WCCB has bagged Asia Environmental Enforcement Award. Earlier it had received this award in 2018 in the same category.

Hence, the correct option is (D).

49. Indian writer Kritika Pandey has won the regional award for Asia of the prestigious Commonwealth Short Story Prize for this year.

The writer was selected for her work titled 'The Great Indian Tee and Snakes'. The Commonwealth Short Story Prize is awarded for the best unpublished short fiction, every year. She had also been earlier nominated for the Pushcart Prize. To be eligible for the award, one must be a commonwealth citizen aged above 18 years.

Hence, the correct option is (A).

50. The Arjuna Awards are given by the Ministry of Youth Affairs and Sports, Government of India to recognize outstanding achievement in National sports. Instituted in 1961, the award carries a cash prize of ₹ 500,000, a bronze statue of Arjuna and a scroll. Varun Singh Bhati (Para-Athletics) is the recipient of the Arjun Award 2017.

Hence, the correct option is (D).

51. Here, the pattern is,

$86 = (8 \times 6) + (8 + 6) = 48 + 14 = 62$

Similarly,

$49 = (4 \times 9) + (4 + 9) = 36 + 13 = 49$

Thus, 49 is related to 49.

'Hence, the correct option is (B).

52. The pattern here is:

$$62 = \frac{62}{2} = 31$$

$$31 \times 5 = 155$$

Similarly,

$$58 = \frac{58}{2} = 29$$

$$29 \times 5 = 145$$

Thus, 58 is related to 145.

Hence, the correct option is (C).

53. The optical glass used in the construction of spectacles is made of flint glass.

- The main use of flint glass is in the manufacture of lenses, prisms, and other optical instruments.
- Flint glass is considered softer glass than any other glass.

Hence, the correct option is (A).

54. In the case of the concave mirror, when the object is between the focus and the pole, the image formed is virtual, erect, and enlarged. That's why a concave mirror is used as a shaving glass.

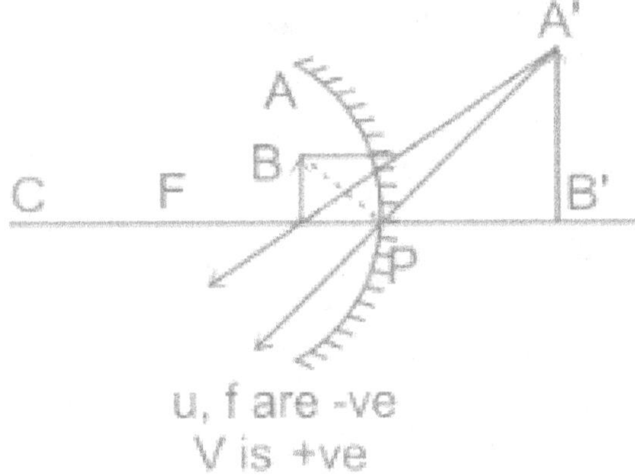

Hence, the correct option is (B).

55. In figure (b), elements of the 1st column are interchanged. In figure (c), elements of the 2nd column are interchanged. In figure (d), elements of the 3rd column are interchanged.

So,

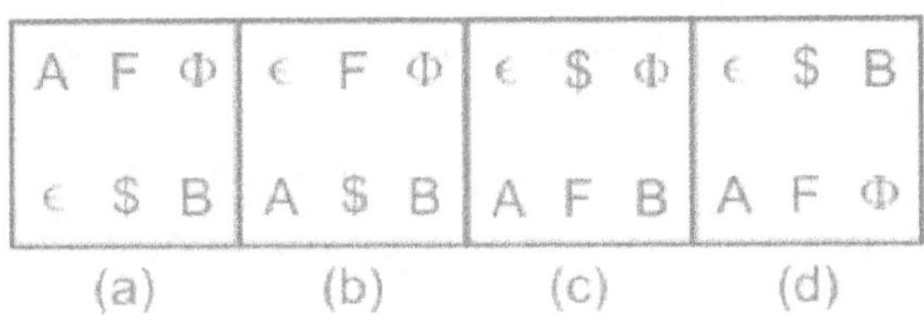

Hence, the correct option is (B).

56. In the above series, symbols present at the corners are rotating in the clockwise direction, and every time it rotates, the new symbol introduced at the centre and symbol from the right corner is removed, also symbol at the centre moves down in the next step. Thus, the answer figure is,

Hence, the correct option is (D).

57. Tie, Shirt and Shoe are all separate items, entirely different from each other.

The Venn diagram given below depicts the relationship among Tie, Shirt and Shoe-

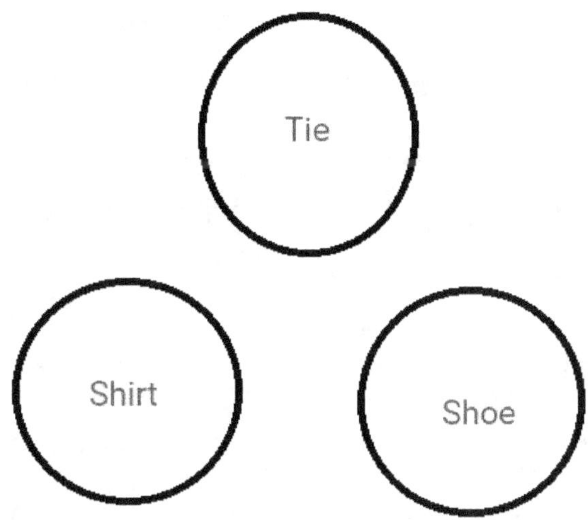

Hence, the correct option is (A).

58. Dictionary is a type of book. But printer is different from both dictionary and book.

The Venn diagram given below depicts the relationship among Dictionary, Book and Printer-

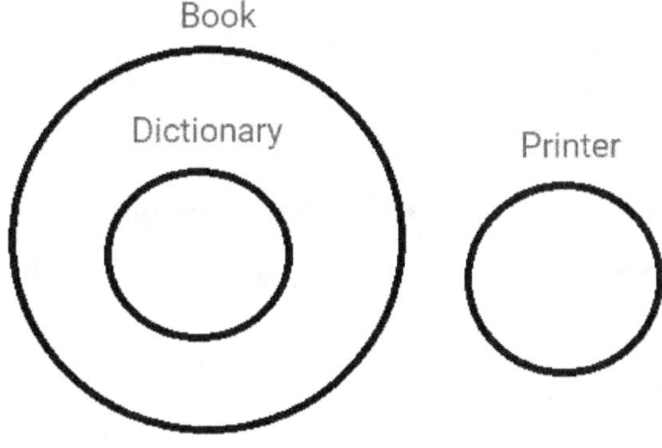

Hence, the correct option is (C).

59. The least possible Venn diagram for the given statements is as follows

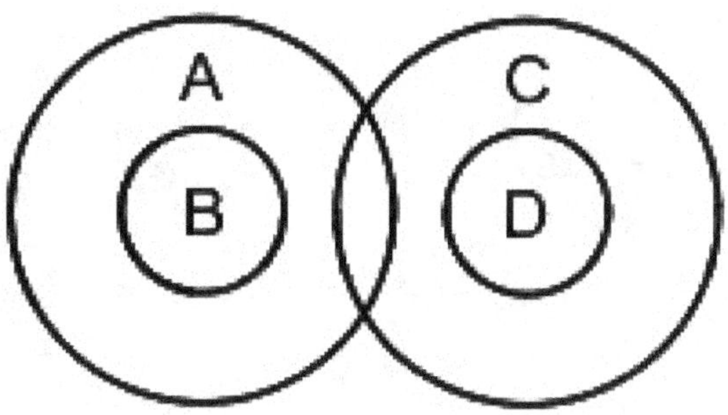

Conclusions:

(i) Some B can be C → False (only A are B, nothing else can be B)

(ii) Some D are A → False (Only C are D, nothing else can be D)

Therefore, none of the conclusion follows.

Hence, the correct option is (D).

60. The least possible Venn diagram for the given statements is as follows,

Conclusions:

I. At least some mechanics are not plumbers is a possibility → True (Only a few plumbers are mechanics)

II. All electricians are mechanics is a possibility → True (Possibility is true as shown below)

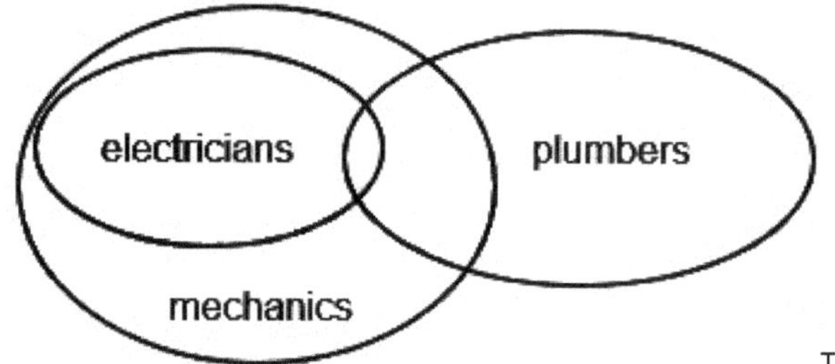

Thus, both conclusions I and II follow.

Hence, the correct option is (C).

61. Given series:

Split like this $(3.4, 4, 4.6, 5.2)(9.3, 9.8, 10.3, 10,8)$

$(3.4, 4, 4.6, 5.2)$

$3.4 + 0.6 = 4$

$4 + 0.6 = 4.6$

$4.6 + 0.6 = 5.2$

$5.2 + 0.6 = 5.8$

$(9.3, 9.8, 10.3, 10,8)$

$9.3 + 0.5 = 9.8$

$9.8 + 0.5 = 10.3$

$10.3 + 0.5 = 10.8$

$10.8 + 0.5 = 11.3$

Hence, the correct option is (A).

62. We have:

$102 = 121 - 19$

$\Rightarrow 84 = 102 - 18$

$\Rightarrow 71 = 84 - 13$

$\Rightarrow 59 = 71 - 12$

$\Rightarrow 52 = 59 - 7$

Therefore, $? = 52 - 6 = 46$

Hence, the correct option is (D).

63. On counting the number of triangles in the given figure we find that there are 11 triangles in the given figure.

Hence, the correct option is (B).

64. Answer figure (A) in which question figure is hidden/embedded.

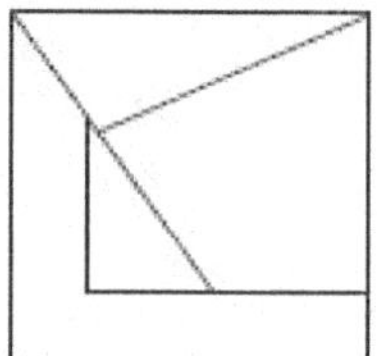

Hence, the correct option is (A).

65. 20th June 1837 means 1836 complete years + first 5 months of the year 1837 + 20 days of June.

1600 years give no odd days.

200 years give 3 odd days.

36 years give (36 + 9) or 3 odd days.

Thus 1836 years give 6 odd days.

From 1st January to 20th June there are 3 odd days.

Odd days: January 3, February 0, March 3, April 2, May 3, June 6 = 17

Thus the total number of odd days = 6 + 3 or 2 odd days

This means that the 20th of June fell on 2nd day commencing from Monday.

The required day was Tuesday.

Hence, the correct option is (B).

66.

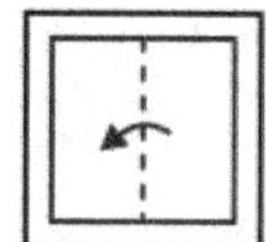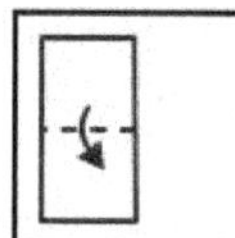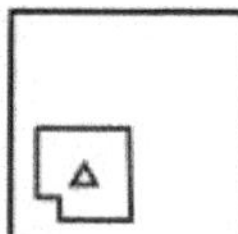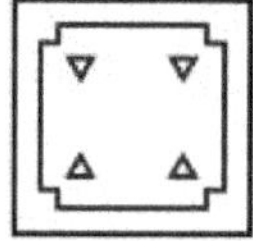

Hence, the correct option is (A).

67.

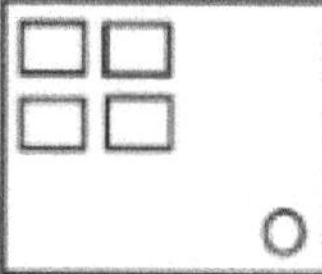

Hence, the correct option is (A).

68.

Alpha bets	A	B	C	D	E	F	G	H	I	J	K	L	M
Positional value	1	2	3	4	5	6	7	8	9	10	11	12	13
Positional value	26	25	24	23	22	21	20	19	18	17	16	15	14
Alpha bets	Z	Y	X	W	V	U	T	S	R	Q	P	0	N

Opposite letters are used in code language as:

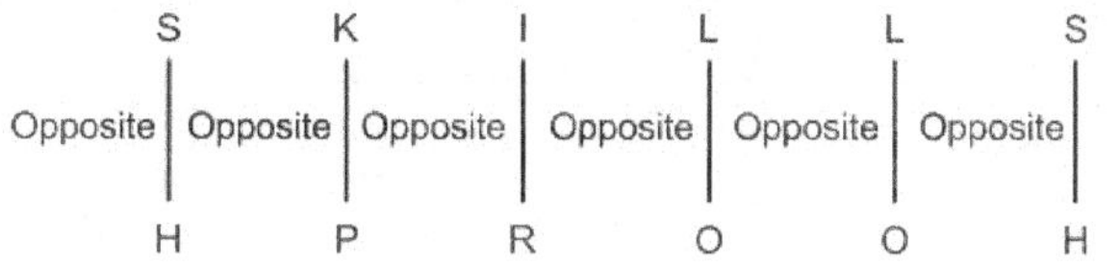

Similarly,

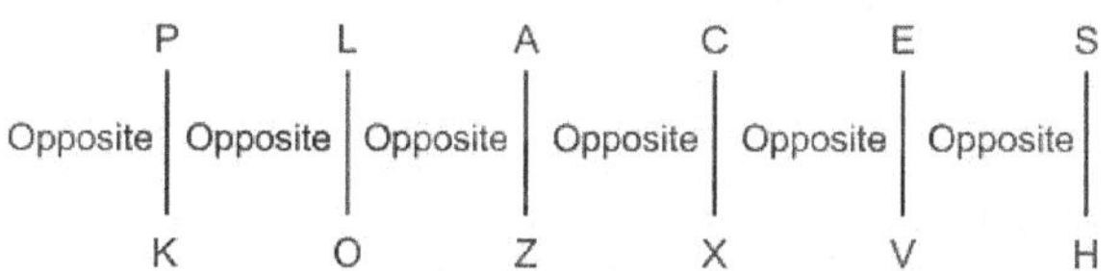

Thus, KOZXVH is the correct answer.

Hence, the correct option is (A).

69.

Alpha bets	A	B	C	D	E	F	G	H	I	J	K	L	M
Positional value	1	2	3	4	5	6	7	8	9	10	11	12	13
Positional value	26	25	24	23	22	21	20	19	18	17	16	15	14
Alpha bets	Z	Y	X	W	V	U	T	S	R	Q	P	0	N

Here, Code for consonants is their place value and code for vowels is the place value of opposite alphabet.

SECRETE is written as 1922318222022.

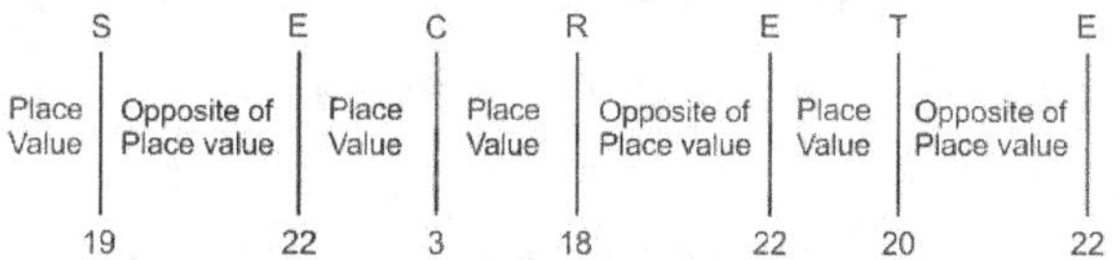

And, SOUND is written as 19126144.

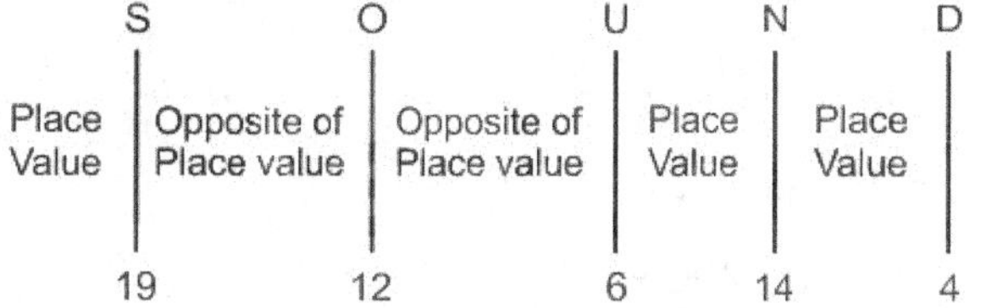

Similarly, NOISE be written in the same language-

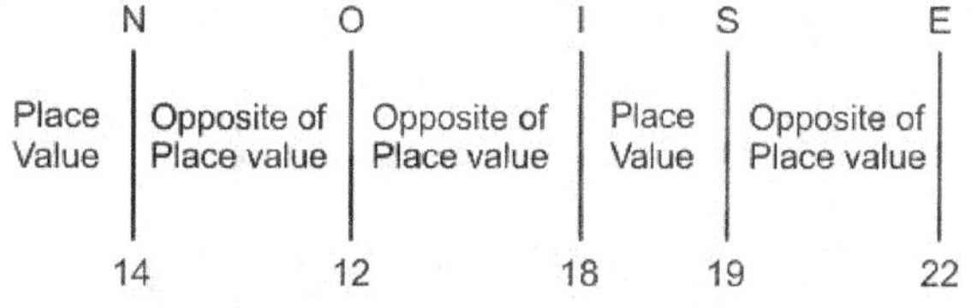

Thus, 1412181922 is the correct answer.

Hence, the correct option is (C).

70. According to the dictionary order,

Terrific → Trauma → Troll → Trouble → Truth

So, the correct option is 3, 4, 2, 5, 1.

Hence, the correct option is (C).

71. After arranging as per the dictionary order, we get:

Greasepaint → Greasy → Greater → Grebe → Grecian

So, the correct option is 3, 5, 2, 4, 1.

Hence, the correct option is (D).

72. From the following relationship diagram, Radhika is the mother of Devraj.

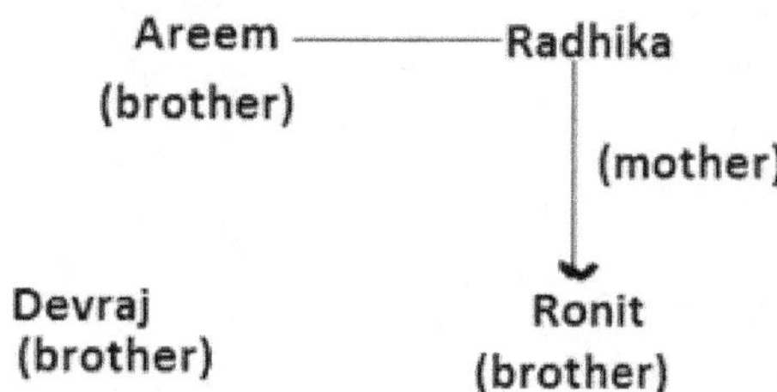

Hence, the correct option is (A).

73. By using the symbols in the table given below, we can draw the following family tree:

Symbol in Diagram	Meaning
◯	Female
☐	Male
═	Married Couple
—	Siblings
│	Difference of a generation

According to the given information,

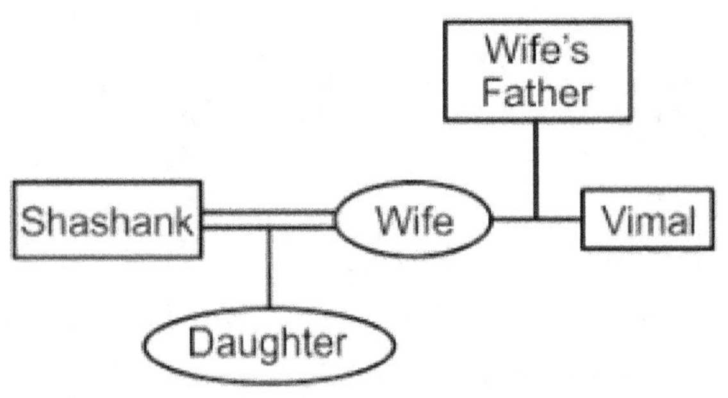

Here,

Shashank's daughter's mother → Shashank's wife ;

Shashank's wife's father → Shashank's father-in-law;

Father-in-law's son → Shashank's brother-in-law

So, Vimal is Shashank's brother-in-law.

Hence, the correct option is (B).

74. All of them except Bear belong to the cat family.

Hence, the correct option is (C).

75.

Alphabets	A	B	C	D	E	F	G	H	I	J	K	L	M
Positional value	1	2	3	4	5	6	7	8	9	10	11	12	13
Positional value	26	25	24	23	22	21	20	19	18	17	16	15	14
Alphabets	Z	Y	X	W	V	U	T	S	R	Q	P	O	N

The pattern followed here is,

D - 4 = Z, Z - 4 = V, V - 4 = R

G - 4 = C, C - 4 = Y, Y - 4 = U

Q - 4 = M, M - 4 = I, I - 3 = F

R - 4 = N, N - 4 = J, J - 4 = F

Hence, the correct option is (C).

76. The listed price that means the marked price of the article is Rs. 7600.
Discount = 10%.
After 10% discount price became = $\left(\frac{90}{100}\right)$ × 7600 = 6840
The final selling price is 5814.
2nd discount = (6840 - 5814) = 1026
The additional discount is given on the price Rs. 6840 = $\left(\frac{1026}{6840}\right)$ × 100 = 15%
∴ 15% additional discount must be given to bring the net selling price to Rs. 5,814.
Hence, the correct option is (C).

77. Average of A, B, C, D and E is 40 years.

So, $\frac{A+B+C+D+E}{5} = 40$

$A + B + C + D + E = 200$

$A + B = 70$

$C + D = 84$

$E = 200 - 70 - 84$

$= 200 - 154$

$= 46$

Hence, the correct option is (A).

78. Growth of CO_2 from power sector during 2005 to $2009 = 800 - 500 = 300$ (Just take values of 2009 and 2005 and subtract them)

Percentage growth $= \left\{\frac{(Value\ in\ 2009)-(Value\ in\ 2005)}{(Value\ in\ 2005)}\right\} \times 100\%$

Percentage growth $= \frac{(800-500)}{500} \times 100\%$

$= \frac{300}{500} \times 100 = 60\%$

Hence, the correct option is (A).

79. Percentage Growth: $= \left\{\frac{(Value\ in\ 2009)-(Value\ in\ 2005)}{(Value\ in\ 2005)}\right\} \times 100\%$

Power: $\% = \frac{(800-500)}{500} \times 100 = 60\%$

Industry: $\% = \frac{(450-200)}{200} \times 100 = 125\%$

Commercial: $\% = \frac{(320-150)}{150} \times 100 = 113\%$

Agriculture: $\% = \frac{(200-80)}{80} \times 100 = 150\%$

Domestic: $\% = \frac{(180-100)}{100} \times 100 = 80\%$

So, the maximum growth in CO_2 is Agriculture.

Hence, the correct option is (D).

80. Total emissions of CO_2 in $2005 = 500 + 200 + 150 + 80 + 100 = 1030$

Total emissions of CO_2 in $2009 = 800 + 450 + 320 + 200 + 180 = 1950$

Percentage growth $= \left\{\frac{(Value\ in\ 2009)-(Value\ in\ 2005)}{(Value\ in\ 2005)}\right\} \times 100\%$

$\%$ increased $= \frac{(1950-1030)}{1030} \times 100 = 89.32\%$

Hence, the correct option is (A).

81. In 2005 to 2006: $\frac{100}{500} \times 100 = 20\%$

In 2006 to 2007: $\frac{50}{600} \times 100 = 8.33\%$

In 2007 to 2008: $\dfrac{50}{650} \times 100 = 7.69\%$

In 2008 to 2009: $\dfrac{100}{700} \times 100 = 14.28\%$

Average Annual growth rate $= \dfrac{50.30}{4} = 12.57\%$

Hence, the correct option is (A).

82. % contribution of the power sector to total CO_2 emissions in the year $2008 = \dfrac{700}{1700} \times 100 = 41.18\%$

Hence, the correct option is (B).

83. As we know,

If a person completes a piece of work in 'n' days, then work of 1 day is $\dfrac{1}{n}$ part of work.

Time taken by Ganesh and Bhima complete a work $= 6$ days

The part of the work that is completed by Ganesh and Bhima in 1 day $= \dfrac{1}{6}$

Time taken by Ganesh to complete a work $= 10$ days

The part of work that is completed by Ganesh in 1 day $= \dfrac{1}{10}$

Now, we first find the part of work completed by Bhima in 1 day

$= \dfrac{1}{6} - \dfrac{1}{10}$

$= \dfrac{(10-6)}{60}$

$= \dfrac{4}{60}$

$= \dfrac{1}{15}$

$\therefore$ Bhima completes the whole work in 15 days.

Hence, the correct option is (D).

84. Let the number be x.

$\left(\dfrac{1}{5}\right) \times \left(\dfrac{3}{4}\right) \times \left(\dfrac{1}{3}\right) \times x = 24$

$\Rightarrow x = 24 \times 20$

$\Rightarrow x = 480$

So, 20% of $x = \left(\dfrac{20}{100}\right) \times 480 = 96$

$\therefore$ The required number is 96.

Hence, the correct option is (C).

85. Given:

Mahesh is 6 years older than Suresh.

Let be assume the age of Mahesh and Suresh is 9x and 7x respectively.

$\Rightarrow$ 9x - 7x = 6

$\Rightarrow$ 2x = 6

$\Rightarrow$ x = 3

$\Rightarrow$ Age of Mahesh = 3 × 9

= 27 years

$\therefore$ The required result will be 27 years.

Hence, the correct option is (C).

86. Let the given triangle be $\triangle ABC$, as shown below,

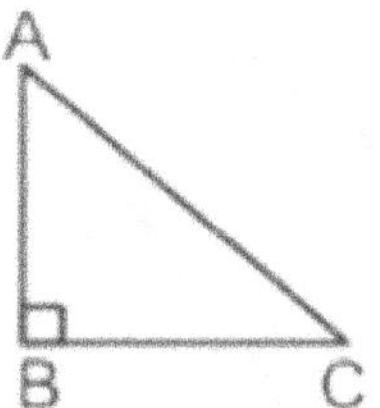

$\Rightarrow BC = $ base $= (u^2 - v^2)$

$\Rightarrow AC = $ hypotenuse $= (u^2 + v^2)$

According to Pythagoras theorem,

$(AC)^2 = (AB)^2 + (BC)^2$

$\Rightarrow (u^2 + v^2)^2 = (AB)^2 + (u^2 - v^2)^2$

$\Rightarrow u^4 + v^4 + 2u^2v^2 = (AB)^2 + u^4 + v^4 - 2u^2v^2$

$\Rightarrow (AB)^2 = 4u^2v^2$

$\Rightarrow AB = 2uv$

Now,

Area of triangle $= \dfrac{1}{2} \times$ base $\times$ heigh

$\dfrac{1}{2} \times BC \times AB = 2016$

$\Rightarrow (u^2 - v^2) \times uv = 2016$

$\Rightarrow uv(u + v)(u - v) = 32 \times 7 \times 9$

We can write,

$uv(u + v)(u - v) = 16 \times 9\sqrt{2} \times 7\sqrt{2}$

Thus, we get, $u = 8\sqrt{2}$ and $v = \sqrt{2}$

$\therefore$ Perimeter of triangle:

$= AB + BC + AC = 2uv + u^2 - v^2 + u^2 + v^2$

$= 2uv + 2u^2 = 32 + 256 = 288$ units

Hence, the correct option is (B).

87. Given,

a is predecessor of b.

$\therefore b = a - 1$

Now,

$a - b = a - (a - 1)$

$= a - a + 1$

$= 1$

$b - a = (a - 1) - a$

$= a - a - 1$

$= -1$

So, the value of $(a - b)$ and $(b - a)$ are 1 and -1.

Hence, the correct option is (B).

88. Given:

Rishu saves $x\%$ of her income

Increase in her income $= 26\%$

Increase in her expenditure $= 20\%$

Increase in saving $= 50\%$

As we know,

Income $=$ Saving $+$ Expenditure

Let income of Rishu be 100

Saving of Rishu $= 100 \times \left(\dfrac{x}{100}\right)$

$= x$

Expenditure of Rishu $= 100 - x$

Rishu's salary after increment $= 100 \times \left(\dfrac{126}{100}\right)$

$= 126$

Rishu's expenditure after increment $= (100 - x) \times \dfrac{120}{100}$

$= (100 - x) \times \dfrac{6}{5}$

New Saving $= 126 - (100 - x) \times \dfrac{6}{5} \dots (i)$

New saving after increment $= x \times \dfrac{150}{100}$

New saving after increment $= \dfrac{3x}{2} \dots (ii)$

From equation (i) and equation (ii)

$\Rightarrow 126 - (100 - x) \times \dfrac{6}{5} = \dfrac{3x}{2}$

$\Rightarrow 126 - 120 + \dfrac{6x}{5} = \dfrac{3x}{2}$

$\Rightarrow 6 = \left(\dfrac{3x}{2}\right) - \left(\dfrac{6x}{5}\right)$

$\Rightarrow 6 = \dfrac{(15x - 12x)}{10}$

$\Rightarrow x = 20$

$\therefore$ The value of x is 20.

Hence, the correct option is (C).

89. Given:

Length of road = 1200 m

Time taken to cross a road = 10 min

Formula Used:

Speed $= \dfrac{Distance}{Time}$

Speed $= \dfrac{1200 \times 60}{10 \times 1000} = 7.2$ km/hr

$\therefore$ The speed of the person is 7.2 km/hr.

Hence, the correct option is (D).

90. Given:

A person divides a certain amount among his three sons in the ratio $= 3 : 4 : 5$

If he had divided this amount in the ratio $= \dfrac{1}{3} : \dfrac{1}{4} : \dfrac{1}{5}$

The person who had got the lowest share earlier would get Rs. 1188 more

Let money get by first, second and third son be $3x$, $4x$ and $5x$ respectively

Total share $= 3x + 4x + 5x = 12x$

Here first son got minimum share $= 3x$

If person had divided total amount in the ratio $= \dfrac{1}{3} : \dfrac{1}{4} : \dfrac{1}{5}$

LCM of 3, 4 and $5 = 60$

Ratio of First, second and third $= \left(\dfrac{1}{3}\right) \times 60 : \left(\dfrac{1}{4}\right) \times 60 : \left(\dfrac{1}{5}\right) \times 60$

$= 20 : 15 : 12$

Share of first student $= \left(\dfrac{12x}{47}\right) \times 20$

$= \dfrac{240x}{47}$

According to the question,

$\Rightarrow \left(\dfrac{240x}{47}\right) - (3x) = 1188$

$\Rightarrow \dfrac{(240x - 141x)}{47} = 1188$

$$\Rightarrow \frac{99x}{47} = 1188$$

$$\Rightarrow x = 12 \times 47$$

$$\Rightarrow x = 564$$

Total amount $= 12x$

$$= 12 \times 564$$

$$= \text{Rs. } 6768$$

∴ The total amount is Rs. 6768.

Hence, the correct option is (C).

91. Rows & Columns are data organized in a spreadsheet. A column is a vertical series of cells in a chart, table, or spreadsheet. A row is the range of cells that go across (horizontal) the spreadsheet/worksheet. Rows are identified by numbers e.g. row 1, row 5.

Hence, the correct option is (C).

92. In Microsoft Word you can insert a table with up to 63 columns, that is the limit to the number of columns allowed in a Word document.

Hence, the correct option is (B).

93. Statistical calculations and preparation of tables and graphs can be done using Power Point, Notepad, Adobe Photoshop Excel.

Hence, the correct option is (B).

94. The process of arranging the items of a column in some sequence or order is known as sorting. it is the process of arranging the items of a column in some sequence or order is known as sorting.

Hence, the correct option is (C).

95. A wizard found in the Microsoft Excel program that takes users step-by-step through the process of creating a chart in Microsoft Excel. The Chart Wizard is accessible on the "Insert Menu", then you choose "Chart". See also wizard. Select a range of data, click the button and Excel produces an embedded chart.

Hence, the correct option is (D).

96. The maximum font-size available in Microsoft Word 2010 from the dropdown list is 72; however the font size can be set up to 1638 by typing the size manually for the font.

Hence, the correct option is (B).

97. Data analytics is the science of examining raw data with the purpose of drawing conclusions about that information. Data analytics is used in many industries to allow companies and organizations to make better business decisions and in the sciences to verify or disprove existing models or theories.

Hence, the correct option is (A).

98. When a web browser is launched, it will automatically open at least one web page. This is the browser's home page, which is also called its start page.

Hence, the correct option is (C).

99. Tower model Refers to a computer in which the power supply, motherboard, and mass storage devices are stacked on top of each other in a cabinet. The main advantage of tower models is that there are fewer space constraints, which makes the installation of additional storage devices easier.

Hence, the correct option is (C).

100. Wireless fidelity is the full form of Wi-Fi.

- Wi-Fi is a wireless local area network.
- It was introduced in 1997.
- It allows an electronic device to exchange data wirelessly using radio waves.
- Wi-Fi provides services in private homes, businesses, as well as in public spaces.
- Wi-Fi positioning systems use the positions of Wi-Fi hotspots to identify a device's location.

Hence, the correct option is (B).

General Awareness/Current Affairs

Q.1 Who has been appointed as the new Director-General of the Sashastra Seema Bal on June 2022?

A. Sujoy Lal Thaosen   **B.** Sanjay Arora

C. Sanjeev Sharma   **D.** Ranjeet Singh Rana

Q.2 The Buxa Tiger Reserve in West Bengal is threatened by the ongoing:

[SSC MTS, 2021]

A. Hematite mining   **B.** Magnetite mining

C. Dolomite mining   **D.** Copper mining

Q.3 Which was the venue of the 'Semicon India Conference-2022'?

A. Mumbai   **B.** New Delhi

C. Bengaluru   **D.** Chennai

Q.4 In 2022, India has nominated which dance form to be inscribed on UNESCO's intangible cultural heritage list?

A. Loor   **B.** Garba

C. Khor   **D.** Ghoomar

Q.5 What was the theme of International Girls in ICT Day 2022 which is observed annually on the fourth Thursday in April?

A. Access and safety

B. Inspiring the Next Generation

C. Case For Change, Connected Women, IoT and Tech4Girls

D. Powering Change: Women in Innovation and Creativity

Q.6 The assembly of Haryana, which hasbeen constituted after the election ofOctober, 2019 :

[HTET PGT - Computer Science, 2020]

A. 12th   **B.** 13th   **C.** 14th   **D.** 15th

Q.7 Which bank has signed an MoU with the Central Board of Direct Taxes (CBDT) and Central Board of Indirect Taxes and Customs (CBIC) for tax collection?

A. Kotak Mahindra Bank

B. Dhanlaxmi Bank

C. Federal Bank

D. DCB Bank

Q.8 Abhijit Sen, who passed away on August 29, 2022, was related to which field?

A. Geography   **B.** Psychology

C. Biology   **D.** Economics

Q.9 In which of the following national parks the eight African cheetahs is shifted?

[Delhi Forest Guard, 2020]

A. Kuno Palpur National Park

B. Jim Corbett National Park

C. Ranthambore National Park

D. Kaziranga National Park

Q.10 Which medal did Devendra Jhajharia win in World Para Athletics Grand Prix 2022?

A. Gold   **B.** Silver

C. Bronze   **D.** None of the above

Q.11 Who among the following was the chief economic advisor to the Government of India as of August 2020?

[SSC MTS, 2021]

A. Krishnamurthy Subramanian

B. Ajay Bhushan Pandey

C. Atanu Chakraborty

D. Rajeev Kumar

Q.12 Who among the following is known as the 'Gandhi of Uttarakhand'?

A. Govind Ballabh Pant

B. Hemwati Nandan Bahuguna

C. Indramani Badoni

D. Badri Dutt Pandey

Q.13 Who is known as the 'Encyclopaedia of Uttarakhand'?

A. Manglesh Dabral   **B.** Shiv Prasad Dabral

C. Viren Dangwal   **D.** Govind Chatak

Q.14 The credit for discovering the Valley of Flowers goes to:

A. William Smith   **B.** Margaret Laigi

C. Richard Holdsworth   **D.** Frank Smythe

Q.15 On 26th November, 1949, which of the following provisions of the Constitution of India came into effect?

A. Citizenship

B. Elections (Article-324)

C. Provisional Parliament

D. Fundamental Rights

[Maharashtra Public Service Commission, 2018]

A. A, B and C   **B.** B, C and D

C. A and C   **D.** A and B

Q.16 In which of the following cases did the Supreme Court of India pronounce the verdict that the basic structure of the constitution cannot be amended by the parliament?

[Maharashtra Public Service Commission, 2018]

A. Shankari Prasad vs Union of India

B. Golaknath vs State of Punjab

C. Kesavananda Bharti vs State of Kerala

D. Minerva Mills Ltd. vs Union of India

Q.17 Which model of workers' participation in Management is working in India?

A. Quality circles   **B.** Joint consultation

C. Co-determination   **D.** Self-management

Q.18 Poverty studies have been often criticized by sociologists for:

A. Taking a limited view of poverty

B. Defining it in terms of the poverty line

C. Not recognizing unequal sharing in family

D. All the above

Q.19 According to whom, 'the ideological superstructure is not merely a reflection of the economy but also in the part condition of its existence?

A. L. Althusser   **B.** A. Giddens

C. K. Marx   **D.** J. Habermas's

Q.20 Which one of the following is the most noticeable characteristic of the Mediterranean climate?
[Indian Military Academy (IMA), 2019], [Officers Training Academy (OTA), 2019]

A. Limited geographical extent

B. Dry summer

C. Dry winter

D. Moderate temperature

Q.21 Which one of the following rivers takes a 'U' turn at Namcha Barwa and enters India?
[Indian Military Academy (IMA), 2019], [Officers Training Academy (OTA), 2019]

A. Ganga   **B.** Tista

C. Barak   **D.** Brahmaputra

Q.22 Which one of the following Indian States has no international boundary?
[Indian Military Academy (IMA), 2019], [Officers Training Academy (OTA), 2019]

A. Bihar   **B.** Chhattisgarh

C. Uttarakhand   **D.** Meghalaya

Q.23 Which one of the following Novels is not written by Shailesh Matiyani?

A. Kabutarkhana   **B.** Kameene

C. Jaymala   **D.** Mahabhoj

Q.24 Who among the following has not been an editor of 'Almora Akhbar'?

A. Buddhi Ballabh Pant

B. Munshi Imtiyaz Ali

C. Jeeva Nand Joshi

D. Sri Dev Suman

Q.25 Who is the author of the book named "Man Eaters of Kumaon"?

A. Thomas Mann   **B.** Romain Rolland

C. Jim Corbett   **D.** Philip Roth

Q.26 Which of the following is/are a feature of Chhau dance?

1. Chhau is a style performed exclusively by men from the triangular area of Bihar, Bengal and Orissa.

2. The Chhau mask is made of artificial clay.

3. The Chhau dancer makes lightning body movements known as Chamak.

A. 1 and 2 only   **B.** 2 and 3 only

C. 1 and 3 only   **D.** All of the above

Q.27 Which of the following is/are a feature of Kathputli?

1. It is a form of string puppetry.

2. These puppets wear long trailing skirts and do not have legs.

3. Their costumes and headgears are designed in the medieval Rajasthani style of dress.

A. 1 and 2 only   **B.** 2 and 3 only

C. 1 and 3 only   **D.** 1, 2 and 3

Q.28 Which of the following is correct about Pavakoothu?

1. Pavakoothu is a form of Glove puppet from Tamil Nadu.

2. It came into existence during the 18th century due to the influence of Kathakali.

3. The head and the arms are carved of wood and joined together with a thick cloth, cut and stitched into a small bag.

A. 1 and 2   **B.** 2 and 3

C. 1 and 3   **D.** All of the above

Q.29 Dilwara Temple is located at:

A. Jaipur   **B.** Udaipur   **C.** Jodhpur   **D.** Mt. Abu

Q.30 Where is Patwon ki haweli located?

A. Jodhpur   **B.** Jaisalmer

C. Kota   **D.** Udaipur

Q.31 The headquarter of Rajasthan Institute of Cooperative Education and Management (RISEM) is located at:

A. Jaipur   **B.** Jaisalmer

C. Chittorgarh   **D.** Kota

Q.32 Who remained the highest-placed Indian batsman at the fourth position in the latest ICC Test rankings issued in January 2021?

A. David Warner   **B.** Kane Williamson

C. Virat Kohli   **D.** Rishabh Pant

Q.33 Who among the following cricket player has won the ICC men's ODI player of the decade award, one of the ICC Awards of the Decade?

A. Virat Kohli   **B.** Brett Lee

C. Chris Gayle   **D.** Stuart Broad

Q.34 Ishwar Pandey is related to which of the following sports?

A. Hockey   **B.** Football

C. Cricket   **D.** Badminton

Q.35 Which of the following Committee recommended for Panchayati Raj System in India?
[HSSC Canal Patwari, 2021]

A. Singhvi Committee

B. Punchhi committee

C. Balwantrai Mehta Committee

D. None of the above

Q.36 The chairmanship/presidency of the UN Security Council rotates among the Council Members-

A. Every 6 months   **B.** Every 3 months
C. Every year   **D.** Every month

Q.37 Which of the following statements relating to the International Labor Organisation (ILO) is incorrect?

A. Social security was one of the agendas of ILO when it was found.

B. In 2003, ILO launched a Global Campaign on "Social Security and Coverage for All".

C. Due to a lack of consensus, social security was not included as one of the human rights under the Universal Declaration of Human Rights (UDHR), 1948.

D. ILO mandate of extension of social security measures was restated in 1944 in the Declaration of Philadelphia to provide a basic income to all in need of such protection and comprehensive medical care.

Q.38 The International Monetary Fund (IMF) works to foster which of the following?

1. Global monetary cooperation
2. Secure financial stability
3. Facilitate international trade
4. Reduction of poverty around the world

Select the correct answer using the code given below:

A. 1 and 2 only   **B.** 2 and 3 only
C. 1, 2 and 4 only   **D.** 1, 2, 3 and 4

Q.39 What is Vermicompost?
A. Inorganic fertilizer
B. Toxic substance
C. Organic bio fertilizer
D. Synthetic fertilizer

Q.40 In which form the chemical compound RDX is used?
A. As an composition
B. As an reactor
C. As an explosive
D. As an nuclear weapon

Q.41 Bio-chemical compounds are used as....
A. Skin Treatments   **B.** Food preservatives
C. Cooking Oils   **D.** All of the above

Q.42 Who invented the modern mercury thermometer with a standardized scale?
A. Anders Celsius
B. Galileo Galilei
C. Grand Duke
D. Daniel Gabriel Fahrenheit

Q.43 Which of the following instruments is used to determine the area of irregular plots in a map?
A. Mapometer   **B.** Cartometer
C. Segmometer   **D.** Planimeter

Q.44 Which of the following orbiters had detected water molecules on the moon surface?
A. Luna 9   **B.** Lunar Orbiter 1
C. Chandrayaan-2   **D.** Chang'e 5

Q.45 The Kalinga war caused guilt and huge penitence to Ashoka, because of which he started to used "Dhammaghosha" instead of "Bherighosha". Here, the term "Dhammaghosha" signifies which of the following?
A. Military conquest
B. Cultural annihilation
C. Conquest by regional tribes
D. Conquest by Brahmanical traditions

Q.46 Who of the following was/were economic critic/ critics of colonialism in India?
1. Dadabhai Naoroji
2. G. Subramania Iyer
3. R. C. Dutt
A. 1 only   **B.** 1 and 2 only
C. 2 and 3 only   **D.** 1,2 and 3

Q.47 Match the following:

	Provinces		Capital
A.	Central Province	1.	Patliputra
B.	Uttarapatha	2.	Toshali
C.	Prachya	3.	Taxila
D.	Dakshinapatha	4.	Suvarnagiri
E.	Avanti Rastra	5.	Ujjain

A. A(3), B(5), C(1), D(4), E(2)
B. A(1), B(4), C(3), D(5), E(2)
C. A(1), B(3), C(2), D(4), E(5)
D. A(4), B(3), C(4), D(2), E(5)

Q.48 Benjamin Netanyahu has been nominated for the 2021 Nobel Peace Prize. He is the Prime Minister of which country?
A. Israel   **B.** Turkey   **C.** Yemen   **D.** Oman

Q.49 Who has been conferred with the Swami Brahmanand Award 2021?
A. Anand Kumar
B. Asha Bhosle
C. Dr Rajendra Kishore Panda
D. P Sainath

Q.50 The Abel Prize for 2021 was jointly awarded to___.
A. Prof. Shankar Balasubramanian and Prof. David Klenerman
B. László Lovász and Avi Wigderson
C. Alfred V. Aho and Jeffrey David Ullman
D. Nitin Rakesh and Jerry Wind

Reasoning

Q.51 Direction: Select the related letters from the given alternatives.
EAC : KGI : : HDF : ?
A. PLN   **B.** KIJ   **C.** FBD   **D.** NJL

Q.52 Direction: Select the related word from the given alternatives.
Window : Pane : : Book : ?
A. Glass   **B.** Page   **C.** Cover   **D.** Novel

Q.53 In the following question, select the odd number pair from the given alternatives.

A. 416   **B.** 925   **C.** 257   **D.** 164

Q.54 Direction: Identify the mirror image of

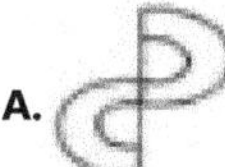 **A.** 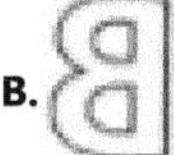 **B.**  **C.**  **D.**

Q.55 Direction: Identify the mirror image of the following figure.

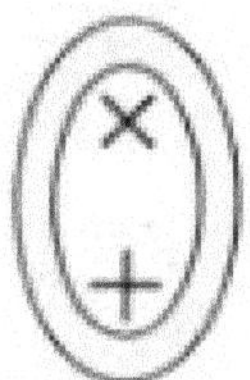

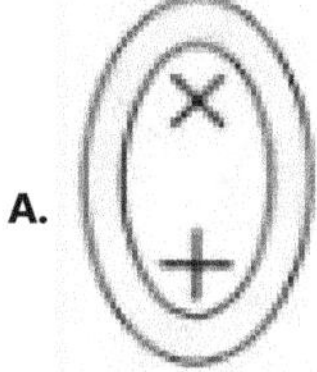 **A.**   **B.** 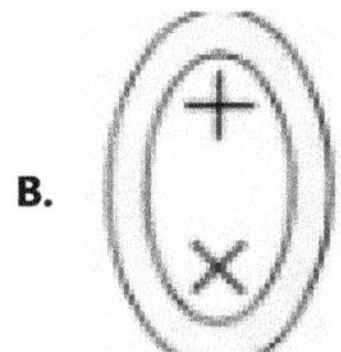

C. 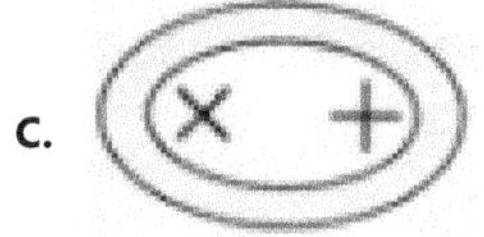   **D.** 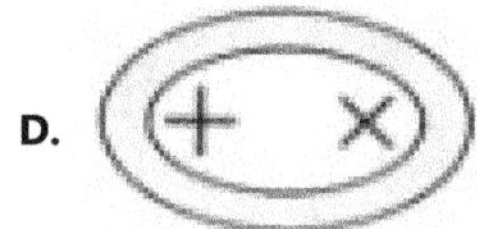

Q.56 Direction: Choose the figure from the options that would follow next in the given series.

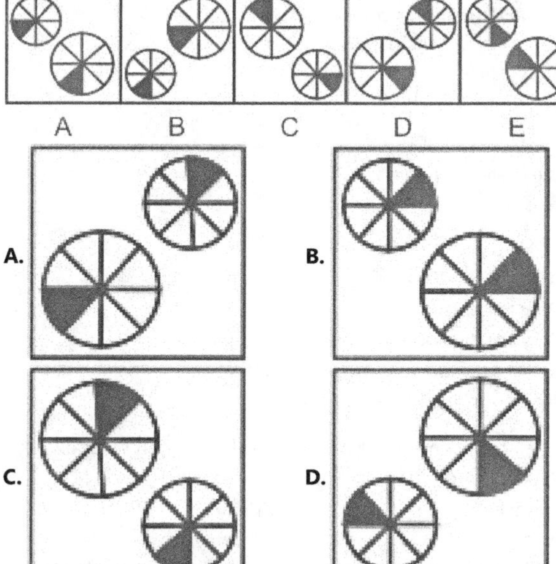

Q.57 Select the correct combination of mathematical signs to replace (*) signs and to balance the given equation.

18 * 2 * 864 * 24

A. × + =   **B.** = ÷ +   **C.** × = ÷   **D.** + = −

Q.58 Direction: From the given alternatives, select the word which CANNOT be formed using the letters of the given word.

FEARLESS

A. GRASS   **B.** RESEAL
C. LESSER   **D.** ERASE

Q.59 W introduced herself to U by saying that you are the daughter-in-law of my husband's father's wife. How are U and W related to each other?

A.   U is W' s husband's brother's wife
B.   U is W's husband's sister
C.   W is U's husband's sister
D.   W is U's brother's wife

Q.60 Select the Venn diagram that best represents the given set of classes.

Words, Synonyms, Antonymous

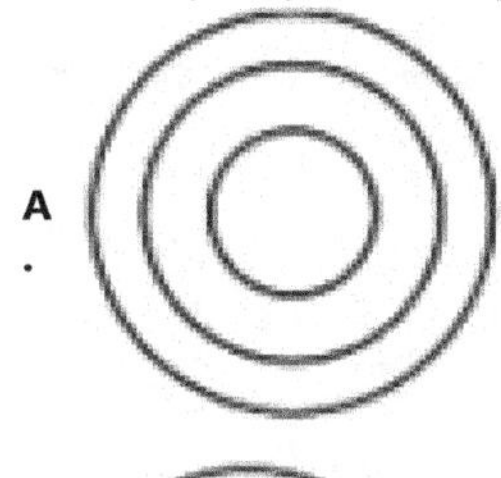 

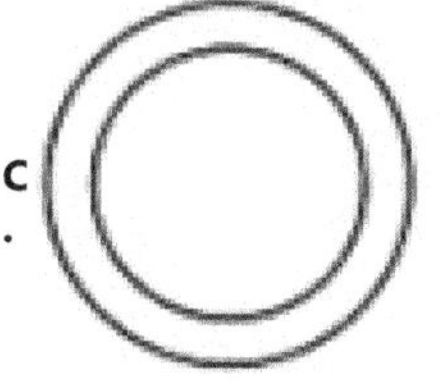 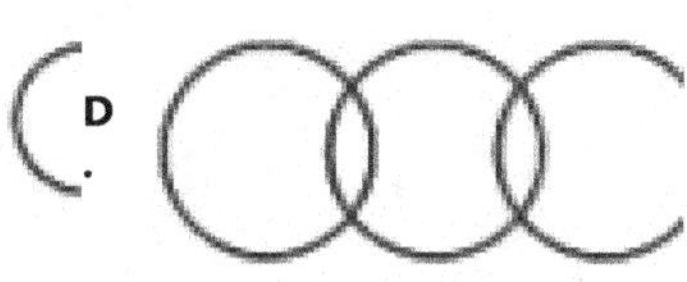

Q.61 Direction: In the following question below are given some statements followed by some conclusions based on those statements. Taking the given statements to be true even if they seem to be at variance from commonly known facts. Read all the conclusions and then decide which of the given conclusion logically follows the given statements.

Statements:

I. Some J are M.

II. Some Q are J.

Conclusions:

I. No M is Q.

II. Some M are J.

A.   Both conclusion I and II follows
B.   Neither conclusion follows
C.   Only conclusion II follows
D.   Only conclusion I follows

Q.62 Select the option that is true about the Statements and Conclusions given:

Statements:

All A's are B.

Some B's are D.

Some A's are C.

Some E's are B's as well as D's.

Conclusions:

i. Some C's are B.

ii. Some E's are A.

A. If only conclusion I follows

B. If only conclusion II follows

C. If both conclusion I and II follows

D. If none of the conclusion I and II follows

Q.63 Direction: Which number will replace the question mark (?) in the following series?

$$17, 51, 58, 116, 123, 123, ?$$

[SSC Sub Inspector (CPO), 2020]

A. 150 **B.** 120 **C.** 130 **D.** 140

Q.64 Direction: Which number will replace the question mark (?) in the following series?

$$2430, ?, 270, 90, 30, 10$$

[SSC Sub Inspector (CPO), 2020]

A. 800 **B.** 805 **C.** 810 **D.** 540

Q.65 From the given answer figures, select the one in which question figure is hidden/embedded. (rotation is not allowed).

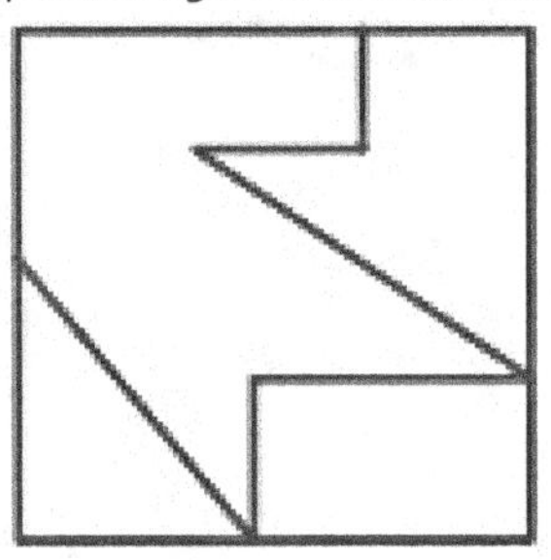

A.

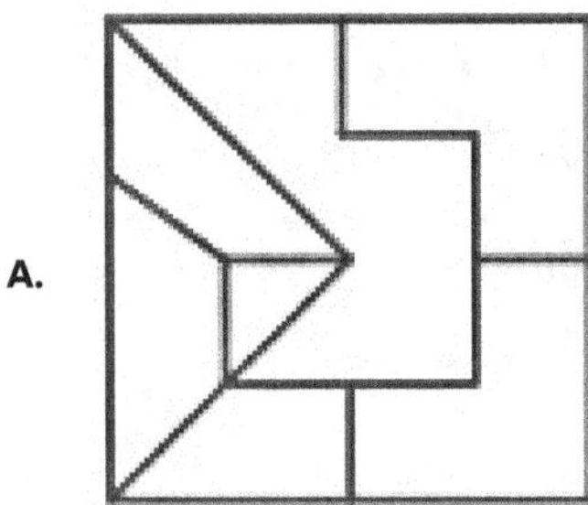

B.

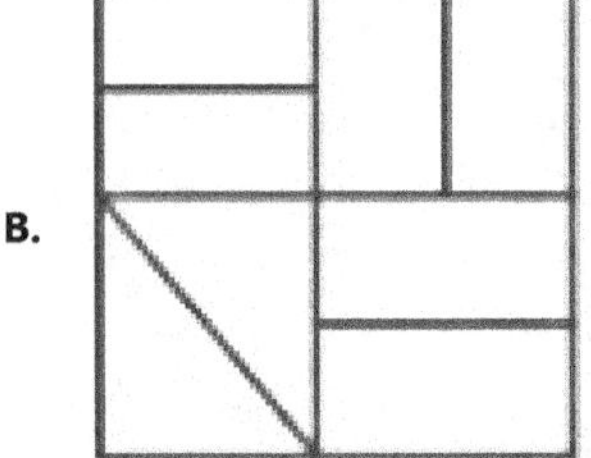

C.

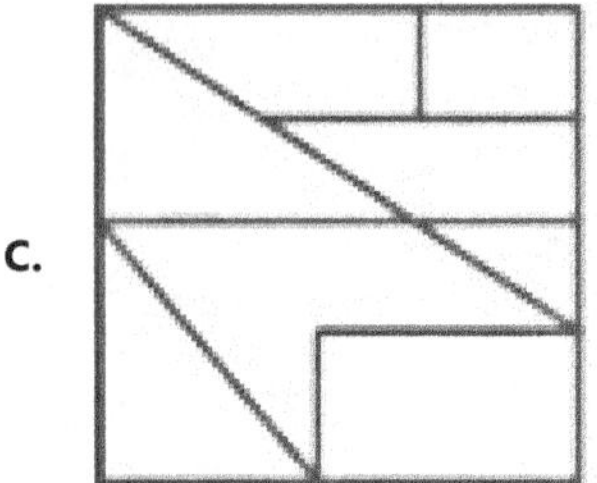

D.

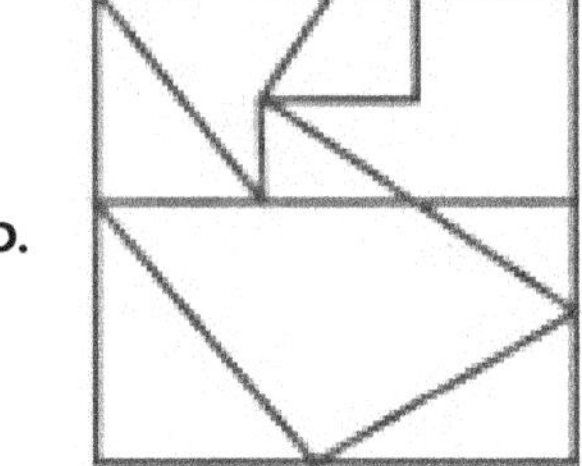

Q.66 Which of the answer figure is not made up only by the components of the question figure?

Question figure :

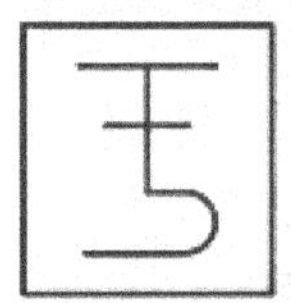

Answer figures :

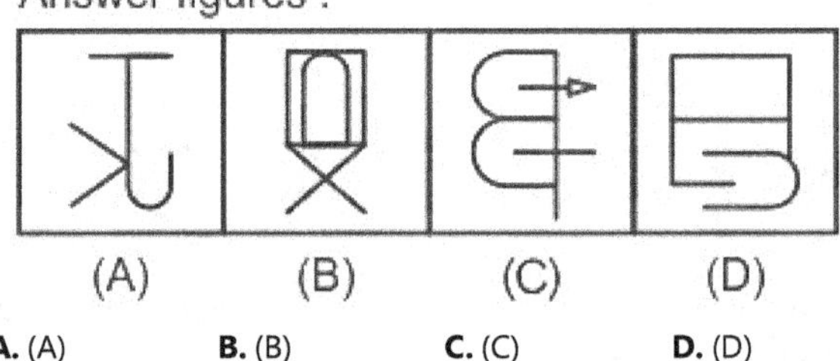

(A) (B) (C) (D)

A. (A) **B.** (B) **C.** (C) **D.** (D)

Q.67 Direction: In this question, two statements are given followed by two conclusions. Choose the conclusion(s) which best fit(s) logically.

Statements:

1) Some cups are books.

2) Some books are shirts.

Conclusions:

I. Some cups are shirts.

II. All shirts are books.

A. Only conclusion II follows

B. Only conclusion I follows

C. Neither conclusion I nor II follows

D. Both conclusions I and II follow

Q.68 If 27th December 2009 was a Thursday, then what day of the week was it on 1st March 2010?

A. Thursday **B.** Friday

C. Sunday **D.** Monday

Q.69 A piece of paper is folded and punched as shown below in the question figures. From the given answer figures, indicate how it will appear when opened?

 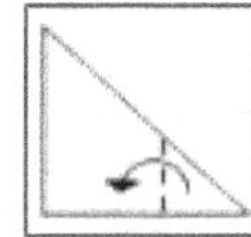 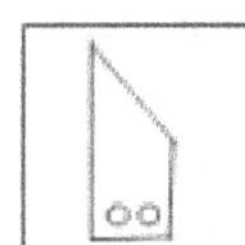

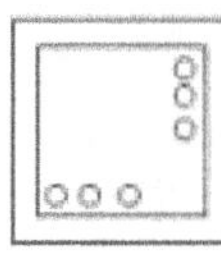 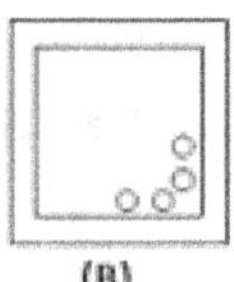

(A)   (B)

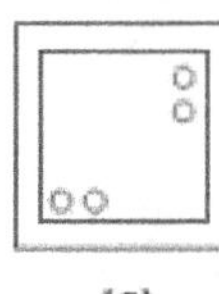 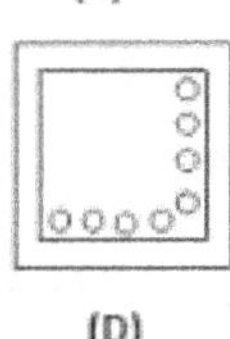

(C)   (D)

A. A   **B.** B   **C.** C   **D.** D

Q.70 In a code language, If STIMULI is written as 7 INFORMATION is written as 11, then how will GRANULES be written in the same language?

[SSC Selection Post Phase IX, 2020]

A. 17   **B.** 8   **C.** 12   **D.** 9

Q.71 In a code language, if CLOSURE is written as 312151921185, then how will INFLUENCE be written in the same language?

[SSC Selection Post Phase IX, 2020]

A. 9146122151435   **B.** 9136122151335
C. 8146122051435   **D.** 1847122151435

Q.72 Direction: Read the following information carefully and answer the questions given below it.

(i) Govind is shorter than Ashish but taller than Kamal.

(ii) Naren is shorter than Kamal.

(iii) Jayant is taller than Naren.

(iv) Ashish is taller than Jayant.

Who among them is the shortest?

[RRB (NTPC), 2017]

A. Ashish   **B.** Govind   **C.** Kamal   **D.** Naren

Q.73 Four letter-clusters have been given, out of which three are alike in some manner and one is different. Select the letter cluster that is different.

[SSC CGL, 2021]

A. *FBXT*   **B.** *TPLH*   **C.** *CYUQ*   **D.** *NJFA*

Q.74 Renu starts from a point and walks for 10 km towards East, she then turns towards her right and walks for 5 km. She again turns towards her left and walks 10 km and then turns right and walks for 5 km and stops. In which direction is the final point from the initial point?

A. South-North   **B.** South-East
C. North-East   **D.** North-West

Q.75 From the given alternatives, find the word which can be formed from the letters used in the given word.
ANECDOTAL
A. FATAL   **B.** DENTAL
C. ANTIDOTAL   **D.** ANCIPITAL

Numerical Ability

Q.76 A person borrows certain amount of money at the rate of 2.5% per month. If he pays Rs. 13110 after 6 months to clear his dues then find the amount of interest paid by the person.
A. Rs. 1840   **B.** Rs. 1690   **C.** Rs. 1710   **D.** Rs. 1660

Q.77 Two pipes A and B can fill a tank in 15 hours and 18 hours, respectively. Both pipes are opened simultaneously to fill the tank. In how many hours will the empty tank be filled?

[SSC Sub Inspector (CPO), 2020]

A. $7\frac{2}{11}$ **B.** $9\frac{2}{11}$ **C.** $10\frac{2}{11}$ **D.** $8\frac{2}{11}$

Q.78 In how many ways can the letters of the word SOFTWARE be arranged so that all the vowels be together?

[UP Police Sub Inspector, 2017]

A. 102   **B.** 360
C. 4320   **D.** None of the above

Q.79 A boatman rows 1.5 km against the stream for 17.25 minutes and down the stream in 8.5 min. What is the speed of man in still water?

A. 8 kmps   **B.** 2.2 mps   **C.** 16 kmph   **D.** 4 kmph

Q.80 If $15 - 15 \div 15 \times 6 = x$, then x is:

[Jawahar Navodaya Entrance Class VI, 2020]

A. 6   **B.** 0   **C.** 9   **D.** 84

Q.81 $\frac{3}{8} \div \left(\frac{5}{3} - \frac{1}{6}\right) + \frac{5}{8}$ equals:

[Jawahar Navodaya Entrance Class VI, 2020]

A. $\frac{3}{8}$ **B.** $2\frac{5}{8}$ **C.** $\frac{7}{8}$ **D.** $1\frac{1}{8}$

Ques (82-86):Direction: The table below shows the number of students admitted to different colleges I, II, III, IV and V in a particular session in various disciplines. Refer to the table below to answer the questions:

Colleges	Discipline Capacity				
	MBA	B.Tech	B.Sc.	B.Com.	B.A.
	200	200	400	300	500
I	185	200	312	281	486
II	190	183	348	215	414
III	198	191	364	291	484
IV	170	178	178	199	429
V	167	199	377	276	412

Q.82 What is the total percentage of seats vacant in college III against its total capacity?
A. 6.8%   **B.** 5.3%   **C.** 3.9%   **D.** 4.5%

Q.83 What is the difference in the percentage of students admitted in M.B.A. of Colleges II and IV?

A. 10%   **B.** 12%   **C.** 15%   **D.** 20%

Q.84 Which of the following colleges has the highest number of vacant seats in B.Com. and B.A. discipline?

A. II   **B.** III   **C.** IV   **D.** V

Q.85 What is the approximate difference between the percentage of students admitted to a discipline in respective colleges showing the lowest admission to B.Sc. and the highest admission in B.A.

A. 19%   **B.** 25%   **C.** 34%   **D.** 29%

Q.86 How many seats in all disciplines taken together are vacant in colleges II and III?

A. 278   **B.** 322
C. 612   **D.** None of these

Q.87 $x^3 + x^2 + 16$ is exactly divisible by x, where x is a positive integer. The number of all such possible values of x is:
[Indian Military Academy (IMA), 2020]

A. 3   **B.** 4   **C.** 5   **D.** 6

Q.88 The value of $\dfrac{40 - \frac{3}{4} \text{ of } 32}{37 - \frac{3}{4} \text{ of } (34 - 6)}$ is :
[SSC Sub Inspector (CPO), 2020]

A. 0   **B.** $\frac{-1}{2}$ **C.** 1   **D.** $\frac{1}{2}$

Q.89 A can do a piece of work in 10 days and B can do it in 15 days. Number of days to complete the work if they work together is:

A. 6 days   **B.** 9 days   **C.** 7 days   **D.** 5 days

Q.90 A mixture contains milk and water in the ratio $9:8$. If 10 liters of water is added to it, the ratio of milk and water becomes $51:47$. Find the original quantity of milk in the mixture.

A. 306 liters   **B.** 272liters
C. 282 liters   **D.** 305 liters

Computer Awareness

Q.91 Press _______ key to open the help window in MS Word 2007 document.

A. F1   **B.** F2   **C.** F9   **D.** F11

Q.92 MS Office, Photoshop and Animagic are examples of:
A. Device driver
B. Application software
C. System software
D. Operating system

Q.93 Which among the following software is not a product of Microsoft?
A. OpenOffice
B. Outlook
C. Access
D. Visual studio express

Q.94 Assigning names to text or to positions in an MS Word document is called _______.
A. Word Count   **B.** Bookmark
C. Named word   **D.** Cross-reference

Q.95 Which of the following term is related with legends in MS Excel?
A. Clipart   **B.** Wood art   **C.** Operator   **D.** Chart

Q.96 The sections within a document that appear in the top and the bottom margins are known as:
A. Scroll bars
B. Header and Footer
C. Quick Access Toolbar and Status bar
D. Ruler and Taskbar

Q.97 What is the number one concern about cloud computing?
A. Too expensive   **B.** Security concerns
C. Too many platforms   **D.** Accessibility

Q.98 Which of the following is a scientific computing language?
A. BASIC   **B.** COBOL
C. FORTRAN   **D.** PASCAL

Q.99 One who gains unauthorized access, destroys vital data, denies legitimate user's service or causes problems for their targets is called-
[Madhya Pradesh Public Service Commission (MPPSC), 2019]
A. White Hat Hacker
B. Cracker
C. Programmer
D. Database Administrator

Q.100 A high-speed internet connection or wideband transmission is known as:
A. Dial-up Network   **B.** Digital transmission
C. Wide Area Network   **D.** Broadband Network

// Smart Answer Sheet //

Correct — Indicates percentage of students who answered questions correctly.

Skipped — Indicates percentage of students who skipped questions.

Q.	Ans.	Correct / Skipped	Q.	Ans.	Correct / Skipped	Q.	Ans.	Correct / Skipped	Q.	Ans.	Correct / Skipped	Q.	Ans.	Correct / Skipped
1	A	86.63 % / 11.92 %	17	B	76.54 % / 19.26 %	33	A	84.34 % / 12.45 %	49	A	44.82 % / 30.39 %	65	C	76.36 % / 22.76 %
2	C	12.34 % / 84.22 %	18	D	40.79 % / 44.73 %	34	C	82.25 % / 16.77 %	50	B	61.7 % / 35.59 %	66	C	76.77 % / 22.6 %
3	C	61.37 % / 31.93 %	19	A	21.53 % / 72.78 %	35	C	46.2 % / 43.4 %	51	D	64.43 % / 34.83 %	67	C	59.85 % / 37.28 %
4	B	64.36 % / 34.68 %	20	B	67.54 % / 30.05 %	36	D	56.59 % / 34.08 %	52	B	68.94 % / 30.75 %	68	B	40.88 % / 39.37 %
5	A	89.54 % / 10.05 %	21	D	80.29 % / 17.94 %	37	C	27.66 % / 69.96 %	53	C	51.43 % / 30.99 %	69	D	17.96 % / 70.06 %
6	C	50.77 % / 47.03 %	22	B	66.33 % / 32.88 %	38	D	42.67 % / 36.79 %	54	B	67.3 % / 30.62 %	70	B	81.64 % / 11.81 %
7	B	56.89 % / 42.39 %	23	C	40.56 % / 30.02 %	39	C	79.83 % / 19.65 %	55	A	14.39 % / 69.28 %	71	A	61.27 % / 36.31 %
8	D	81.05 % / 11.7 %	24	D	16.64 % / 75.48 %	40	C	52.6 % / 47.21 %	56	D	48.96 % / 44.95 %	72	D	58.9 % / 34.8 %
9	A	83.9 % / 13.28 %	25	C	52.24 % / 39.55 %	41	D	83.29 % / 10.37 %	57	C	54.75 % / 31.01 %	73	D	69.88 % / 30.01 %
10	B	88.24 % / 10.64 %	26	C	59.86 % / 32.81 %	42	D	54.52 % / 37.83 %	58	A	81.17 % / 16.69 %	74	B	56.69 % / 34.17 %
11	A	12.15 % / 83.41 %	27	D	27.02 % / 72.18 %	43	D	54.93 % / 41.4 %	59	A	47.08 % / 44.67 %	75	B	69.48 % / 30.45 %
12	C	87.51 % / 12.42 %	28	B	50.15 % / 49.46 %	44	C	64.03 % / 30.22 %	60	B	60.87 % / 38.46 %	76	C	69.59 % / 30.19 %
13	B	47.0 % / 37.58 %	29	D	80.93 % / 15.39 %	45	B	64.68 % / 31.87 %	61	C	88.46 % / 10.43 %	77	D	65.01 % / 30.92 %
14	D	62.08 % / 37.19 %	30	B	46.88 % / 49.8 %	46	D	84.87 % / 10.43 %	62	A	51.09 % / 43.83 %	78	C	40.09 % / 41.72 %
15	A	41.39 % / 39.53 %	31	A	80.64 % / 14.65 %	47	C	42.39 % / 32.41 %	63	C	88.8 % / 10.92 %	79	B	68.76 % / 31.0 %
16	C	44.28 % / 51.53 %	32	C	81.04 % / 11.58 %	48	A	67.73 % / 31.95 %	64	C	50.46 % / 47.72 %	80	C	50.74 % / 48.72 %

Q.	Ans.	Correct		Q.	Ans.	Correct		Q.	Ans.	Correct		Q.	Ans.	Correct		Q.	Ans.	Correct
		Skipped				Skipped				Skipped				Skipped				Skipped
81	C	47.44 %		85	B	52.0 %		89	A	85.86 %		93	A	83.38 %		97	B	18.17 %
		43.74 %				31.68 %				13.79 %				11.37 %				77.89 %
82	D	77.15 %		86	B	59.94 %		90	A	44.88 %		94	B	52.07 %		98	C	69.26 %
		21.02 %				37.41 %				47.27 %				38.57 %				30.66 %
83	A	77.8 %		87	C	65.02 %		91	A	89.97 %		95	D	13.61 %		99	B	11.61 %
		12.43 %				34.06 %				10.02 %				67.6 %				78.95 %
84	C	79.67 %		88	C	47.38 %		92	B	83.71 %		96	B	52.99 %		100	D	25.07 %
		12.51 %				47.86 %				12.86 %				38.11 %				73.49 %

Performance Analysis

Avg. Score (%)	41.0%
Toppers Score (%)	74.0%
Your Score	

//Hints and Solutions//

1. Sujoy Lal Thaosen has been recently appointed as the new Director-General of the Sashastra Seema Bal.

New Delhi, June 2022 (PTI) IPS officer Sujoy Lal Thaosen took charge as the new director-general (DG) of the Sashastra Seema Bal (SSB), which guards Indian frontiers with Nepal and Bhutan. Thaosen, a 1988-batch Indian Police Service (IPS) officer of the Madhya Pradesh cadre, was handed over the baton by officiating DG and ITBP chief Sanjay Arora at the headquarters of the force in R K Puram.

Hence, the correct option is (A).

2. The Buxa Tiger Reserve in West Bengal is threatened by the ongoing dolomite mining.

Dolomite:

- Dolomite is a mineral found in various parts of Madhya Pradesh and West Bengal.
- It is used extensively in steel making industry.
- Dolomite makes the iron less rigid.
- Dolomite is used as a substitute for Limestone in the cement making industry.

Hence, the correct option is (C).

3. Prime Minister Narendra Modi inaugurated Semicon India Conference-2022 in Bengaluru. The consumption of semiconductors is expected to cross USD 110 billion by 2030 and India has the world's fastest-growing start-up ecosystem. It was organized by India Semiconductor Mission in partnership with industry associations. India Semiconductor Mission (ISM) is an Independent Business Division within Digital India Corporation having administrative and financial autonomy to formulate strategies for developing the semiconductor ecosystem.

Hence, the correct option is (C).

4. India has nominated the dance form Garba to be inscribed on UNESCO's intangible cultural heritage list in 2022.

In 2021, 'Durga Puja' was included in the UNESCO intangible cultural heritage representative.

India was elected by UNESCO to serve on the distinguished Intergovernmental Committee of the 2003 Convention for the Safeguarding of the Intangible Cultural Heritage in July 2022.

Hence, the correct option is (B).

5. The theme of International Girls in ICT Day 2022 was Access and Safety. It is celebrated every year on the fourth Thursday in April. International Girls in ICT Day aims to inspire a global movement to increase the representation of girls and women in technology.

Hence, the correct option is (A).

6. The 14th assembly of Haryana, which has been constituted after the election of October, 2019.

The results were announced on 24 October 2019. The Bharatiya Janata Party emerged as the single largest party and formed the government in a post-poll alliance with the Jannayak Janta Party and seven Independent MLAs.

Hence, the correct option is (C).

7. Dhanlaxmi Bank has signed a pact with the Central Board of Direct Taxes (CBDT) and Central Board of Indirect Taxes and Customs (CBIC) for tax collection on April 2022. This MoU will help customers to pay their direct taxes and GST payments and other indirect taxes through the branch network and digital platforms of the bank. The bank has been authorized by the Reserve Bank of India (RBI) based on a recommendation from the Controller General of Accounts for the collection of various taxes.

Hence, the correct option is (B).

8. Abhijit Sen, one of India's leading agricultural economists passed away on August 29, 2022 at the age of 72. Abhijit Sen was a member of the Planning Commission of India from 2004 to 2014 during the tenure of former Prime Minister Manmohan Singh.

Hence, the correct option is (D).

9. Eight African cheetahs from Namibia in South Africa have been relocated to Kuno Palpur National Park in Madhya Pradesh.

After the Cheetahs arrive in the National Park, they will stay in smaller enclosures during the quarantine phase before being shifted to the bigger ones. From 1952 onwards, cheetahs gradually started becoming extinct in India, then in 2009 the 'African Cheetah Introduction Project in India' was started.

Hence, the correct option is (A).

10. Indian javelin thrower, Devendra Jhajharia has clinched a silver medal in the World Para Athletics Grand Prix 2022 in Morocco.

Paralympics gold medalist Devendra Jhajharia threw the javelin to a distance of 60.97 meters to capture the silver. He is a three-time Paralympics medalist.

Hence, the correct option is (B).

11. Krishnamurthy Subramanian was the chief economic advisor to the Government of India as of August 2020.

The government of India appointed Krishnamurthy Subramanian as the Chief Economic Advisor (CEA) on 7 December 2018. He is the 17th Chief Economic Adviser to the Government of India. He will have a tenure of three years. He is currently working as an Associate Professor at the Indian School of Business (ISB), Hyderabad. He also serves on the boards of Bandhan Bank, the National Institute of Bank Management, and the RBI Academy.

Hence, the correct option is (A).

12. Indramani Badoni is a politician, freedom fighter and social activist from Uttarakhand.

- He was born on 25th December 1924 in the Akhodi village of Tehri Garhwal.
- He is best known for his leading role in the Uttarakhand statehood movement.
- He was the architect of the 1994 state movement.

- He is popularly called the 'Gandhi of Uttarakhand' due to his practice of non-violence and satyagraha.

- He was a founding member of the regional political party Uttarakhand Kranti Dal.

- He had started the movement to make Uttarakhand a separate state.

- He was honoured with the Uttarakhand Ratna award (posthumously) in 2016.

Hence, the correct option is (C).

13. Shiv Prasad Dabral is known as the 'Encyclopaedia of Uttarakhand'. The noted historian Shiv Prasad Dabral was born on 12th November 1912 in the Pauri Garhwal district of Uttarakhand. He is the author of the monumental history of Uttarakhand in 18 volumes, 2 collections of poetry, 9 plays, and several edited volumes in Hindi and Garhwali. His Uttarakhand ka Itihaas (History of Uttarakhand) is widely used by scholars as reference work.

Hence, the correct option is (B).

14. The credit for the discovery of the Valley of Flowers goes to the British mountaineer Franks S. Smythe, R.L. Holdsworth, and Eric Shipton who incidentally reached this valley after a successful expedition of Mount Kamet in 1931. Smythe wrote the book "The Valley of Flowers" in 1938.

- The Valley of Flowers is situated in Bhyundar Valley at an elevation of 3,658 meters above sea level.

- The Valley of Flowers National Park is the second core zone of the Nanda Devi Biosphere Reserve.

- The Valley of Flowers National Park is an Indian national park, located in North Chamoli and Pithoragarh, in the state of Uttarakhand, and is known for its meadows of endemic alpine flowers and the variety of flora.

- The Valley of flowers was declared as the National Park of India in the year 1982 and it is now a UNESCO world heritage site.

Hence, the correct option is (D).

15. A, B and C all three of these provisions of the Constitution of India came into effect on 26th November, 1949.

The provisions of the constitution of India which came into effect on 26th November 1949 are below:

- Citizenship.

- Elections.

- Provisional Parliament.

- Temporary and transitional provisions.

- Short title contained in Articles 5, 6, 7, 8, 9, 60, 324, 366, 367, 379, 380, 388, 391, 392, 393.

Fundamental Rights came into effect on 26 Jan 1950.

Hence, the correct option is (A).

16. In Kesavananda Bharti vs State of Kerala case, the Supreme Court of India pronounce the verdict that the basic structure of the constitution cannot be amended by the parliament.

In the Keshavananda Bharti case, SC overruled its judgment in the Golak Nath case (1967). It upheld the validity of the 24th Amendment Act (1971) and stated that Parliament is empowered to abridge or take away any of the Fundamental Rights.

At the same time, it laid down a new doctrine of the basic structure of the constitution. The parliament reacted to it by enacting the 42nd Constitution Amendment Act, 1976, in which the Supreme Court held that the constituent power of Parliament under Article 368 does not enable it to alter the basic structure of the constitution.

Hence, the correct option is (C).

17. Joint consultation is a formal system of communication between the management of an organization and the employees' representatives used prior to making decisions affecting the workforce, usually effected through a joint consultative committee.

Hence, the correct option is (B).

18. Two classic sociological approaches to poverty and social stratification are structural-functionalism and conflict theory. Many sociologists often criticize poverty studies because they taking a limited view of poverty, defining it in terms of the poverty line, not recognizing unequal sharing in family, the division of labour and cash nexus of commercial relationships.

Hence, the correct option is (D).

19. According to L. Althusser, "the ideological superstructure is not merely a reflection of the economy but also in the part condition of its existence".

The superstructure of society includes the culture, ideology, norms and identity of the people who live there. In addition, it refers to social institutions, the political structure, and the state—or the governing system of society.

Hence, the correct option is (A).

20. The characteristics of the Mediterranean Climate includes dry and hot summer, with cold and rainy winters.

- The regions which are located in the Western Part of the Continent in the between 30-45 degrees North and South of the Equator.

- Pressure belts are anticyclonic, meaning they rotate clockwise in the Northern Hemisphere, and anti-clockwise in the Southern Hemisphere.

- Anti-cyclonic conditions are accompanied by a clearer sky.

- Rainfall isn't even but the regions with Mediterranean climate experience winter rainfalls.

- Places with Mediterranean Climate - Central Chile, California, Mediterranean Basin, Western Cape of South Africa, Western and South Australia.

Hence, the correct option is (B).

21. The river Brahmaputra originates on the Angsi Glacier which is located on the Northern Side of the Himalayas in Burang, Tibet.

- It flows as Yarlung Tsangpo River flowing into Southern Tibet, breaking through the Himalayas creating great gorges.

- Tsangpo or Brahmaputra takes a U-turn at Namcha Barwa before entering Arunachal Pradesh, where it is called Dihang or Siang River.

- Further, the Dihang river meets Dibang and Lohit Rivers at the front of the Assam Valley flowing southwest through it.

- It is here that the river is called the Brahmaputra River.

- Right Bank Tributaries of Brahmaputra - Subansiri, Kameng, Manas and Sankosh.

- Left Bank Tributaries of Brahmaputra - Burhi Dihing, Dhansari (South) and Kalang.

- Subansiri which with its origin in Tibet is an antecedent river, meaning it maintains its original pattern and course despite any changes in the underlying rock topography.

Hence, the correct option is (D).

22. Chhattisgarh is the Indian States has no international boundary.

- Other states having no international boundary include Telangana, Haryana, Jharkhand, and Madhya Pradesh.

- Bihar shares its borders with Nepal.

- Uttarakhand shares its borders with Nepal and China.

- Meghalaya shares its borders with Bangladesh.

Hence, the correct option is (B).

23. Jaymala is a novel written by the author Braj Kishore Dixit. He is also known as Brajesh.

Shailesh Matiyani is a famous Hindi writer and poet from the Indian state of Uttarakhand. He was born in the Almora district of Uttarakhand. 'Shailesh Matiyani Smriti Katha Puraskar' was started in Madhya Pradesh in his name. Kabutarkhana, Kameene, and Mahabhoj are novels written by Shailesh Matiyani.

Hence, the correct option is (C).

24. Sri Dev Suman has not been an editor of 'Almora Akhbar'. He was a social activist from the Tehri District of Uttarakhand. He was born at Jaul village patti Bamund of Tehri Garhwal.

- Almora Akhbar was the first and the only letter of Kumaon to be published continuously from 1871 to 1918.

- Almora newspaper was a contemporary of the leading English newspaper 'Pioneer'.

- During the long lifespan of 48 years, Almora newspaper was edited by Budhi Ballabh Pant, Munshi Imtiyaz Ali, Jeeva Nand Joshi, Sadanand Sanwal, Vishnu Dutt Joshi, and after 1913 Badridatta Pandey.

- After Badridatta Pandey became the editor of Almora newspaper in the year 1913, the circulation of the newspaper increased.

- The credit of linking Almora newspaper with the freedom movement also goes to Badridutt Pandey.

Hence, the correct option is (D).

25. Jim Corbett, a hunter-nationalist is the author of the book "Man-Eaters of Kumaon" written in 1944. This book gives details about the experiences that Corbett had in the Kumaon region of India from the 1900s to the 1930s. During this period, he was hunting man-eating Bengal tigers and Indian leopards. It contains ten fascinating stories of tracking and shooting man-eaters in the Indian Himalayas. The stories also contain incidental information on flora, fauna and village life.

Hence, the correct option is (C).

26. Chhau is a style performed exclusively by men from the triangular area where Bihar, Bengal and Orissa meet. So, Statement 1 is correct. This is the tribal belt of India home to the tribal groups of Bhulya, Santhals, Mundas, Hos and Oraons.

Chhau Mask: The masks they use vary depending on the style of Chhau practised, Seraikella Chhau or Purulia Chhau. In the third form of Chhau, Mayurbhanj Chhau, masks are not worn. The Chhau mask is made of potters' clay (Matti Ghada) over which layers of muslin are pasted followed by paper (kagaz chitano). So, Statement 2 is incorrect. Using a delicate wooden chisel, different features of the mask are polished the nose, eyes, ears, chin and lips. Once it is dried it is painted in pastel colours (kahij lepa). Then the mask is separated from the clay model and fully dried in the sun. Finally, the mask is worn with a highly decorated head-dress of tinsel, pearls, coloured paper and artificial flowers. The masks acquire a whole range of expression with every twist and turn of the body. Accompanied by the huge dhamsa drums and two energetic dhol players who provoke and encourage the dancers. The Chhau dancer makes lightning body movements known as chamak. So, Statement 3 is correct.

Hence, the correct option is (C).

27. The traditional marionettes of Rajasthan are known as Kathputli. Kathputli is a string puppet. So, Statement 1 is correct. Kathputli is a combination of two Rajasthani language words Kath meaning wood and Putli meaning a doll.

Characteristics of Kathputli:

- Kathputli means a puppet that is made entirely from wood.

- However, it is made out of wood, cotton cloth, and metal wire.

- These puppets are large colorfully dressed dolls.

- Their costumes and headgears are designed in the medieval Rajasthani style of dress. So, Statement 3 is correct.

- The Kathputli is accompanied by a highly dramatized version of the regional music.

- Facial Features: Oval faces, large eyes, arched eyebrows, and large lips.

- These puppets wear long trailing skirts and do not have legs. So, Statement 2 is correct.

- Puppeteers manipulate them with two to five strings which are normally tied to their fingers and not to a prop or support.

Hence, the correct option is (D).

28. The traditional glove puppet play of Kerala is called Pavakoothu. So, Statement 1 is incorrect.

It came into existence during the 18th century due to the influence of Kathakali, the famous classical dance-drama of Kerala, on puppet performances. So, Statement 2 is correct.

The height of a puppet varies from one to two feet. The head and the arms are carved of wood and joined together with a thick cloth, cut and stitched into a small bag. So, Statement 3 is correct. The face of the puppets is decorated with paints, small and thin pieces of gilded tin, the feathers of the peacock, etc.

The manipulator puts his hand into the bag and moves the hands and head of the puppet. The musical instruments used during the performance are Chenda, Chengiloa, Ilathalam and Shankhathe conch.

The theme for Glove puppet plays in Kerala is based on the episodes from either the Ramayana or the Mahabharata.

Hence, the correct option is (B).

29. Dilwara Temple is a renowned Jain temple in India.

- It is located near Mount Abu, in Sirohi District, Rajasthan's only hill station.
- It is also called Delvada Temples.
- It was built between the 11th and 16th centuries.
- There are five temples and each has its unique identity.
- All are famous for their pure white marble and intricate marble carvings.

Hence, the correct option is (D).

30. The Patwon Ji ki Haveli is an interesting piece of Architecture and is the most important among the Havelis in Jaisalmer. This is precisely because of two things, first that it was the first haveli erected in Jaisalmer and second, that it is not a single haveli but a cluster of 5 small Havelis.

Hence, the correct option is (B).

31. Rajasthan Institute of Cooperative Education and Management:

- It is a premier training institute.
- With a view to developing human resources mainly in the cooperative sector.
- Equipping people with techniques of professional and modern management.
- The Institute was registered in 1990.
- It is located in Jaipur.

Hence, the correct option is (A).

32. Virat Kohli remained the highest-placed Indian batsman at the fourth position in the latest ICC Test rankings issued on 30 Jan 2021.

Cheteshwar Pujara moved up one place to 6th.

Test vice-captain Ajinkya Rahane is the other Indian batsman in the top-10 on the eighth spot.

New Zealand captain Kane Williamson continued to lead the batting charts.

Hence, the correct option is (C).

33. Virat Kohli has been awarded the ICC men's ODI player of the decade Award.

He also won Sir Garfield Sobers award for the best male cricketer of the past decade.

Other ICC awards of the decade:

Mahendra Singh Dhoni won the ICC Spirit of Cricket Award of the decade.

Ellyse Perry a female all-rounder cricketer from Australia won the following awards:

- ICC female cricketer of the decade.
- ICC women ODI cricketer of the decade.
- Women's T20 Cricketer of the decade.

Hence, the correct option is (A).

34. Ishwar Chand Pandey is a former Indian cricketer who played for Madhya Pradesh.

He was a right-arm medium-fast bowler who was the leading wicket-taker of the 2012-13 Ranji Trophy.

He played for India A and was selected in the Indian Test and ODI squads for the New Zealand tour of 2014.

He was bought by the Chennai Super Kings in the 2014 IPL auction for Rs 1.5 crores and was bought by Rising Pune Supergiants in the 2016 and 2017 editions of IPL.

Ishwar Pandey was born in Rewa, Madhya Pradesh.

Hence, the correct option is (C).

35. Balwantrai Mehta Committee recommended for Panchayati Raj System in India.

Balwantrai Mehta Committee:

- In January 1957, the Government of India appointed a committee to examine the working of the Community Development Programme (1952) and the National Extension Service (1953) and to suggest measures for their better working.
- The chairman of this committee was Balwant Rai G Mehta.

Hence, the correct option is (C).

36. The presidency of the United Nations Security Council rotates on a monthly basis alphabetically among all of the members based on their English name.

Hence, the correct option is (D).

37. Statement 1 is correct. One of the major aims and purpose with which ILO was set up was the extension of social security worldwide which was clearly set out in the Preamble to the ILO Constitution (1919).

Statement 2 is correct. Post-2003, ILO has set up a dedicated department to cater to Social security-related initiatives: the Social Security Department which has explored, analyzed, and piloted various ways and means to extend the coverage of health care systems and basic universal cash benefits, notably to people in the informal economy. And, ILO launched a Global Campaign on "Social Security and Coverage for All".

Statement 3 is incorrect. In accordance with this Social security was declared as a basic human right under the Universal Declaration of Human Rights (UDHR), 1948.

Statement 4 is correct. ILO mandate of extension of social security measures was restated in 1944 in the Declaration of Philadelphia to provide a basic income to all in need of such protection and comprehensive medical care.

Hence, the correct option is (C).

38. The International Monetary Fund (IMF) is an organization of 189 countries, working to foster global monetary cooperation, secure financial stability, facilitate international trade, promote high employment and sustainable economic growth, and reduce poverty around the world.

- Created in 1945, the IMF is governed by and accountable to the 189 countries that make up its near-global membership.
- The IMF's primary purpose is to ensure the stability of the international monetary system – the system of exchange rates and international payments that enables countries (and their citizens) to transact with each other.

Hence, the correct option is (D).

39. Vermicompost is ideal organic manure for better growth and yield of many plants. It contains water-soluble nutrients and is an excellent, nutrient-rich organic fertilizer and soil conditioner.

- It is used in farming and small scale sustainable, organic farming.
- Vermicomposting can also be applied for the treatment of sewage.

Hence, the correct option is (C).

40. It is also known as cyclonite or hexogen. The chemical name for RDX is 1,3,5-trinitro-1,3,5-triazine. It is a white powder and is very explosive. RDX is used as an explosive and is also used in combination with other ingredients in explosives.

Hence, the correct option is (C).

41. A biochemical compound is any carbon-based compound that is found in living things. Biochemical compounds make up the cells and tissues of living things. They are also involved in all life processes, including making and using food for energy.

Hence, the correct option is (D).

42. Daniel Gabriel Fahrenheit invented the modern mercury thermometer with a standardized scale. Daniel Gabriel Fahrenheit FRS was a physicist, inventor, and scientific instrument, maker.

Fahrenheit was born on 24 May 1686, Gdansk, Poland, then a predominantly German-speaking city in the Pomeranian Voivodeship of the Polish–Lithuanian Commonwealth.

Hence, the correct option is (D).

43. A planimeter is used to determine the area of irregular plots in a map. A planimeter, also known as a platometer. It is a measuring instrument used to determine the area of an arbitrary two-dimensional shape.

Hence, the correct option is (D).

44. ISRO's Chandrayaan-2 orbiter has detected water molecules on the moon surface.

There was widespread lunar hydration and unambiguous detection of OH and H2O signatures on the moon between 29 degrees north and 62 degrees north latitude. The findings were published in Current Science Journal. The formation of hydroxyl or water molecules occurs due to a process called space weathering.

Hence, the correct option is (C).

45. After Ashoka's coronation, he fought only a major war known as the Kalinga war.

The massacre in this war filled him with grief. This war caused great suffering to the people of Kalinga, the priests, monks who filled Ashoka with great penitence. He, then started to use "Dhammaghosha" instead of "Bherighosha" & adopted the policies of cultural annihilation rather than attacking kingdoms physically. This step became one of the causes responsible for the decline of the Mauryan empire.

Hence, the correct option is (B).

46. Dadabhai Naoroji, G. Subramania Iyer, R. C. Dutt were famous economic critique.

- Amongst the famous economic critique Dadabhai Naoroji, G. Subramania Iyer, R. C. Dutt who studied the economic relationship between the British Empire and India, Dadabhai Naoroji was the most prominent.
- He popularized the drain theory in his book "Poverty and Un-British Rule in India".
- They explained the colonial structure in all its three aspects of domination through trade, industry and finance.

Hence, the correct option is (D).

47. The Mauryan empire was one of the greatest empires which ruled on India.

It has great historical significance. The rule of Mauryas ruled from 322-185 B.C. & under them, the majority of India remained united as a single state by the great founder emperor Chandragupta Maurya. With the help of Chanakya, Chandragupta Maurya laid the foundation of this great Mauryan empire.

Hence, the correct option is (C).

48. Israeli Prime Minister Benjamin Netanyahu and Abu Dhabi Crown Prince Mohammed bin Zayed Al Nahyan have been nominated for the 2021 Nobel Peace Prize. They have been

nominated for their roles in establishing diplomatic ties between their countries It was announced in September 2020 that Donald Trump has been nominated for the Prize following his efforts to broker peace between Israel and the UAE.

Hence, the correct option is (A).

49. Mathematician Anand Kumar has been conferred with the Swami Brahmanand Award 2021 for his contribution in the field of education through his Super 30 initiative.

The award carries Rs. 10,000 in cash, a bronze medal, a bronze statue of Swami Brahmanand, and a certificate. The award is given every year to people who have done special work in the education sector or for the welfare of the cow.

Hence, the correct option is (A).

50. The Abel Prize 2021 was awarded to Avi Wigderson, and Laszlo Lovasz.

László Lovász is a mathematician of Alfréd Rényi Institute of Mathematics (ELKH, MTA Institute of Excellence) and Eötvös Loránd University in Budapest, Hungary, and Avi Wigderson a mathematician of the Institute for Advanced Study, Princeton, USA.

Hence, the correct option is (B).

51.

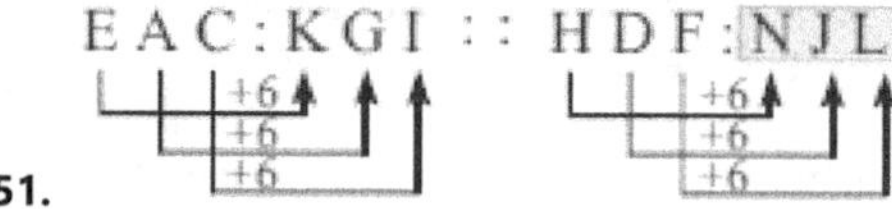

As we can see in the given figure it is clear that NJL will come in the place of ?.

Hence, the correct option is (D).

52. The pane is just a sheet of Glass in the window, many sheets make a window.

Similarly, Page is just a single sheet in a book, many pages make a book.

Window : Pane : : Book : Page

Hence, the correct option is (B).

53. The given series follows the following pattern,

$$257 \Rightarrow 5^2 - 3^2 = 25 - 9 \to 259 \text{ not } 257$$
$$416 \Rightarrow 2^2 - 4^2 = 4 - 16 \to 416$$
$$925 \Rightarrow 3^2 - 5^2 = 9 - 25 \to 925$$
$$164 \Rightarrow 4^2 - 2^2 = 16 - 4 \to 164$$

Thus 257 is the odd number.

Hence, the correct option is (C).

54. The correct mirror image of the given figure when the mirror is held at the right side is:

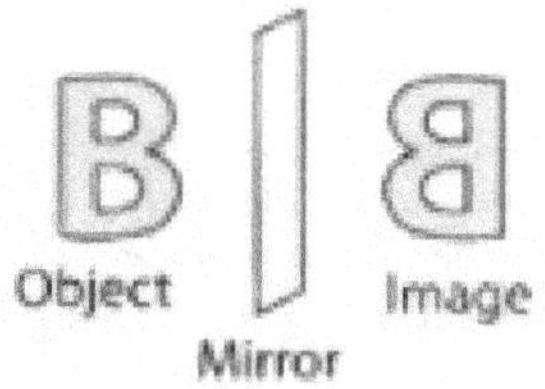

Hence, the correct option is (B).

55. The correct mirror image of the given figure when the mirror is held at the right side is:

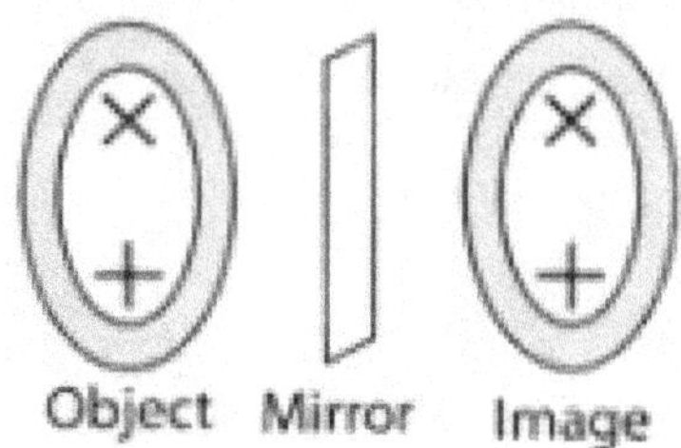

Hence, the correct option is (A).

56. The logic follows here is:

Both the larger and the smaller circle move to the adjacent corner Anticlockwise in each turn.

Also, the shading in the smaller circle moves 1, 2, 3, 4, 5, ... steps anticlockwise sequentially and the shading in the larger circle moves 1, 2, 3, 4, 5,... steps clockwise sequentially.

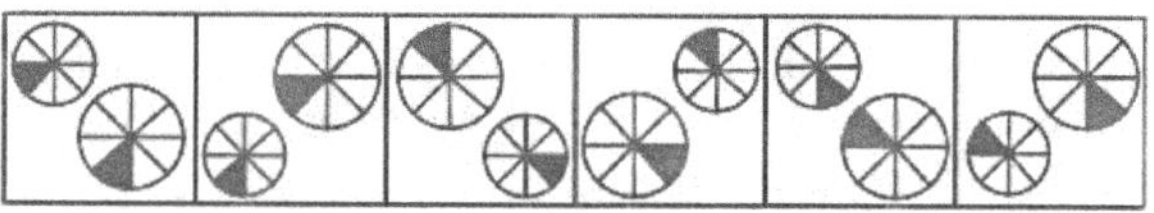

Hence, the correct option is (D).

57. By checking each option:

Option (C) →

18 × 2 = 864 ÷ 24

36 = 36

Option (A) →

18 × 2 + 864 = 24

36 + 864 ≠ 24

Option (B) →

18 = 2 ÷ 864 + 24

18 ≠ 24.002

Option (D) →

18 + 2 = 864 - 24

20 ≠ 840

Hence, the correct option is (C).

58. (A) GRASS – FEARLESS (Cannot be formed because G is missing)

(B) RESEAL – FEARLESS (Can be formed)

(C) LESSER – FEARLESS (Can be formed)

(D) ERASE – FEARLESS (Can be formed)

So, the correct answer is "GRASS".

Hence, the correct option is (A).

59. The best possible diagram from the given information is,

Symbol in Diagram	Meaning
○	Female
□	Male
·········	Married Couple
———	Siblings
|	Difference of A Generation

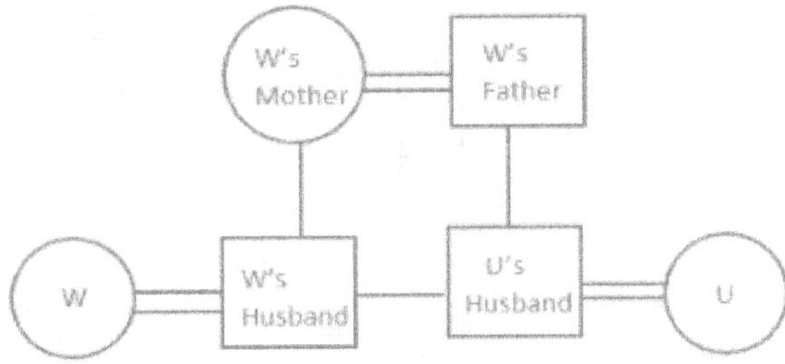

'U is W's husband's brother's wife' is the correct answer.

Hence, the correct option is (A).

60. A word with nearly same meaning is called a synonym and a word with opposite meaning is an antonym.

So,

Synonyms and Antonyms are words.

The correct Venn diagram is,

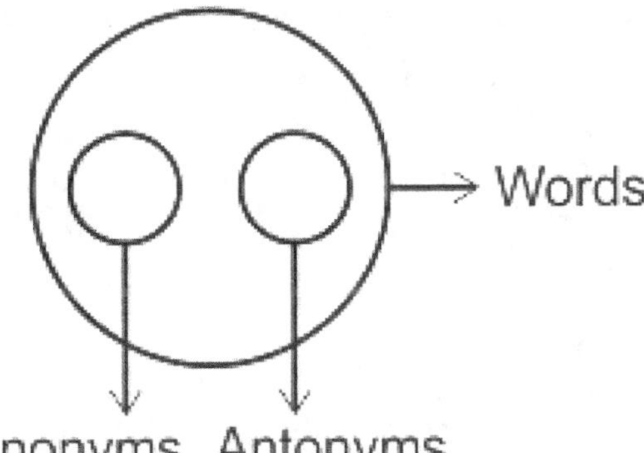

Hence, the correct option is (B).

61. The least possible Venn diagram is:

I. No M is Q. → False (As, there is no definite relation between M and Q. Hence, false)

II. Some M are J. → True (As, Some J are M → Some M are J)

So, only conclusion II follows.

Hence, the correct option is (C).

62. The least possible Venn diagram is:

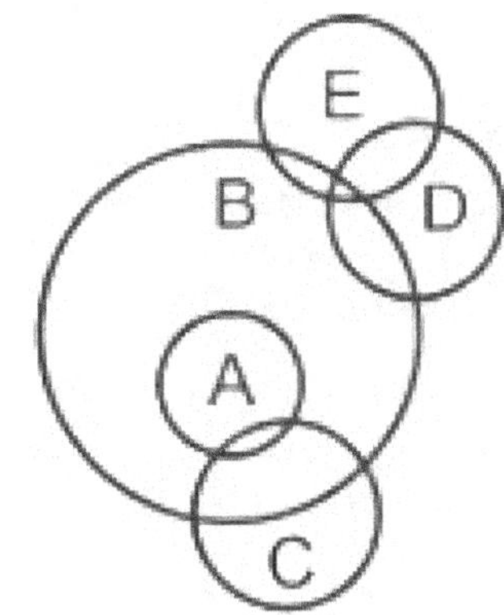

i. Some C's are B. → True (As, all A's are B and some A's are C → Some C's are B)

ii. Some E's are A. → False (As, there is no definite relation between E and A. Hence, false)

So, only conclusion I follows.

Hence, the correct option is (A).

63. Pattern is as follows:

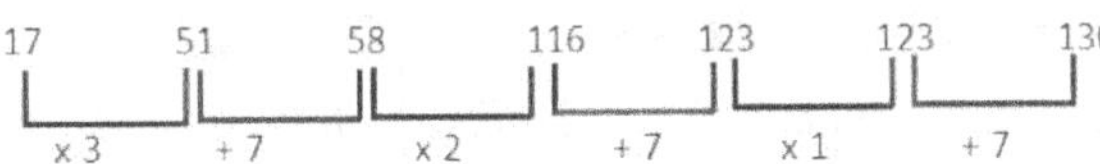

So, 130 will come in place of question mark (?).

Hence, the correct option is (C).

64. Given series,

$2430, ?, 270, 90, 30, 10$

Pattern followed here is:

$$2430 \div 3 = 810$$
$$810 \div 3 = 270$$
$$270 \div 3 = 90$$
$$90 \div 3 = 30$$
$$30 \div 3 = 10$$

So, 810 will replace the question mark (?).
Hence, the correct option is (C).

65. Shape in option (C) is embedded in given figure.

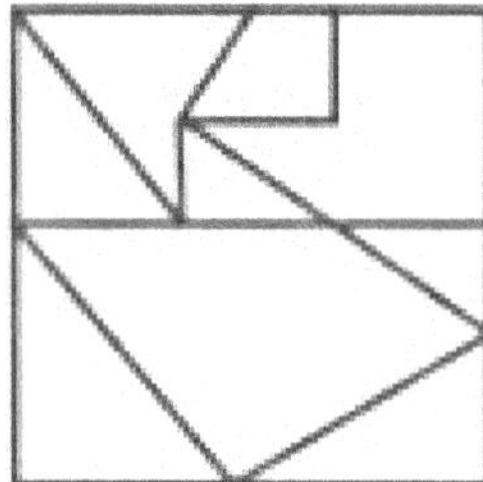

Hence, the correct option is (C).

66. The answer figure is not made up only by the components of the question figure is '(C)'.

Clearly, an arrow symbol is there in figure (C) which is not present in the question figure.

Hence, the correct option is (C).

67. The least possible venn diagram is:

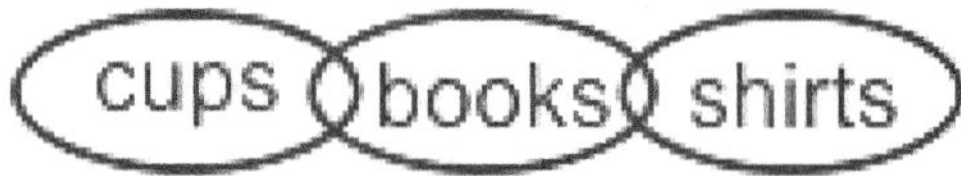

I. Some cups are shirts. → False (It can be possible, but it is not definite)

II. All shirts are books. → False (It can be possible, but it is not definite)

So, neither conclusion I nor II follow.

Hence, the correct option is (C).

68. As 2010 is not a leap year, there are 28 days in February in 2010

So, the total number of days between 27th December 2009 to 1st March 2010 = 4 + 31 + 28 + 1

= 64

= (7 × 9) + 1

So, the total number of odd days = 1

Thus, as 27th December 2009 was a Thursday, then on 1st March 2010 it was Thursday + 1 = Friday.

Hence, the correct option is (B).

69. After punching the paper when we open the paper we will find the following figure.

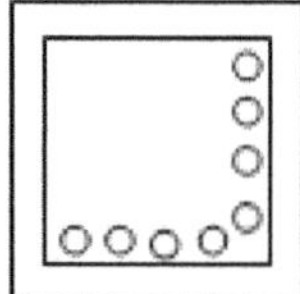

Hence, the correct option is (D).

70. Logic: Here, every word is coded as the number of letters in that word.

⇒ In the word 'STIMULI', there are 7 letters. So, code is 7.

⇒ In the word 'INFORMATION', there are 11 letters. So, code is 11.

So, the code for the word 'GRANULES' is 8 as there are 8 letters in this word.

Thus, GRANULES will be written as 8.

Hence, the correct option is (B).

71.

Alpha bets	A	B	C	D	E	F	G	H	I	J	K	L	M
Positional value	1	2	3	4	5	6	7	8	9	10	11	12	13
Positional value	26	25	24	23	22	21	20	19	18	17	16	15	14
Alpha bets	Z	Y	X	W	V	U	T	S	R	Q	P	O	N

Logic: Each letter of the word 'CLOSURE' is coded as its respective numerical position in alphabetical order.
Position of each letter of the word 'CLOSURE' is -
C → 3, L → 12, O → 15, S → 19, U → 21, R → 18, E → 5
Therefore code of CLOSURE is- 312151921185
Similarly, the word 'INFLUENCE' will be coded as-
I → 9, N → 14, F → 6, L → 12, U → 21, E → 5, N → 14, C → 3, E → 5
Thus, INFLUENCE will be written as- 9146122151435.
Hence, the correct option is (A).

Q.72 According to the given information,

(i) Govind is shorter than Ashish but taller than Kamal.

Ashish > Govind > Kamal

(ii) Naren is shorter than Kamal.

Kamal > Naren (Ashish > Govind > Kamal > Naren)

(iii) Jayant is taller than Naren.

Jayant > Naren

(iv) Ashish is taller than Jayant.

Ashish > Jayant

Combining the above statements there can be two possibilities:

Ashish > Govind > Kamal > Jayant > Naren

Ashish > Jayant > Govind > Kamal > Naren

In both cases Naren is the shortest.

Hence, the correct option is (D).

73. According to the English alphabet series and its positional value:

Alphabets	A	B	C	D	E	F	G	H	I	J	K	L	M
Positional Value	1	2	3	4	5	6	7	8	9	10	11	12	13
Positional Value	26	25	24	23	22	21	20	19	18	17	16	15	14
Alphabets	Z	Y	X	W	V	U	T	S	R	Q	P	O	N

The pattern followed here is:

$$FBXT \rightarrow F - 4 = B, B - 4 = X, X - 4 = T$$

$$TPLH \rightarrow T - 4 = P, P - 4 = L, L - 4 = H$$

$$CYUQ \rightarrow C - 4 = Y, Y - 4 = U, U - 4 = Q$$

$$NJFA \rightarrow N - 4 = J, J - 4 = F, F - 5 = A$$

Hence, the correct option is (D).

74. The diagram will be,

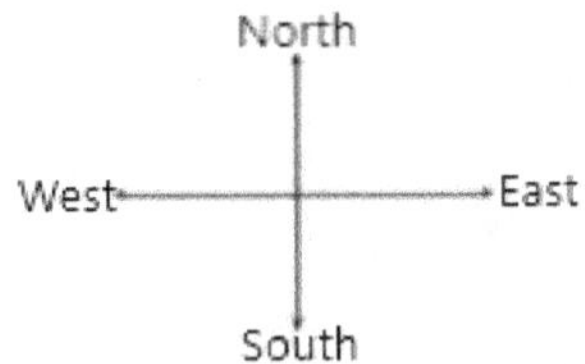

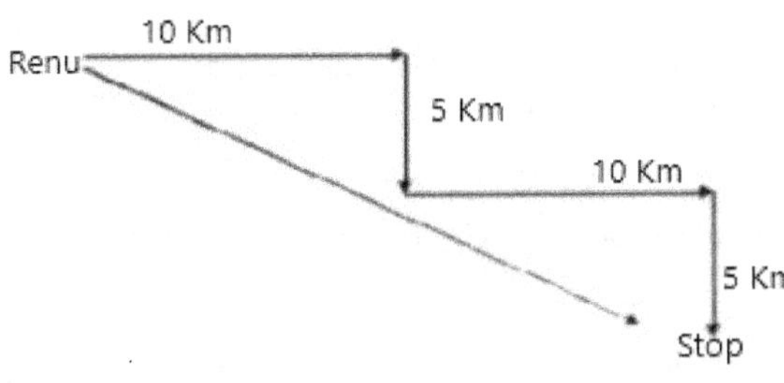

Hence, the correct option is (B).

75. 1) FATAL - the letter F is not present in ANECDOTAL, so it can't be formed.

2) DENTAL - it can be formed.

3) ANTIDOTAL - the letter I is not present in ANECDOTAL, so it can't be formed.

4) ANCIPITAL - the letter C is not present in ANECDOTAL, so it can't be formed.

So, the word DENTAL can be formed from the letters used in ANECDOTAL.

Hence, the correct option is (B).

76. Given:

Rate of interest $= 2.5\%$ per month

Amount paid after 6 months $=$ Rs. 13110

Amount, $A = P + SI$

Simple interest, $SI = \dfrac{P \times R \times T}{100}$

Where $P \rightarrow$ Principal, $R \rightarrow$ rate of interest, $T \rightarrow$ time

Suppose the sum borrowed be Rs. x

$$SI = \frac{x \times 2.5 \times 6}{100} = 0.15x$$

$$A = x + 0.15x = 1.15x$$

$$1.15x = 13110$$

$$\Rightarrow x = 11400$$

$$\Rightarrow \text{Amount of interest} = 0.15 \times 11400$$

$$= \text{Rs. } 1710$$

Hence, the correct option is (C).

77. Given,

Pipe A can fill in 15 hours.

Pipe B can fill in 18 hours.

Tank filled by Pipe A in 1 hour $= \dfrac{1}{15}$

Tank filled by Pipe B in 1 hour $= \dfrac{1}{18}$

Tank filled by both Pipes in 1 hour $= \left(\dfrac{1}{15}\right) + \left(\dfrac{1}{18}\right)$

$$= \frac{11}{90}$$

Time taken By both pipes to fill the tank $= \dfrac{90}{11}$

$$= 8\frac{2}{11} \text{ hours}$$

$\therefore$ Time taken by both pipes is $8\dfrac{2}{11}$ hours.

Hence, the correct option is (D).

78. Given:

The given word = SOFTWARE

Formula used:

Arrangement of n letter of a word

Case 1:- If there were no repeating letters $= n!$

Case 2:- If there were "r" letter of one kind $= \dfrac{n!}{r!}$

Keeping all the vowel at one place and consider it as one vowel

$\Rightarrow$ SFTWR(OAE)

Here, $n = 6$ and number of vowel $= 3$

All letter can be arranged in $6!$ ways and Vowel can be arranged in 3! ways

Total number of ways to arrange the word
$= 6! \times 3! = 6 \times 5 \times 4 \times 3 \times 2 \times 1 \times 3 \times 2 \times 1 = 4320$

$\therefore$ Total number of ways to arrange the word $= 4320$

Hence, the correct option is (C).

79. Given:

A boatman rows $1.5\ km$ against the stream for 17.25 minutes.

A boatman rows $1.5\ km$ downstream for 8.5 minutes.

We know that:

$$\text{Speed of boat} = \frac{(\text{Upstream speed} + \text{Downstream speed})}{2}$$

Upstream speed of man $= \dfrac{1500}{17.25 \times 60} = 1.45\ m/s$

Downstream speed of man $= \dfrac{1500}{8.5 \times 60} = 2.94\ m/s$

Speed of the boat in still water $= \dfrac{1.45 + 2.94}{2} = 2.2\ m/s$

$\therefore$ The speed of the boat in still water is $2.2\ m/s$.

Hence, the correct option is (B).

80. Given,:

$15 - 15 \div 15 \times 6 = x$

$x = 15 - 15 \times \dfrac{1}{15} \times 6$

$x = 15 - 15 \times \dfrac{1}{15} \times 6$

$x = 15 - 6$

$x = 9$

Hence, the correct option is (C).

81. Given:

$\dfrac{3}{8} \div \left(\dfrac{5}{3} - \dfrac{1}{6}\right) + \dfrac{5}{8}$

$= \dfrac{3}{8} \div \left(\dfrac{10-1}{6}\right) + \dfrac{5}{8}$

$= \dfrac{3}{8} \div \dfrac{9}{6} + \dfrac{5}{8}$

$= \dfrac{3}{8} \times \dfrac{6}{9} + \dfrac{5}{8}$

$= \dfrac{3}{2 \times 4} \times \dfrac{2 \times 3}{9} + \dfrac{5}{8}$

$= \dfrac{1}{4} + \dfrac{5}{8}$

$= \dfrac{7}{8}$

Hence, the correct option is (C).

82. Total seat in all disciplines for college III = 200 + 200 + 400 + 300 + 500 = 1600

Total vacant seats in respective discipline of college III are (200 - 198) + (200 - 191) + (400 - 364) + (300 - 291) + (500 - 484) = 2 + 9 + 36 + 9 + 16 = 72

$\therefore$ The total percentage of seats vacant in college III against its total capacity $= \left(\dfrac{72}{1600}\right) \times 100 = 4.5\%$

Hence, the correct option is (D).

83. Percentage of student admitted in MBA of College II $= \left(\dfrac{190}{200}\right) \times 100 = 95\%$

Percentage of student admitted in MBA of College IV $= \left(\dfrac{170}{200}\right) \times 100 = 85\%$

$\therefore$ Required difference = 95 - 85 = 10%

Hence, the correct option is (A).

84. Total number of seats in B.Com. and B.A = 300 + 500 = 800

College	B.Com	B.A
Capacity	300	500
I	281	486
II	215	414
III	291	484
IV	199	429
V	276	412

The number of vacant seats in college I for B.Com. and B.A = Total - Seat filled = 19 + 14 = 33 or 800 - (281 + 486) = 33

The number of vacant seats in college II for B.Com. and B.A = 85 + 86 = 171

The number of vacant seats in college III for B.Com. and B.A = 9 + 16 = 25

The number of vacant seats in college IV for B.Com. and B.A = 101 + 71 = 172

The number of vacant seats in college V for B.Com. and B.A = 24 + 88 = 112

$\therefore$ The highest number of vacant seats in B.Com. and B.A. discipline was in college IV.

Hence, the correct option is (C).

85. Lowest admission in BSc was in college IV i.e., 290 out of total 400 seats.

$\Rightarrow$ The percentage of students admitted in BSc. $= \left(\dfrac{290}{400}\right) \times 100 \approx 72\%$

Highest admission in B.A was in college I i.e., 486 out of total 500 seats.

$\Rightarrow$ The percentage of students admitted in B.A. $= \left(\dfrac{486}{500}\right) \times 100 \approx$ 97%

$\therefore$ Approximate difference = 97 - 72 = 25%

Hence, the correct option is (B).

86. For college II, Distribution of seats in all disciplines

MBA	B.Tech	B.Sc	B.Com	B.A.
200	200	400	300	500

Seat filled in College II in all disciplines

II	190	183	348	215	414

$\therefore$ Seat vacant in all disciplines = Total - Seat filled

MBA	B.Tech	B.Sc	B.Com	B.A.
10	17	52	85	86

Similarly for College III,

Seat filled in College III in all disciplines

III	198	191	364	291	484

$\therefore$ Seat vacant in all disciplines = Total - Seat filled

MBA	B.Tech	B.Sc	B.Com	B.A.
2	9	36	9	16

$\therefore$ Total seat vacant in both the colleges = (10 + 17 + 52 + 85 + 86) + (2 + 9 + 36 + 9 + 16) = 322

Hence, the correct option is (B).

87. Given:

$x^3 + x^2 + 16$ is exactly divisible by x, where x is a positive integer.

Let a number N be equal to $x^3 + x^2 + 16$.

$$N = x^3 + x^2 + 16$$

Now divide $\dfrac{N}{x}$

$$\dfrac{N}{x} = \dfrac{x^3 + x^2 + 16}{x}$$

$$\Rightarrow x^2 + x + \left(\dfrac{16}{x}\right)$$

As N is divisible by x so 16 must be divisible by x.

Values of x that can divide 16 are $1, 2, 4, 8$ and 16.

So, there are total 5 values of x that can divide N without leaving the remainder.

Hence, the correct option is (C).

88. Given,

$$\dfrac{40 - \frac{3}{4} \text{ of } 32}{37 - \frac{3}{4} \text{ of } (34 - 6)}$$

$$= \dfrac{40 - \frac{3}{4} \times 32}{37 - \frac{3}{4} \text{ of } 28}$$

$$= \dfrac{(40 - 24)}{(37 - 21)}$$

$$= \dfrac{16}{16}$$

$$= 1$$

$\therefore$ The required value is 1.

Hence, the correct option is (C).

89. Given,

A can do work in 10 days.

A's 1 day's work $= \dfrac{1}{10}$

B can do work in 15 days.

B's 1 day's work $= \dfrac{1}{15}$

(A + B)'s 1 day's work $= \dfrac{1}{10} + \dfrac{1}{15}$

$$= \dfrac{(3 + 2)}{30}$$

$$= \dfrac{1}{6}$$

$\therefore$ Together they can complete work in 6 days.

Hence, the correct option is (A).

90. Let the quantity of milk and water be $9x$ liters and $8x$ liters respectively.

As per the given details,

$$\dfrac{9x}{8x + 10} = \dfrac{51}{47}$$

$$\Rightarrow 423x = 408x + 510$$

$$\Rightarrow 423x - 408x = 510$$

$$\Rightarrow 15x = 510$$

$$\Rightarrow x = \dfrac{510}{15}$$

$$\Rightarrow x = 34$$

$\therefore$ Original quantity of milk in the mixture $= 9x = 9 \times 34$

$= 306$ liters

Hence, the correct option is (A).

91.

- The Help button in Word is too small that will be easily ignored. Actually the Help button stays in the top right corner of the window.
- Shortcut key F1 to enable the Help window.

Other important keys and their functions:

Shortcut Keys	Functions
F2	Moves text or object
F9	Updates all the field codes in the current selection
F11	Moves to the next Field
F12	Displays the Save As dialog box.

Hence, the correct option is (A).

92.

- MS Office, Photoshop, and Animagic are examples of Application software

- MS Office is a software bundle provided by Microsoft.

- It includes software like MS Word, MS Excel, MS Powerpoint, MS Outlook, MS Access, MS One Note, and others.

Hence, the correct option is (B).

93.

- Apache OpenOffice is an open-source office productivity software suite. It is one of the successor projects of OpenOffice.org and the designated successor of IBM Lotus Symphony.

- Outlook, Access, Visual studio express, Windows are developed by Microsoft.

Hence, the correct option is (A).

94.

- Assigning names to text or to positions in an MS Word document is called Bookmark.

- A bookmark in MS Word serves the same purpose as the bookmark you put in place in a book.

- The bookmark marks a place that you want to find easily, and one that you want to return to when you need it.

- The definition of bookmark in MS Word is a specific word, section, or location in your Word document that you want to name and identify for future reference.

- In Word, bookmarks are saved with the document file. Therefore, you can assign bookmarks with the same name in different files.

- Names of bookmarks must begin with a letter of the alphabet, they can contain only letters, numbers, and the underscore, and cannot contain spaces or punctuation marks.

- Adding bookmarks in Word is also easy.

- All you have to do is mark the location in the document, and then go to the toolbar menu and click "Insert">"Bookmark".

- You'll need to select a name for your bookmark so that you can easily find it later on.

Hence, the correct option is (B).

95.

- Legend is the space located on the plotted area of the chart in excel. It has Legend keys which are connected to the data source. Legend will appear automatically when we insert a chart in excel.

- The legend identifies the visual elements used to distinguish different groups of data on the graph.

- The legend helps you evaluate the effects of grouping. For example, the legend in the preceding graph shows the attributes of the symbols and connect lines used to represent the Control and Education groups.

Show or hide a legend:

1. Click the chart in which you want to show or hide a legend. This displays the Chart Tools, adding the Design, Layout, and Format tabs.

2. On the Layout tab, in the Labels group, click Legend.

3. Do one of the following: To hide the legend, click None.

Hence, the correct option is (D).

96. The header is a section of the document that appears in the top margin, while the footer is a section of the document that appears in the bottom margin.
Headers and footers generally contain information such as the page number, date, and document name.
Headers and footers can help keep longer documents organized and make them easier to read. Text entered in the header or footer will appear on each page of the document.

To insert a header or footer:

- Select the Insert tab.

- Click either the Header or Footer command. A drop-down menu will appear.

- From the drop-down menu, select Blank to insert a blank header or footer, or choose one of the built-in options.

Hence, the correct option is (B).

97. Security is the primary concern about cloud computing. This is the main for many IT departments to refrain from using cloud computing. Some things that put the security of cloud computing to be concerned are: Theft or loss of intellectual property.

Hence, the correct option is (B).

98. Scientific languages include Maple, Python, FORTRAN, ALGOL, APL, J, Julia, and R. Fortran is a general-purpose, compiled imperative programming language that is especially suited to numeric computation and scientific computing.

Hence, the correct option is (C).

99. One who gains unauthorized access destroys vital data, denies legitimate user's service, or causes problems for their targets is called a cracker.

Crackers are often malicious and have many means at their disposal for breaking into a system.

Hence, the correct option is (B).

100. The term broadband commonly refers to high-speed Internet access that is always on and faster than traditional dial-up access.

Broadband includes several high-speed transmission technologies such as Digital Subscriber Line (DSL).

Hence, the correct option is (D).

General Awareness/Current Affairs

Q.1 Who has been appointed as a director in the Prime Minister's Office (PMO) in August 2022?

A. Shweta Singh

B. Ravi Kumar

C. Ruchi Mishra

D. Anoop Kumar Pathak

Q.2 Who presided over an emergency session of the General Assembly to discuss Russia's military operations in Ukraine?

A. Abdulla Shahid

B. Volkan Bozkir

C. Antonio Guterres

D. Kofi Annan

Q.3 Who among the following has been awarded for Ramon Magsaysay Award, 2018?

[Super TET Paper - I, 2019]

A. Bharat Vatwani

B. Bruce Rittmann

C. Robert Langlands

D. Richard H. Thaler

Q.4 Who is the head of the Labour Ministry's commission, which recommended a basic living wage?

A. Santosh Kumar Gangwar

B. C V Ananda Bose

C. Apurva Chandra

D. Alok Kumar Mathur

Q.5 What is the name of the digital platform that would be used to track the beneficiaries for COVID vaccination in India?

A. Atmanirbhar System

B. Arogya Setu System

C. COWIN System

D. Serum System

Q.6 Who has won the gold medal in the 52 kg category at the Women's World Boxing Championships 2022?

A. MC Mary Kom

B. Pinki Jangra

C. Sarjubala Devi

D. Nikhat Zareen

Q.7 Which country was host the 44th FIDE Chess Olympiad 2022?

A. Russia   **B.** France   **C.** Italy   **D.** India

Q.8 Where was the first Regional Toys Fair held in May 2022?

A. Varanasi

B. Bengaluru

C. Kanchipuram

D. Kolkata

Q.9 Consider the following statements with respect to 'News Broadcasting & Digital Standards Authority (NBDSA).

1. It is an autonomous body under the Ministry of Information and Broadcasting

2. The Authority may initiate proceedings on its own and take action in respect to any matter falling within its regulations

Select the correct statement.

A. 1 only

B. 2 only

C. Both 1 and 2

D. Neither 1 nor 2

Q.10 Jharkhand CM Hemant Soren has launched Jharkhand ___ Policy 2022 in Ranchi on 13th September 2022?

A. Farmer's

B. Sports

C. Unskilled Labour

D. All of the above

Q.11 Which bank has signed an MoU with the Indian Air Force (IAF) to manage the salary accounts of the defence personnel in July 2022?

A. Axis Bank

B. Kotak Mahindra Bank

C. State Bank of India

D. HDFC Bank

Q.12 Alluvial soils vary in nature from sandy loam to clay. They are generally:

[Indian Military Academy (IMA), 2021], [Officers Training Academy (OTA), 2021]

A. poor in potash and rich in phosphorus

B. poor in both potash and phosphorus.

C. rich in both potash and phosphorus.

D. rich in potash and poor in phosphorus.

Q.13 Who among the following was the Chairman of the National Commission for Review of the Working of the Constitution (2000)?

[Indian Military Academy (IMA), 2021], [Officers Training Academy (OTA), 2021]

A. Justice M.N. Venkatachaliah

B. Justice J.S. Verma

C. Justice Ranganath Mishra

D. Justice Y.K. Sabharwal

Q.14 Who among the following founded the Marathi newspaper 'Kesari'?

[Indian Military Academy (IMA), 2021], [Officers Training Academy (OTA), 2021]

A. Lokmanya Tilak

B. Vallabhbhai Patel

C. Lala Lajpat Rai

D. Mahatma Gandhi

Q.15 That India is a secular state is implied in the phrase:

A. Social justice

B. Dignity of the individuals

C. Equality of status

D. Liberty of faith and worship

Q.16 What type of body is the Central Information Commission?

A. Constitutional body **B.** Quasi-Judicial body
C. Statutory body **D.** Executive body

Q.17 Geometric mean can be used to find out:
[Uttarakhand Public Service Commission (UKPSC), 2011]

A. Population Growth **B.** Growth rate of GNP
C. Both (A) and (B) **D.** None of them

Q.18 The first finance minister of Independent india was:
[Uttarakhand Public Service Commission (UKPSC), 2011]

A. Sri Gulzari Lal Nanda
B. Sri John Mathai
C. Sri Krishnamachari
D. Smt. Sarojini Naidu

Q.19 Which of the following is not a direct tax in India?
[Uttarakhand Public Service Commission (UKPSC), 2011]

A. Income tax **B.** Wealth tax
C. Estate duty **D.** Sales tax

Q.20 'Those Days' is the translated version of a Sahitya Akademi Award winning historical novel originally written by:
[SSC Sub Inspector (CPO), 2020]

A. Sumitranandan Pant
B. Nandita Das
C. Bhartendu Harishchandra
D. Sunil Gangopadhyay

Q.21 Which of the following books is not authored by Nirad C. Chaudhuri?
[SSC Sub Inspector (CPO), 2020]

A. A Passage to India
B. Autobiography of an Unknown Indian
C. The Continent of Circe: An Essay on People of India
D. Scholar Extraordinary

Q.22 Which among the following books was written by B.R. Ambedkar?
[SSC Sub Inspector (CPO), 2020]

A. The New Economic Menace of India
B. Satyarth Prakash
C. Annihilation of Caste
D. Savitri

Q.23 Where was 'Kheer Bhavani Mela' 2019 celebrated in India?
A. Manipur
B. West Bengal
C. Jammu and Kashmir
D. Jharkhand

Q.24 Bathukamma Utsav, 2019 was held in which state of India?
A. Arunachal Pradesh **B.** Himachal Pradesh
C. Meghalaya **D.** Telangana

Q.25 Sabarimala Temple is located:
A. Kerala **B.** Karnataka
C. Tamil Nadu **D.** Odisha

Q.26 Which city of Rajasthan is famous for yellow stone business?
[Rajasthan Police Constable, 2020]

A. Kota **B.** Jaisalmer
C. Ajmer **D.** Chittorgarh

Q.27 Which of the following district of Rajasthan is considered an ideal place for cement industry?
[Rajasthan Police Constable, 2020]

A. Hanumangarh **B.** Jaisalmer
C. Ajmer **D.** Chittorgarh

Q.28 In which city in Rajasthan is the chhatri of eighty-four pillars located?
[Rajasthan Police Constable, 2020]

A. Bundi **B.** Alwar **C.** Ramgarh **D.** Jodhpur

Q.29 Which of the following clubs was declared the winner of the second-tier Women's Championship by England's Football Association (FA) in June 2020?
A. Aston Villa **B.** Birmingham City
C. Liverpool **D.** West Ham

Q.30 Ms. Sonia Lather is associated with which of the following sports?
[Haryana Primary Teacher (PRT), 2020]

A. Wrestling **B.** Kabaddi
C. Atheletics **D.** Boxing

Q.31 With which sport do you associate the name of Koneru Humpy ?
A. Chess **B.** Volleyball
C. Table Tennis **D.** Basketball

Q.32 Article 359 of the Constitution authorizes the president of India to suspend the right to move any court for the enforcement of Fundamental Rights during :
A. A National Emergency
B. A failure of constitutional machinery in States
C. A financial emergency
D. None of Above

Q.33 Which of the following statement is/are correct?
1. Non-Aligned Movement(NAM) was established in 1961 in Belgrade, SR Serbia Yugoslavia.
2. Indian Prime Minister Jawaharlal Nehru also contributed to the established NAM.

A. 1 only **B.** 2 only
C. Both 1 and 2 **D.** Neither 1 nor 2

Q.34 Period of geopolitical tension between the Soviet Union and the United States said to be Cold War Era, in which duration?
A. 1914-1919 **B.** 1939-1945
C. 1947-1991 **D.** 1991-2001

Q.35 Which of the following statement is/are correct?

1. The eastern alliance North Atlantic Treaty Organisation (NATO), which came into existence in April 1949.

2. The western alliance, known as the Warsaw Pact, was led by the Soviet Union, which was created in 1955.

A. 1 only
B. 2 only
C. Both 1 and 2
D. Neither 1 nor 2

Q.36 Which one of the following elements is present in the green pigment of leaves?

[UPSC Central Armed Police Forces AC, 2017]

A. Magnesium
B. Iron
C. Calcium
D. Copper

Q.37 Leakage of which one of the following gases had caused Bhopal Gas Tragedy in the year 1984.

[UPSC Central Armed Police Forces AC, 2017]

A. Methyl isocyanate
B. Hexamethylene diisocyanate
C. Isophorone diisocyanate
D. Isothitxyanate

Q.38 Which of the following diseases are caused by the consumption of water contaminated by mercury and nitrate?

[UPSC Central Armed Police Forces AC, 2017]

A. Minamata disease and Osteoporosis
B. Osteoporosis and Blue Baby Syndrome
C. Minamata disease and Blue Baby Syndrome
D. Osteoporosis and Minamata disease

Q.39 Zika virus was named after the Zika Forest of which country?

A. Nigeria
B. Angola
C. Nicaragua
D. Uganda

Q.40 According to the Researchers, the first-ever stable ring of pure carbon consists of how many atoms?

A. 18
B. 60
C. 80
D. 108

Q.41 Which one of the following is not correct with regard to a peasant?

A. The peasant represents little tradition
B. The peasants in India are predominantly represented by the middle strata of the caste hierarchy
C. The peasants are dependents on land for the mainstay of their livelihood
D. Though the peasants are dependent on the land for the mainstay of their livelihood, they resort to several other activities for their livelihood security

Q.42 Which one of the following Indian places receives minimum rainfall in a year?

[Indian Military Academy (IMA), 2020], [Officers Training Academy (OTA), 2020]

A. Jodhpur
B. Leh
C. New Delhi
D. Bengaluru

Q.43 Timber vegetation is generally not found in which of the following regions?

[Indian Military Academy (IMA), 2020], [Officers Training Academy (OTA), 2020]

A. Subtropical region
B. Temperate region
C. Alpine region
D. Tundra region

Q.44 The Isotherm Line, which divides India North-South in almost two equal parts in the month of January, is:

[Indian Military Academy (IMA), 2020], [Officers Training Academy (OTA), 2020]

A. 10° C
B. 25° C
C. 15° C
D. 20° C

Q.45 Consider the following statements regarding the European Union:

1. The European Union is a group of 18 countries that operate as a cohesive economic and political block.

2. The EU has developed an internal single market through a standardized system of laws that apply in all member states in matters, where members have agreed to act as one.

Which of the statements given above is/are correct?

A. 1 only
B. 2 only
C. Both 1 and 2
D. Neither 1 nor 2

Q.46 Which of the following describe correctly the Group of Seven Countries (G-7)?

A. They are developing countries
B. They are industrialized countries
C. They are holding Atomic Bomb technology
D. They are the countries that can launch their own satellites

Q.47 Which of the following country is not a member of the SAARC?

A. Myanmar
B. Bhutan
C. Nepal
D. Maldives

Q.48 Which Indian theatre artist is to be conferred the prestigious French honor, Knight of the Order of Arts and Letters?

A. Naseeruddin Shah
B. Sanjana Kapoor
C. Girish Karnad
D. Lillete Dubey

Q.49 Veteran writer and conservationist Sugathakumari, who passed away, was from which state?

A. Karnataka
B. Tamil Nadu
C. Kerala
D. Andhra Pradesh

Q.50 Who has been nominated to the board of the Global Alliance for Vaccines and Immunisation (GAVI) from India?

A. Rajiv Kumar
B. Narendra Modi
C. Harsh Vardhan
D. Amitabh Kant

Reasoning

Ques (51-52):Directions: In the following question, select the related word/letters/numbers from the given alternatives.

Q.51 $21:3::574:?$
A. 23
B. 82
C. 97
D. 113

Q.52 $LNPQ:TVXY::CEGH:?$
A. *JLNP*
B. *FHJM*
C. *KMPT*
D. *KMOP*

Q.53 The focal length of a plane mirror is:

A. zero　　　　　　　　　**B.** infinite

C. very less　　　　　　　**D.** indefinite

Q.54 The Mirror formula is:

A. f = u + v　　　　　　　**B.** $f = \frac{1}{u} + \frac{1}{v}$

C. $f = \frac{u+v}{uv}$　　　　　　**D.** $\frac{1}{f} = \frac{1}{u} + \frac{1}{v}$

Q.55 Direction: Which figure is not following the same sequence as followed by figures in question figure?

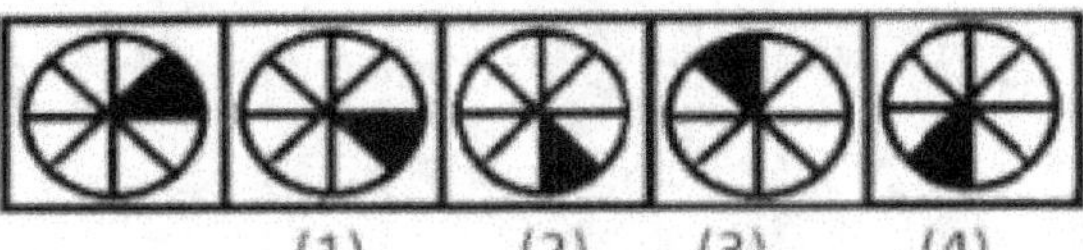

A. (1)　　　**B.** (2)　　　**C.** (3)　　　**D.** (4)

Q.56 Direction: Find the answer figure from alternatives which are numbered from 1 to 4 by using the sequence of set of figures given in question figure.

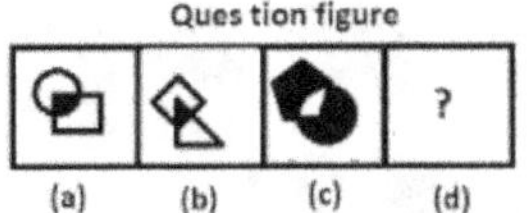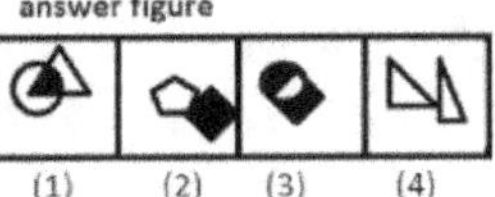

A. (1)　　　**B.** (2)　　　**C.** (3)　　　**D.** (4)

Q.57 Identify the diagram which best represents the relationship among the classes given below.

Alphabets, Numbers, Vowels, Consonants

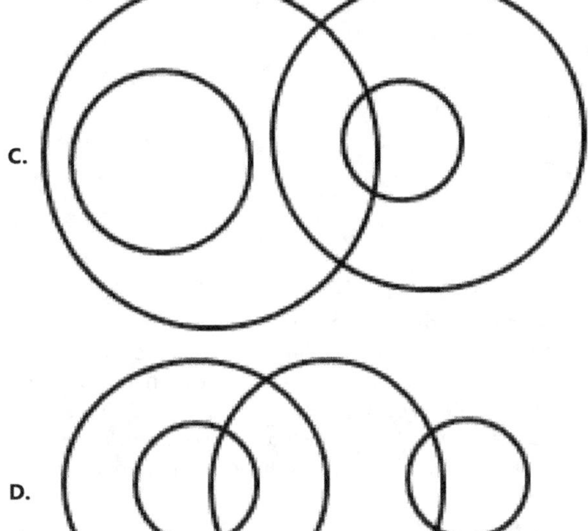

Q.58 Direction: Identify the diagram which best represents the relationship among the classes given below -

student, teacher, school

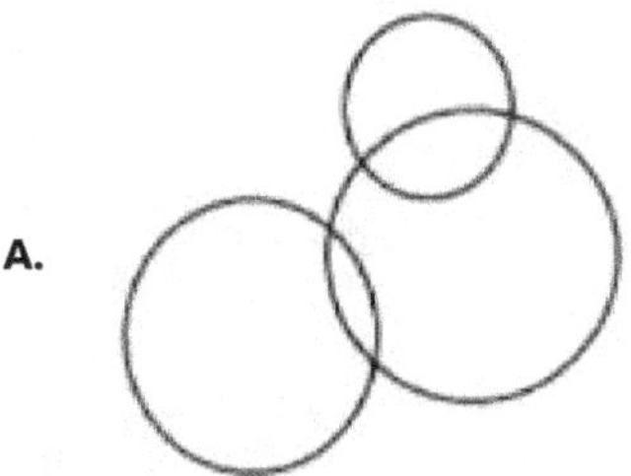

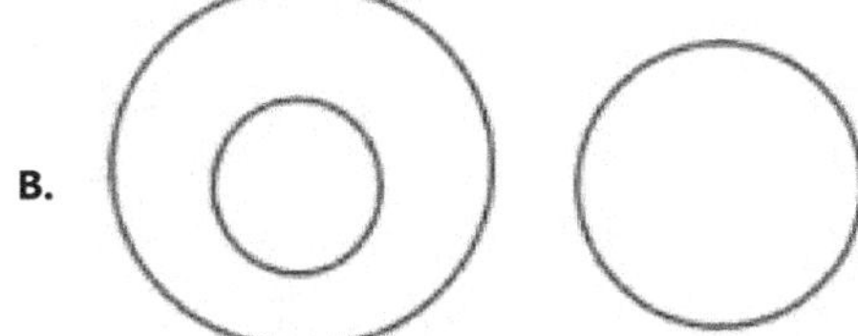

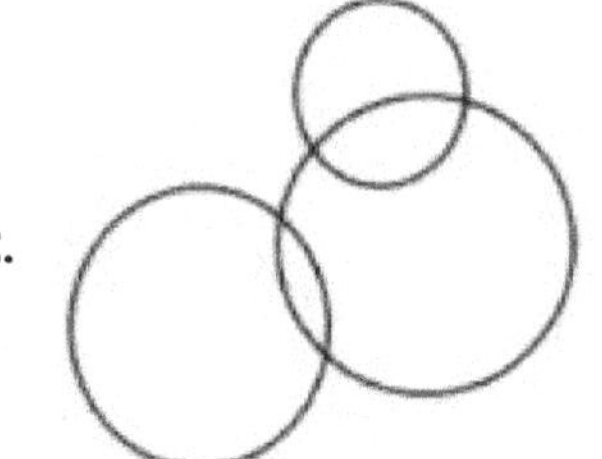

D. 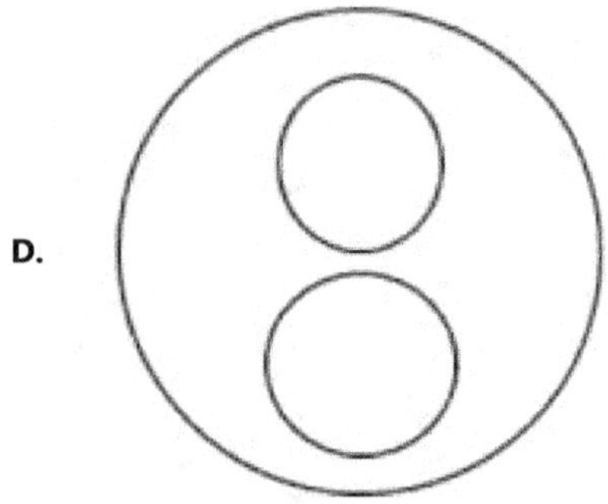

 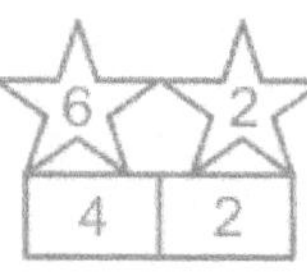 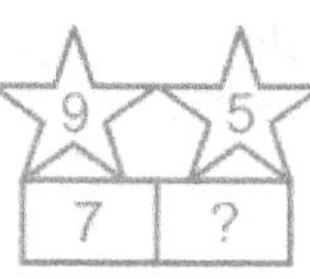

A. 2   **B.** 4   **C.** 5   **D.** 6

Q.64 Direction: Select a figure from amongst the four alternatives that when placed in the blank space (?) of the question figure will complete the pattern. (Rotation is not allowed).

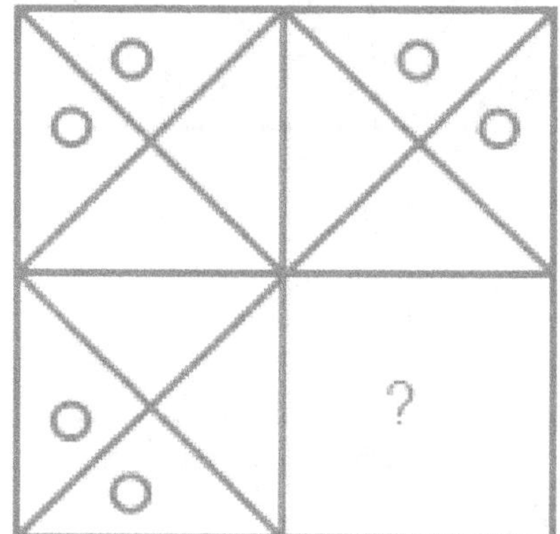

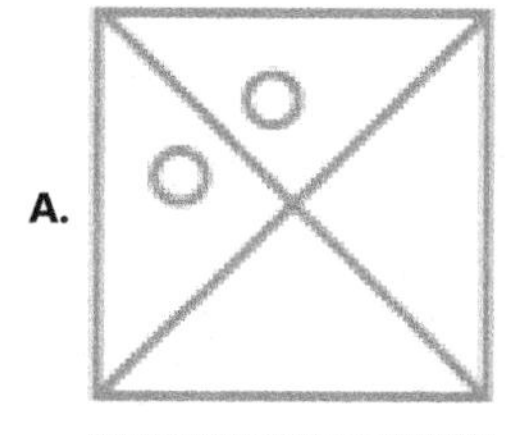 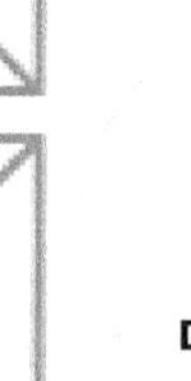 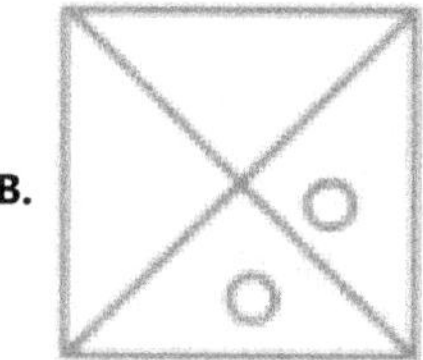

A.   **B.**

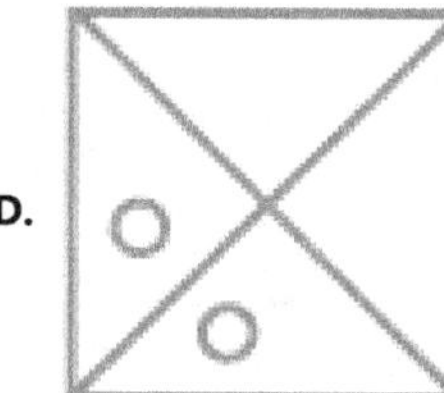

C.   **D.**

Q.59 Direction: In the question below are given two statements followed by two conclusions numbered I and II. You have to take the given statements to be true even if they seem to be at variance with commonly known facts. Read all the conclusions and then decide which of the given conclusions logically follows from the given statements disregarding commonly known facts.

Statements:

Some red which are green is yellow

All green is black

Conclusions:

I. Some black are not yellow

II. Some red are black

A. Only conclusion I follows

B. Only conclusion II follows

C. Either conclusion I or II follows

D. Neither conclusion I nor II follows

Q.60 Direction: In each question below are given three statements followed by two conclusions numbered I and II. You have to take the given two statements to be true even if they seem to be at variance with commonly known facts and then decide which of the given conclusions logically follows from the statements, disregarding commonly known facts.

Statements:

Some bananas are soaps.

Some powders are soaps.

All detergents are powders.

Conclusions:

I. Some soaps are detergents.

II. No soaps are detergents.

A. Only I follows

B. Only II follows

C. Either I or II follows

D. Neither I and II follows

Q.61 Complete the series choosing the missing number:

5, 15, 45, 135, _____

A. 455   **B.** 395   **C.** 305   **D.** 405

Q.62 Complete the following series.

19, 24, 30, 37, 45,__?

A. 57   **B.** 64   **C.** 49   **D.** 54

Q.63 Direction: Study the given pattern carefully and select the number that can replace the question mark (?) given in it.

Q.65 If January 1 is a Friday, what is the first day of the month of March in a leap year?

A. Tuesday   **B.** Wednesday

C. Thursday   **D.** Friday

Q.66 Choose a figure which would most closely resemble the unfolded form of Figure (Z).

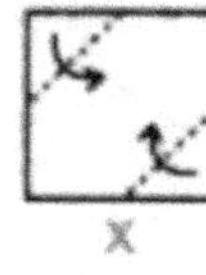 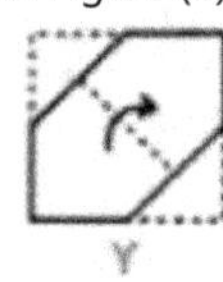 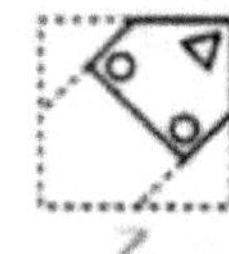

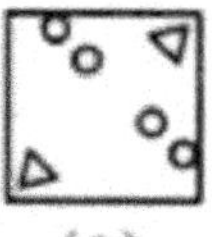 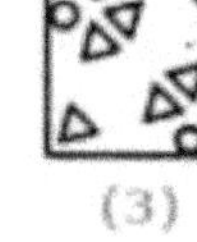

(1)   (2)   (3)   (4)

A. (1)   **B.** (2)   **C.** (3)   **D.** (4)

Q.67 Find out which of the figures (1), (2), (3), and (4) can be formed from the pieces given in figure (X).

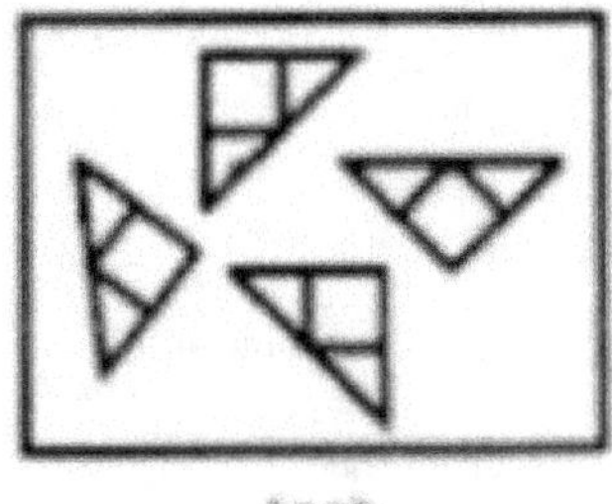

(X)

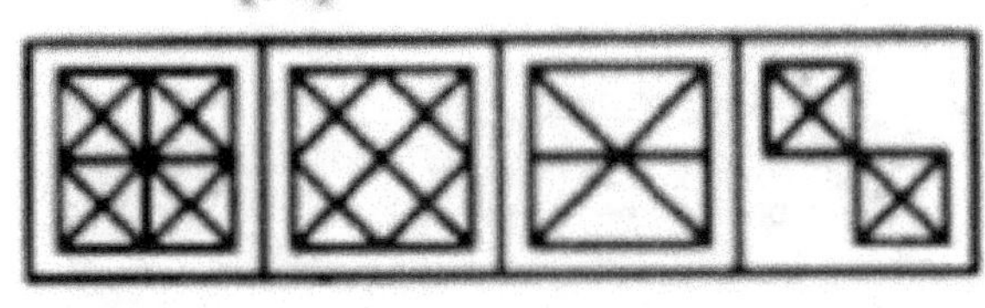

(1)　　(2)　　(3)　　(4)

A. (1)　　**B.** (2)　　**C.** (3)　　**D.** (4)

Q.68 If B = 25, SUN = 27, then CAR = ?

A. 54　　**B.** 59　　**C.** 56　　**D.** 49

Q.69 In certain code, "LIFE" is written as "3965", then how must "FUN" be written?

A. 635　　**B.** 634　　**C.** 633　　**D.** 629

Q.70 Among P, Q, R, S, and T each having different weights, S is heavier than P and R. T is lighter than P. Who is the lightest?

A. P
B. Q
C. R
D. Data inadequate

Q.71 Dino selected the 9th camera from the left in a row of 60 cameras. How many cameras will be present on the right side of Dino's selected camera?

A. 52　　**B.** 51　　**C.** 53　　**D.** 54

Q.72 P is the father of Q, but Q is not his son. S is the wife of P. R is the son of S. How is Q related to S?

A. Brother
B. Daughter
C. Father
D. Cannot be determined

Q.73 Pointing to a photograph, X said, "He is the only son of my sister's daughter". How is the person in the photograph related to X?

A. Nephew
B. Grandson
C. Granddaughter
D. Can't be determined

Q.74 Find the odd number word from the given alternative.

A. Cabbage
B. Papaya
C. Gourd
D. Cucumber

Q.75 Given below are four pairs of words out of which three are alike in some way or the other, while one is different. Select the different word pair.

[Rajasthan Police Constable, 2020]

A. High - Low
B. Easy - Hard
C. Brave - Coward
D. Black - Shiny

Numerical Ability

Q.76 10%, 20% and 25% of consecutive discounts will be equal to which single discount?

A. 55%　　**B.** 45%　　**C.** 40%　　**D.** 46%

Q.77 The average age of three boys is 15 years. If their age is in the ratio of $3:5:7$, what will be the age of the youngest boy?

A. 5 Year　　**B.** 9 Year　　**C.** 7 Year　　**D.** 8 Year

Ques (78-82):Direction: Study the following table to answer these question.

The number of watches of different companies sold in various shops in a year.

Shop Name	No. of watches sold		
	Titan	Sonata	Fastrack
A	750	850	680
B	920	670	960
C	1050	470	850
D	710	780	820

Q.78 What percentage of the total number of watches sold by shop A were Titan watches?

A. 29.9　　**B.** 32.89　　**C.** 38.15　　**D.** 28.67

Q.79 The total number of watches sold by shop D is what percentage of the total number of watches sold by shop B?

A. 78.91　　**B.** 81.67　　**C.** 90.59　　**D.** 93.48

Q.80 By what percentage is the number of Fastrack watches sold by shop C more than the number of Fastrack watches sold by shop A?

A. 15　　**B.** 835　　**C.** 25　　**D.** 20

Q.81 In which shop the average number of watches was sold the highest?

A. A　　**B.** B　　**C.** C　　**D.** D

Q.82 The number of Sonata watches sold by Shop B is what percent of the total number of Sonata watches sold by all shops together?

A. 28.32　　**B.** 22.69　　**C.** 27.52　　**D.** 24.19

Q.83 It takes 10 hours for a person to travel a distance. If he reduces his speed by 20%, then what is the percentage increase in the time taken to cover the same distance?

[UP Police Sub Inspector, 2017]

A. 33.33%
B. 20%
C. 25%
D. Can not be determined

Q.84 Write four more rational numbers in the following pattern
$$\frac{1}{-6}, \frac{2}{-12}, \frac{3}{-18}, \frac{4}{-24}$$

[RRB/RRC Group D, 2018]

A. $\dfrac{5}{6}, \dfrac{7}{8}, \dfrac{9}{10}, \dfrac{11}{12}$

B. $\dfrac{5}{30}, \dfrac{6}{36}, \dfrac{7}{42}, \dfrac{8}{48}$

C. $\dfrac{5}{-6}, \dfrac{6}{-12}, \dfrac{7}{-18}, \dfrac{8}{-24}$

D. $\dfrac{5}{-30}, \dfrac{6}{-36}, \dfrac{7}{-42}, \dfrac{8}{-48}$

Q.85 The ratio of the present age of Riti and her father is $6:13$. After 4 years the age of her father will be double of her age. what was the age of her father at the time of her birth?

A. 24   **B.** 28   **C.** 32   **D.** 26

Q.86 Walls (excluding roofs and floors) of 5 identical rooms having a length, breadth and height 6 m, 4 m and 2.5 m respectively are to be painted. Out of five rooms, two rooms have one square window each having a side of 2.5 m. Paints are available only in cans of 1 litre, and 1 litre of paint can be used for painting 20 square metres. The number of cans required for painting is:

[Indian Military Academy (IMA), 2018]

A. 10   **B.** 12   **C.** 13   **D.** 14

Q.87 The highest four-digit number which is divisible by each of the numbers 16, 36, 45, 48 is:

[Indian Military Academy (IMA), 2018]

A. 9180   **B.** 9360   **C.** 9630   **D.** 9840

Q.88 What percent of 1 day is 37 minutes 45 sec?

A. 2.62%   **B.** 2.1%   **C.** 2.69%   **D.** 0.25%

Q.89 A, B, and C can do a work in 24, 16 and 12 days respectively. How many days will it take them to complete the work, if the three of them decide to work together?

A. $5\frac{1}{3}$ days   **B.** $5\frac{2}{3}$ days   **C.** $5\frac{1}{2}$ days   **D.** $5\frac{3}{4}$ days

Q.90 When x is added to each of $9,\ 15,\ 21$ and 31, the numbers so obtained are in proportion. What is the mean proportional between the numbers $(3x - 2)$ and $(5x + 4)$?

[SSC CGL, 2020]

A. 30   **B.** 42   **C.** 35   **D.** 20

Computer Awareness

Q.91 Which of the following documents appears blurred behind the text?

A. Background   **B.** Watermark
C. Front land   **D.** Image

Q.92 What is the shortcut key to copy files from one folder to another?

A. Shift + C   **B.** Alt + C   **C.** Ctrl + C   **D.** None

Q.93 What is the shortcut key to print a document in Microsoft Word?

A. Ctrl+Shift+F12   **B.** Ctrl + Shift + P
C. Ctrl + F12   **D.** None of these

Q.94 What is the maximum number of Zoom you can do in Excel?

A. 400   **B.** 500   **C.** 600   **D.** 3000

Q.95 What is the shortcut key to hyperlink?

A. Ctrl + P   **B.** Ctrl + K
C. Ctrl + A   **D.** None of these

Q.96 If you want to send a message to many people at the same time, then what will you use?

A. Macro   **B.** Mail merge
C. Both (A) and (B)   **D.** None of these

Q.97 What is Facebook?

A. Social networking website
B. Any book
C. Face with a book
D. Internet

Q.98 What are web browser cookies?

A. It is a virus that is downloaded from the internet
B. It is a small file that contains user browsing data
C. It is an application needed for playing audio or video files
D. It verifies files that are downloaded for viruses

Q.99 In www.Google.com, www stands for:

A. Web World Wide
B. World Wide Web
C. Wide World Web
D. World Wide Weblinks

Q.100 WLAN stands for ________.

A. Wireless Local Area Network
B. Wire Lost Area Network
C. Wireless Local Ambiguity Network
D. Wired Local Area Network

// Smart Answer Sheet //

Correct — Indicates percentage of students who answered questions correctly.

Skipped — Indicates percentage of students who skipped questions.

Q.	Ans.	Correct / Skipped	Q.	Ans.	Correct / Skipped	Q.	Ans.	Correct / Skipped	Q.	Ans.	Correct / Skipped	Q.	Ans.	Correct / Skipped
1	A	78.15 % / 11.09 %	17	C	54.14 % / 30.58 %	33	C	29.81 % / 68.54 %	49	C	61.29 % / 37.41 %	65	A	46.61 % / 37.77 %
2	A	17.21 % / 82.38 %	18	B	57.98 % / 31.99 %	34	C	68.08 % / 30.29 %	50	C	40.9 % / 34.07 %	66	B	65.46 % / 32.63 %
3	A	59.26 % / 39.95 %	19	C	77.39 % / 19.09 %	35	D	50.84 % / 47.86 %	51	B	84.23 % / 14.19 %	67	B	58.65 % / 32.86 %
4	B	18.6 % / 80.35 %	20	D	10.23 % / 84.85 %	36	A	84.48 % / 14.25 %	52	D	81.74 % / 13.32 %	68	B	76.45 % / 10.77 %
5	C	59.02 % / 39.32 %	21	A	49.06 % / 31.96 %	37	A	80.69 % / 14.76 %	53	B	50.43 % / 30.94 %	69	A	66.07 % / 30.43 %
6	D	41.69 % / 46.81 %	22	C	25.86 % / 73.67 %	38	C	89.2 % / 10.26 %	54	D	76.18 % / 21.17 %	70	D	80.1 % / 19.25 %
7	D	45.06 % / 50.59 %	23	C	88.29 % / 10.39 %	39	D	61.77 % / 37.31 %	55	C	21.49 % / 72.62 %	71	B	80.85 % / 17.37 %
8	A	18.39 % / 76.24 %	24	D	88.17 % / 10.14 %	40	A	58.42 % / 38.0 %	56	C	76.11 % / 21.79 %	72	B	54.21 % / 38.59 %
9	B	44.45 % / 54.18 %	25	A	61.42 % / 36.69 %	41	C	53.94 % / 41.9 %	57	B	84.29 % / 12.96 %	73	B	88.07 % / 10.32 %
10	B	66.69 % / 31.05 %	26	B	58.95 % / 35.18 %	42	B	49.06 % / 42.89 %	58	D	64.6 % / 32.62 %	74	B	68.05 % / 31.16 %
11	A	62.48 % / 36.58 %	27	D	78.09 % / 19.12 %	43	D	50.34 % / 31.13 %	59	B	46.68 % / 51.11 %	75	D	67.55 % / 30.39 %
12	D	48.25 % / 49.56 %	28	A	61.31 % / 33.71 %	44	D	69.83 % / 30.15 %	60	C	87.03 % / 10.75 %	76	D	82.12 % / 17.39 %
13	A	11.34 % / 69.98 %	29	A	13.66 % / 68.83 %	45	B	20.7 % / 74.62 %	61	D	83.8 % / 14.36 %	77	B	44.89 % / 54.25 %
14	A	55.0 % / 36.43 %	30	D	41.29 % / 41.66 %	46	B	42.69 % / 46.09 %	62	D	80.49 % / 12.92 %	78	B	51.54 % / 36.11 %
15	D	52.17 % / 38.93 %	31	A	81.78 % / 16.67 %	47	A	45.19 % / 35.33 %	63	A	41.58 % / 51.13 %	79	C	63.6 % / 32.17 %
16	C	45.44 % / 42.99 %	32	A	48.47 % / 36.92 %	48	B	69.42 % / 30.49 %	64	B	67.83 % / 31.96 %	80	C	44.29 % / 38.0 %

Q.	Ans.	Correct		Q.	Ans.	Correct		Q.	Ans.	Correct		Q.	Ans.	Correct		Q.	Ans.	Correct
		Skipped				Skipped				Skipped				Skipped				Skipped
81	B	63.14 %		85	B	10.03 %		89	A	88.33 %		93	A	52.16 %		97	A	44.63 %
		33.31 %				85.82 %				11.32 %				36.3 %				53.54 %
82	D	58.67 %		86	B	54.17 %		90	C	66.36 %		94	A	88.43 %		98	B	27.61 %
		40.48 %				36.74 %				31.02 %				10.46 %				69.13 %
83	C	21.23 %		87	B	67.36 %		91	B	64.49 %		95	B	81.94 %		99	B	79.29 %
		72.02 %				30.15 %				31.72 %				14.23 %				18.42 %
84	D	86.0 %		88	A	40.61 %		92	C	41.2 %		96	B	67.16 %		100	A	79.31 %
		13.34 %				49.83 %				42.73 %				30.91 %				13.58 %

Performance Analysis

Avg. Score (%)	53.0%
Toppers Score (%)	58.0%
Your Score	

//Hints and Solutions//

1. Indian Foreign Service (IFS) officer Shweta Singh was on 2 August 2022 appointed as a director in the Prime Minister's Office (PMO).

- She is a 2008-batch IFS officer.
- The Appointments Committee of the Cabinet (ACC) approved Singh's appointment for a period of three years from the date of her joining.

Hence, the correct option is (A).

2. The UN held an emergency session of the General Assembly to discuss Russia's military operations in Ukraine. UNGA President Abdulla Shahid presided over the 11th Emergency Special Session of the General Assembly, at the UN Headquarters in New York. The UN Security Council voted to hold the special emergency session of UNGA. India abstained from voting on the resolution.

Hence, the correct option is (A).

3. Bharat Vatwani has been awarded for Ramon Magsaysay Award, 2018.

Bharat Vatwani is an Indian psychiatrist in Mumbai. He was awarded Ramon Magsaysay Award in 2018 for leading the rescue of thousands of mentally ill street paupers to treat and reunite them with their families. Bharat Vatwani and his wife established Shraddha Rehabilitation Foundation in 1988, aimed at rescuing mentally-ill persons living on the streets; providing free shelter, food, and psychiatric treatment; and reuniting them with their families.

Hence, the correct option is (A).

4. A one-member commission was created under the Labour Ministry's Central Advisory Contract Labour Board (CACLB), to prepare an action plan for the welfare and development of guest and contract workers during the COVID-19 pandemic.

Veteran IAS officer C V Ananda Bose, who was in-charge of the commission, has recommended payment of a basic living wage in the event of employment loss. He also sought to establish Labour Authority of India as a nodal body.

Hence, the correct option is (B).

5. The Union Ministry of health and Family welfare has issued guidelines on mass Covid-19 vaccination drive in the country.

The Ministry has stated that COVID Vaccine Intelligence Network (Co-WIN) system would be used track the beneficiaries for COVID vaccination. In the first phase of vaccination, the Government has decided to vaccinate nearly 30 crore people.

Hence, the correct option is (C).

6. India's Nikhat Zareen has won the gold medal in the 52 kg category at the Women's World Boxing Championships. She defeated Thailand's Jitpong Jutamas in the fly-weight final in Istanbul, Turkey on May 19. With this win, Nikhat becomes the fifth Indian women's boxer after Mary Kom, Sarita Devi, Jenny RL and Lekha KC to win a gold at the World Championships.

Hence, the correct option is (D).

7. India was host the 44th FIDE Chess Olympiad 2022. It was originally scheduled to be hosted in Russia. FIDE has recently announced that it pulled out from Russia following the Ukraine invasion. After the announcement, Tamil Nadu government and All-India Chess Federation made a joint bid to host the tournament It is the first time that India is hosting FIDE Chess Olympiad since its inception in 1927.

Hence, the correct option is (D).

8. The first Regional Toys Fair was organised in Varanasi at Deendayal Hastkala Sankul Trade Facilitation Centre & Museum from 27th -30th May, 2022 by the office of Development Commissioner Handicrafts, Ministry of Textiles in association with Export Promotion Council for Handicrafts (EPCH).

Hence, the correct option is (A).

9. Out of the given statements, only statement 2 is correct.

It is an independent body set up by the News Broadcasters & Digital Association (NBDA). It serves as a representative of private television news, current affairs and digital broadcasters.

Statement 1 is Incorrect .

The Authority may initiate proceedings on its own and issue notice or take action in respect to any matter which falls within its regulations. This can also be through complaints referred to the Authority by the Ministry of Information & Broadcasting or any other governmental body, or by anyone else via its website.

Statement 2 is correct.

Hence, the correct option is (B).

10. Jharkhand CM Hemant Soren has launched Jharkhand Sports Policy 2022 in Ranchi on 13th September 2022.

- This policy is aimed at reducing bottlenecks in the path of sportspersons in excelling at national and international events.
- The sports policy made for five years is the second such policy framework in Jharkhand.
- The last such policy was made in 2007.

Hence, the correct option is (B).

11. Axis Bank has signed an MoU with the Indian Air Force (IAF) to manage the salary accounts of the defence personnel in July 2022.

These salary accounts will have benefits such as a personal accident cover of up to Rs 56 lakh & air accident cover of Rs crore among others. The bank will offer a 'defence service salary package' under its 'Power Salute' initiative.

Axis Bank Limited:

CEO: Amitabh Chaudhry

Headquarters: Mumbai

Founded:1993, Ahmedabad

Hence, the correct option is (A).

12. The correct answer is rich in potash and poor in phosphorus.

Alluvial soil:

- Mostly available soil in India (about 43%) covers an area of 143 sq. km.
- Widespread in northern plains and river valleys.
- In peninsular-India, they are mostly found in deltas and estuaries.
- Humus, lime, and organic matters are present.
- Highly fertile.
- Indus-Ganga-Brahmaputra plain, Narmada-Tapi plain, etc are examples.
- They are depositional soil – transported and deposited by rivers, streams, etc.
- Sand content decreases from west to east of the country.
- New alluvium is termed as Khadar and old alluvium is termed as Bhangar.
- Its color is Light Grey to Ash Grey.
- Its texture is Sandy to silty loam or clay.
- Wheat, rice, maize, sugarcane, pulses, oilseed, etc are cultivated mainly.

Hence, the correct option is (D).

13. Justice M.N. Venkatachaliah was the Chairman of the National Commission for Review of the Working of the Constitution (2000).

Justice M.N. Venkatachaliah is the former (25th) Chief Justice of India.

- The National Commission to Review the Working of the Constitution was set up by Government Resolution dated 22 February 2000 under the Chairmanship of Justice M.N. Venkatachaliah.
- The Commission submitted its report in two volumes to the Government on 31st March 2002.
- The Commission observed that where a treaty is entered into by the Union Government concerning a matter in the State List vitally affecting the interests of the States no prior consultation is made with them.

Hence, the correct option is (A).

14. Lokmanya Tilak founded the Marathi newspaper 'Kesari'.

The Kesari newspaper is a Marathi-language Indian newspaper.

- The newspaper was initially founded in 1881 by a prominent personality of the Indian Independence Movement, Lokmanya Bal Gangadhar Tilak.
- The Kesari newspaper was originally started as a co-operative effort by Agarkar (the paper's first editor), Chiplunkar, and Tilak, and was published along with Tilak's English newspaper, the Mahratta, to encourage people to rise against the oppressive regime of the time, instead of being submissive.

- the Kesari is still published from the original offices in Pune. Reporting local, national, and international news, the paper today is still one of the leading dailies of Maharashtra.

Hence, the correct option is (A).

15. Indian constitution declares India a secular state this means that the state regards religion as a private affair of the citizen and does not discriminate on this basis.

- The meaning of secular means India does not establish any specific religion/one religion as the Official.
- Under secularism, no one country has the power to punish or discriminate against people on the basis of religion they want to follow.
- According to the Indian Constitution, each and every person has a right to profess, practice, and propagate the religion as he /she believes in.
- So, it means that in India there is a Liberty of faith and worship, which implies India's secular state.

Hence, the correct option is (D).

16. The Central Information Commission is a statutory body formed under the Right to Information Act 2005.

Central Information Commission is not a constitutional body but an independent body, which looks into complaints and appeals pertaining to offices, public sector undertakings, financial institutions, etc., under the government and the Union territories.

- Established: 12th October 2005
- Headquarters: New Delhi
- Term of office of CIC and IC: 5 years or 65 years, whichever is earlier.

Hence, the correct option is (C).

17. Geometric mean can be used to find out both population Growth and growth rate of GNP.

The geometric mean is often used for a set of numbers whose values are meant to be multiplied together or are exponential in nature, such as a set of growth figures: values of the human population or interest rates of a financial investment over time. The geometric mean is used in finance to calculate average growth rates and is referred to as the compounded annual growth rate.

Hence, the correct option is (C).

18. The first finance minister of Independent india was Sri John Mathai.

John Matthai CIE was an economist who served as India's first Railway Minister and subsequently as India's Finance Minister, taking office shortly after the presentation of India's first Budget, in 1948. He presented two Budgets as India's Finance Minister, but resigned following the 1950 Budget in protest against the increasing power of the Planning Commission and P. C. Mahalanobis.

Hence, the correct option is (B).

19. Estate duty is not a direct tax in India.

Estate duty was a form of tax which was levied on the total value of the property held by an individual calculated at the time of his / her demise. It was payable at the time when the deceased individual's property was passed on to the successors. However, in 1985, estate duty law was abolished in India.

Direct taxes are taxes that are directly paid to the government by the taxpayer. These taxes are applied on individuals and organizations directly by the government. For example: Income tax, Corporation Tax, Wealth Tax, etc.

Indirect taxes are those applied on the manufacture or sale of goods and services. These are initially paid to the government by an intermediary, who then adds the amount of tax paid to value of the goods / services and passes on the total amount to the end user. Examples : Sales tax, service tax, excise duty.

Hence, the correct option is (C).

20. 'Those Days' is the translated version of a Sahitya Akademi Award winning historical novel originally written by Sunil Gangopadhyay.

'Those Days' was originally written as Sei Samoy. Sunil Gangopadhyay won the Sahitya Akademi award for Those Days in 1982.

Important Novels:

- Atma Prakash (1966)
- Purba Paschim (1989)
- Prothom Alo (1996)

Hence, the correct option is (D).

21. A Passage to India is not authored by Nirad C. Chaudhuri.

Nirad C. Chaudhuri, born in Kishorganj, East Bengal, British India (now in Bangladesh), Bengali author and scholar who was opposed to the withdrawal of British colonial rule from the Indian subcontinent and the subsequent rejection of Western culture in independent India. He dedicated his first book, The Autobiography of an Unknown Indian (1951), to the memory of the British Empire.

Hence, the correct option is (A).

22. Annihilation of Caste (1936) was written by Dr. BR Ambedkar, also called Babasaheb Ambedkar.

He was the chairman of the Drafting Committee of the Constituent Assembly and played a crucial role in framing the Indian Constitution. The motive behind writing this book is to draw mass attention towards the depressed class and measures to remove untouchability.

Few important books of Dr. Ambedkar:

- Mook Nayak (weekly) 1920
- Janta (weekly) 1930
- The Untouchables 1948
- Buddha Or Karl Marx 1956

Hence, the correct option is (C).

23. Kheer Bhavani Mela is a popular fair held in Jammu and Kashmir. This Mela is one of the biggest religious festivals of Kashmiri Pandits, it is held annually on Jyeshtha Ashtami.
Hence, the correct option is (C).

24. This festival celebrated in the state of Telangana between 28 September to 6 October 2019 is also known as the 'Festival of Flowers'.
Hence, the correct option is (D).

25. Sabarimala is a famous Hindu temple located in the Periyar Tiger Sanctuary in Kerala. It has the largest annual pilgrimage in the world, which attracts about 2 crore devotees every year.

Sabarimala is a wonderful link between Shaivites and Vaishnavites. In Malayalam, 'Shabarimala' means mountain.

There is a temple of Lord Ayyappan in Sabarimala.
Hence, the correct option is (A).

26. Jaisalmer city of Rajasthan is famous for its yellow stone business.

The town of Jaisalmer has been built to the East and the North of the famous Jaisalmer fort which crowns the city. Jaisalmer is also called the 'Golden City' because the Yellowstone is the most common material one can find in the architecture of this city. The yellow golden sand gives a golden shadow to the city and its neighboring areas. The peculiar yellow stone found in Jaisalmer is world-famous for its art, cultural and historical heritage. It has been used in the Sonar fort and many other historical monuments.

Hence, the correct option is (B).

27. Chittorgarh district of Rajasthan is considered an ideal place for the cement industry.

The raw materials for making cement are lime, gypsum, and coal. This raw material is easily available in the Chittorgarh district of Rajasthan. Rajasthan ranks second in cement production in the country after Andhra Pradesh. The first cement factory in Rajasthan was established by ACC in 1915 at Lakheri (Bundi). Presently there are 19 large-scale cement factories, 4 medium size and 104 small-scale cement factories in Rajasthan. Chittorgarh and Sawai Madhopur are the most suitable districts for the localization of the cement industry.

Hence, the correct option is (D).

28. Eighty-four pillared chhatri or "84-pillared cenotaph" is located in the Bundi district of Rajasthan. It was built in 1740 by Rao Raja Anirudh, the Maharaja of Bundi, as a memorial to his foster brother Deva. Under whose love and guidance the prince grew up. He loved Dev very much, thus he built an 84-pillared cenotaph in his honor. It is also widely known as the "Umbrella of the Music Queen". It is said that all 84 beams cannot be counted at once.

Hence, the correct option is (A).

29. Chelsea has been awarded the Women's Super League title.

Aston Villa was declared the winner of the second-tier Women's Championship by England's Football Association (FA) on 5 June 2020.

Bottom-placed Liverpool, whose men's team are two wins away from securing a first top-flight crown in 30 years, will be relegated to the second-tier for the 2020-21 season.

Hence, the correct option is (A).

30. Sonia Lather is an Indian boxer.

She was a silver medallist at the 2016 AIBA Women's World Boxing Championships and a twice silver medallist at the Asian Amateur Boxing Championships.

Hence, the correct option is (D).

31. Koneru Humpy is from Gudivada, Andhra Pradesh, India.

In 2002, she became the youngest woman ever to achieve the title of Grandmaster at the age of 15 years.

In 2003 she was awarded Arjuna Award.

In 2007 she was awarded Padma Shri.

She is an Asian games gold medalist winning 2 gold medals in the individual and mixed category that were held in Doha.

Hence, the correct option is (A).

32. Where a Proclamation of Emergency is in operation, the President may by order declare that the right to move any court for the enforcement of such of 1[the rights conferred by Part III (except articles 20 and 21)] as may be mentioned in the order and all proceedings pending in any court for the enforcement of the rights so mentioned shall remain suspended for the period during which the Proclamation is in force or for such shorter period as may be specified in the order.

Hence, the correct option is (A).

33. The Non-Aligned Movement (NAM) was founded in 1961 in Belgrade, SR Serbia Yugoslavia.

Indian Prime Minister Jawaharlal Nehru also contributed to the established name.

The Non-Aligned Movement (NAM) is a forum of 120 developing world states that are not formally aligned with or against any major development bloc. After the United Nations, it is the largest grouping of states around the world.

Belgrade in 1961 through the initiative of Indian Prime Minister Jawaharlal Nehru, Ghana's President Dr. Sukmano, Indonesian President Sukarno, Egyptian President Gamal Abdel Nasser and Yugoslav President Josip Broz Tito, drawing on the principles agreed at the Bandung Conference in 1955 The Non-Aligned Movement was founded in , SR Serbia, Yugoslavia. Hence, both the statements are correct.

Hence, the correct option is (C).

34. Period of geopolitical tension between the Soviet Union and the United States said to be Cold War Era, in 1947-1991.

The Cold War was a period of geopolitical tension between the Soviet Union and the United States and their respective allies, the Eastern Bloc and the Western Bloc, after World War II.

The period is generally considered to span 1947 to the 1991 dissolution of the Soviet Union.

The term "cold" is used because there was no large-scale fighting directly between the two superpowers, but they each supported major regional conflicts known as proxy wars.

The West was led by the United States as well as the other First World nations of the Western Bloc that were generally liberal democratic but tied to a network of authoritarian states, most of which were their former colonies.

Hence, the correct option is (C).

35. The western alliance North Atlantic Treaty Organisation (NATO), which came into existence in April 1949. So, statement 1 is not correct.

The eastern alliance, known as the Warsaw Pact, was led by the Soviet Union which was created in 1955. So, statement 2 is not correct.

The North Atlantic Treaty Organization, also called the North Atlantic Alliance, is an intergovernmental military alliance between 30 European and North American countries. The organization implements the North Atlantic Treaty that was signed on 4 April 1949.

Hence, the correct option is (D).

36. In the green pigment of leaves magnesium is present. Magnesium is needed during photosynthesis for chlorophyll to capture sun energy, i.e., magnesium is required to give green colour to leaves.

Hence, the correct option is (A).

37. Bhopal gas tragedy happened due to leakage of Methyl Isocyanate gas. It was the deadliest gas tragedy in the history of India. It destroyed the life of many generation of the people.

On 3 December 1984, Methyl isocyanate(Chemical formula- CH_3NCO or C_2H_3NO situated in Bhopal, Madhya Pradesh. After this tragedy, the government of India enacted a Public Liability Insurance Act (1991). Recently on 7th May 2020, another major gas leak incident occurred from the styrene plant owned by South Korean electronics giant LG in R. R. Venkatapuram village on the outskirts of Visakhapatnam.

Hence, the correct option is (A).

38. Minamata disease caused by the mercury contaminated water. It was first discovered in Minamata city of japan that's why it is called as Minamata Disease.

Blue baby syndrome caused by the nitrate contaminated water. Hence, the correct option is (C).

39. Zika virus was first detected in Uganda in 1947 by the scientists when they were researching on yellow fever. Zika Virus was named after the Zika Forest of Uganda. In the local language word, Zika means overgrown. In the research, scientists came across a different and apparently harmless virus transmitted by mosquitoes to monkeys and they named it as Zika.

Hence, the correct option is (B).

40. Oxford University and IBM Research Labs chemists have achieved that the first ring-shaped stable molecule of pure carbon is a circle of 18 atoms. The work was published in a recent issue "Science". Circular carbon molecules are known as cyclocarbons and the smallest such ring comprises 18 atoms which are predicted to be stable.

Hence, the correct option is (A).

41. The peasants are dependents on land for the mainstay of their livelihood. A peasant is a pre-industrial agricultural labourer or a farmer with limited land-ownership, especially one living in the Middle Ages under feudalism and paying rent, tax, fees, or services to a landlord.

Hence, the correct option is (C).

42. The place in India receiving the lowest rainfall is Leh.

- The average annual precipitation in these regions is less than 50 cms. The cities like Jaisalmer in Rajasthan and Leh in Ladakh receive the least rainfall.

- India mainly receives rainfall from the Monsoons which lasts from June-September. Overall, India receives an average of 200-300 mm of rainfall over the country as a whole with the largest values observed during the monsoon season.

- The average annual rainfall in India is about 300–650 millimeters.

- The rainy season in India is affected by the humid southwest summer monsoon.

- The South of India typically receives more rainfall.

Hence, the correct option is (B).

43. Timber vegetation is generally not found in Tundra region.

- Timber is a type of wood that has been processed into beams and planks.

- It is also known as 'lumber' in the US and Canada.

- Any wood capable of yielding a minimum dimensional size can be termed timber or lumber. It is a stage in the process of wood production.

- Timbers are used for structural purposes. Those woods which are adapted for building purposes are timbers. Finished timber is supplied in standard sizes for the industry.

- Timber is used for building houses and making furniture.

- The Timber vegetation is generally found in the Subtropical, Temperate, and Alpine regions.

- The tundra is a treeless polar desert found in the high latitudes in the polar regions, primarily in Alaska, Canada, Russia, Greenland, Iceland, and Scandinavia, as well as sub-Antarctic islands. The region's long, dry winters feature months of total darkness and extremely frigid temperatures.

Hence, the correct option is (D).

44. The Isotherm Line, which divides the India North-South into almost two equal parts in January is 20°C.

- Isotherms are the lines that connect points of equal temperature on weather maps, so at every point along a given isotherm, the temperature values are the same.

- Isotherms help to visualize and to interpret the horizontal temperature distribution of an area by showing the patterns of temperature on a weather or oceanography map.

- Constructing the map of isotherms is an elementary step in the temperature data analysis, and the process, in general, is known as contouring.

- It can even be done for other parameters like barometric pressure (isobars), dew point temperature (isodrosotherms), geopotential height (isohypses), wind speed (isotachs), and salinity (isohalines). Isotherms are always smooth, labeled with the values, and mostly parallel to each other.

- The isotherm of 20°C runs roughly parallel to the Tropic of Cancer.

Hence, the correct option is (D).

45. The European Union is a group of 28 countries that operate as a cohesive economic and political block.

- So statement 1 is not correct.

19 of these countries use EURO as their official currency.

9 EU members (Bulgaria, Croatia, Czech Republic, Denmark, Hungary, Poland, Romania, Sweden, and the United Kingdom) do not use the euro.

The EU grew out of a desire to form a single European political entity to end centuries of warfare among European countries that culminated with World War II and decimated much of the continent.

The EU has developed an internal single market through a standardized system of laws that apply in all member states in matters, where members have agreed to act as one.

- So statement 2 is correct.

Hence, the correct option is (B).

46. The Group of 7 is a group consisting of Canada, France, Germany, Italy, Japan, the United Kingdom and the United States. These countries, with the 7 largest advanced economies in the world, represent more than 62% of the global net wealth. They are industrialized economies.

Hence, the correct option is (B).

47. Myanmar is not a member of the SAARC. All the members of the SAARC are; Afghanistan, Bangladesh, Bhutan, India, Nepal, the Maldives, Pakistan and Sri Lanka.

Hence, the correct option is (A).

48. Veteran theatre personality and the daughter of Bollywood star Shashi Kapoor, artist Sanjna Kapoor is to be presented with the French honour, Knight of the Order of Arts and Letters. The award is conferred on her for the outstanding contribution the artist has made to the theatre arts.

The Culture Minister of France, Franck Riester, who is currently on an official visit to India, is expected to confer the prestigious award on Sanjna Kapoor in a proposed ceremony. Sanjana Kapoor acted in several plays and revived the Prithvi Theatre in Mumbai, which was founded by her parents in tribute to Prithviraj Kapoor. She also co-founded an organization called Junoon, which increases the reach of theatre and the arts.

Hence, the correct option is (B).

49. Renowned Malayalam poet, conservationist and women's rights activist Sugathakumari passed away at the age of 86.

The writer has released 15 collections of much-acclaimed poems. Sugathakumari was also the first chairperson of the Kerala State Women Commission and led the launch of Kudumbashree Missions. She had received various awards including the Padma Shri, the Saraswati Samman among others.

Hence, the correct option is (C).

50. Union Minister of Health and Family Welfare Harsh Vardhan has been nominated by the Global Alliance for Vaccines and Immunisation (GAVI) as a member on the GAVI Board.

The Minister is to succeed Mr. Myint Htwe of Myanmar and will represent the South East Area Regional Office (SEARO)/ Western Pacific Regional Office (WPRO) constituency from 1st January 2021 until 31st December 2023.

Hence, the correct option is (C).

51. Here, $21:3$ is given in the form of $7x:x$.

So, $574 = 7 \times ?$

$$\Rightarrow ? = \frac{574}{7} = 82$$

Hence, the correct option is (B).

52. Here, the pattern is:

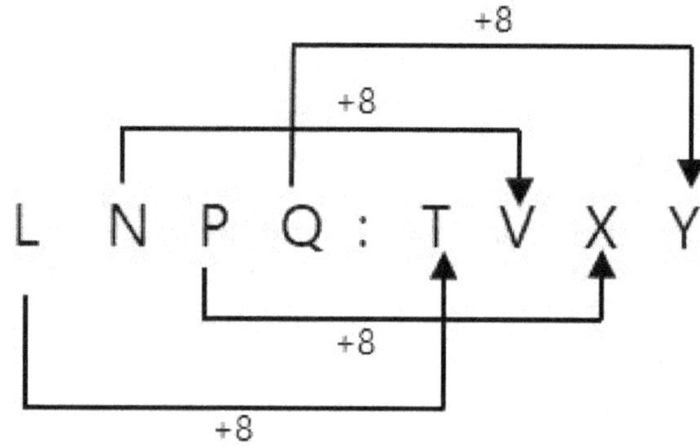

Similarly,

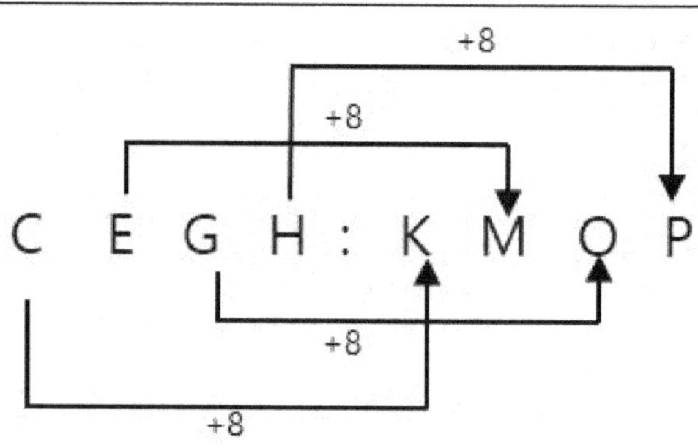

Thus, $CEGH$ is related to $KMOP$.

Hence, the correct option is (D).

53. The focal length of a plane mirror is infinite.

Since the plane mirror is a part of an infinitely large spherical mirror, therefore the radius of curvature and focal length of the plane mirror is Infinity.

Hence, the correct option is (B).

54. The Mirror formula is $\dfrac{1}{f} = \dfrac{1}{u} + \dfrac{1}{v}$.

where, f = focal length, v = the distance of the image from the mirror, and u = the distance of the object from the mirror.

Mirror Formula: The following formula is known as the mirror formula, which represents the relation between focal length, image distance, and object distance.

Hence, the correct option is (D).

55. In each step, one space is shaded in clockwise direction.

According to figure only figure (3) is not shaded in clockwise direction.

Hence, the correct option is (C).

56. Like in 1st two figures common area is shaded, in next set of figures common area is not shaded.

Hence, the correct option is (C).

57. Vowels and consonants are parts of alphabets while numbers are not alphabets.

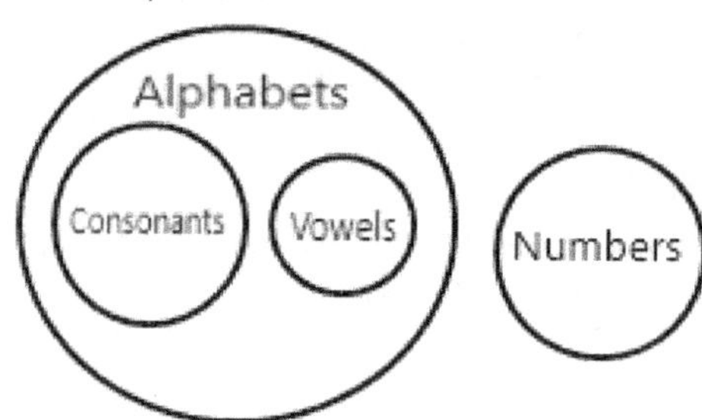

Hence, the correct option is (B).

58. Both teachers and students are part of the school. Also, no student can be a teacher.

Hence, the correct option is (D).

59. The least possible diagram for the given statements is as follows:

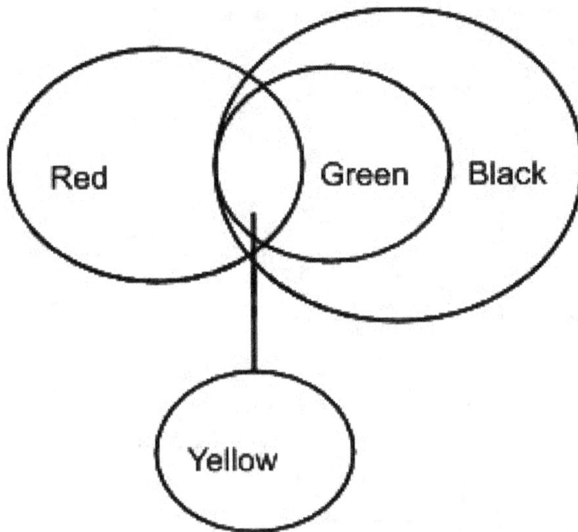

Conclusions:

I. Some black are not yellow → False (It is possible but not definite)

II. Some red are black → True (All green are black and some red are green). Therefore, only conclusion II follows.

Hence, the correct option is (B).

60. The least possible Venn diagram for the given statements is as follows.

Conclusions:

I. Some soaps are detergents → False (It is possible but not definite)

II. No soaps are detergents → False (It is possible but not definite)

Here some + not condition form a complementary pair.

Therefore, Either conclusion I or II follows.

Hence, the correct option is (C).

61. The series 5, 15, 45, 135, _____ followed the pattern

⇒ 5 × 3 = 15

⇒ 15 × 3 = 45

⇒ 45 × 3 = 135

Similarly

⇒ 135 × 3 = 405

∴ The missing number is 405.

Hence, the correct option is (D).

62. Given

19, 24, 30, 37, 45,__?

⇒ 19 + 5 = 24

⇒ 24 + 6 = 30

⇒ 30 + 7 = 37

⇒ 37 + 8 = 45

⇒ 45 + 9 = 54

∴ The complete series is 19, 24, 30, 37, 45, 54.

Hence, the correct option is (D).

63. The pattern follows left to right:

1st diagram: 3 × 2 = 6 and 2 + 4 = 6

2nd diagram: 4 × 2 = 8 and 6 + 2 = 8

Similarly,

3rd diagram: 9 + 5 = 14

Let the missing number be 'a'.

So, 7 × a = 14

⇒ a = 14 ÷ 7

⇒ a = 2

Hence, the correct option is (A).

64. The figure from amongst the four alternatives that when placed in the blank space (?) of the figure will complete the pattern when rotation is not allowed, is shown below:

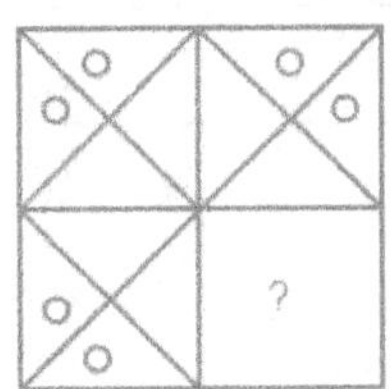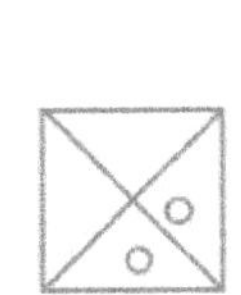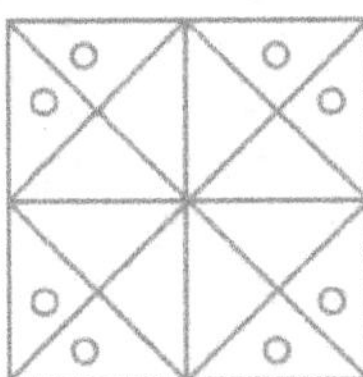

Hence, the correct option is (B).

65. Given:

January 1 is a Friday.

A leap year

Total number of days from January 1 to March 1

= 31 + 29 + 1

= 61 days

(February in leap years = 29 days) = 61 ÷ 7

= 8 weeks and 5 odd days

So, the fifth day from Friday = Tuesday

Hence, the correct option is (A).

66.

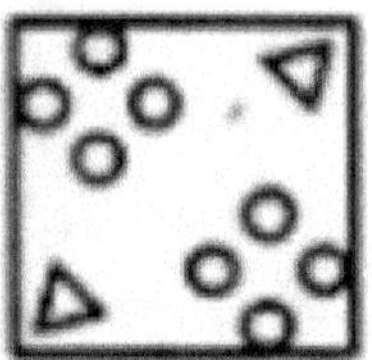

Figure (2), would most closely resemble the unfolded form of Figure (Z).

Hence, the correct option is (B).

67.

Figure (2) can be formed from the pieces given in figure (X).

Hence, the correct option is (B).

68. B = 25 i.e., the position number of B from the right end or in reverse order.

SUN = 8+6+13 = 27

So, CAR = 24+26+9 = 59

Hence, the correct option is (B).

69. According to the given coding language,

A	B	C	D	E	F	G	H	I	J	K	L	M
1	2	3	4	5	6	7	8	9	10	11	12	13
Z	Y	X	W	V	U	T	S	R	Q	P	O	N
26	25	24	23	22	21	20	19	18	17	16	15	14

L = 12 (1 + 2) = 3
I = 9
F = 6
E = 5
Similarly,
F = 6
U = 21 (2 + 1) = 3
N = 14 (1 + 4) = 5
So, FUN corresponds to 635.

Hence, the correct option is (A).

70. According to the given information,

P > T and S > P, R

Therefore, we cannot determine who is the lightest.

Hence, the correct option is (D).

71. Total number of cameras $=$ Position of the camera from right $+$ Position of the camera from left

$60 =$ Position of Dino's camera from right $+9$

Position of Dino's camera from right $= 60 - 9 = 51$

Therefore, there will be 51 cameras on the right-hand side of his selected camera.

Hence, the correct option is (B).

72. P is the father of Q, but Q is not his son,

Q is the daughter of P (male).

Also, S is the wife of P. R is the son of S,

Q (female) and R (male) are siblings.

Thus, Q is the daughter of S.

Hence, the correct option is (B).

73. The diagram according to the question,

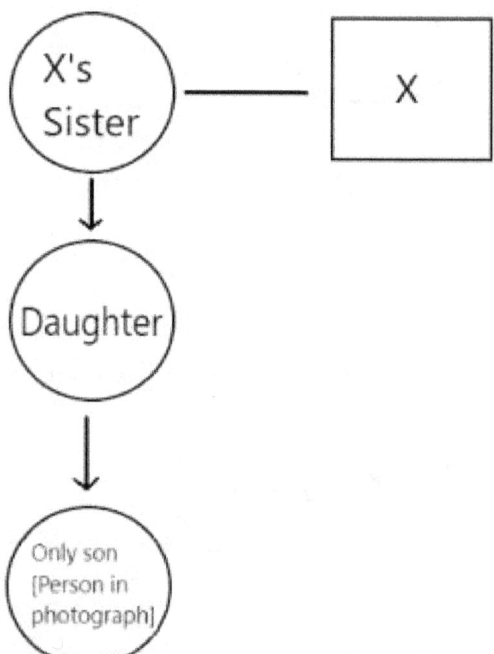

Therefore, from the above family tree, the person in the photograph is the grandson of X.

Hence, the correct option is (B).

74. All of them except Papaya are vegetables, while papaya is fruit.

Hence, the correct option is (B).

75. Except option (D) all are antonyms of the first word in a pair of words.

Black - Shiny → Black is not the antonym of Shiny.

High - Low → High is an antonym of Low.

Easy - Hard → Easy is an antonym of Hard.

Brave - Coward → Brave is an antonym of Coward.

Hence, the correct option is (D).

76. Given,
$10\%, 20\%$ and 25% consecutive discounts.
As we know,
Consecutive discount for $x\%$ and $y\% = [x + y - \frac{xy}{100}]$
Consecutive discount for 10% and 20% discounts $= 10 + 20 - [\frac{(10\times20)}{100}] = 28\%$
Consecutive discount for 28% and 25% discounts $= 28 + 25 - [\frac{(28\times25)}{100}] = 46\%$
$\therefore$ The value of single discount is 46%.

Hence, the correct option is (D).

77. Let the age of three boys be $3x, 5x$ and $7x$ respectively. And the average age is 15 years.

While the average age $= \frac{3x+5x+7x}{3}$

$15 = \frac{15x}{3}$

$\Rightarrow x = 3$

Therefore, the youngest boy's age $= 3 \times 3 = 9$ Year

Hence, the correct option is (B).

78. From the table,

Total watches sold in shop A $= 750 + 850 + 680 = 2280$

Titan watches sold in shop A $= 750$

Required percentage $= \frac{750}{2280} \times 100 = 32.89\%$

$\therefore 32.89\%$ of total numbers of watches sold by shop A were Titan watches.

Hence, the correct option is (B).

79. From the table,

No. of watches sold				
Shop Name	Titan	Sonata	Fastrack	Total number of watches sold
B	920	670	960	920+670+960=2550
D	710	780	820	710+780+820=2310

Required percentage $= \frac{2310}{2550} \times 100\% = 90.588\% \approx 90.59\%$

$\therefore$ The total number of watches sold by shop D is 90.59% of total number of watches sold by shop D.

Hence, the correct option is (C).

80. From the table,

The number of Fastrack watches sold by shop $A = 680$

The number of Fastrack watches sold by shop $C = 850$

The increase in the sale of Fastrack watches
$= 850 - 680 = 170$

Required percentage $= \frac{170}{680} \times 100\% = 25$

$\therefore$ Number of Fastrack watches sold by shop C is more than the number of Fastrack watches sold by shop A by 25%.

Hence, the correct option is (C).

81. From the table,

No. of watches sold					
Shop Name	Titan	Sonata	Fastrack	Total number of watches sold	The average number of watches sold
A	750	850	680	750+850+680=2280	22803=760
B	920	670	960	920+670+960=2550	25503=850
C	1050	470	850	1050+470+850=2370	23703=790
D	710	780	820	710+780+820=2310	23103=770

$\therefore$ The average number of watches sold in shop B was the highest.

Hence, the correct option is (B).

82. From the table,

Total number of Sonata watches sold by all shops together $= 850 + 670 + 470 + 780 = 2770$

The number of Sonata watches sold by shop $B = 670$

Required percentage $= \frac{670}{2770} \times 100\% = 24.187\% \approx 24.19\%$

$\therefore$ The number of Sonata watches sold by Shop B is 24.19% of the total number of Sonata watches sold by all shops together.

Hence, the correct option is (D).

83. Given:

Let, speed be x km/hour.

It takes 10 hours to travel the distance.

That means total distance = 10x km

Latter speed $= x\left\{\frac{(100-20)}{100}\right\} = \left(\frac{4x}{5}\right)$ km/hour

Time taken to cover the whole distance at this speed

is $\dfrac{10x}{\left(\frac{4x}{5}\right)}$ = 12.5 hour

Time increase = (12.5 – 10) hours = 2.5 hours

Percentage increase in time taken = $\left(\dfrac{2.5}{10}\right)$ × 100 = 25%

Hence, the correct option is (C).

84. $\dfrac{1}{-6}, \dfrac{2}{-12}, \dfrac{3}{-18}, \dfrac{4}{-24}, \dfrac{5}{-30}, \dfrac{6}{-36}, \dfrac{7}{-42}, \dfrac{8}{-48}$

Numerators are consecutive natural numbers and denominators are successive multiples of 6.

Hence, the correct option is (D).

85. Given:

The ratio of the present age of Riti and her father $= 6:13$.

After 4 years the age of her father $=$ double of Riti's age.

Let, her present age is $6x$ and that of her father is $13x$.

After 4 years her age will be $(6x + 4)$.

After 4 years her father's age will be $(13x + 4)$.

Accordingly,

$(13x + 4) = 2 \times (6x + 4)$

$\Rightarrow 13x + 4 = 12x + 8$

$\Rightarrow 13x - 12x = 8 - 4$

$\Rightarrow x = 4$

Riti's present age is $(6 \times 4) = 24$ years

And her father's present age is $(13 \times 4) = 52$

At the time of her birth, her father's age was $(52 - 24) = 28$ years

∴ The age of her father was 28 years at the time of her birth.

Hence, the correct option is (B).

86. Given:

Length of room = l = 6 m

Breadth of room = b = 4 m

Height of room = h = 2.5 m

⇒ Total area of walls of 1 room = 2lh + 2bh = 30 + 20 = 50 m²

⇒ Total area of walls in 5 identical rooms = 5(50) = 250 m²

Now, two rooms have one square window each of side 2.5 m,

⇒ Area of the two windows = 2 × (2.5)² = 12.5 m²

⇒ Total area to be painted = 250 – 12.5 = 237.5 m²

∵ Area of 20 m² can be painted in 1 can,

∴ Total no. of cans required = $\dfrac{237.5}{20}$ = 11.875 ≅ 12

Hence, the correct option is (B).

87. We can write,

⇒ 16 = 2⁴

⇒ 36 = 2² × 3²

⇒ 45 = 3² × 5

⇒ 48 = 2⁴ × 3

LCM of the numbers = Product of highest powers of prime factors = 2⁴ × 3² × 5 = 720

Now, Highest 4-digit number = 9999

On dividing 9999 by 720, remainder = 639

∴ Required number = 9999 - 639 = 9360

Hence, the correct option is (B).

88. 37 min 45 sec $= \dfrac{151}{4}$ min

1 days $= 24$ hrs $= 24 \times 60$ min

$\Rightarrow \dfrac{151}{4 \times 24 \times 60} \times 100 = 2.62\%$

Hence, the correct option is (A).

89. Given,

A can do the work in 24 days.

B can do the work in 16 days.

C can do the work in 12 days.

Efficiency $= \dfrac{\text{Total work}}{\text{Time taken}}$

LCM of $24, 16$ and $12 = 48 =$ Total work

Efficiency of $A = \dfrac{48}{24} = 2$ units/day

Efficiency of $B = \dfrac{48}{16} = 3$ units/day

Efficiency of $C = \dfrac{48}{12} = 4$ units/day

Total efficiency of A, B and C together $= (2 + 3 + 4) = 9$ units/day

Time taken by A, B and $C = \dfrac{48}{9} = \dfrac{16}{3} = 5\dfrac{1}{3}$ days

∴ Time taken if all of them work together is $5\dfrac{1}{3}$ days.

Hence, the correct option is (A).

90. Given:

When x is added to each of $9, 15, 21$ and 31, the numbers so obtained are in proportion.

As we know,

If a, b, c and d are in proportion, then $\dfrac{a}{b} = \dfrac{c}{d}$

Mean proportion of two numbers a and b is $\sqrt{ab}$

According to Question,

$\dfrac{(9+x)}{(15+x)} = \dfrac{(21+x)}{(31+x)}$

$\Rightarrow (9 + x)(31 + x) = (15 + x)(21 + x)$

$\Rightarrow x^2 + 40x + 279 = x^2 + 36x + 315$

$\Rightarrow 4x = 36$

$\Rightarrow x = 9$

Mean proportion of $(3x - 2)$ and $(5x + 4) =$
$\sqrt{\{(3 \times 9 - 2)(5 \times 9 + 4)\}}$

$= \sqrt{(25 \times 49)}$

$= 35$

$\therefore$ Mean proportional between the numbers $(3x - 2)$ and $(5x + 4)$ is 35.

Hence, the correct option is (C).

91. The watermark appears faintly (or blurred) in the background on every page of your document, except for the title page.

Hence, the correct option is (B).

92. Ctrl + C is the shortcut key to copy files from one folder to another. Hold down Ctrl and press X to cut or C to copy. Right-click the item's destination and choose Paste. You can right-click inside a document, folder, or nearly any other place. Hold down Ctrl and press V to paste.

Hence, the correct option is (C).

93. Ctrl+Shift+F12 prints a document in Microsoft Word.

Hence, the correct option is (A).

94. You can zoom in the workbook by moving the slider to the right. It will change the only view of the workbook. You can have maximum of 400% zoom in.

Hence, the correct option is (A).

95. Ctrl+K is a keyboard shortcut that varies depending on the program used. For example, in certain programs, Ctrl+K is used to insert a hyperlink, and in some browsers, Ctrl+K focuses on the search bar.

Hence, the correct option is (B).

96. If you want to send a message to many people at the same time, then you can use mail merge. Mail Merge is a useful tool that allows you to produce multiple letters, labels, envelopes, name tags, and more using information stored in a list, database, or spreadsheet.

Hence, the correct option is (B).

97.

- Social networking is the use of internet-based social media sites to stay connected with friends, family, colleagues, customers, or clients.

- Social networks provide instant communication and offer the opportunity to share information with people from any part of the world and with which we shared some type of interest.

- Facebook is a social networking site that makes it easy for you to connect with family and friends online. Originally designed for college students, Facebook was created in 2004 by Mark Zuckerberg while he was enrolled at Harvard University.

- Facebook is a popular free social networking website that allows registered users to create profiles, upload photos and video, send messages and keep in touch with friends, family, and colleagues.

Other social networking sites and their founders:

Social networking sites	Founders
Twitter	Jack Dorsey, Evan Williams, Biz Stone, Noah Glass
Instagram	Kevin Systrom
Whats App	Jan Koum, Brian Acton

Hence, the correct option is (A).

98.

- Cookies are messages that web servers pass to your web browser when you visit websites.

- Your browser stores each message in a small file called a cookie.

- When you request another page from the server, your browser sends the cookie back to the server.

- These files typically contain information about your visit to the web page, as well as any information you've volunteered, such as your name and interests.

- The term cookie is an allusion to a Unix program called Fortune cookie that produces a different message, or fortune, each time it runs.

- Cookies are also used for online shopping.

- Online stores often use cookies that record any personal information you enter, as well as any items in your electronic shopping cart, so that you don't need to re-enter this information each time you visit the site.

- Servers can use cookies to provide personalized web pages.

- When you select preferences at a site that uses this option, the server places the information in a cookie. When you return, the server uses the information in the cookie to create a customized page for you.

- The website that creates a cookie can read it, so other servers do not have access to your information. Additionally, web servers can use only information that you provide or choices that you make while visiting the website as content in cookies.

Hence, the correct option is (B).

99. WWW stands for World Wide Web.

The World Wide Web is all the resources and users on the internet that are using the Hypertext Transfer Protocol (HTTP).

World Wide Web was created by Timothy Berners Lee in 1989 in CERN in Geneva.

Hence, the correct option is (B).

100. WLAN stands for "Wireless Local Area Network".

It is a wireless computer network that allows devices to connect and communicate wirelessly within a limited area.

It is also referred to as LAWN (local area wireless network).

WLANs use radio waves.

Hence, the correct option is (A).

General Awareness/Current Affairs

Q.1 Which country has won gold medal in men's table tennis event at the 2022 Commonwealth Games in Birmingham on 2 August 2022 ?

A. Malaysia

B. Canada

C. India

D. South Africa

Q.2 Where was the International Conference on Climate Change held in December 2018?

[Super TET Paper - I, 2019]

A. Kankun (Mexico)

B. Durban (South Africa)

C. Katowice (Poland)

D. Doha (Qatar)

Q.3 Who among the following introduced the Preventive Detention Bill in 1950 in the Indian parliament?

A. Baldev Singh

B. Narahar Vishnu Gadgil

C. Sardar Patel

D. Jawahar Lal Nehru

Q.4 Which company has signed a Memorandum of Understanding (MoU) with SIDBI to accelerate e-commerce for small industries in August 2022?

A. Flipkart **B.** Zomato **C.** Myntra **D.** ONDC

Q.5 Special ASEAN-India Foreign Ministers' Meeting (SAIFMM) will be held on the 16th and 17th June 2022 in ______________.

A. New Delhi, India

B. Islamabad, Pakistan

C. Dhaka, Bangladesh

D. Colombo, Sri Lanka

Q.6 Which of the following rail corridors has been acquired by Adani Ports and Special Economic Zone (APSEZ)?

A. Sarguja Rail Corridor

B. Howrah-Haldia Rail Corridor

C. Eastern Dedicated Freight Corridor

D. North-South Dedicated Freight Corridor

Q.7 India's first 'Amrit Sarovar' has come up in which state?

A. Gujarat

B. Punjab

C. Odisha

D. Uttar Pradesh

Q.8 Which edition of Chartered Accountant's Day was observed on 1 July 2022?

A. 70th **B.** 72th **C.** 74th **D.** 76th

Q.9 The Union Government has authorised which bank for issue and encash Electoral Bonds through its 29 Authorized Branches from 1–10 th of July 2022?

A. State Bank of India

B. Axis Bank

C. ICICI Bank

D. HDFC Bank

Q.10 Who assassinated W.C. Rand, the Plague Commissioner of Pune in 1897?

A. Ganesh Savarkar

B. Chapekar Brothers

C. Vasudev Balwant Phadke

D. Chiplunkar Brothers

Q.11 The Indian Railways has placed a purchase order for 39,000 wheels for LHB coaches from the manufacturer of which of the following country in July 2022?

A. Ukraine

B. China

C. Russia

D. Germany

Q.12 Who is the first woman of the world who climbed Mount Everest successfully from the Kangshung side?

[Rajasthan Teachers Eligibility Test - Level 1 Primary Level (RTET), 2021]

A. Bachendri Pal

B. Santosh Yadav

C. Premlata Agrawal

D. Arunima Sinha

Q.13 Who was the first Indian astronaut?

[Rajasthan Teachers Eligibility Test - Level 1 Primary Level (RTET), 2021]

A. Kalpana Chawla

B. Sunita Williams

C. Rakesh Sharma

D. Raja Cheri

Q.14 Which deity (Lok Devta) of Rajasthan is known as 'Deity of camels'?

[Rajasthan Teachers Eligibility Test - Level 1 Primary Level (RTET), 2021]

A. Goga ji

B. Ramdev ji

C. Pabu ji

D. Bhomia ji

Q.15 Match the following:

	Rights		Articles
1.	Right to Equality	(A).	21
2.	Right to Freedom	(B).	14
3.	Right to Property	(C).	19
4.	Right to Life	(D).	300A

A. 1(C), 2(B), 3(A), 4(D)

B. 1(B), 2(C), 3(D), 4(A)

C. 1(B), 2(C), 3(A), 4(D)

D. 1(C), 2(B), 3(D), 4(A)

Q.16 Which of the following is not a feature of Indian federalism?

A. Indian federalism is based on Canadian model of federalism.

B. The word federalism is mentioned in article 1 under the Indian Constitution.

C. KC Wheare described Indian federalism as Quasi federalism.

D. Federalism is a part of basic structure.

Q.17 Malinowski's functionalism is often termed as

A. Individualistic functionalism
B. Collective functionalism
C. Fundamental functionalism
D. Psychological functionalism

Q.18 The Doctoral thesis of Dr. Ambedkar is entitled as:

[UGC NET Sociology, 2020]

A. Ancient Indian Commerce
B. State and minorities Annihilation of caste
C. Commercial Relations of India
D. The problem of Rupee: Its origin and its solution

Q.19 Depeasantization essentially means

[UGC NET Sociology, 2020]

A. The Shrinking size of peasant's practices or small producers from the land
B. The condition in which a person or community takes up corporate farming
C. The condition in which a person changes his occupation and marriage pattern
D. The condition in which a person becomes a millionaire

Q.20 Which one of the following pairs is/are not correctly matched?

Name of the author	Title of the Book
1. R.C. Dutt	Economic History of India
2. Bal Gangadhar Tilak	The Drain of Wealth and Indian Nationalism at the turn of the century
3. W. Digly	Prosperous British India
4. V. Anstey	The Economic Development of India

A. 1 and 2 only
B. 2 only
C. 1 and 3 only
D. 2 and 3 only

Q.21 Who wrote the Natyashastra?

A. Bharat
B. Chanakya
C. Kalhana
D. Sudraka

Q.22 Whose autobiography is "My Life"?

A. Nelson Mandela
B. Bill Clinton
C. Margaret Thatcher
D. J.M. Lyngdoh

Q.23 Which state is associated with the "Chaitra Jatra Festival" held annually?

A. Chhattisgarh
B. Andra Pradesh
C. Karnataka
D. Odisha

Q.24 In which style are the temples of Bhubaneswar and Puri built?

A. Nagar
B. Dravid
C. Besar
D. None of these

Q.25 Consider the following historical sites:

1. Ajanta Caves
2. Lepakshi Temple
3. Sanchi Stupa

Which of the above sites/murals are also known for painting?

A. Only 1
B. Only 1 and 2
C. 1, 2 and 3
D. No one

Q.26 The correct match is:

1	Lohagarh Fort	a	Jaisalmer
2	Jaigarh Fort	b	Rajsamand
3	Kumbhalgarh Fort	c	Jaipur
4	Sonar Fort	d	Bharatpur

A. 1-c, 2-d, 3-b, 4-a
B. 1-b, 2-c, 3-d, 4-a
C. 1-d, 2-c, 3-a, 4-b
D. 1-d, 2-c, 3-b, 4-a

Q.27 Where is Albert Hall Museum of Rajasthan located?

A. Jaipur
B. Jaisalmer
C. Jodhpur
D. Jhunjhunu

Q.28 The Centre for Cellular and Molecular Biology is situated at:

A. Patna
B. Jaipur
C. Hyderabad
D. New Delhi

Q.29 Who among the following is NOT a recipient of Rajiv Gandhi Khel Ratna 2020?

A. Vinesh Phogat
B. Rohit Sharma
C. Mariyappan Thangavelu
D. Mirabai Chanu

Q.30 In which city is the summer Olympic Games 2024 to be held?

[Bihar Police SI, 2019]

A. Los Angeles
B. London
C. Beijing
D. Paris

Q.31 Which Indian player won the first Olympic Medal in badminton?

A. Kidambi Srikanth
B. Saina Nehwal
C. Prakash Padukone
D. P. Gopichand

Q.32 Which two Indian Presidents died while in Office?

i. Zakir Hussain
ii. Rajendra Prasad
iii. Fakhruddin Ali Ahmed
iv. A.P.J Abdul Kalam

[HSSC Canal Patwari, 2021]

A. ii and iv **B.** iii and iv **C.** i and iii **D.** i and iv

Q.33 Which among the following is/are examples of Mauryan Art & Architecture:

1. Yakshini at Didarganj.
2. Lion Capital at Sarnath.
3. Seated Buddha at Sarnath.
4. Caves in Barabar hills.

Select the correct answer using the code:

A. 1 and 2 only
B. 1,2,3 and 4
C. 2,3 and 4
D. 1,2 and 4

Q.34 Which of the following changes was/were introduced by the Montagu - Chelmsford Reforms?

1. Montagu-Chelmsford Reforms introduced by the colonial government in British India to introduce self-governing institutions gradually in India.

2. Bicameral legislature was introduced at the centre.

A. 1 only
B. 2 only
C. Both 1 and 2
D. Neither 1 nor 2

Q.35 Choose the correct order in which the following committees were established.

1. Alagh Committee

2. Lakdawala committee

3. C.Rangrajan committee

4. Tendulkar committee

Choose the correct option-

A. 2-3-4-1
B. 1-2-4-3
C. 2-4-3-1
D. 1-4-3-2

Q.36 Which one of the following reactions is the main cause of the energy radiation from the sun?

A. Fusion reaction
B. Fission reaction
C. Chemical reaction
D. Diffusion reaction

Q.37 If excess fertilizers are applied to a plant without water the plant will-

A. Be stunted in growth
B. Develop modifications
C. Die due to plasmolysis
D. Remain unaffected

Q.38 What is the unit of Nervous system?

A. Brain
B. Spinal Cord
C. Neuron
D. Nerves

Q.39 The process that they do to avoid spoiling of products

A. Pasteurization
B. Precipitation
C. Purification
D. None of these

Q.40 Which of the following anti-satellite missile is tested by India on 27 March 2019?

A. Mission Antriksh
B. Mission Gagan
C. Mission Shakti
D. Mission Destruction

Q.41 Which state of India became first to reserve a government job for HIV positive candidates?

A. Uttar Pradesh
B. Mizoram
C. Kerala
D. Maharashtra

Q.42 Which of the following is a erosional feature by river?

A. Loess
B. U-shaped valley
C. V-shaped valley
D. Natural levee

Q.43 Which of the following is true about the Indian ocean currents:

1. It is mostly driven by the monsoon wind

2. Seasonal reversal is found in the northern part

3. Agulhas is a cold current near the east African coast

A. 1,2 and 3
B. 1 and 2
C. 2 and 3
D. 1and 3

Q.44 The invisible line joins the North pole to the South Pole is called:

A. Meridian
B. Latitude
C. Equator
D. Axial plane

Q.45 Which country released a commemorative postage stamp on 75th anniversary of UN?

A. USA
B. India
C. Russia
D. China

Q.46 Consider the following statements regarding the Hague Convention on the Civil Aspects of International Child Abduction:

1. The convention seeks to return children abducted or retained overseas by a parent to their country of habitual residence.

2. The convention applies to the child, up to the age of 18 years.

3. All the members of the United Nations are the party to the Hague Convention.

Which of the statements given above is/are correct?

A. 1 and 2 only
B. 1, 2 and 3
C. 1 only
D. 2 and 3 only

Q.47 Consider the following statements regarding the World Trade Organization.

1. The World Trade Organization is an international body that deals with the rules of trade between nations.

2. The World Trade Organization (WTO) has chosen Italian's former finance minister Ngozi Okonjo-Iweala as its first female leader.

Which of the statements given above is/are correct?

A. 1 only
B. 2 only
C. Both 1 and 2
D. Neither 1 nor 2

Q.48 Which sports award is given by the Government ofMaharashtra?

A. Shiv Chhatrapati State Lifetime SportsAchievement Award
B. Shiv Chhatrapati State Sports Award
C. Shiv Chhatrapati State AdventureSports Award
D. All of the above

Q.49 Cash prize of Dronacharya Award is:

A. Rupees Five Lakhs
B. Rupees four Lakhs
C. Rupees ten Lakhs
D. Rupees Twenty Lakhs

Q.50 _______given for Outstanding Performance in Sports and Games, is the second-highest sporting honour of India.

A. Arjuna Award
B. Padma Award
C. Dhyanchand Lifetime AchievementAward
D. Major Dhyan Chand Khel Ratna Award

Reasoning

Q.51 A man starts from a point, walks 4 miles towards the north and turns left and walks 6 miles, turns right and walks for 3 miles and again turns right and walks 4 miles and takes rest for 30 minutes. He gets up and walks straight 2 miles in the

same direction and turns right and walks one mile. What is the direction he is facing?

A. North
B. West
C. South-east
D. South

Ques (52-53):Direction: In the following question, select the related word from the given alternatives.

Q.52 RST : QPO :: MNO : ?

A. YZA
B. GHI
C. BAC
D. LKJ

Q.53 APPEAR : FUUJFW : : GRIND : ?

A. LWNSI
B. ISNWL
C. LNWSI
D. LINWS

Q.54 Select the odd word pair from the given alternatives.

A. Akbar
B. Humayun
C. Jahangir
D. Alauddin Khalji

Q.55 Direction: A mirror is placed on the line NM, and then which of the Answer Figures is the right image of the given Question Figure?

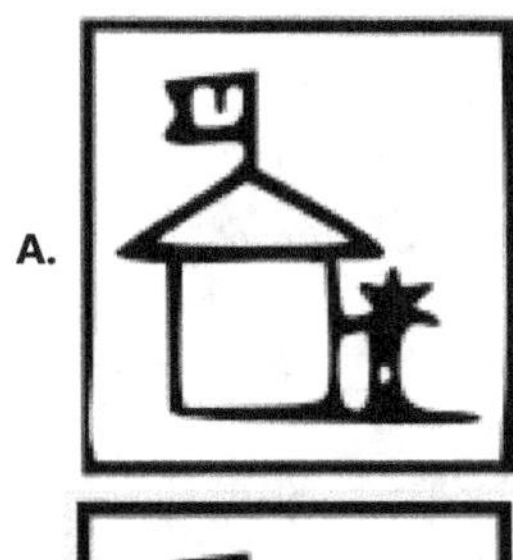

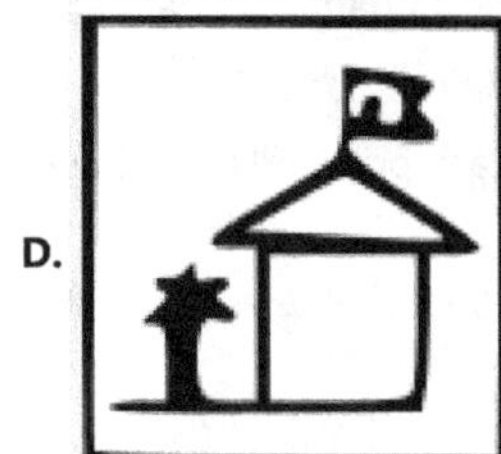

Q.56 Direction: A mirror is placed on the line MN, and then which of the Answer Figures is the right image of the given Question Figure?

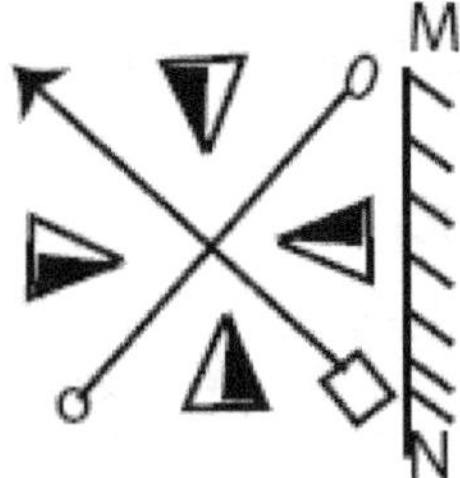

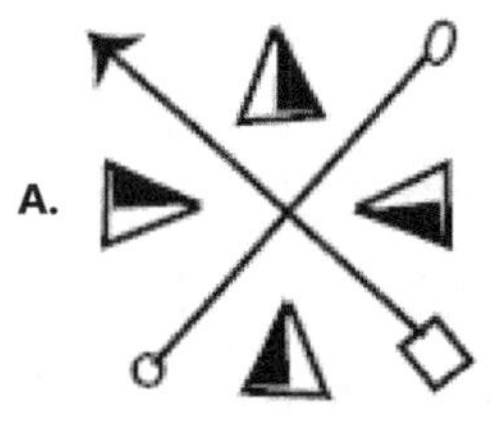

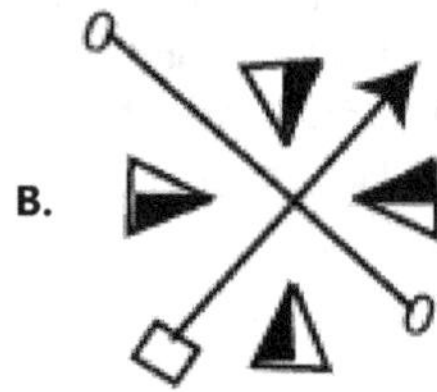

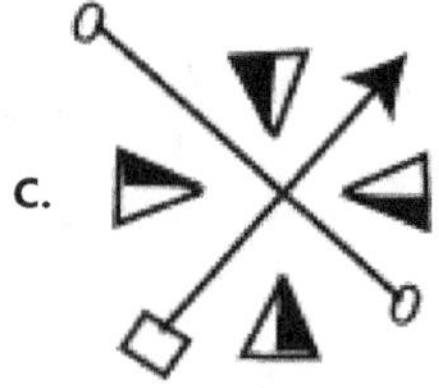

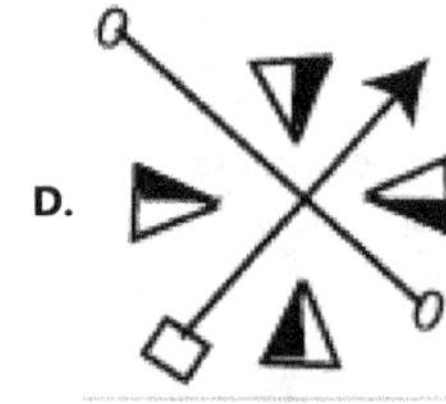

Q.57 Direction: Which figure will come next in the series.

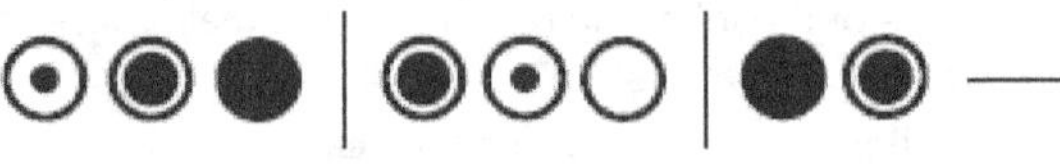

A. ● **B.** ◉ **C.** ⊙ **D.** ○

Q.58 If, ' + ' is coded as ' $ ', ' × ' is coded as ' # ', ' ÷ ' is coded as ' @ ', ' − ' is coded as ' ! ' then what is the value of

95 @ 5 $ 46 ! 3 # 27

A. −18
B. −21
C. −16
D. −14

Q.59 In the following question, select the word which cannot be formed using the letters of the given word.

MALINTERDIGITATION

A. Male
B. Inter
C. Action
D. Line

Q.60 In the following question below are given some statements followed by some conclusions. Taking the given statements to be true even if they seem to be at variance from commonly known facts, read all the conclusions, and then decide which of the given conclusion logically follows the given statements.

Statements:

1. Some cups are tables.

2. Some tables are chairs.

Conclusions:

I. Some chairs are not cups.

II. Some chairs are tables.

A. Only conclusion (I) follows
B. Only conclusion (II) follows
C. Both conclusions follow
D. Neither conclusion (I) nor conclusion (II) follows

Q.61 Arrange the given words in the sequence in which they occur in the dictionary.

1. Decisive

2. Dethrone

3. Decision

4. Demand

5. Dearth

A. 5 1 4 3 2
B. 1 5 4 2 3
C. 5 3 1 4 2
D. 1 5 3 2 4

Q.62 Direction: Which number will replace the question mark (?) in the following number series ?

34, 42, 50, 56, 62, 66, ?

[SSC Sub Inspector (CPO), 2020]

A. 68   **B.** 72   **C.** 66   **D.** 70

Q.63 Direction: Which number will replace the question mark (?) in the following number series ?

24, 61, 122, 213, ?

[SSC Sub Inspector (CPO), 2020]

A. 343   **B.** 334   **C.** 337   **D.** 340

Q.64 Direction: Choose the options figure in which the problem figure is hidden/embedded.

Question Figure:

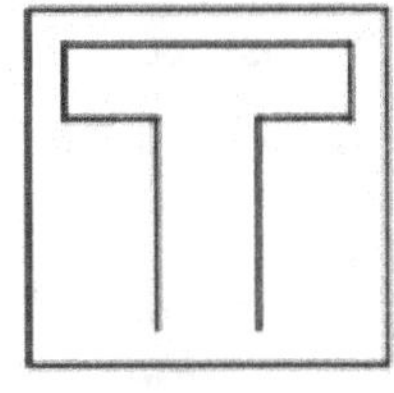

A. 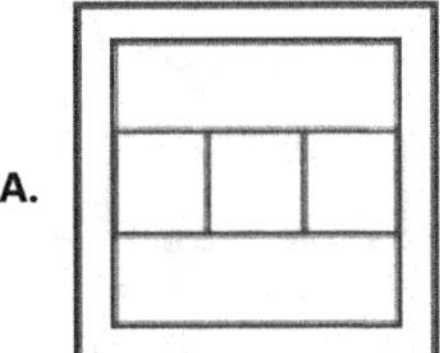   **B.** 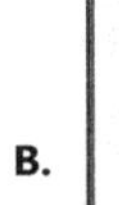

C. 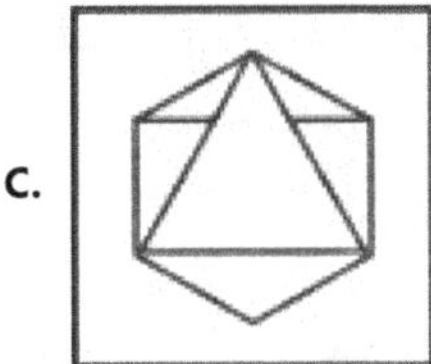   **D.** 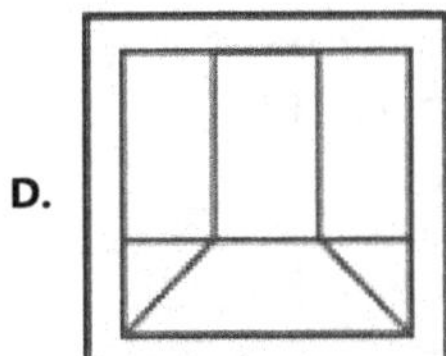

Q.65 Direction: Select the option in which the given figure (X) is embedded (rotation is NOT allowed).

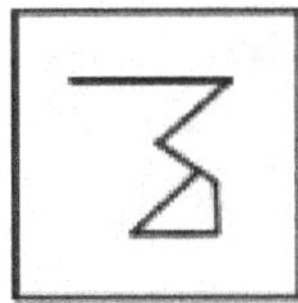

X

[SSC Sub Inspector (CPO), 2020]

A.    **B.** 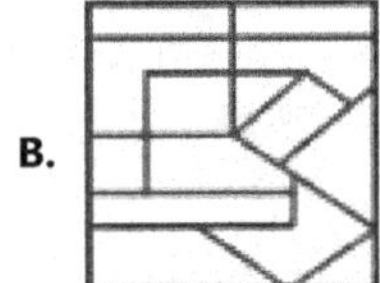

C. 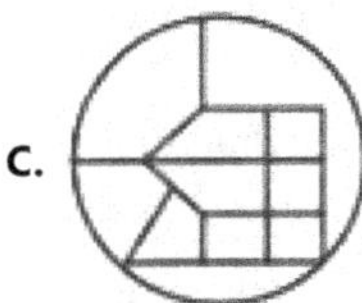   **D.** 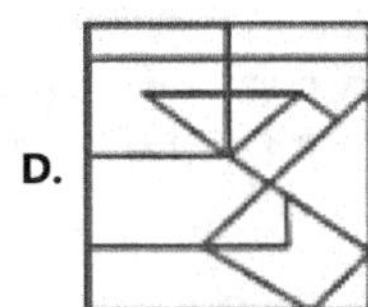

Q.66 Direction: Read the given statement(s) and conclusions carefully and select which of the conclusions logically follow(s) from the statement(s).

Statements:

I. Some napkins are papers.

II. Some napkins are cloth.

Conclusions:

1. Some cloth are napkins.

2. Some papers are cloth.

A. Neither 1 nor 2 follows

B. Conclusion 1 alone follows

C. Conclusion 2 alone follows

D. Both 1 and follows

Q.67 The angle between the minute hand and the hour hand of a clock when the time is 4:20 is:

[Uttarakhand Public Service Commission (UKPSC), 2016]

A. 5°   **B.** 10°   **C.** 20°   **D.** 0°

Q.68 The following question consists of a set of three figures X, Y and Z showing a sequence of folding of a piece of paper. Figure (Z) shows the manner in which the folded paper has been cut. These three figures are followed by four answer figures from which you have to choose a figure which would most closely resemble the unfolded form of a figure (Z).

Choose a figure which would most closely resemble the unfolded form of Figure (Z).

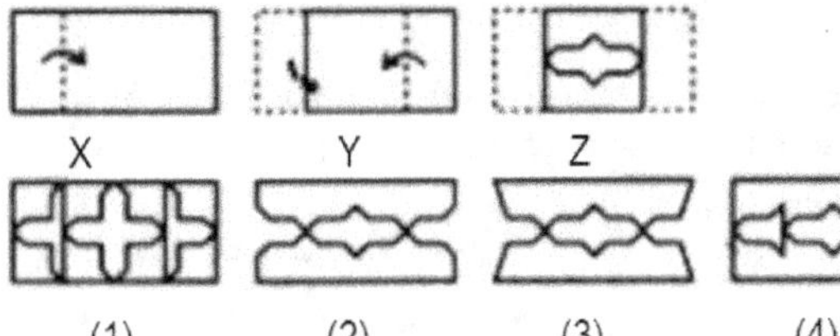

A. (1)   **B.** (2)   **C.** (3)   **D.** (4)

Q.69 In code language, 'ROLLER' is written as 'TQNJCP', then how will 'DOCILE' be written as in that language?

[SSC Selection Post Phase IX, 2019]

A. FPEHID   **B.** FPFGJC

C. FQEGJC   **D.** EPFGKD

Q.70 In a code language, if 'MOUNT' is coded as '166', then how will 'ROUND' be coded in the same language?

[SSC Selection Post Phase IX, 2019]

A. 146   **B.** 142   **C.** 144   **D.** 140

Q.71 Five newly born babies were weighed by the doctor. Infant A was lighter than infant B. Infant C was lighter than

infant D. Infant B was lighter than infant D but heavier than infant E. Which infant was the heaviest?

A. Infant E **B.** Infant D **C.** Infant B **D.** Infant C

Q.72 Pointing towards a girl, Gitesh said, "She is the only daughter of my daughter-in-law". How is the girl related to Gitesh?

A. Daughter **B.** Niece
C. Sister **D.** Grand daughter

Ques (73-74):Direction: Read the given statement and conclusions carefully. Assuming that the information given in the statement is completely true, even if it differs from commonly known facts, decide which of the given conclusions follow/s the statement?

Q.73 Statement: Some basketball players are women.

Conclusions:

(i) Some basketball players are not women.

(ii) Not all basketball players are women.

[Rajasthan Police Constable, 2020]

A. Only conclusion (i) follows.
B. Only conclusion (ii) follows.
C. Both conclusion (i) and conclusion (ii) follow.
D. Neither conclusion (i) nor conclusion (ii) follows.

Q.74 Statement: All pianists are good at dance.

Conclusions:

(i) All people who are good at dance are pianists.

(ii) Some people who are good at dance are pianists.

[Rajasthan Police Constable, 2020]

A. Only conclusion (i) follows.
B. Only conclusion (ii) follows.
C. Both conclusion (i) and conclusion (ii) follow.
D. Neither conclusion (i) nor conclusion (ii) follows.

Q.75 Direction: Choose the word from the alternatives that are most similar to the set of given words.

Almonds, Cashew, Walnuts

[Rajasthan Police Constable, 2020]

A. Banana **B.** Apple
C. Apricot **D.** Watermelon

Numerical Ability

Q.76 A bank offers the business loan at simple interest, rate of interest for 1st 2 years is 8% for the next 3 years it is 10% and for the period beyond 5 years it is 12.5% per annum. If a person took the loan of Rs. $20\,L$ and paid Rs. $36.7\,L$ after some years. Find the number of years after which he repaid the loan:

A. 7 years **B.** 9 years **C.** 8 years **D.** 10 years

Q.77 A pipe can fill a tank with water in 20 hours but due to leakage at the tank in it's bottom, it takes 40 hours to fill the tank. In what time the leakage will empty the fully filled tank.

A. 40 hours **B.** 30 hours **C.** 60 hours **D.** 5 hours

Q.78 In how many ways can an interview panel of 3 members be formed from 2 engineers, 3 psychologists and 4 managers if at least 1 psychologist must be included?

A. 56 **B.** 64 **C.** 72 **D.** 84

Q.79 The value of $8 - 3 \div 6$ of $2 + \left(4 \div 4 \text{ of } \dfrac{1}{4}\right) \div 8 + \left(4 \times 8 \div \dfrac{1}{4}\right) \times \dfrac{1}{8}$ is:

[SSC Sub Inspector (CPO), 2020]

A. $-\dfrac{97}{4}$ **B.** $\dfrac{7}{4}$ **C.** $-\dfrac{7}{4}$ **D.** $\dfrac{97}{4}$

Q.80 In one hour, a boat goes 11 km along the stream or 5 km against the stream. Find the speed of the boat in still water.

A. 3 km/hr **B.** 6 km/hr **C.** 5 km/hr **D.** 8 km/hr

Q.81 The value of $3 \div 18$ of $3 \times 6 + 21 \times 6 \div 18 - 3 \div 2 + 3 - 3 \div 9$ of 3×9 is:

[SSC CGL, 2020]

A. $\dfrac{29}{6}$ **B.** $\dfrac{41}{9}$ **C.** $\dfrac{47}{6}$ **D.** $\dfrac{35}{9}$

Q.82 The value of $\left(2.\overline{4} \times 0.\overline{6} \times 30 \times 0.\overline{16}\right) \times \left[0.\overline{27} \times \left(0.\overline{83} \div 0.\overline{16}\right)\right]$ is:

[SSC CGL, 2020]

A. $0.\overline{11}$ **B.** $1.\overline{36}$ **C.** 11.3 **D.** $1.\overline{814}$

Ques (83-87):Direction: The Pie chart shows the percentage of visitors visited in the sanctuary on different days in a week (except Saturday).

Total number of persons visiting on a sanctuary in six days of a week $= 72600$

Percentage of visitors visited in Sancturay

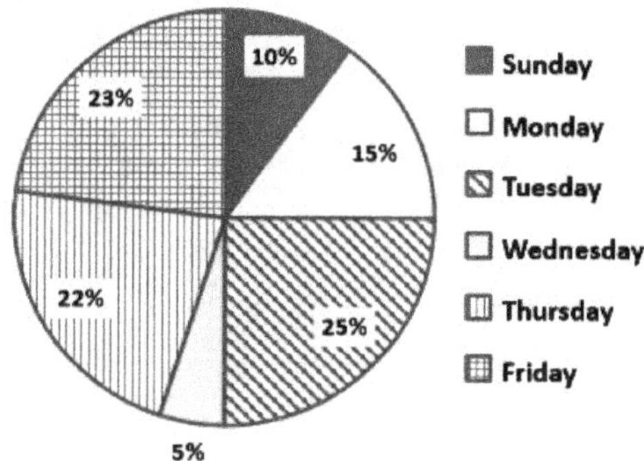

Q.83 If 20%, 30%, and 16.67% of the total number of visitors visited in the sanctuary on Monday, Wednesday and Friday respectively are female then find the total number of female visitors on those days together?

A. 6850 **B.** 8650 **C.** 6050 **D.** 6520

Q.84 The number of visitors visited in the sanctuary on Friday is how much percent is more than the number of visitors visited in Monday?

A. 66.66% **B.** 100% **C.** 53.33% **D.** 33.33%

Q.85 What is the respective ratio between the number of visitors in Wednesday to the number of visitors on Friday visited in the sanctuary?

A. 2 : 13   **B.** 5 : 23   **C.** 9 : 11   **D.** 23 : 5

Q.86 What is the average number of person visited in the sanctuary over the six days in a week?

A. 11470   **B.** 12100   **C.** 13100   **D.** 10470

Q.87 If 25% of the total number of visitors visited on Sunday is equal to the number of visitors visited in another sanctuary in a week, out of them two-fifth part are female. What is the total number of female visitors who visited another sanctuary?

A. 1726   **B.** 726   **C.** 826   **D.** 3630

Q.88 Joseph scored 8 marks fewer than Amit in an examination. Kumar scored 12 marks more than Amit. In total, they scored 205 marks. What was the score of Joseph?

[Jawahar Navodaya Entrance Class VI, 2018]

A. 67   **B.** 79   **C.** 59   **D.** 75

Q.89 A vessel contains 2.5 liters of water and 10 liters of milk. 20% of the contents of the vessel are removed. To the remaining contents, x liters of water is added to reverse the ratio of water and milk. Then y liter of milk is added again to reverse the ratio of water and milk. Find y.

A. 120   **B.** 200   **C.** 150   **D.** 100

Q.90 3 men or 5 women can complete the work in 12 days then in how many days 3 men and 7 women will complete the same work?

A. 5 days   **B.** 8 days   **C.** 10 days   **D.** 15 days

Computer Awareness

Q.91 Which of the following is the shortcut in Microsoft Word to insert a link?

A. Ctrl+I   **B.** Ctrl+K   **C.** Ctrl+U   **D.** Ctrl+N

Q.92 What was the default font in MS Word 2007?

A. Calibri   **B.** Times New Roman
C. Arial   **D.** Cambria

Q.93 Anti-virus is installed in a computer to:

A. Safeguard the computer from virus
B. Safeguard the computer from fire
C. Improve the memory size
D. Install other programs

Q.94 Which of the following appears dimly behind main body text?

A. Watermark   **B.** Background
C. Water colour   **D.** Layout

Q.95 Which of the following is grid of cells made up of horizontal and vertical columns?

A. Formula bar   **B.** OneNote
C. Worksheet   **D.** Page

Q.96 In MS Word 2019, table option comes under the______ menu.

A. file   **B.** review   **C.** insert   **D.** layout

Q.97 Which algorithm is used to decide the path to transfer the packets from source to destination?

A. Routing   **B.** Pathing
C. Selecting   **D.** Directing

Q.98 Which of the following denotes http://www.yahoo.com?

A. Web site   **B.** URL
C. Web page   **D.** Home page

Q.99 Full form of DNS.

A. Domain name system
B. Driving name system
C. Domain navigation system
D. None of the above

Q.100 Which of the following refers to a small, single-site network?

A. LAN   **B.** DSL   **C.** RAM   **D.** USB

// Smart Answer Sheet //

Correct — Indicates percentage of students who answered questions correctly.

Skipped — Indicates percentage of students who skipped questions.

Q.	Ans.	Correct / Skipped
1	C	80.68 % / 17.58 %
2	C	24.91 % / 72.36 %
3	C	61.86 % / 30.28 %
4	D	65.47 % / 30.71 %
5	A	87.27 % / 10.79 %
6	A	23.31 % / 76.43 %
7	D	44.93 % / 48.57 %
8	C	87.86 % / 11.7 %
9	A	88.74 % / 10.99 %
10	B	43.52 % / 53.62 %
11	B	68.59 % / 30.16 %
12	B	81.47 % / 12.31 %
13	C	88.03 % / 10.42 %
14	C	66.94 % / 31.33 %
15	B	47.81 % / 32.74 %
16	B	62.31 % / 33.32 %
17	A	62.4 % / 35.1 %
18	D	54.47 % / 36.38 %
19	A	43.76 % / 52.03 %
20	B	67.04 % / 30.26 %
21	A	66.33 % / 33.52 %
22	B	46.37 % / 53.14 %
23	D	68.76 % / 30.24 %
24	A	68.22 % / 30.98 %
25	B	45.4 % / 42.1 %
26	D	80.97 % / 17.09 %
27	A	61.42 % / 38.24 %
28	C	79.19 % / 11.3 %
29	D	87.59 % / 11.34 %
30	D	47.64 % / 38.69 %
31	B	66.62 % / 32.45 %
32	C	47.04 % / 48.09 %
33	D	29.11 % / 70.68 %
34	C	67.53 % / 30.79 %
35	B	69.36 % / 30.61 %
36	A	82.79 % / 13.9 %
37	C	66.82 % / 32.63 %
38	C	64.22 % / 35.41 %
39	A	54.21 % / 43.81 %
40	C	43.79 % / 37.57 %
41	C	42.89 % / 33.98 %
42	C	42.14 % / 49.94 %
43	B	66.43 % / 30.78 %
44	A	61.7 % / 30.97 %
45	B	29.91 % / 67.84 %
46	C	49.95 % / 31.25 %
47	A	47.05 % / 42.03 %
48	D	87.92 % / 10.11 %
49	A	41.07 % / 35.69 %
50	A	78.33 % / 13.1 %
51	D	87.64 % / 11.26 %
52	D	54.39 % / 30.57 %
53	A	61.9 % / 35.05 %
54	D	54.85 % / 33.3 %
55	C	44.08 % / 34.45 %
56	D	69.29 % / 30.2 %
57	C	53.58 % / 43.06 %
58	C	47.68 % / 32.74 %
59	C	81.84 % / 17.47 %
60	B	40.95 % / 31.49 %
61	C	21.24 % / 70.0 %
62	D	69.17 % / 30.82 %
63	D	67.48 % / 30.51 %
64	B	66.24 % / 32.75 %
65	D	44.91 % / 51.3 %
66	B	26.26 % / 71.63 %
67	B	42.67 % / 42.69 %
68	B	43.31 % / 32.09 %
69	C	53.51 % / 46.07 %
70	C	85.62 % / 10.88 %
71	B	61.76 % / 36.11 %
72	D	57.19 % / 34.65 %
73	D	55.42 % / 33.23 %
74	B	44.17 % / 43.02 %
75	C	79.63 % / 18.54 %
76	C	53.92 % / 33.87 %
77	A	45.0 % / 44.7 %
78	B	45.49 % / 38.04 %
79	D	42.13 % / 51.29 %
80	D	47.84 % / 33.15 %

Q.	Ans.	Correct / Skipped
81	C	77.34 % / 19.32 %
82	C	78.28 % / 13.43 %
83	C	10.69 % / 71.76 %
84	C	63.71 % / 34.35 %

Q.	Ans.	Correct / Skipped
85	B	68.31 % / 30.96 %
86	B	79.88 % / 14.14 %
87	B	43.48 % / 46.73 %
88	C	81.05 % / 10.06 %

Q.	Ans.	Correct / Skipped
89	A	12.93 % / 84.86 %
90	A	78.21 % / 14.12 %
91	B	82.56 % / 11.74 %
92	A	58.09 % / 35.67 %

Q.	Ans.	Correct / Skipped
93	A	54.55 % / 33.87 %
94	A	84.58 % / 10.52 %
95	C	79.55 % / 12.04 %
96	C	78.86 % / 14.18 %

Q.	Ans.	Correct / Skipped
97	A	53.9 % / 44.35 %
98	B	86.08 % / 12.03 %
99	A	86.63 % / 12.75 %
100	A	87.9 % / 10.12 %

Performance Analysis

Avg. Score (%)	48.0%
Toppers Score (%)	57.0%
Your Score	

//Hints and Solutions//

1. The Indian men's table tennis team clinched the gold medal at the 2022 Commonwealth Games in Birmingham on 2 August 2022.

- India defeated Singapore by 3-1 in the final.
- This is India's third gold medal at the CWG in the men's team event having earlier won in 2010 and 2018.
- On 2 August 2022 , the Indian women's lawn bowls team also won its first-ever gold at the Commonwealth Games.

Hence, the correct option is (C).

2. The International Conference on Climate Change held in December 2018 was held at Katowice in Poland.

The 2018 United Nations Climate Change Conference, more commonly referred to as the Katowice Climate Change Conference or COP24, was the 24th Conference of the Parties to the United Nations Framework Convention on Climate Change. It was held between 2 and 15 December 2018 in Katowice, Poland. The conference was held in the International Congress Centre. The president of COP24 was Michał Kurtyka. The conference also incorporated the fourteenth meeting of the parties for the Kyoto Protocol (CMP14), and the third session of the first meeting of the parties for the Paris Agreement (CMA1-3 or CMA1.3) which agreed on rules to implement the Agreement. The conference's objective was to have a full implementation of the Paris agreement.

Hence, the correct option is (C).

3. The first preventive detention bill of Independent India was moved in 1950 by Sardar Patel. Patel had said that he had several sleepless nights before deciding if it was necessary to introduce the bill. Consequently, the Preventive Detention Act, 1950 was enacted by the Parliament on 26th February 1950.

Hence, the correct option is (C).

4. ONDC has signed a Memorandum of Understanding (MoU) with SIDBI for the coordination of functions of institutions engaged in similar activities in August 2022.

- The partnership is aimed to change the landscape of MSMEs by bringing them into the ONDC network and accelerating their participation in eCommerce.
- The MoU was signed by Sivasubramanian Ramanan, Chairman & MD of SIDBI and T Koshy, MD & CEO of ONDC.

Hence, the correct option is (D).

5. Special ASEAN-India Foreign Ministers' Meeting (SAIFMM) will be held on the 16th and 17th June 2022 in New Delhi, India to commemorate 30 years of ASEAN-India Dialogue Relations. In recognition of this milestone, the year 2022 is being celebrated as the ASEAN-India Friendship Year as announced by ASEAN and Indian leaders at the 18th ASEAN-India Summit in October 2021.

Hence, the correct option is (A).

6. Adani Ports and Special Economic Zone (APSEZ)'s composite scheme to acquire Sarguja Rail Corridor Pvt Ltd (SRCPL) has been approved by the National Company Law Tribunal (NCLT). It will be effective from the appointed date of April $1,2021$. Once consolidated, SRCPL will add Rs. 450 crore or five percent of APSEZ's total Ebitda (earnings before interest, tax, depreciation, and amortisation).

Hence, the correct option is (A).

7. India's first 'Amrit Sarovar' has come up in Uttar Pradesh's Rampur.

India's first "Amrit Sarovar" was inaugurated by the Union Minister for Minority Affairs Mukhtar Abbas Naqvi on 13 May 2022.

PM Narendra Modi had called for having at least 75 ponds in every district in the 75th year of India's Independence, calling them 'Amrit Sarovar'.

Hence, the correct option is (D).

8. 74th edition of Chartered Accountant's Day was observed on 1 July 2022.

The day is celebrated by Institute of Chartered Accountants of India (ICAI). ICAI was established by the Parliament of India in 1949. It is the second-largest accounting and statutory body across the globe. In India, ICAI is the only licensing and regulatory body for the financial audit and accounting profession.

Hence, the correct option is (C).

9. The Union Government has authorized the State Bank of India to issue and encashes Electoral Bonds through its 29 Authorized Branches from 1–10 th of July 2022.

The Electoral Bonds will be valid for fifteen calendar days from the date of issue and no payment will be made to any payee Political Party if the Electoral Bond is deposited after the expiry of the validity period.

Hence, the correct option is (A).

10. Chapekar Brothers assassinated W.C. Rand, the Plague Commissioner of Pune in 1897.

On 22 June 1897, brothers Damodar Hari Chapekar and Balkrishna Hari Chapekar assassinated British officer W.C. Rand and his military escort, Lieutenant Ayerst, in Pune, Maharashtra. This was the first case of militant nationalism in India after the revolt of 1857.

Hence, the correct option is (B).

11. The Indian Railways has placed a purchase order for 39,000 wheels for LHB Coaches from the Chinese manufacturer Taiyuan against a global tender." Due to the ongoing war between Russia and Ukraine, the supplies against the ongoing contracts with the firms from Russia and Ukraine have been affected. The contract rate is 1.68% higher than the rate per wheel given in a Ukrainian firm's earlier Letter of Acceptance (LoA).

Hence, the correct option is (B).

12. Santosh Yadav is the first woman of the world who climbed Mount Everest successfully from the Kangshung side.

Santosh Yadav:

- Santosh Yadav is a female mountaineer from India.

- She was born in Rewari district of Haryana in 1967.

- She is the first woman in the world to climb Mount Everest twice. She is awarded by the Padma Shri. The first woman to climb Mt. Everest from Kangshung Face (Eastern Facing side of Mt. Everest).

- She was the first Indian woman to climb Everest twice.

- She climbed the peak first in May 1992 and then again in May 1993 with an Indo-Nepalese Team.

- She has also been awarded the Tenzing Norgay National Adventure award in 1994.

Hence, the correct option is (B).

13. Rakesh Sharma was the first Indian astronaut.

- In 1984, former Indian Air Force pilot Rakesh Sharma became the first Indian citizen to travel into space.

- He was selected as a cosmonaut for a space mission launched jointly by the Indian Space Research Organisation (ISRO) and the Soviet Intercosmos space program.

- On April 3, 1984, he flew aboard the Soviet Soyuz T-11 rocket to the space station Salyut 7.

- Prior to becoming a cosmonaut, the seasoned IAF test pilot had flown 21 combat missions in a MiG-21 during the Bangladesh war of 1971.

Hence, the correct option is (C).

14. Pabu ji deity (Lok Devta) of Rajasthan is known as 'Deity of camels'.

Pabu ji is a folk god of Rajasthan who is worshipped in Rajasthan and adjoining regions, Gujarat and Sindh (Pakistan). He is worshipped as the protector of animals and is worshipped in Rajasthan when camels are sick.

Hence, the correct option is (C).

15. Fundamental rights are the rights that are essential for human survival.

The Indian Constitution accommodates fundamental rights which are Justiciable subject to reasonable restrictions.

There are six fundamental rights namely:

1. Right to Equality (Article 14-18)
2. Right to freedom (Article 19-22)
3. Right against exploitation (Article 23 and 24)
4. Right to freedom of religion (Article 25-28)
5. Cultural and educational rights (Article 29 and 30)
6. Rights to constitutional remedies (Article 32)

Hence, the correct option is (B).

16. The word federalism is not mentioned in Article 1 of the Indian Constitution. Article 1 describes India as a union of states.

Federalism can be formed through integration (US) or dissolution (Canada). Indian federalism resembles the "Canadian model". It is not the result of an agreement between the states and the states have no right to secede from the federation. It is an indestructible union of destructive states. Casey describes it as "quasi-federalism". Granville Austin called this "cooperative federalism" (the need for national integrity and unity). Unitary bias means central domination in financial powers, central grants, NITI Aayog.

Hence, the correct option is (B).

17. Bronislaw Malinowski functionalism is often termed as individualistic functionalism for he defined functionalism as a theory of transformation of the organic which includes individual needs that are met to derive cultural necessities. For Malinowski, human beings have certain psychological needs which require an organized and collective response from the members of the society. The individual needs include food, shelter, safety, relaxation, movement, growth and reproduction.

Hence, the correct option is (A).

18. The book 'The problem of Rupee: Its origin and its solution' was authored by Dr B.R Ambedkar in 1923. The book talks about the Indian economy, banking system and raises currency question in British India which led to the creation of the Reserve Bank of India.

Hence, the correct option is (D).

19. Depeasantization refers to a situation of deagrarinization in which peasants lose their economic capacity, social coherence and demographically shrink in size. Many peasants give up their part of the land by selling them in order to fulfil the demands of everyday life like the construction of new houses or buying a new vehicle, for marriage expenditure or to get new furniture.

Hence, the correct option is (A).

20.

Name of the author	Title of the Book
R.C. Dutt	• Romesh Chandra Dutt, a retired ICS officer, published The Economic History of India at the beginning of the 20th century in which he examined in minute detail the entire economic record of colonial rule since 1757.
Dadabhai Naoroji	• Poverty and Unbritish Rule in India book was written by Dadabhai Naoroji.
W. Digly	• 'Prosperous' British India, more completely titled Prosperous' British India: A Revelation from Official Records, was a book published in 1901 by British author William Digby that described the economic conditions prevailing in British India in the latter half of the nineteenth century under British rule.
V. Anstey	• The Economic Development of India by V. Anstey lucidly explains the journey of the

| | | Indian economy pre and post-independence and its gradual transition to a relatively market-friendly economy today. | | | fort.
It is second oldest fort in Rajasthan which built by Rajput kings around 1156. |

Hence, the correct option is (B).

21. Natyashastra is a detailed treatise and handbook on dramatic art that deals with all aspects of classical Sanskrit theatre. It is believed to be written by Brahman sage Bharata. It has largely influenced dance, music and literary traditions in India. The composition date of Natyashastra is unknown, estimates vary between 500 BCE to 500 CE.

Hence, the correct option is (A).

22. My Life is a 2004 autobiography written by former President of the United States Bill Clinton, who left office on January 20, 2001. It was released on June 22, 2004. The book was published by the Knopf Publishing Group; the book sold in excess of 2,250,000 copies. Clinton had received what was at the time the world's highest book advance fee, believed to have been worth US$12 million; at the announcement of media personality Oprah Winfrey's future weight loss book, it was said that her undisclosed advance fee had broken this record. In April 2008, the Clintons' tax records confirmed that the advance for My Life was actually $15 million.

Hence, the correct option is (B).

23. The Chaitra Jatra festival is held every year at the "Tara Tarini hill temple" on the Tuesday of the Hindu month of Chaitra. Tara Tarini Pahari Temple is located in Kumari Pahari on the banks of river Rushikulya. It is a major center of Shakti Puja in Odisha. Tara Tarini hill temple is one of the four major ancient Tantra Peeths and Shakti Peethas in India.
Hence, the correct option is (D).

24. Jagannath Temple is located in Puri district of Odisha state. The famous Lingaraj Temple in Bhubaneswar and Sun Temple in Konark are located in this state. All these temples are built in the Nagara style.
Hence, the correct option is (A).

25. The evidence of mural painting in Ajanta caves and Lepakshi temple is quite clear but the evidence of mural painting in Sanchi Stupa is not clear. The pylons surrounding the stupa are filled with pictures of Buddha's life events and Jataka tales and are ornate from bottom to top. Toranas cannot be considered as part of stupas
Hence, the correct option is (B).

26.

Fort Name	Place	Other Features
Lohagarh Fort	Bharatpur	Suraj Mal, Jat king of Bharatpur built this fort.
Jaigarh Fort	Jaipur	It is located in famous 'Cheel ka Teela' of the Aravalli range. It was built by Jai Singh II
Kumbhalgarh Fort	Rajsamand	It was built by Rana Kumbha in 15th century. It is included in world heritage site of hill forts of Rajasthan.
Sonar Fort	Jaisalmer	It is primarily known as Jaisalmer

Hence, the correct option is (D).

27. Albert Hall Museum or the Central Museum sited amid the gardens of Ram Niwas Bagh in Jaipur.

- It is one of the oldest museums in the state of Rajasthan.
- This museum was designed by Colonel Sir Swinton Jacob in 1876 for the purpose of greeting King Edward VII, Prince of Wales on his visit to India.
- After ten years, it was opened to the public.
- Since 1969, the galleries on the ground floor of the museum have been thoroughly rebuilt and remodelled.
- The Albert Hall Museum is modelled on the Albert Museum of London and represents the Indo-Saracenic style of architecture.

Hence, the correct option is (A).

28. The Centre for Cellular and Molecular Biology is situated at Hyderabad.

The Center for Molecular Biology (CMB) was established in the fall of 2002 with funding provided by Smith College and the Howard Hughes Medical Institute. The goal of the Center for Molecular Biology is to provide first-class support for molecular biology research, training, and education to all that are interested in the Smith community.

Hence, the correct option is (C).

29. Among the options, only Mirabai Chanu is NOT a recipient of Rajiv Gandhi Khel Ratna 2020.

Mirabai Chanu is an Indian weightlifter.

- She was honored with the Rajiv Gandhi Khel Ratna in 2018.

Rajiv Gandhi Khel Ratna 2020 winners:

- Rohit Sharma (Cricket)
- Mariyappan Thangavelu (Paralympian)
- Manika Batra (Table Tennis)
- Vinesh Phogat (Wrestler)
- Rani Rampal (Hockey)

Hence, the correct option is (D).

30. The summer Olympic Games 2024 to be held in Paris.

- Paris will become the second city to host the Olympics three times, after London (1908, 1948, and 2012).
- It was previously the host in the year 1900 and 1924. The year 2024 will mark the centenary of the Paris Games of 1924.
- These will be the sixth Olympic Games hosted by France (three summers and three winters).

- Paris was elected as the host city on September 13, 2017, at the 131st IOC Session in Lima, Peru.

- Paris is the capital of France.

- Currencies: Euro, CFP franc.

Hence, the correct option is (D).

31. Saina Nehwal is an Indian player who won the first Olympic medal in badminton.

- A former world number 1, she has won over 24 international titles, including eleven titles in the Superseries.

- While she reached the 2nd world ranking in 2009, it was only in 2015 that she was able to cross the number 1 world ranking, becoming the only female player from India and after Prakash Padukone, the second Indian player to achieve this feat.

- Three times at the Olympics, she has represented India, earning a bronze medal in her second appearance.

- She is the first Olympic medal-winning Indian badminton player, the first Indian to reach the final of the BWF World Championship, and the only Indian to win the BWF or Junior World Championships.

- She became the first Indian female to win a 4-star tournament in 2006 and the youngest Asian.

- She became the first Indian to win two Commonwealth Games singles gold medals (2010 and 2018).

Srikanth Kidambi is an Indian badminton player who ranked in the BWF rankings in April 2018 as world number 1.

Pullela Gopichand is a former player of Indian badminton who is the Indian Badminton team's, Chief National Coach. In 2001, he won the All England Open Badminton Championships, becoming the second Indian, after Prakash Padukone, to achieve this feat.

Prakash Padukone is a former Indian badminton player; who was ranked World number 1 in 1980.

Hence, the correct option is (B).

32. Two presidents Zakir Hussain and Fakhruddin Ali Ahmed died while in office.

- Zakir Hussain was the 3rd president of India, from 13 May 1967 until his death on 3 May 1969.

- He also served as the Governor of Bihar as well as the Vice-President of India.

- Fakhruddin Ali Ahmed was an Indian lawyer and politician who served as the fifth President of India from 1974 to 1977.

Hence, the correct option is (C).

33. The Maurya Empire was a strong power founded by Chandragupta Maurya who ruled ancient India between 32 BC and 180 BC.

In the Maurya period, stone art emerged as the major medium for Indian artists to create art forms. Prior to this, wood was the main material for most art forms. Mauryan art was originally a

royal art. The use of pillars, stupas, caves, sculpture, pottery were typical examples of Mauryan art.

The life-size standing image of Yakshini in Didarganj, properly chauried is a fine example of the sculpture tradition of the Maurya period. Therefore, statement 1 is correct.

The Lion Capital was discovered at Sarnath near Varanasi (U.P), commonly known as the Sarnath Lion Capital. So, statement 2 is correct.

It was a classic example of the Sarnath school of sculpture that emerged during the Gupta period, not the Maurya period. So, statement 3 is not correct.

The four caves in the Barabar Hills (Lomas Rishi Cave) were dedicated by Ashoka to the Ajivika monks of the Ajivika sect. So, statement 4 is correct.

Hence, the correct option is (D).

34. The Montagu-Chelmsford Reforms or more briefly known as Mont-Ford Reforms were reforms introduced by the colonial government in British India to introduce self-governing institutions gradually in India.

The reforms take their name from Edwin Montagu, the Secretary of State for India during the latter parts of the First World War, and Lord Chelmsford, Viceroy of India between 1916 and 1921. The reforms were outlined in the Montagu-Chelmsford Report prepared in 1918 and formed the basis of the Government of India Act 1919. These are related to constitutional reforms.

The important features of this act were:

- The Imperial Legislative Council at the centre was now to consist of two houses- the Central Legislative Assembly and the Council of State.

- The provinces were to follow the Dual Government System or Dyarchy. So, both are correct.

Hence, the correct option is (C).

35. Alagh Committee-

Planning Commission had appointed YK Alagh Committee in July 1977. Committee submitted its report in January 1979. This committee used the "Calorie" criteria for the measurement of Poverty. This committee used the "Calorie" criteria for the measurement of Poverty.

- For Rural area - 2400 calorie

- For Urban area- 2100 calorie

Lakdawala Committee-

Planning Commission in September 1989 appointed D.T.Lakadwala Committee. Committee submitted its report in January 1993. Lakadwala committee used the Alagh committee's method but it declared separate poverty lines for each state, rural as well as urban. Committee used the Uniform Recall Period method. The government used this method from 1997 to 2011 for the measurement of poverty.

Tendulkar Committee-

Planning Commission in December 2005 appointed Suresh Tendulkar Committee. Committee submitted its report in December 2009. It rejected the use of Calorie as criteria to measure poverty. It accepted Food, Health, Education, Clothing as a component in the poverty line basket. It used the data of the 61st round of NSSO.

- For Rural area- Rs. 446.68
- For Urban area- Rs. 578.8
- The above data was for the 2004-2005 year.
- For the 2009-2010 year
- Rural- Rs. 673
- Urban- Rs. 860

C.Rangarajan Committee-

In 2012 government-appointed committee under C.Rangarajan to measure poverty in the country. Committee submitted its report in 2014.

This committee recommended using the Lakdawala Committee method to measure Poverty.

This committee used the calorie criteria to measure the poverty.

- For Rural- 2155 Calorie
- For Urban- 2090 Calorie

It used the separate poverty line for a separate state.

Hence, the correct option is (B).

36. A fusion reaction is the main cause of energy radiation from the sun.

Fusion powers stars and produces virtually all elements in a process called nucleosynthesis. The Sun is a main-sequence star, and, as such, generates its energy by nuclear fusion of hydrogen nuclei into helium. In nuclear physics, nuclear fusion is a reaction in which two or more atomic nuclei are combined to form one or more different atomic nuclei

Hence, the correct option is (A).

37. If excess fertilizers are applied to a plant without water the plant will die due to plasmolysis.

If excess fertilizer is added to the soil then the soil will become hypertonic as compared to the cell sap of the roots of the plant. Thus, the water will flow out of the roots through the process of exosmosis. The roots will become plasmolyzed and excessive loss of water may kill the plants.

Hence, the correct option is (C)

38. The units which make up the nervous system are called nerve cells or neurons. Therefore, neuron is the functional and structural unit of nervous system. Neuron is the largest cell in the body.

Hence, the correct option is (C).

39. Pasteurization or pasteurisation is a process in which packaged and non-packaged foods are treated with mild heat, usually to less than 100 °C, to eliminate pathogens and extend shelf life.

Hence, the correct option is (A).

40. India successfully conducted its first anti-satellite (ASAT) missile test on 27 March 2019 destroying low earth orbit satellite in space by using a missile that covered a distance of 300 km to engage the target. Let us tell you that India became the fourth country to acquire such type of modern capability. The codename of anti-satellite (ASAT) is Mission Shakti.

Hence, the correct option is (C).

41. The Kerala State Aids Control Society (KSACS) announced to reserve a government job for HIV positive candidates. A vacancy has been reserved in the office of KSACS for HIV positive candidates for the post of coordinator. The reason behind is that the presence of such a person will improve coordination and communication with groups at risk and ensure effective prevention.

Hence, the correct option is (C).

42. The landscape is being continuously worn away by two processes – weathering and erosion. Erosion is the wearing away of the landscape by different agents like water, wind, and ice.

- At higher gradients, downward, vertical erosion is more dominant. This produces V-shaped valleys
- The V-shaped valley is typical of one that has been carved by flowing water.
- The erosion is more pronounced when the water flow is a heavy one, and the water carries suspended particles (sedimentary load).

Hence, the correct option is (C).

43. The ocean current is a general movement of a mass of water in a fairly defined direction over great distances. Base on the temperature characteristics it can be categorized as warm and cold current. It can be broadly categorized into Atlantic ocean current, Pacific ocean current, and Indian ocean current. The currents in the northern portion of the Indian Ocean differ entirely from the general pattern of circulation.

- The currents in the northern portion of the Indian Ocean differ entirely from the general pattern of circulation.
- They change their direction from season to season in response to the seasonal rhythm of the monsoons.
- In the northern section of the Indian Ocean, there is a clear reversal of currents between winter and summer.
- In winter, the north equatorial current and the south equatorial current flow from east to west.
- The northeast monsoons drive the water along the coast of the Bay of Bengal to circulate in an anti-clockwise direction.
- Similarly, along the coasts of the lands bordering the Arabian Sea, an anticlockwise circulation of currents develops.

Therefore, statements 1 and 2 are correct.

Hence, the correct option is (B).

44. Both longitude and latitude are angles measured with the center of the earth as an origin. Longitude is an angle from the prime meridian, measured to the east (longitudes to the west are negative). Latitudes measure an angle up from the equator (latitudes to the south are negative).

- The line joining the north and south pole is called Prime Meridian.
- A (geographic) meridian (or line of longitude) is half of an imaginary great circle on the Earth's surface.
- It is a coordinate line terminated by the North Pole and the South Pole, connecting points of equal longitude, as measured in angular degrees east or west of the Prime Meridian.

Hence, the correct option is (A).

45. The Indian government released a commemorative postage stamp on the 75th anniversary of the United Nations. S Jaishankar, External Affairs Minister was the chief guest at the event. "As a founding member of the United Nations, India is invested with its heart and soul, right from the crafting of the principles of the UN Charter to being in the forefront of keeping its peace," the external affairs minister said.

Hence, the correct option is (B).

46. Hague Convention on the Civil Aspects of International Child Abduction is a multilateral treaty that came into existence on 1st December 1983.

The convention seeks to protect children from the harmful effects of abduction and retention across international boundaries by providing a procedure to bring about their prompt return.

The convention is intended to enhance the international recognition of rights of custody and access arising in place of habitual residence and to ensure the prompt return of the child who is wrongfully removed or retained from the place of habitual residence.

It seeks to return children abducted or retained overseas by a parent to their country of habitual residence for the courts of that country to decide on matters of residence and contact.

So, Statement 1 is correct.

The convention shall apply to any child, up to the age of 16 years who is a habitual resident of any of the contracting states.

So, Statement 2 is not correct.

Over 90 countries are party to the Convention. Despite pressure from the US and European countries, India (a UN member) is yet to ratify it.

So, Statement 3 is not correct.

Hence, the correct option is (C).

47. The WTO's 164 members unanimously selected the 66-year-old development economist to serve a four-year term as director-general.

The appointment came after new United States President Joe Biden endorsed her candidacy, which had been blocked by former President Donald Trump.

Okonjo-Iweala, formerly Nigeria's finance minister, had a 25-year career at the World Bank, where she rose to the number-two position of managing director. She holds both US and Nigerian citizenship.

The World Trade Organization is an international body that deals with the rules of trade between nations. So statement 1 is correct.

At its heart are the WTO agreements, negotiated among the bulk of the world's nations and ratified in their legislatures.

Hence, the correct option is (A).

48. Sports awards given by Government of Maharashtra:

1. Shiv Chhatrapati State Lifetime Sports Achievement Award
2. Shiv Chhatrapati State Sports Award (Best Sports Coach) and Jijamata Award (Women Sports Coach)
3. Shiv Chhatrapati State Sports Award (Player)
4. Shiv Chhatrapati State Adventure Sports Award
5. Shiv Chhatrapati State Sports Award (Specially Abled Player)

Hence, the correct option is (D).

49. The nature of this award is a memento, certificate, blazer and cash of Rupees Five Lakhs. Dronacharya Award is given to motivate thecoaches who have coached the playerswho have done outstanding performanceat the international level and made thecountry proud.

Hence, the correct option is (A).

50. Arjuna Award given for Outstanding Performance in Sports and Games, is the second-highest sporting honour of India. The nature of this award is a memento, certificate, blazer and cash of Rupees Fifteen Lakhs.

Hence, the correct option is (A).

51.

Now the man is facing south.

Hence, the correct option is (D).

52.

Alphabet	A	B	C	D	E	F	G	H	I	J	K	L	M
Position value	1	2	3	4	5	6	7	8	9	10	11	12	13
Alphabet	Z	Y	X	W	V	U	T	S	R	Q	P	O	N
Position value	26	25	24	23	22	21	20	19	18	17	16	15	14

R – 1 = Q

S - 3 = P

T - 5 = O

Likewise, M - 1 = L, N - 3 = K & O - 5 = J

Therefore, LKJ is the required word.

Hence, the correct option is (D).

53.

Alphabet	A	B	C	D	E	F	G	H	I	J	K	L	M
Position value	1	2	3	4	5	6	7	8	9	10	11	12	13
Alphabet	Z	Y	X	W	V	U	T	S	R	Q	P	O	N
Position value	26	25	24	23	22	21	20	19	18	17	16	15	14

A+4=F   Similarly, G+4=L

P+4=U   R+4=W

P+4=U   I+4=N

E+4=J   N+4=S

A+4=F   D+4=I

R+4=W

So we can see the pattern that is being followed above.

Therefore the answer to the problem is LWNSI.

Hence, the correct option is (A).

54. Akbar, Humayun, and Jahangir all three belong to the Mughal dynasty while Alauddin Khalji belongs to the Khalji dynasty.

Hence, the correct option is (D).

55.

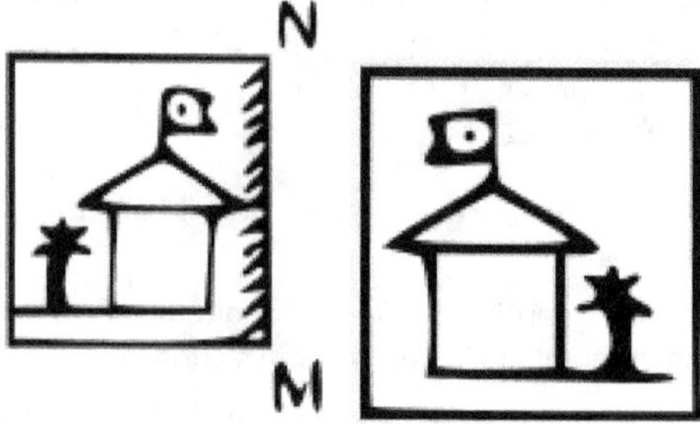

Hence, the correct option is (C).

56.

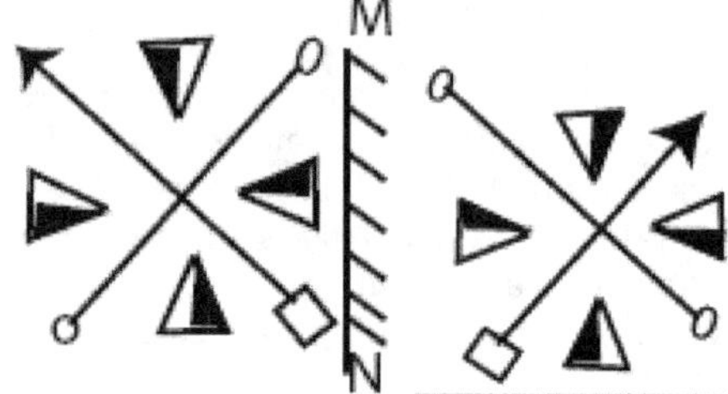

Hence, the correct option is (D).

57. In this series, the shaded part inside the circle gets larger and then smaller.

Hence, the correct option is (C).

58. After simplifying the equation with the given symbols we get:

$$95 @ 5 \$ 46 ! 3 \# 27 = 95 \div 5 + 46 - 3 \times 27$$

$$\Rightarrow \left(\frac{95}{5}\right) + 46 - (3 \times 27)$$

This equation will be simplified by BODMAS. So,

$$\Rightarrow 19 + 46 - 81 = -16$$

Hence, the correct option is (C).

59. The word 'Action' cannot be formed using the letters of the given word as there is no 'C' in the given word.

Hence, the correct option is (C).

60. The least possible Venn diagram for the given statements is as follows,

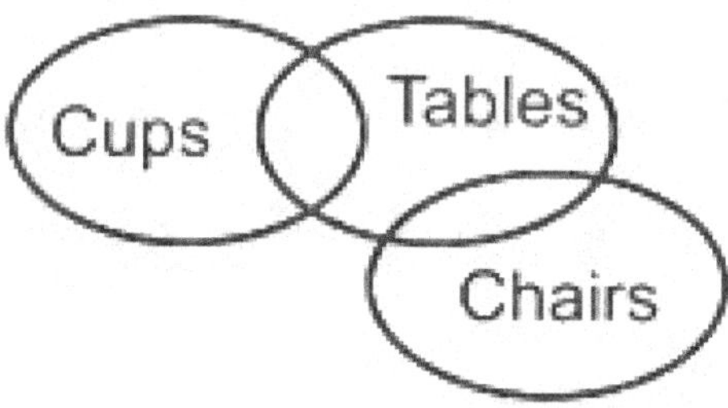

Conclusions:

I. Some chairs are not cups → not follows.

II. Some chairs are tables → follow.

So, only conclusion II follows.

Hence, the correct option is (B).

61. According to the sequence in the dictionary:

5. Dearth

3. Decision

1. Decisive

4. Demand

2. Dethrone

So, "5 3 1 4 2" is the correct answer.

Hence, the correct option is (C).

62. Given series is: $34, 42, 50, 56, 62, 66, ?$

The pattern followed here is:

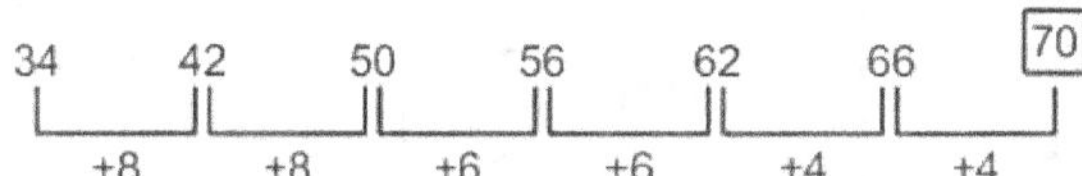

Hence, the correct option is (D).

63. The logic follows here is:

$$3^3 - 3 = 27 - 3 = 24$$
$$4^3 - 3 = 64 - 3 = 61$$
$$5^3 - 3 = 125 - 3 = 122$$
$$6^3 - 3 = 216 - 3 = 213$$

Similarly,

$$7^3 - 3 = 343 - 3 = 340$$

Hence, the correct option is (D).

64. Given,

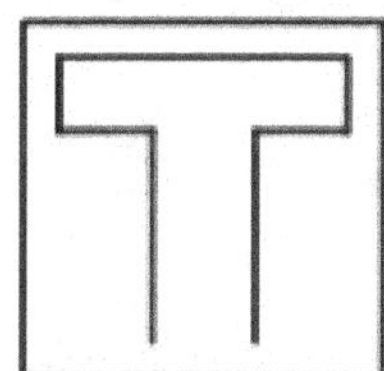

The given figure is hidden/embedded in

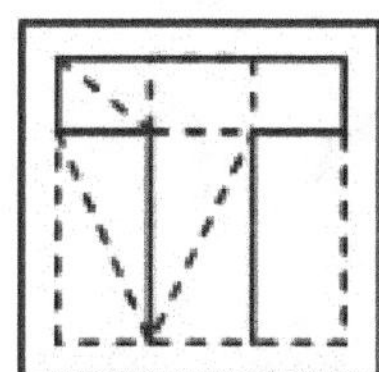

So, the correct answer is

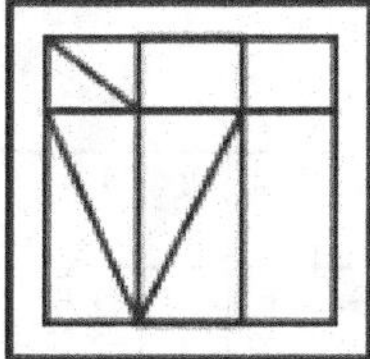

Hence, the correct option is (B).

65. The highlighted portion in the below given image represents the hidden figure:

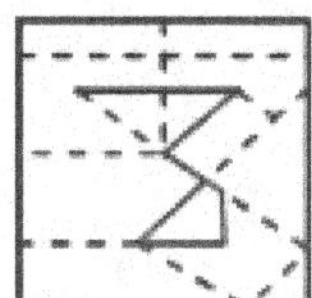

Hence, the correct option is (D).

66. The least possible venn diagram is:

1. Some cloth are napkins → True (As, Some napkins are cloth, so some cloth are napkins)

2. Some papers are cloth → False (As, Some napkins are papers and Some napkins are cloth → So, it is not definite that Some papers are cloth)

So, conclusion 1 alone follows.

Hence, the correct option is (B).

67. This question can be approached as follows,

For an hour, hour hand rotates $30°$.

so for every 60 min $= 30°$

for every 1 min $= \frac{1}{2}$

For 20 min $= \frac{1}{2} \times 20$

For 20 min $= 10°$

Therefore, $10°$ is the correct answer.

Hence, the correct option is (B).

68.

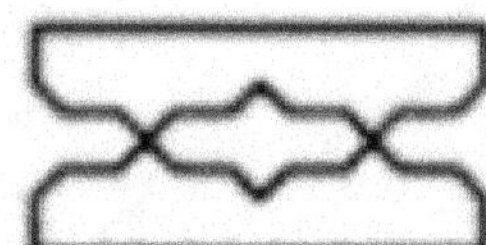

On unfolding figure Z we get a similar pattern as provided in figure (2).

Hence, the correct option is (B).

69. The logic is:

Alpha bets	A	B	C	D	E	F	G	H	I	J	K	L	M
Positional value	1	2	3	4	5	6	7	8	9	10	11	12	13
Positional value	26	25	24	23	22	21	20	19	18	17	16	15	14
Alpha bets	Z	Y	X	W	V	U	T	S	R	Q	P	O	N

$$R \xrightarrow{+2} T \quad O \xrightarrow{+2} Q \quad L \xrightarrow{+2} N \quad L \xrightarrow{-2} J \quad E \xrightarrow{-2} C \quad R \xrightarrow{-2} P$$

Similarly,

$$D \xrightarrow{+2} F \quad O \xrightarrow{+2} Q \quad C \xrightarrow{+2} E \quad I \xrightarrow{-2} G \quad L \xrightarrow{-2} J \quad E \xrightarrow{-2} C$$

Hence, the correct option is (C).

70. The logic is:

Alpha bets	A	B	C	D	E	F	G	H	I	J	K	L	M
Positional value	1	2	3	4	5	6	7	8	9	10	11	12	13
Positional value	26	25	24	23	22	21	20	19	18	17	16	15	14
Alpha bets	Z	Y	X	W	V	U	T	S	R	Q	P	O	N

MOUNT = 13 + 15 + 21 + 14 + 20 = 83 and 83 × 2 = 166

Similarly,

ROUND = 18 + 15 + 21 + 14 + 4 = 72 and 72 × 2 = 144

Hence, the correct option is (C).

71. According to the given information:

(1) Infant A was lighter than infant B, i.e.,

$$A < B$$

(2) Infant C was lighter than infant D, i.e.,

$$C < D$$

(3) Infant B was lighter than infant D but heavier than infant E, i.e.,

$$E < B < D$$

On combining all the statements, we get:

$$E < B < D; A < B; C < D$$

Thus, D is heavier than C and B. Also, as D is heavier than B, implies, D is heavier than both A and E.

So, infant D is the heaviest.

Hence, the correct option is (B).

72. Preparing the family tree using the following symbols:

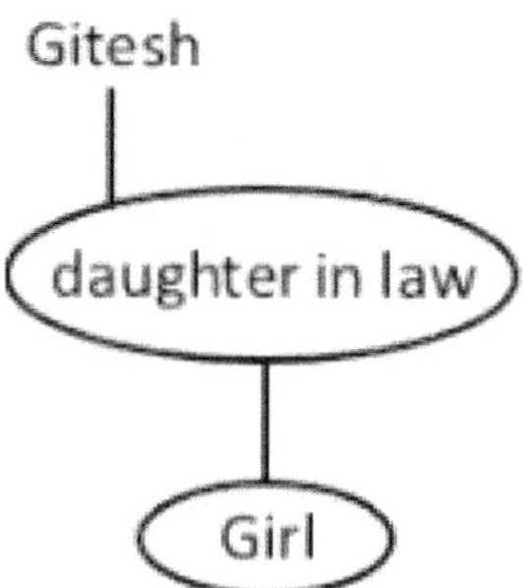

Symbol in Diagram	Meaning
◯	Female
☐	Male
═	Married Couple
—	Siblings
		Difference of a generation

A possible tree diagram will be:

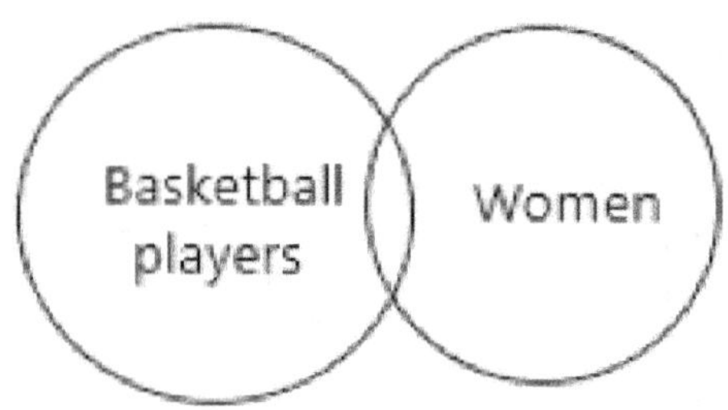

So, Girl is grand daughter of Gitesh.

Hence, the correct option is (D).

73. The least possible Venn diagram is as follows:

Conclusions:

(i) Some basketball players are not women. → False (We do not have any information about the other basketball player they can be women or men.)

(ii) Not all basketball players are women.→ False (This is a possibility but we cannot say definitely.)

So, neither conclusion (i) nor conclusion (ii) follows.

Hence, the correct option is (D).

74. The least possible Venn diagram is as follows:

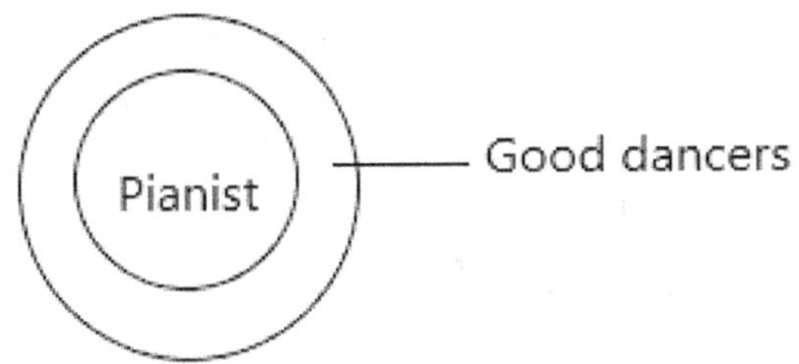

Conclusions:

(i) All people who are good at dance are pianists. → False (We cannot say that all good dancer are pianists.)

(ii) Some people who are good at dance are pianists. → True (As all pianists are good dancer means some of the good dancers are pianists.)

So, only conclusion (ii) follows.

Hence, the correct option is (B).

75. The set of given words are Almonds, Cashews, Walnuts all are dry fruits.

Apricot is the most similar to that set of words. Remaining Banana, Apple, and Watermelon different from Apricot.

Hence, the correct option is (C).

76. Given:

The rate of interest for 1st 2 years is 8%

For the next 3 years it is 10%

For the period beyond 5 years it is 12.5%

Principal $= Rs\, 20\, L$

Amoun paid $= Rs\, 36.7\, L$

Amount $= P + SI$

Simple Interest, $SI = \dfrac{P \times R \times T}{100}$

Where $P \to$ Principal, $R \to$ rate of interest, $T \to$ time

Total $SI = A - P = 36.7\, L - 20L$

Total $SI = 16.7\, L$

SI for first 2 years $= 20\, L \times 2 \times \dfrac{8}{100} = 3.2\, L$

SI for next 3 years $= 20\, L \times 3 \times \dfrac{10}{100} = 6\, L$

So, total SI for the first 5 years $= 9.2\, L$

Then, the rest of the interest is obtained at the rate of 12.5%

Remaining interest $= 16.7\, L - 9.2\, L = 7.5\, L$

SI for next N years $= 20\, L \times N \times 12.5\% = 7.5\, L$

$N = 7.5\, L \times \dfrac{8}{20}\, L \quad (12.5\% \to \dfrac{1}{8}\, in$ fraction $)$

$N = 3$

That is, total years $= 2 + 3 + 3 = 8$ years.

Hence, the correct option is (C).

77. Given

Tank filled in 20 hours

Tank filled in 40 hours due to leakage.

Let the tank empty in x hours due to leakage.

Tank filled in 1 hour without leakage $= \left(\dfrac{1}{20}\right)$

Tank empty in 1 hour $= \left(\dfrac{1}{x}\right)$

Tank filled in 1 hour with leakage $= \left(\dfrac{1}{40}\right)$

According to question

Tank filled in 1 hour with leakage = Tank filled in 1 hour - Tank empty in 1 hour due to leakage

$\left(\dfrac{1}{40}\right) = \left(\dfrac{1}{20}\right) - \left(\dfrac{1}{x}\right)$

$\Rightarrow \left(\dfrac{1}{x}\right) = \left(\dfrac{1}{20}\right) - \left(\dfrac{1}{40}\right)$

$\Rightarrow \left(\dfrac{1}{x}\right) = \dfrac{(2-1)}{40}$

$\Rightarrow \left(\dfrac{1}{x}\right) = \left(\dfrac{1}{40}\right)$

$\Rightarrow x = 40$

$\therefore$ The tank will empty in 40 hours.

Hence, the correct option is (A).

78. The ways of arranging n different things $= n!$

The ways of arranging n things, having r same things and rest all are different $= \dfrac{n!}{r!}$

The number of ways of arranging the n arranged thing and m arranged things together $= n! \times m!$

The number of ways for selecting r from a group of $n(n > r) = {}^nC_r$

The selection can be done in the ways:

Case 1: 1 psychologist out of 3 and 2 other professionals out of $6(2$ engineers $+4$ managers)

Aumber of ways $= {}^3C_1 \times {}^6C_2 = 3 \times 15 = 45$

Case $2:$ 2 psychologists out of 3 and 1 other professional out of $6(2$ engineers $+4$ managers)

Number of ways $= {}^3C_2 \times {}^6C_1 = 3 \times 6 = 18$

Case $3:3$ psychologist out of 3 and no other professional out of $6(2$ engineers $+4$ managers)

Number of ways $= {}^3C_3 = 1$

Thus, total number ways $N = 45 + 18 + 1 = 64$

Hence, the correct option is (B).

79. Given,

$$8 - 3 \div 6 \text{ of } 2 + \left(4 \div 4 \text{ of } \frac{1}{4}\right) \div 8 + \left(4 \times 8 \div \frac{1}{4}\right) \times \frac{1}{8}$$

$$= 8 - 3 \div 12 + (4 \div 1) \div 8 + (4 \times 8 \times 4) \times \frac{1}{8}$$

$$= 8 - \frac{1}{4} + 4 \div 8 + 16$$

$$= 8 - \frac{1}{4} + \frac{1}{2} + 16$$

$$= \frac{(32 - 1 + 2 + 64)}{4}$$

$$= \frac{97}{4}$$

$\therefore$ The required value is $\dfrac{97}{4}$.

Hence, the correct option is (D).

80. Let speed of boat and stream be x km/hr and y km/hr.

Downstream speed = (x + y) km/hr

Upstream speed = (x – y) km/hr

According to the question,

(x + y) = 11 km/hr....(1)

(x – y) = 5 km/hr...(2)

Adding equation (1) and equation (2), we get

2x = 16

$\Rightarrow$ x = 8

$\therefore$ Speed of the boat in still water is 8 km/hr.

Hence, the correct option is (D).

81. Given:

$$3 \div 18 \text{ of } 3 \times 6 + 21 \times 6 \div 18 - 3 \div 2 + 3 - 3 \div 9 \text{ of } 3 \times 9$$

Using the BODMAS rule to solve the above expression, we get

$$= 3 \div 54 \times 6 + 21 \times 6 \div 18 - 3 \div 2 + 3 - 3 \div 27 \times 9$$

$$= \frac{3}{54} \times 6 + 21 \times \frac{1}{3} - \frac{3}{2} + 3 - \frac{3}{27} \times 9$$

$$= \frac{1}{18} \times 6 + 21 \times \frac{1}{3} - \frac{3}{2} + 3 - \frac{1}{9} \times 9$$

$$= \frac{1}{3} + 7 - \frac{3}{2} + 3 - 1$$

$$= \left(\frac{1}{3} - \frac{3}{2}\right) + 9$$

$$= \frac{(54 + 2 - 9)}{6}$$

$$= \frac{47}{6}$$

Hence, the correct option is (C).

82. Given:

$$\left(2.\overline{4} \times 0.\overline{6} \times 30 \times 0.\overline{16}\right) \times [0.\overline{27} \times \left(0.\overline{83} \div 0.\overline{16}\right)]$$

Using the BODMAS rule to solve the above expression, we get

$$= \left(\frac{22}{9} \times \frac{2}{3} \times 30 \times \frac{1}{6}\right) \times \left[\frac{5}{18} \times \left(\frac{5}{6} \div \frac{1}{6}\right)\right]$$

$$= \left(\frac{22}{9} \times \frac{2}{3} \times 30 \times \frac{1}{6}\right) \times \left[\frac{5}{18} \times \left(\frac{5}{6} \times 6\right)\right]$$

$$= \left(\frac{22}{9} \times \frac{2}{3} \times 30 \times \frac{1}{6}\right) \times \left[\frac{25}{18}\right]$$

$$= \left(\frac{22}{9} \times 10 \times \frac{1}{3}\right) \times \frac{25}{18}$$

$$= \frac{22}{9} \times 5 \times \frac{1}{3} \times \frac{25}{9}$$

$$= \left(\frac{2750}{243}\right)$$

$$= 11.31$$

$\therefore$ the value of $\left(2.\overline{4} \times 0.\overline{6} \times 30 \times 0.\overline{16}\right) \times [0.\overline{27} \times \left(0.\overline{83} \div 0.\overline{16}\right)]$ is 11.31.

Hence, the correct option is (C).

83. Given:

Total number of visitors in a week $= 72600$

Name of days	Percentage of visitors visited on different days in a week
Sunday	10%
Monday	15%
Tuesday	25%
Wednesday	5%
Thursday	22%
Friday	23%

Percentage of female visitors visited on Monday $= 20\%$

Percentage of female visitors visited on Wednesday $= 30\%$

Percentage of female visitors visited on Friday $= 16.67\%(\frac{1}{6}$ in fraction)

Number of visitors visited on Monday $= 72600 \times 15\% = 10890$

Number of female visitors on Monday $= 10890 \times 20\% = 2178$

Number of visitors visited on Wednesday $= 72600 \times 5\% = 3630$

Number of female visitors on Wednesday $= 3630 \times 30\% = 1089$

Number of visitors visited on Friday $= 72600 \times 23\% = 16698$

Number of female visitors on Friday $= 16698 \times 16.67\% = 2783$

Total female visitors $= (2178 + 1089 + 2783) = 6050$

$\therefore$ Total female visitors on those days is 6050.

Hence, the correct option is (C).

84. Given:

Total number of visitors in a week $= 72600$

Name of days	Percentage of visitors visited on different days in a week
Sunday	10%
Monday	15%
Tuesday	25%
Wednesday	5%
Thursday	22%
Friday	23%

Number of visitors visited on Monday $= 72600 \times 15\% = 10890$

Number of visitors visited on Friday $= 70400 \times 23\% = 16698$

Difference $= (16698 - 10890) = 5808$

Required percentage $= \frac{5808}{10890} \times 100\% = 53.33\%$

$\therefore$ Required percentage is 53.33%.

Hence, the correct option is (C).

85. Given:

Total number of visitors in a week $= 72600$

Name of days	Percentage of visitors visited on different days in a week
Sunday	10%
Monday	15%
Tuesday	25%
Wednesday	5%
Thursday	22%
Friday	23%

We know that:

If ratio of A and B is $= x : y$

$\therefore \dfrac{A}{B} = \dfrac{x}{y}$

Number of visitors visited on Wednesday $= 72600 \times 5\% = 3630$

Percentage of visitors visited in Sanctuary on Friday $= 72600 \times 23\% = 16698$

Required ratio $= 3630 : 16698 = 5 : 23$

$\therefore$ The ratio of the number of visitors on Wednesday to the number of visitors on Friday is $5 : 23$.

Hence, the correct option is (B).

86. Given:

Total number of visitors in a week $= 72600$

Name of days	Percentage of visitors visited on different days in a week
Sunday	10%
Monday	15%
Tuesday	25%
Wednesday	5%
Thursday	22%
Friday	23%

$$\text{Average} = \frac{\text{Sum of total quantity}}{\text{Total number of quantities}}$$

Total number of visitors visited in Sanctuary $= 72600$

Required average $= \dfrac{72600}{6} = 12100$

$\therefore$ Required average 12100.

Hence, the correct option is (B).

87. Given:

Total number of visitors in a week $= 72600$

Name of days	Percentage of visitors visited on different days in a week
Sunday	10%
Monday	15%
Tuesday	25%
Wednesday	5%
Thursday	22%
Friday	23%

25% of the visitors visited on Sunday $=$ The number of visitors visited another sanctuary in a week

Part of female visitors in other sanctuary $= \dfrac{2}{5}$th part

Number of visitors visited on Sunday $= 72600 \times 10\% = 7260$

Number of visitors in other sanctuary $= 7260 \times 25\% = 1815$

Female visitors $= 1815 \times \dfrac{2}{5} = 726$

$\therefore$ Number of female visitors visited other sanctuary are 726.

Hence, the correct option is (B).

88. Let the score of Amit be x marks, then

Joseph's Score $= x - 8$

Kumar's score $= x + 12$

Total marks scored by them $= 205$

$\therefore x + x - 8 + x + 12 = 205$

$\Rightarrow 3x + 4 = 205$

$\Rightarrow 3x = 205 - 4$

$\Rightarrow 3x = 201$

$\Rightarrow x = \dfrac{201}{3}$

$\Rightarrow x = 67$

$\therefore$ Joseph's score $= x - 8 = 67 - 8 = 59$

Hence, the correct option is (C).

89. Given:

The initial quantity of water in vessel $= 2.5$ liters

And the initial quantity of milk in vessel $= 10$ liters

The ratio of milk and water $= 10 : 2.5$

$= 4 : 1$

Amount of mixture removed $= \left(\dfrac{20}{100}\right) \times (10 + 2.5) = \left(\dfrac{1}{5}\right) \times 12.5$

$= 2.5$ litres

Amount of milk removed $= 2.5 \times \left(\dfrac{4}{5}\right) = 2$ litres

Amount of water removed $= 2.5 \times \left(\dfrac{1}{5}\right) = 0.5$ litres

Now, After adding x litres of water the ratio of milk and water get reversed,

$\dfrac{(10-2)}{(2.5-0.5+x)} = \dfrac{1}{4}$

$\Rightarrow \dfrac{8}{(2+x)} = \dfrac{1}{4}$

$\Rightarrow 8 \times 4 = 2 + x$

$\Rightarrow x = 32 - 2$

$\Rightarrow x = 30$

Now, Quantity of water $= (2.5 - 0.5 + 30)$ liters $= 32$ liters

And, Quantity of milk $= (10 - 2)$ liters $= 8$ liters

Then, After adding y litres of milk the ratio of milk and water get reversed,

$\dfrac{(8+y)}{32} = \dfrac{4}{1}$

$\Rightarrow 8 + y = 32 \times 4$

$\Rightarrow 8 + y = 128$

$\Rightarrow y = 120$

$\therefore$ The value of y is 120.

Hence, the correct option is (A).

90. Given,

3 men or 5 women can complete the work in 12 days.

Work done by 3 men = Work done by 5 women

1 men $= \dfrac{5}{3} \times$ women

Now, 3 men $+7$ women $= 3 \times \left(\dfrac{5}{3}\right) + 7$ women $= 12$ women

As we know,

$W_1 \times D_1 = W_2 \times D_2$

$\therefore 5 \times 12 = 12 \times D_2$

$\Rightarrow D_2 = 5$ days

Hence, the correct option is (A).

91.

- Microsoft Word is a word processor developed by Microsoft.
- It was released on October 25, 1983, under the name Multi-Tool Word for Xenix system.
- The commercial versions of Word are licensed as a standalone product or as a component of Microsoft Office or Windows RT.

Shortcut Keys (Word)	Function
Ctrl+I	Italicize highlighted selection.
Ctrl+K	Insert link.
Ctrl+U	Underline highlighted selection.
Ctrl+N	Open new/blank document.

Hence, the correct option is (B).

92. Calibri was the default font in MS Word 2007.

- The normal template of Word 2007 uses a default font, Calibri.
- Calibri font is 11 point font size by default.
- Calibri is a sans-serif typeface family.

From Word 1993 until Word 2007 Times New Roman was the default font.

- Times New Roman font is 12 point font size by default.

Important fonts in MS Word: Times New Roman, Arial, Cambria, Serif.

Hence, the correct option is (A).

93.

- Antivirus is installed in a computer to safeguard the computer from viruses.
- Antivirus software helps protect your computer against malware and cybercriminals. Antivirus software looks at data - web pages, files, software, applications - travelling over the network to your devices.
- It searches for known threats and monitors the behaviour of all programs, flagging suspicious behaviour.
- Most antivirus programs incorporate both automated and manual filtering abilities. The instant scanning option may check files - downloaded from the Internet, discs that are embedded into the PC, and files that are made by software installers.
- The programmed scanning process may likewise check the entire hard drive on a day-to-day basis. The manual scanning system enables you to check single documents or even to scan the complete network at whatever point you feel it is necessary.
- Virus: A computer virus is a piece of software that can 'infect' a computer, install itself and copy itself to other computers, without the user's knowledge or permission. It usually attaches itself to other computer

programs, data files, or the boot sector of a Hard drive. Malware, Trojan horse, Worm are some of the viruses.

Hence, the correct option is (A).

94. A watermark is a faded background image or text that displays behind the text in a document.

- A watermark indicates a company or the document's status or importance.
- Watermark option is present under the Design tab.

The Page Layout Tab contains all the options that allow users to arrange document pages based on need.

Hence, the correct option is (A).

95.

- The worksheet is a grid of cells made up of horizontal and vertical columns.
- Gridlines are the horizontal and vertical lines on the screen that separate cells in a spreadsheet.
- OneNote is a note-taking program for free-form information gathering and multi-user collaboration.
- OneNote is a product of Microsoft.
- A page or virtual page is a fixed-length contiguous block of virtual memory.
- It is the smallest unit of data for memory management in a virtual memory operating system
- The formula bar is a toolbar at the top of the Microsoft Excel spreadsheet window that we can use to enter or copy an existing formula into cells or charts.

Hence, the correct option is (C).

96. In MS Word 2019 table option comes under the Insert menu.

- Options like Pictures, Icons, Clip Art, Chart, etc. comes under the Insert menu.

The list of File menu commands is Info, New, Open, Save, Print, Share, etc.

The list of Layout menu commands is Margins, Orientation. Size etc.

The list of Review menu commands is Thesaurus, Spelling and Grammer, Word count, etc.

Hence, the correct option is (C).

97. Routing is the process of selecting a path for traffic in a network, or between or across multiple networks.

Hence, the correct option is (A).

98. A Uniform Resource Locator (URL), commonly informally termed a web address (a term which is not defined identically) is a reference to a web resource that specifies its location on a computer network and a mechanism for retrieving it.

Hence, the correct option is (B).

99. DNS stands for Domain Name System. The internet world is completely based on IP (Internet Protocol) address. To access any website you need to know its IP address which is a long numeric code and is not possible to learn. Now, here comes the role of DNS. A DNS is an internet service that translates a domain name into a corresponding IP address. The domain name used here is alphabetic and can be easily remembered.

For example, www.example.com is a domain name of a site. And with the help of DNS, it will get translated into its IP address 198.105.232.4.
Hence, the correct option is (A).

100. LAN is a local area network that is used to refer to a small single-site network. LAN is confined to a small building, room or group of buildings, however, one LAN can be connected to other LAN's over any distance via telephone line and radio waves.
Hence, the correct option is (A).

General Awareness/Current Affairs

Q.1 The Hoysaleshwara Temple is an aspirant for the tag of World Heritage Site is located at which of the following state?

A. Himachal Pradesh **B.** Karnataka

C. Odisha **D.** Maharashtra

Q.2 Who among the following unveiled the logo, theme, and website of India's G20 Presidency on 8 November 2022?

A. President Droupadi Murmu

B. PM Narendra Modi

C. Vice President Jagdeep Dhankar

D. Anurag Thkur

Q.3 Vinesh Phogat is recently honouredwith which National Award ?

[HTET PGT - Computer Science, 2020]

A. Dronacharya Award

B. Arjuna Award

C. Rajiv Gandhi Khel Ratna Award

D. Dhyanchand Award

Q.4 Which of the following country has granted a patent to an 'artificial intelligence system' relating to a "food container based on fractal geometry" innovation?

A. Canada **B.** South Africa

C. Australia **D.** Russia

Q.5 Who has been appointed as the Managing Director and Chief Executive Officer of SBI General Insurance Company Limited in July 2022?

A. T Raja Kumar

B. Paritosh Tripathi

C. Vijay Shekhar Sharma

D. Gyanesh Bharti

Q.6 When 'India Water Week' 2019 was celebrated?

[Haryana Primary Teacher (PRT), 2020]

A. 15 January to 21 January

B. 22 March to 26 March

C. 2 October to 8 October

D. 24 September to 28 September

Q.7 As of 2022, which country is the largest bilateral lender to Sri Lanka?

A. China **B.** India **C.** Australia **D.** USA

Q.8 44th International Chess Olympiad will be held in which of the following Indian state from July 28 to August 10, 2022?

A. Karnataka **B.** Kerala

C. Tamil Nadu **D.** Telangana

Q.9 Who has been appointed as the new CEO of Data Security Council of India in September 2022?

A. Anurag Thakur **B.** Tushar Mehta

C. Sudha Murti **D.** Vinayak Godse

Q.10 Which state launched the Mukhya Mantri Bagwani Bima scheme portal on April 2022 To compensate for the damage caused to the crops due to adverse weather and natural calamities?

A. Uttar Pradesh **B.** Tamil Nadu

C. Gujarat **D.** Haryana

Q.11 The International version of which government application has been launched by the Union IT Minister?

A. UMANG

B. FAME

C. SWACHH BHARAT

D. m-AWAS

Q.12 Which Bharat Ratna recipient's birthday is celebrated as Engineer's Day?

A. Abdul Kalam Azad **B.** J R D Tata

C. M Visvesvaraya **D.** C V Raman

Q.13 Who was the first Indian to go into space?

A. Rakesh Sharma **B.** Ramesh Sharma

C. Suresh Sharma **D.** Mahesh Sharma

Q.14 Who is known as the "Father of Dogri" language?

A. Ram Nath Shastri

B. Padma Sachdev

C. Prem Nath Dogra

D. Ghulam Nabi Khayal

Q.15 The Central Government shall appoint the Director of CBI on the recommendation of a three-member committee consisting of

1. the Prime Minister as Chairperson

2. the Union Home Minister

3. the Leader of Opposition in the Lok Sabha

4. the Leader of Opposition in the Rajya Sabha

5. the Chief Justice of India or Judge of the Supreme Court (SC) nominated by him

Select the correct answer using the code given below:

A. 1, 3 and 5 **B.** 2, 4 and 5

C. 1, 2 and 3 **D.** 1, 3, 4 and 5

Q.16 Which of the following were not included in the ORIGINAL Indian Constitution?

A. Socialist **B.** Secular

C. Integrity **D.** All of the above

Q.17 The capital that is consumed by an economy or a firm in the production process is known as:

A. Capital loss   **B.** Production cost
C. Dead-weight loss   **D.** Depreciation

Q.18 Economic problems arise because
A. Wants are unlimited
B. Resources are scarce
C. Scare resources have alternative uses
D. All of the above

Q.19 Which perspective is based on the assumption that Indian society is unique and the Indian social institutions can be better studied through the texts?
A. Subaltern
B. Indological
C. Civilzational
D. Structural/Functional

Q.20 Who wrote the great literary work 'Mricchakatika'?

[RRB (NTPC), 2020]

A. Kalidasa   **B.** Shudraka
C. Harsha   **D.** Bhaasa

Q.21 Who is the author of the book 'Republic'?

[RRB (NTPC), 2020]

A. Leo Tolstoy   **B.** Leo Tolstoy
C. Plato   **D.** TS Eliot

Q.22 Which of the following is an ancient Buddhist text?

[RRB (NTPC), 2020]

A. Vishnu Purana   **B.** Raghuvamsam
C. Ritusamhara   **D.** Abhidharma kosha

Q.23 With respect to Guru Nanak, consider the following statements.
I. Established a centre at Kartarpur named Dera Baba Nanak on the river Ravi.
II. The sacred space thus created by Guru Nanak was known as dharmsal.
III. Before his death Guru appointed Lehna as his successor.
Choose the correct statements.
A. I and II
B. II and III
C. I and III
D. All the statements are correct

Q.24 Match the List 1 with List 2 and select the correct answer from the given options.

List- I	List- II
a. Parijatapaharanam	1. Nandi Thimmana
b. Panduranga Mahathyam	2. Gangadevi
c. Kalahasti Mahatyam	3. Tenali Ramalinga
d. Madura Vijayam	4. Dhurajati

A. a-1, b-3, c-4, d-2   **B.** a-2, b-4, c-3, d-1
C. a-2, b-4, c-3, d-1   **D.** a-2, b-1, c-3, d-4

Q.25 The Telia Rumal of which state was given the Geographical Indication (GI) tag?
A. Telangana   **B.** Odisha

C. Jharkhand   **D.** Punjab

Q.26 Which Indian State/ UT has won the Khelo India Youth Games Champions trophy, 2020?
A. Haryana   **B.** Maharashtra
C. Gujarat   **D.** Karnataka

Q.27 The ban on which Indian sports federation has been lifted recently by its International Regulator, ahead of Tokyo Olympics 2020?
A. Athletic Federation of India
B. Archery Association of India
C. All India Tennis Association
D. All India Football Federation

Q.28 Kobe Bryant, who recently died in a helicopter crash, was a legendary personality of which sports?
A. Cricket   **B.** Basket ball
C. Football   **D.** Boxing

Q.29 The tomb of Ibrahim Lodi is situated at:
A. Panipat   **B.** Gurugram
C. Mahendragarh   **D.** Rohtak

Q.30 There is a sports school at the place named Rai of Sonipat district of Haryana, what is the name of the school?
A. Jawaharlal Nehru Sports School
B. Indira Gandhi Sports School
C. Motilal Nehru Sports School
D. Rajiv Gandhi Sports School

Q.31 In which of the following places, cooperative milk plants are open in Haryana?
A. Ambala   **B.** Rohtak
C. Jind   **D.** All the above

Q.32 How many places of former Prime Minister Atal Bihari Vajpayee were immersed in Haryana?
A. 2   **B.** 4   **C.** 6   **D.** 8

Q.33 Where is the headquarters of the World Trade Organization?
A. New York   **B.** Geneva
C. Madrid   **D.** Paris

Q.34 Which of the following is not related to the World Trade Organization (WTO)?
A. Multifiber Agreement
B. General Agreement on Trade and Services
C. Multilateral Agreement on Investment
D. Agreement on Agriculture

Q.35 Headquarters of UNO are situated at:
A. New York, USA
B. Hague (Netherlands)
C. Geneva
D. Paris

Q.36 Which of the following statements is/are correct about Lysosome?
1. It is called the "suicidal bags" of the cell.

2. The lysosomal membrane is rich in Cardiolipin.

3. They are absent in Erythrocytes.

4. They are basic in nature.

A. 1 and 3 only   **B.** 2 and 4 only
C. 1, 2 and 4 only   **D.** 2, 3 and 4 only

Q.37 Which of the following statements is/are correct concerning Ozone gas?

1. Good ozone is found in the upper part of the atmosphere called the Troposphere.

2. The thickness of the ozone in a column of air from the ground to the top of the atmosphere is measured in terms of Dobson units (DU).

A. 1 only   **B.** 2 only
C. Both 1 and 2   **D.** Neither 1 nor 2

Q.38 Which of the following is/are correct concerning Bharat Stage norms?

1. Bharat stage (BS) emission standards are laid down by the government to regulate the output of air pollutants from the internal combustion engines and spark-ignition engine equipment.

2. The central government has mandated that vehicle makers must manufacture, sell, and register only BS-VI (BS6) vehicles from April 1, 2020.

3. The first emission norms were introduced in India in 1992 for petrol and in 1994 for diesel vehicles.

A. 1 and 2 only   **B.** 2 and 3 only
C. 1 and 3 only   **D.** All of the above

Q.39 According to whom anthropology is a natural science and studies human society, often using the methods of the natural sciences?

A.   Bronisław Kasper Malinowski
B.   Alfred Reginald Radcliffe-Brown
C.   Claude Lévi-Strauss
D.   John Dewey

Q.40 "The problems which scientists selected for study, and their conceptualization, were determined by the values of the scientists." According to Max Weber, this statement refers to:

A. Value Judgement   **B.** Value Neutrality
C. Normative Value   **D.** Value Relevance

Q.41 In which qualitative approach the primary goal is to gain access to individuals' inner world experiences?

A. Case study   **B.** Ethnography
C. Phenomenology   **D.** Grounded theory

Q.42 A geographical indication tag is used to assign certain products corresponding to a specific region. Which among the following is **NOT** the GI tagged product in India?

A. Kadaknath   **B.** Vijayawada Durries
C. Katarni Rice   **D.** Zardalu Mango

Q.43 Which one of the following statements about the atmosphere is correct?

A. The atmosphere has definite upper limit but gradually thins until it becomes imperceptible.

B. The atmosphere has no definite upper limit but gradually thins until it becomes imperceptible.

C. The atmosphere has definite upper limits but gradually thickens until it becomes imperceptible.

D. The atmosphere has no definite upper limits but gradually thickens until it becomes imperceptible.

Q.44 The Pacific Islands from New Guinea south-eastwards to the Fiji Islands group is called?

A. Polynesia   **B.** Melanesia
C. Micronesia   **D.** Australasia

Q.45 With reference to the contribution of 19th century nationalist in the freedom struggle of India, which of the following statements is/are correct?

1. R.C. Dutt called British Colonialism "White man's Burden".

2. Sachidanand Sinha made "the drain" the major theme of his book "The Economic History of India.

A. 1 only   **B.** 2 only
C. Both 1 and 2   **D.** Neither 1 nor 2

Q.46 Which of the following statements is/are correct in context to Kushan rulers:

1. They repaired the Sudarshana lake in Kathiawar region.

2. They supported the development of Mahayana sect of Buddhism.

3. They were the first rulers to issue gold coins.

Select the correct answer using the codes given below:

A. 1,2 and 3   **B.** 2 and 3 only
C. 1 and 3 only   **D.** 2 only

Q.47 British Indian government setup committee for Sargent Plan which was related to:

A.   Famine policy
B.   Education policy
C.   Civil services reforms
D.   Judicial reforms

Q.48 Who won the title "Sportswoman of the Year" at the 2021 Laureus World Sports Awards?

A. Naomi Osaka   **B.** Ashleigh Barty
C. Sofia Kenin   **D.** Simona Halep

Q.49 Who has won the 2021 Booker Prize for Fiction for his novel The Promise?

A.   Anuk Arudpragasam
B.   Damon Galgut
C.   Patricia Lockwood
D.   Marion Hänsel

Q.50 Which of the following CRPF jawan from Rajasthan received the Police Gallantry Award by the President?

A.   Ankit Gupta
B.   Rajendra
C.   Vassundhara Chauhan
D.   Ranjit Singh Gujjar

Reasoning

Q.51 Direction: In following question, select the related word/letters/number from the given alternatives.

Japan : Judo : : Spain : ?

A. Baseball

B. Hockey

C. Table Tennis

D. Bull's Fight

Q.52 Direction: In each of the following questions, select the one which is different from the others.

(A) MIGE   (B) XTQO

(C) RNKI   (D) HDAY

A. MIGE   **B.** RNKI   **C.** HDAY   **D.** XTQO

Q.53 If a mirror is placed on the line AB, then which of the answer figures is the right image of the given figure?

[SSC MTS, 2019], [SSC MTS, 2017]

A. 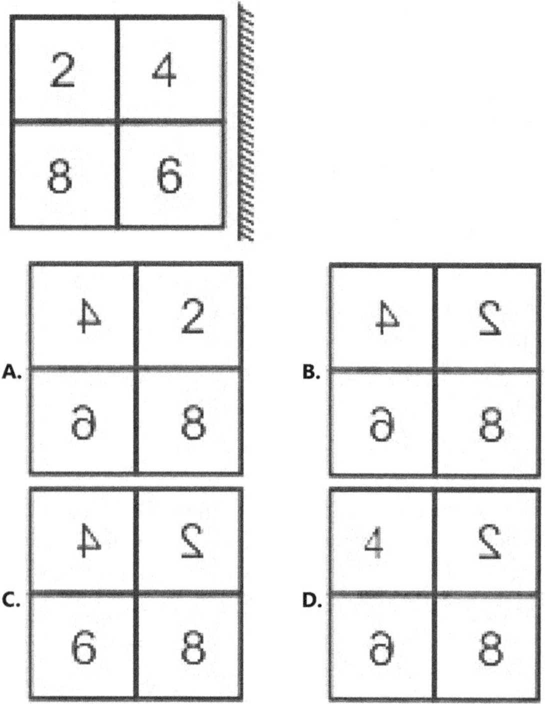

Q.54 Direction: Study the image carefully and choose the correct mirror image.

Ques (55-56):Direction: Select the Answer figure that will complete the series of question figures.

Q.55 Question figure:

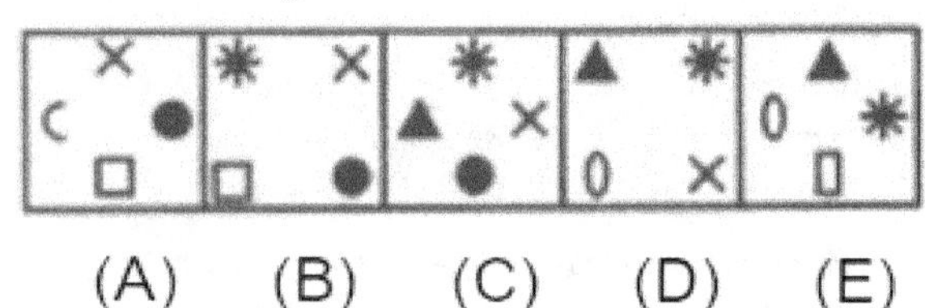

(A)   (B)   (C)   (D)   (E)

Answer figures:

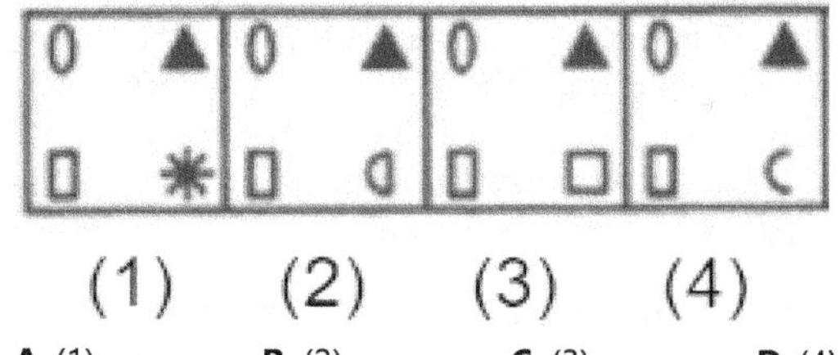

(1)   (2)   (3)   (4)

A. (1)   **B.** (2)   **C.** (3)   **D.** (4)

Q.56 Question figures:

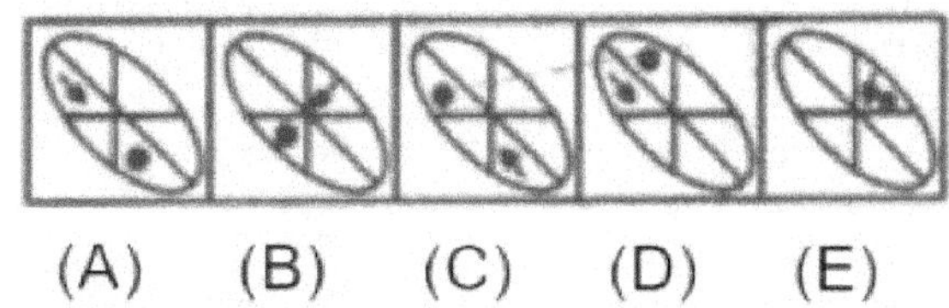

(A)   (B)   (C)   (D)   (E)

Answer figures:

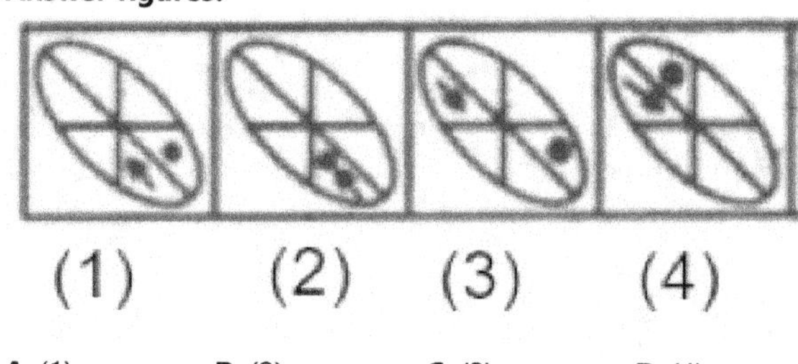

(1)   (2)   (3)   (4)

A. (1)   **B.** (2)   **C.** (3)   **D.** (4)

Q.57 In the given figure, how many are musical toys?

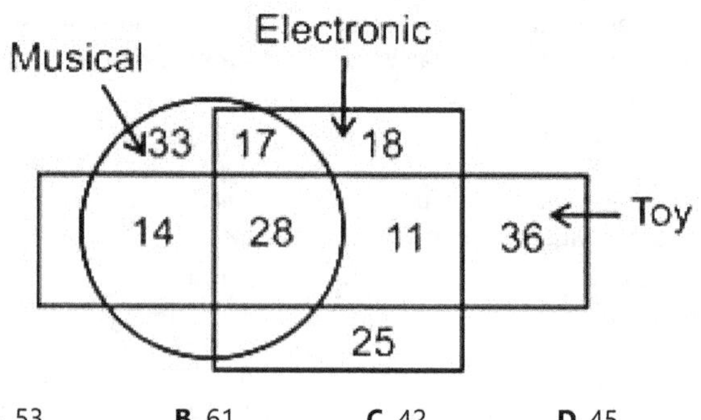

A. 53   **B.** 61   **C.** 42   **D.** 45

Q.58 Identify the diagram that best represents the relationship among the given classes.

Staff, Manager, Worker

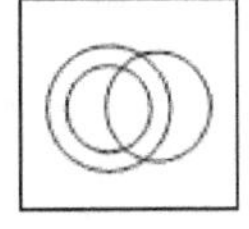
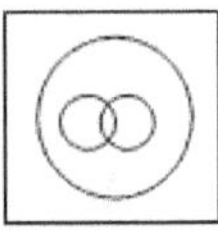
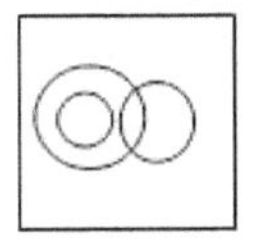
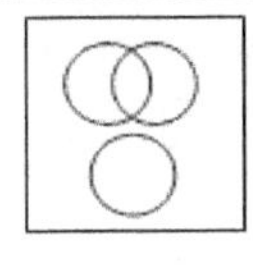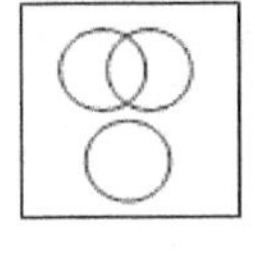

(A) (B) (C) (D)

A. (A)   **B.** (B)   **C.** (C)   **D.** (D)

Ques (59-60):Direction: Select the option that is true about the Statements and Conclusion given:

Q.59 Statement:

No river is sea.

All seas are oceans.

Conclusion:

I. All rivers are oceans.

II. No river is oceans.

[MP Police (Constable), 2017]

A.   Only conclusion II follows
B.   Only conclusion I follows
C.   Neither conclusion I nor conclusion II follows
D.   Both conclusion I and II follows

Q.60 Statement:

No chain is ring.

All rings are bangles.

Conclusion:

I. Some bangles are rings.

II. Some chains are bangles.

[MP Police (Constable), 2017]

A.   Only conclusion II follows
B.   Only conclusion I follows
C.   Neither conclusion I nor conclusion II follows
D.   Both conclusion I and II follows

Q.61 Direction: In the following question, select the number which can be placed at the sign of question mark (?) from the given alternatives.

$$2, 1, \left(\tfrac{1}{2}\right), \left(\tfrac{1}{4}\right), ?$$

A. $\left(\tfrac{1}{3}\right)$ **B.** $\left(\tfrac{1}{8}\right)$ **C.** $\left(\tfrac{2}{8}\right)$ **D.** $\left(\tfrac{1}{16}\right)$

Q.62 In the following question, select the number which can be placed at the sign of question mark (?) from the given alternatives.

4	13
12	4
7	5
20	1
?	9
19	2

A. 3   **B.** 4   **C.** 8   **D.** 20

Q.63 Direction: In the following question, Fig (X) is implicit in exactly one of the four alternative figures [A], [B], [C] and [D]. Find the option that contains figs. (X) as part of it.

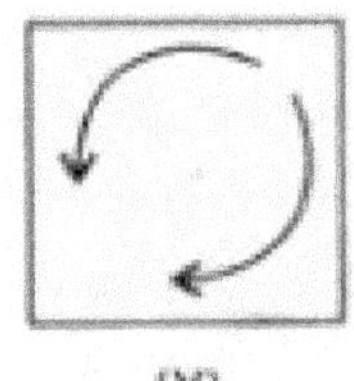

(X)

A.

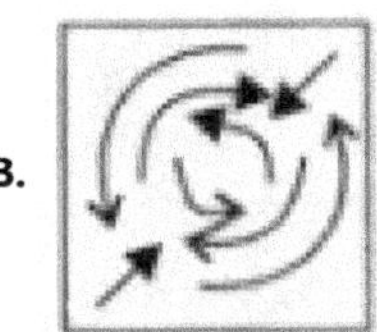
B.

C.

D.

Q.64 Identify the option figure that is embedded in the following figure (rotation not allowed).

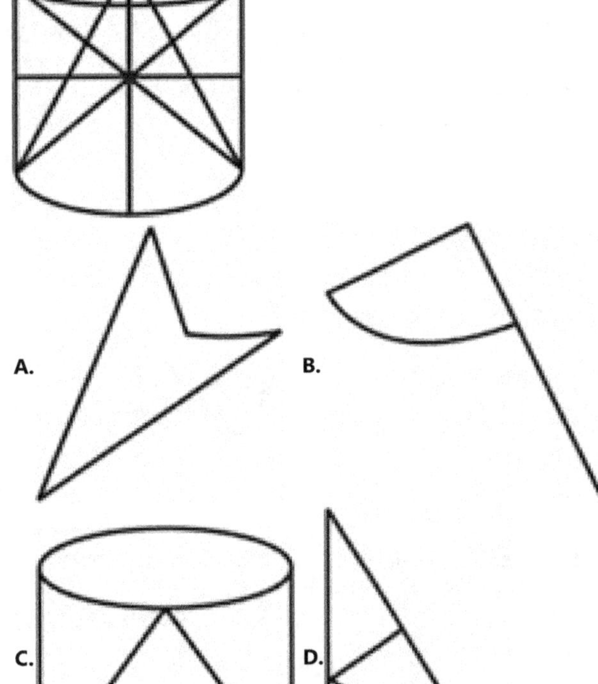

Q.65 What was the day on 25th January 1975?

A. Friday   **B.** Saturday   **C.** Sunday   **D.** Monday

Q.66 A transparent sheet as shown below, carrying a design is folded along the dotted line on either side

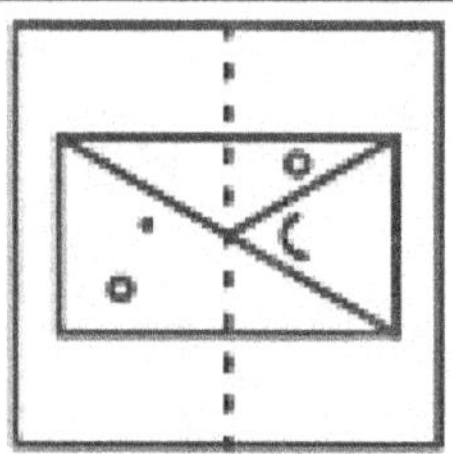

Which one among the following figures resembles the pattern formed after folding the above sheet?

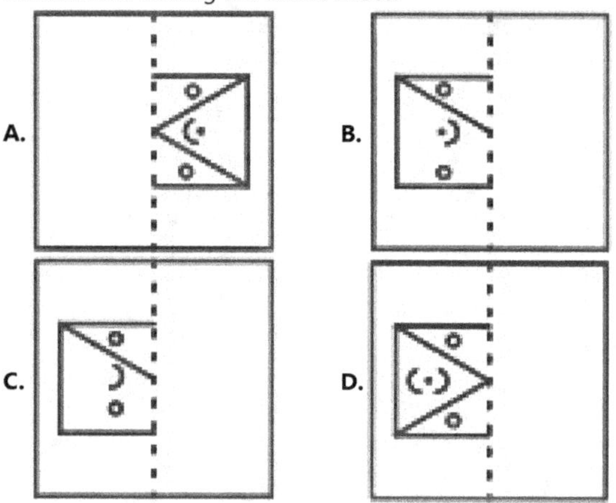

A.   B.   C.   D.

Q.67 There are three sets of figures $W, X, Y,$ and Z showing the sequence of folding of a piece of paper. Some punch holes are made in the final folding Z as shown in the figure. Now the folding Z is unfolded completely.

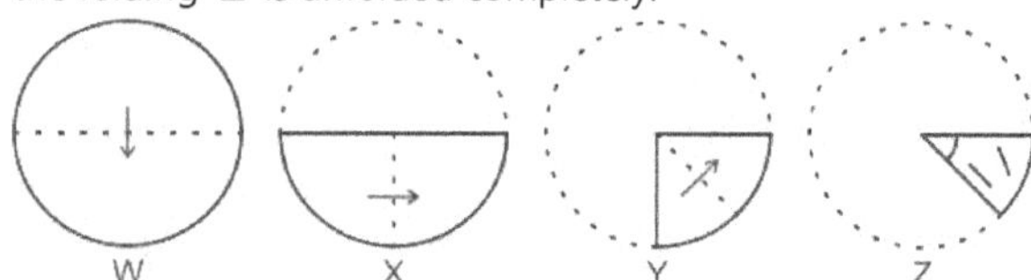

W   X   Y   Z

Which of the following option is correct?

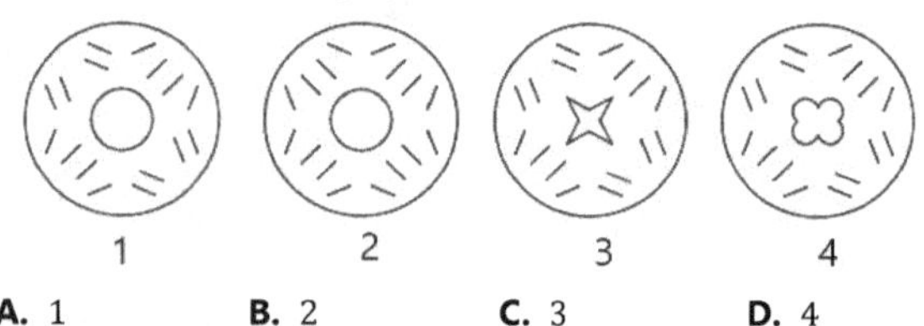

1   2   3   4

A. 1   **B.** 2   **C.** 3   **D.** 4

Q.68 In a code language, MATERIAL is written as NDYLTMGT. How will PURCHASE be written in that language?

[SSC Selection Post Phase IX, 2020]

A. QWUGJDWJ   **B.** QXWJJEYM
C. QWUGICVI   **D.** QXWJIDXL

Q.69 In a code language, if SAILOR is written as 21414192631, then how will MARBLE be written in the same language?

[SSC Selection Post Phase IX, 2020]

A. 1542392322   **B.** 1542392318
C. 1542382522   **D.** 1542392116

Ques (70-71):Direction: Arrange the given words as per dictionary order and select the right option.

Q.70 1. Aqueous
2. Aquarium
3. Aquiline
4. Aquatic
A. 4, 3, 2, 1   **B.** 1, 2, 3, 4   **C.** 2, 4, 1, 3   **D.** 3, 1, 4, 2

Q.71 1. Arise
2. Abysmal
3. Agility
4. Accrue
A. 2, 1, 4, 3   **B.** 3, 4, 2, 1   **C.** 2, 4, 1, 3   **D.** 2, 4, 3, 1

Q.72 Priya is the only daughter of Pravin and Kajal. Nikhil is the father of Rohan and the son-in-law of Kajal. How is Priya related to Nikhil?
A. Daughter   **B.** Granddaughter
C. Niece   **D.** Wife

Q.73 Pointing to a man, Ajay said, "He is the only son of my grandfather who had no daughter". How is Ajay related to that man if Ajay is a male?
A. Uncle   **B.** Father
C. Grandfather   **D.** Son

Q.74 Which one of the following four-letter clusters does NOT belong to the group?

[SSC Constable (GD), 2019]

A. SOPQ   **B.** WTUV   **C.** HEFG   **D.** NKLM

Q.75 Find the odd numbers from the given responses.
A. 48 – 54   **B.** 38 – 44   **C.** 34 – 40   **D.** 32 – 39

Numerical Ability

Q.76 Sonali could not decide between a discount of 30% or two successive discounts of 25% and $5\%,$ both given on shopping of Rs. $2000.$ What is the difference between both the discounts?
A.   Rs.   15
B.   Rs.   25
C.   Rs.   100
D.   There is no difference

Q.77 The average of four consecutive even numbers is $47.$ The largest of these number is:
A. 50   **B.** 48   **C.** 52   **D.** 46

Ques (78-82):Direction: Study the following table chart carefully and answer the questions given beside.

The following table represents the Maximum marks of five subjects and marks obtained by five students in five subjects.

Students	Physics (Out of 75)	Mathematics (Out of 100)	Chemistry (Out of 75)	Biology (Out of 75)	English (Out of 120)
Ragini	56	65	45	38	95
Rohan	60	52	62	55	88

Sohan	50	78	70	58	88
Mohini	55	82	65	66	110
Mohan	42	96	64	72	104

Q.78 Marks obtained by Ragini in Chemistry and Biology together is what percent of the marks obtained by Mohini in Physics and Mathematics together?

A. 66.23%   B. 60.58%   C. 58.34%   D. 54.32%

Q.79 Find the respective ratio of the marks obtained by all the students in Mathematics and marks obtained by all the students in Chemistry.

A. 293 : 351   B. 373 : 306

C. 351 : 293   D. 306 : 373

Q.80 Find the overall percentage of Sohan in all the subjects.

A. 62.7%   B. 58.4%   C. 77.3%   D. 79.1%

Q.81 Find the difference between the percentage of marks obtained by Mohan in English and that of Rohan in Physics.

A. 6.67%   B. 4.59%   C. 5.53%   D. 3.12%

Q.82 Find the sum of marks obtained by Rohan in all the subjects.

A. 515   B. 427   C. 611   D. 317

Q.83 A train moving at the rate of 72 kmph crosses a pole in 20 seconds. How much time will the train require to cross car moving at speed of 18 kmph in opposite direction?

A. 20 s   B. 16 s   C. 10 s   D. 12 s

Q.84 What will come in place of the question mark in the following question?

$$120 \div 40 \text{ of } \frac{1}{4} + \frac{2}{5} \times 3\frac{1}{4} = ?$$

A. $13\frac{3}{10}$ B. $11\frac{1}{9}$ C. $3\frac{1}{10}$ D. $32\frac{3}{11}$

Q.85 If $A:B = 7:3$, find the value of $\frac{AB+B^2}{A^2-B^2}$.

A. $\frac{3}{4}$ B. $\frac{4}{3}$ C. $\frac{7}{3}$ D. $\frac{3}{7}$

Q.86 Find the ages of Anil, Bini, and Chaya in order (in years) as the average age of Anil and Bini is 20 years and if Anil is to be replaced by Chaya, the average would be 19 years and the average age of Chaya and Anil is 21 years.

A. 20, 18, 22   B. 18, 22, 20

C. 22, 18, 20   D. 18, 20, 22

Q.87 There is a path of width 5 m around a circular plot of land whose area is 144π m². The total area of the circular plot including the path surrounding it is:

[Indian Military Academy (IMA), 2018]

A. 349π m²   B. 289π m²   C. 209π m²   D. 149π m²

Q.88 Due to a shortage of labor in a factory, its production decreases by 25%. By how much% should the working period be increased so that production remains the same?

A. $53\frac{1}{3}$%   B. $23\frac{1}{3}$%   C. $40\frac{1}{3}$%   D. $33\frac{1}{3}$%

Q.89 A man and a woman received Rs. 1500 as wages for 20 days for the work they did together. If the efficiency of the man is double the women, then find daily wages of woman.

A. Rs. 25   B. Rs. 50   C. Rs. 500   D. Rs. 100

Q.90 If $I = a^2 + b^2 + c^2$, where a and b are consecutive integers and $c = ab$, then I is:

[Indian Military Academy (IMA), 2020]

A. an even number and it is not a square of an integer

B. an odd number and it is not a square of an integer

C. square of an even integer

D. square of an odd integer

Computer Awareness

Q.91 Which of the following statement is false?

A. You can set different header footer for even and odd pages

B. You can set different page number formats for different sections

C. You can set different header footer for first page of a section

D. You can set different header and footer for last page of a section

Q.92 Text-styling feature of MS word is:

A. WordColor   B. WordFont

C. WordArt   D. WordFill

Q.93 Which one can be used as watermark in a word document.

A. Text   B. Image

C. Both (A) and (B)   D. None

Q.94 Where footnotes appear in a document?

A. End of document   B. Bottom of a Page

C. End of Heading   D. None

Q.95 The ____ feature of MS Excel quickly completes a series of data.

A. auto Complete   B. auto Fill

C. fill Handle   D. sorting

Q.96 What is the shortcut key for save as in Libre Office Writer?

A. Ctrl + Shift + S   B. Ctrl + S

C. F12   D. None of the above

Q.97 ________ is a computer device/program which provide functionality for other device/program.

A. Server   B. Browser

C. USB port   D. Gateway

Q.98 Which device enables movement of data from one network to other network?

A. HUB   B. Repeater   C. Router   D. Modem

Q.99 Internet Explorer is a __________.

A. Web browser

B. Web search engine

C. Hypertext transfer protocol

D. Web data store

Q.100 Which device is required for the Internet connection?

A. Joystick   **B.** Modem

C. CD Drive   **D.** NIC Card

// Smart Answer Sheet //

Correct — Indicates percentage of students who answered questions correctly.

Skipped — Indicates percentage of students who skipped questions.

Q.	Ans.	Correct / Skipped	Q.	Ans.	Correct / Skipped	Q.	Ans.	Correct / Skipped	Q.	Ans.	Correct / Skipped	Q.	Ans.	Correct / Skipped
1	B	64.74 % / 34.16 %	17	D	48.45 % / 31.64 %	33	B	61.77 % / 33.8 %	49	B	62.62 % / 34.53 %	65	B	58.29 % / 41.12 %
2	B	68.5 % / 30.97 %	18	A	89.72 % / 10.22 %	34	C	60.91 % / 32.41 %	50	B	42.99 % / 49.43 %	66	B	69.51 % / 30.04 %
3	C	78.75 % / 10.25 %	19	B	63.33 % / 35.57 %	35	A	64.21 % / 35.17 %	51	D	81.24 % / 15.42 %	67	B	17.0 % / 82.33 %
4	B	67.14 % / 31.26 %	20	B	63.68 % / 31.75 %	36	A	58.44 % / 34.86 %	52	A	65.38 % / 32.41 %	68	B	20.07 % / 78.89 %
5	B	47.44 % / 34.39 %	21	C	51.56 % / 47.37 %	37	B	31.23 % / 67.98 %	53	A	77.77 % / 11.48 %	69	B	57.06 % / 34.55 %
6	D	87.13 % / 12.64 %	22	D	89.38 % / 10.43 %	38	A	78.96 % / 15.14 %	54	B	89.39 % / 10.41 %	70	C	78.74 % / 17.44 %
7	B	42.02 % / 38.93 %	23	D	21.56 % / 68.53 %	39	B	27.46 % / 69.42 %	55	B	15.78 % / 80.01 %	71	D	80.72 % / 18.92 %
8	C	62.03 % / 36.32 %	24	A	30.91 % / 67.56 %	40	A	54.36 % / 40.91 %	56	A	56.12 % / 30.6 %	72	D	54.17 % / 34.49 %
9	D	67.39 % / 31.91 %	25	A	59.07 % / 37.58 %	41	C	22.05 % / 75.43 %	57	C	51.29 % / 35.6 %	73	D	61.69 % / 33.2 %
10	D	77.19 % / 19.65 %	26	B	23.42 % / 67.54 %	42	B	46.44 % / 38.83 %	58	B	58.09 % / 33.17 %	74	A	65.47 % / 31.76 %
11	A	41.64 % / 54.66 %	27	B	52.86 % / 39.16 %	43	B	80.83 % / 17.97 %	59	C	49.3 % / 33.08 %	75	D	68.43 % / 30.72 %
12	C	63.41 % / 30.83 %	28	B	23.68 % / 75.48 %	44	B	50.23 % / 48.92 %	60	B	57.83 % / 36.77 %	76	B	81.04 % / 15.99 %
13	A	42.17 % / 43.01 %	29	A	86.24 % / 13.67 %	45	D	14.1 % / 68.18 %	61	B	64.0 % / 31.53 %	77	A	63.2 % / 33.08 %
14	A	43.91 % / 52.74 %	30	C	42.6 % / 57.24 %	46	D	21.16 % / 74.09 %	62	A	45.54 % / 50.32 %	78	B	50.83 % / 39.94 %
15	A	13.16 % / 67.48 %	31	D	87.75 % / 11.09 %	47	B	64.61 % / 32.34 %	63	C	45.99 % / 30.11 %	79	B	64.68 % / 32.72 %
16	D	66.71 % / 31.54 %	32	A	50.95 % / 32.36 %	48	A	40.9 % / 57.33 %	64	A	47.68 % / 34.56 %	80	C	61.55 % / 38.08 %

Q.	Ans.	Correct / Skipped
81	A	51.13 %
		46.52 %
82	D	87.85 %
		11.36 %
83	B	67.22 %
		31.75 %
84	A	47.32 %
		51.13 %

Q.	Ans.	Correct / Skipped
85	A	54.49 %
		41.77 %
86	C	69.11 %
		30.11 %
87	B	85.22 %
		14.5 %
88	D	69.32 %
		30.44 %

Q.	Ans.	Correct / Skipped
89	A	63.18 %
		30.37 %
90	D	65.55 %
		32.03 %
91	D	82.27 %
		17.08 %
92	C	81.97 %
		17.93 %

Q.	Ans.	Correct / Skipped
93	C	85.92 %
		14.01 %
94	B	80.68 %
		17.73 %
95	B	60.93 %
		31.7 %
96	A	67.94 %
		31.83 %

Q.	Ans.	Correct / Skipped
97	A	56.26 %
		39.45 %
98	C	66.65 %
		30.79 %
99	A	18.09 %
		79.45 %
100	B	66.08 %
		31.63 %

Performance Analysis

Avg. Score (%)	44.0%
Toppers Score (%)	65.0%
Your Score	

//Hints and Solutions//

1. The Hoysaleshwara Temple is an aspirant for the tag of World Heritage Site is located at Karnataka state.

- Tiong Kian Boom, an expert from International Commission on Monuments and Sites (ICOMOS), visited the Hoysaleshwara temple in Halebeedu, Karnataka on September 14, 2022.
- The Hoysala structure is an aspirant for the tag of World Heritage Site, which is given by UNESCO.
- It is a 12th-century Hindu temple dedicated to Lord Shiva.

Hence, the correct option is (B).

2. PM Narendra Modi unveiled the logo, theme, and website of India's G20 Presidency on 8 Nov 2022.

The logo, theme, and website will reflect India's message and overarching priorities to the world. India will assume G20 Presidency on 1 December 2022. G20 is the premier forum for international economic cooperation representing around 85% of the global GDP, and over 75% of the global trade.

Hence, the correct option is (B).

3. Major Dhyan Chand Khel Ratna:

Major Dhyan Chand Khel Ratna Award (formerly Rajiv Gandhi Khel Ratna) is the highest sports award given in India. The award has been named after the best player of India and world hockey, who was a member of the Indian hockey team that won three Olympic gold medals.

Vinesh Phogat:

Vinesh Phogat (born 25 August 1994) is an Indian wrestler. She became the first Indian female wrestler to win gold in both the Commonwealth and Asian Games. She is the only Indian female wrestler to have won multiple medals at the World Wrestling Championships.

Hence, the correct option is (C).

4. South Africa, first time in the world, has granted a patent to an 'artificial intelligence system' relating to a "food container based on fractal geometry" innovation.

The innovation involves interlocking food containers that are easy for robots to grasp and stack.

Hence, the correct option is (B).

5. SBI General Insurance Company Limited has announced Paritosh Tripathi as Managing Director and Chief Executive Officer on July 2022.

He was nominated for the position by the parent company State Bank of India and has succeeded PC Kandpal.

From 2017 to 2020 he was the head of Bancassurance first with SBI Mutual Fund and then with SBI General Insurance.

Hence, the correct option is (B).

6. The 6th India Water Week-2019 (IWW-2019) is to be held at Vigyan Bhawan, New Delhi from 24 to 28 September 2019.

- It is organised by the Ministry of Jal-Shakti, Department of Water Resources, River Development and Ganga Rejuvenation, Government of India.
- The IWW-2019 is being organised with the theme of "Water Cooperation - Coping with 21st Century Challenges".
- The objective of bringing new ideas for mutual cooperation for sustainable water management in the context of changing basin dynamics across administrative boundaries.

Hence, the correct option is (D).

7. India has become the largest bilateral lender to Sri Lanka by disbursing a total of USD 968 million in loans in four months of 2022, surpassing China.

China has maintained its position as the largest bilateral lender to Sri Lanka in the past five years from 2017 to 2021. Asian Development Bank (ADB) has been the largest multilateral lender in the past five years by disbursing an amount of USD 610 million in 2021.

Hence, the correct option is (B).

8. 44th International Chess Olympiad, the world's biggest chess event, will be held at Poonjeri Village in Mamallapuram, from Chennai, Tamil Nadu, from July 28 to August 10, 2022. PM Modi and Chief Minister of Tamil Nadu M K Stalin will attend the grand inaugural ceremony. The official mascot is 'Thambi', a horse clad in the traditional Veshti -Sattai'. The Olympiad was originally scheduled to take place in Russia, but the event is not happening in Russia due to the ongoing Russian-Ukraine war.

Hence, the correct option is (C).

9. Premier industry body Data Security Council of India (DSCI) established by NASSCOM, has appointed its senior vice president Vinayak Godse as the new CEO.

- Godse will be taking over from Rama Vedashree who led DSCI for more than six years.
- Godse will be taking over as the CEO from 1 Oct 2022.
- DSCI Founded: 2008
- Founder: NASSCOM
- Current Chairman: Rajendra S Pawar
- HQ: Noida, Uttar Pradesh

Hence, the correct option is (D).

10. To compensate for the damage caused to the crops due to adverse weather and natural calamities, Haryana has launched the Mukhya Mantri Bagwani Bima scheme portal on April 2022 with an initial corpus of Rs 10 crore for the scheme. The scheme compensates a sum of Rs 30,000 per acre for vegetables and Spices and Rs 40,000 per acre for fruits, which will be compensated to the farmers upon claim via four categories such as 25 per cent, 50 per cent, 75 per cent and 100 per cent based on the survey. The farmer's contribution will be only 5 per cent of the insured amount i.e., Rs 750 per acre for vegetables and Spices and Rs 1000 per acre for fruits.

Hence, the correct option is (D).

11. Union Minister for Electronics and Information Technology, Ravi Shankar Prasad launched the UMANG's international version in coordination with Ministry of External Affairs for select countries including USA, UK, Canada, Australia, UAE, Netherlands, Singapore, Australia and New Zealand.

An online conference was organized to mark the occasion of 3 years of UMANG (Unified Mobile Application for New-age Governance) and a milestone of 2000 plus services. The app will help Indian international students, NRIs and Indian tourists to avail the services of the Government.

Hence, the correct option is (A).

12. Engineers day is observed on September 15 to commemorate the birth anniversary of M Visvesvaraya.

Under his able Dewanship, the state of Mysore saw a major transformation in the realms of Agriculture, Irrigation, Industrialization, Education, Banking, and Commerce.

Hence, the correct option is (C).

13. In 1984, Indian Air Force pilot Rakesh Sharma made history by becoming the first Indian to travel to space.

Mr. Sharma was part of the Soviet Union's Soyuz T-11 expedition, which was launched on April 2, 1984.

He spent nearly eight days orbiting Earth.

Hence, the correct option is (A).

14. Ram Nath Shastri was born on 15 April 1914. He is known as the "Father of Dogri" for his pivotal role in the revival and resurgence of the Dogri language in Jammu and Kashmir.

He was conferred with Padma Shri.

He was a prolific and versatile litterateur who excelled as a Dogri poet, fiction writer, lexicographer, essayist, educationist, dramatist, translator, and editor. Through his writings in various genres, he has succeeded in ushering Dogri language on the national stage.

In the year 2001, India's National Academy of Letters, the highest literary honour was awarded by the Sahitya Akademi Fellowship, awarded by the Sahitya Akademi.

Hence, the correct option is (A).

15. Recently, the Central Government has appointed 'Subodh Kumar Jaiswal' as a new Director of the Central Bureau of Investigation (CBI).

Central Bureau of Investigation (CBI):

- The CBI was set up in 1963 by a resolution of the Ministry of Home Affairs.
- The establishment of the CBI was recommended by the Santhanam Committee on Prevention of Corruption (1962–1964).

- The CBI is not a statutory body. It derives its powers from the Delhi Special Police Establishment Act, 1946.
- The CBI is the main investigating agency of the Central Government.
- The CBI is headed by a Director.
- Appointment of CBI Director:
  - The Lokpal and Lokayuktas Act (2013) amended the Delhi Special Police Establishment Act (1946) and made the following changes with respect to appointment of the Director of CBI:
  - Appointment Committee: The Central Government shall appoint the Director of CBI on the recommendation of a three-member committee consisting of
    - the Prime Minister as Chairperson,
    - the Leader of Opposition in the Lok Sabha and
    - the Chief Justice of India or Judge of the Supreme Court (SC) nominated by him. Therefore, statements 1, 3 and 5 are correct.

Hence, the correct option is (A).

16.

- The Preamble Specifies the source of authority, i.e. the people of India, the system of Government.
- The Preamble of the Constitution is the preface of the constitution and based on the basic structure of the constitution.
- It is constituted on 26 Nov 1949.

Hence, the correct option is (D).

17. The capital that is consumed by an economy or a firm in the production process is known as depreciation. In economics, depreciation is the gradual decrease in the economic value of the capital stock of a firm, nation, or other entity, either through physical depreciation, obsolescence, or changes in the demand for the services of the capital in question.

Hence, the correct option is (D).

18. The economic problem arises from the scarcity of resources. Every economy faces scarcity of resources because their wants are unlimited and their resources (means) are limited. Therefore, the economic problem is the problem of economizing scarce resources. It means making the best use of the available resources.

Hence, the correct option is (A).

19. The Indological approach rested on the assumption that historically, Indian society and culture are unique and that this 'contextually' specificity of Indian social realities could be grasped better through the 'texts'.

Hence, the correct option is (B).

20. Shudraka wrote the great literary work 'Mricchakatika'.

- Mṛcchakatika is a Sanskrit drama written by Shudraka.
- Mṛcchakatika is written in Sanskrit in the 2nd century BC.
- It is is a love story of a worthy Brahmana Charudatta and a courtesan Vasantasena.
- No historical records mention a king by the name Shudraka.
- Other notable works of Shudraka are Vinavasavadatta, Bhana, Padmaprabhritaka.

Hence, the correct option is (B).

21. Plato is the author of the book 'Republic'.

- Plato was an ancient Greek philosopher.
- He was born in 428-7 B.C.E and died in 348-7 B.C.E.
- He was the student of Socrates and the teacher of Aristotle.
- Plato is known for his work "the Republic"

Hence, the correct option is (C).

22. Abhidharma kosha is an ancient Buddhist text.

- It was written in Sanskrit by the Indian Buddhist scholar Vasubandhu.
- Vasubandhu wrote this book before he converted to Mahayana Buddhism.
- The word meaning of the text "Abhidharma kosha" is the storehouse (Kosa) of Abhidharma.
- This text was widely used by schools of Buddhism in India, Tibet and East Asia to teach Buddism.
- It was the main source of Abhidharma and Sravakayana Buddhism for later Mahayana Buddhists.

Hence, the correct option is (D).

23. Established a centre at Kartarpur named Dera Baba Nanak on the river Ravi.

The sacred space thus created by Guru Nanak was known as dharmsal. It is now known as Gurdwar.

Before his death Guru appointed Lehna also known as Guru Angad as his successor.
Hence, the correct option is (D).

24. The correct match is a-1, b-3, c-4, d-2.

Parijatapaharanam is a Telugu poem composed by Nandi Thimmana.

Panduranga Mahathyam is a magnum opus of 16th century poet Tenali Ramalinga.

Dhurajati was a Telugu poet in the court of the king Krishnadevaraya . He wrote Kalahasti Mahatyam.

Madura Vijayam, meaning "The Conquest of Madurai", is a 14th-century C.E Sanskrit poem written by the poet Gangadevi.

Hence, the correct option is (A).

25. Jharkhand's Sohrai Khovar painting and Telangana's Telia Rumal were given the Geographical Indication.

Telia Rumal cloth involves intricate handmade work with cotton loom displaying a variety of designs and motifs in three particular colours — red, black and white.
Hence, the correct option is (A).

26. The Team of Maharashtra dominated the Khelo India Youth Games by clinching the overall trophy for the second time with a huge haul of 256 medals, including 78 gold and 77 silver. Last year, Maharashtra topped the table with 228 medals. The trophy was presented to Maharashtra by the Chief Minister of Assam Sarbananda Sonowal in the presence of Union Sports Minister Kiren Rijju, during the closing ceremony.

The second place was bagged by the state of Haryana with 200 medals and Delhi with 122 medals. Khelo India Youth games has been organised in Assam's Guwahati for the last 13 days.

Hence, the correct option is (B).

27. Recently the World Archery has conditionally lifted the suspension of the Archery Association of India, ahead of Tokyo Olympics 2020. The Archery Association of India had been suspended since August 5th, 2019, following elections in New Delhi on 18th January.

The Indian archery athletes were only allowed to compete under a neutral flag at events that directly affected their qualification chances for the Olympics. After the ban is lifted, Indian archers are allowed to participate in World Archery events. India currently has three men's and one women's quota place at Tokyo 2020.

Hence, the correct option is (B).

28. Kobe Bryant was a 41- year-old American professional basketball player, who recently died in a helicopter crash near Los Angeles. Bryant played in the National Basketball Association (NBA) with the Los Angeles Lakers, throughout his entire career. He entered the NBA directly from high school and had won five NBA championships.

Bryant was on board the helicopter with eight others, including his 13-year-old daughter Gianna Bryant during the crash. The sudden demise of one of the greatest basketball players in history was mourned by basketball enthusiasts all over the world.

Hence, the correct option is (B).

29. The tomb of Ibrahim Lodi is situated at Panipat.

Ibrahim Khan Lodi was an 'Afghan Sultan' of the 'Delhi Sultanate' who became Sultan in 1517 after the death of his father Sikandar Lodi. He was the last ruler of the Lodi dynasty. He was defeated and killed at the Battle of Panipat by Babur's invading army. He died on died 21 April 1526.

Hence, the correct option is (A).

30. Motilal Nehru School of Sports is a boarding school located in Rai in Sonipat district of the Indian state of Haryana. It was founded in July 1973 by the Government of Haryana. It is ranked amongst the top 10 boarding schools in the country as per the education world rankings 2016.

Motilal Nehru School of Sports in Rai, Haryana is known for producing better players. Apart from the army, many students have excelled in national and international sports.

Hence, the correct option is (C).

31. Cooperative milk plants are open in Ambala, Rohtak and Jind in Haryana.

The Dairy Corporation was formed in 1970 which continued active functioning till 31 March 1977. There after it's business was taken over by federation to set up THREE TIER SYSTEM based on Anand Pattern. Since 1 April 1992, the federation has leased out the plants to the Milk Unions. Haryana is one of the most progressive states of India.

Hence, the correct option is (D).

32.

- The ashes of former prime minister Atal Bihari Vajpayee were taken to various states from the national capital today for immersion in rivers across the country as part of the BJP's 'asthi kalash yatra'.

- In Haryana, Chief Minister Manohar Lal Khattar said the ashes would be immersed in rivers at two places, Pehowa in Kurukshetra and Hathnikundin Yamunanagar on 23 August 2018.

Hence, the correct option is (A).

33. The headquarters of the World Trade Organization (WTO) is Geneva, Switzerland.

The WTO has many roles: it operates a global system of trade rules, it acts as a forum for negotiating trade agreements, it settles trade disputes between its members and it supports the needs of developing countries.

Hence, the correct option is (B).

34.

- The term multifiber agreement is not related to the World Trade Organization (WTO).

- It actually governed the global trade in both garments and even textiles from the year 1974 through the year 2004.

- It imposes quotas on an entire amount developing nations can export to the developed nations.

- It is vital to know that this agreement is actually expired on the date 1st January 2005.

Hence, the correct option is (C).

35. The headquarters of the United Nations is a distinctive complex in New York City (USA). The United Nations has three additional, subsidiary, regional headquarters or headquarter districts. These are located in Geneva (Switzerland), Vienna (Austria), and Nairobi (Kenya).

Hence, the correct option is (A).

36. Lysosomes:

- It is called the "suicidal bags" of the cell. Therefore statement 1 is correct.

- It is also known as the is called the perinuclear dense bodies.

- The lysosomal membrane is rich in Sialic acid. Therefore statement 2 is not correct.

- They are absent in Erythrocytes. Therefore statement 3 is correct.

- They are acidic in nature due to the presence of anabolic enzymes. Therefore statement 4 is not correct.

- Acid phosphatase (Enzyme) is used as a marker for the lysosomes.

- Sucrose density gradient centrifugation is used in the isolation of Liposomal fractions.

Functions of lysosomes:

- Autolysis
- Autophagy
- Digestion (intracellular and extracellular)

Gamori staining techniques are used to locate the lysosomes.

Phosphate esters and nucleases are the components of lysosomes.

They are considered the "garbage trucks" of a cell because they remove all unwanted cellular materials.

White blood cells contain the most active lysosomes.

They are involved in Secretion.

They are found in Leukocytes.

Hence, the correct option is (A).

37. Good ozone is found in the upper part of the atmosphere called the stratosphere, and it acts as a shield absorbing ultraviolet radiation from the sun. Therefore, statement 1 is incorrect.

UV rays are highly injurious to living organisms since the DNA and proteins of living organisms preferentially absorb UV rays, and it's high energy breaks the chemical bonds within these molecules.

The thickness of the ozone in a column of air from the ground to the top of the atmosphere is measured in terms of Dobson units (DU). Therefore, statement 2 is correct.

Ozone gas is continuously formed by the action of UV rays on molecular oxygen and also degraded into molecular oxygen in the stratosphere.

There should be a balance between the production and degradation of ozone in the stratosphere. Of late, the balance has been disrupted due to the enhancement of ozone degradation by chlorofluorocarbons (CFCs).

CFCs find wide use as refrigerants. CFCs discharged in the lower part of the atmosphere move upward and reach the stratosphere.

In the stratosphere, UV rays act on them releasing Cl atoms.

- Cl degrades ozone releasing molecular oxygen, with these atoms acting merely as catalysts;

- Cl atoms are not consumed in the reaction.

Therefore, whatever CFCs are added to the stratosphere, they have permanent and continuing effects on Ozone levels.

Although ozone depletion is occurring widely in the stratosphere, the depletion is particularly marked over the Antarctic region.

This has resulted in the formation of a large area of the thinned ozone layer, commonly called the ozone hole.

UV radiation of wavelengths shorter than UV-B is almost completely absorbed by Earth's atmosphere, given that the ozone layer is intact.

But, UV-B damages DNA and mutation may occur. It causes ageing of the skin, damage to skin cells, and various types of skin cancers. In the human eye, the cornea absorbs UV-B radiation, and a high dose of UV-B causes inflammation of the cornea, called snow-blindness, cataracts, etc. Such exposure may permanently damage the cornea.

Recognizing the deleterious effects of ozone depletion, an international treaty, known as the Montreal Protocol, was signed at Montreal (Canada) in 1987 (effective in 1989) to control the emission of ozone-depleting substances.

Subsequently, many more efforts have been made and protocols have laid down definite roadmaps, separately for developed and developing countries, for reducing the emission of CFCs and other ozone-depleting chemicals.

Hence, the correct option is (B).

38. Bharat stage (BS) emission standards are laid down by the government to regulate the output of air pollutants from the internal combustion engines and spark-ignition engine equipment. Therefore, statement 1 is correct.

The first emission norms were introduced in India in 1991 for petrol and in 1992 for diesel vehicles. Therefore, statement 3 is incorrect.

- Followed these, the catalytic converter became mandatory for petrol vehicles and unleaded petrol was introduced in the market.

The central government has mandated that vehicle makers must manufacture, sell, and register only BS-VI (BS6) vehicles from April 1, 2020. Therefore, statement 2 is correct.

- As per BS-VI emission norms, petrol vehicles will have to effect a 25% reduction in their NOx, or nitrogen oxide emissions.

- Diesel engines will have to reduce their HC+NOx (hydrocarbon + nitrogen oxides) by 43%, their NOx levels by 68%, and particulate matter levels by 82%.

- The emission norms of all models of two-wheelers in India are ahead of Europe (2021) and Japan (2022).

- India is the first country to adopt this level of emission norms. (BS-VI norms).

Hence, the correct option is (A).

39. Alfred Reginald Radcliffe-Brown was one of the most eminent anthropologists of the first half of the twentieth century. By example and teaching, he helped to develop and establish modern "social" anthropology as a generalizing, theoretical discipline. Anthropology is the scientific study of humanity, concerned with human behaviour, human biology, and societies, in both the present and past, including past human species.

Hence, the correct option is (B).

40. A value judgment (or value judgement) is a judgment of the rightness or wrongness of something or someone, or of the usefulness of something or someone, based on a comparison or other relativity. As a generalization, a value judgment can refer to a judgment based upon a particular set of values or on a particular value system. A related meaning of value judgment is an expedient evaluation based upon limited information at hand, an evaluation was undertaken because a decision must be made on short notice.

Hence, the correct option is (A).

41. Phenomenology is a form of qualitative approach in which the primary goal is to gain access to individuals' inner world experiences. Phenomenology is the philosophical study of the structures of experience and consciousness.

Hence, the correct option is (C).

42. Vijayawada Durries is not a GI tagged product in India.

A geographical indication (GI) is a name or sign used on certain products which correspond to a specific geographical location or origin (e.g., a town, region, or country). These indications ensure the quality of goods originating from a particular region. Darjeeling Tea was the first GI tagged product in India.

Hence, the correct option is (B).

43. The atmosphere has no definite upper limit but gradually thins until it becomes imperceptible. The atmosphere becomes thinner and thinner with increasing altitude, with no definite boundary between the atmosphere and outer space.

Hence, the correct option is (B).

44. Melanesia is a subregion of Oceania (and occasionally Australasia) extending from the western end of the Pacific Ocean to the Arafura Sea, and eastward to Fiji.

The region includes the four countries of Vanuatu, Solomon Islands, Fiji, and Papua New Guinea.

Hence, the correct option is (B).

45. Sachidanand Sinha called British Colonialism as White man's Burden in the newspaper, Indian People in 1903. So, statement 1 is not correct.

R.C. Dutt made the drain as the major theme of his book The Economic History of India. So, statement 1 is not correct.

Hence, the correct option is (D).

46. Kushanas are one of the branches of the Yue Chi tribes living at the Chinese frontier or in Central Asia. Kujula Kadphises laid the foundation of the Kushana Empire in India. Kadphises II (Viema Kadphises) issued a large number of gold coins and spread his kingdom up to the East of Indus river. The first gold coins were not issued by the Kushanas. These were identical in weight with those issued by the Romans & the Parthians and

have been found at various sites in north India & Central Asia. So, statement 3 is incorrect.

Kanishka was the greatest Kushana ruler. He started a new era known as the Shaka Era (78 AD). Kushans were the great patron of the Mahayana form of Buddhism. Kanishka convened the fourth Buddhist Council at Kundalvana in Kashmir where the doctrines of Mahayana Buddhism were finalised. It was held in Sanskrit. So, statement 2 is correct.

The famous Shaka ruler, Rudradaman I undertook the repairing of Sudarshana lake in Kathiawar region which had been in the use of irrigation for a long time dated back to the Mauryas. So, statement 1 is incorrect.

Hence, the correct option is (D).

47. British Indian government set up a committee for Sargent Plan which was related to Education policy.

It is also known as Sargent Plan after John Sargent, the then Educational Advisor to the Government of India. It proposed the establishment of nursery schools on a voluntary basis for children under six, while from six to fourteen years of age education should be free and compulsory for both boys and girls in a phased program spread over 40 years (1944-1984).

Hence, the correct option is (B).

48. World number two tennis player Naomi Osaka of Japan has been named "Sportswoman of the Year" at the 2021 Laureus World Sports Awards.

This is Osaka's second recognition at the Laureus Sports Awards. She won the "Breakthrough of the Year" award in 2019. Due to the raging COVID-19 pandemic, the 22nd Laureus World Sports Awards was held in a virtual ceremony in Seville, Spain.

Hence, the correct option is (A).

49. South African author Damon Galgut has won the 2021 Booker Prize for Fiction for his novel The Promise.

He won the award in his third appearance on the shortlist after making the cut in 2003 and 2010. He follows in the footsteps of other South African winners Nadine Gordimer and JM Coetzee, and is the first winner from the country since 1999.

Hence, the correct option is (B).

50. Rajendra a CRPF soldier from Rajasthan received Police Gallantry Award.

Assistant commandant Rajendra was awarded the Police Gallantry Award by President. Kumar Rajesh Chandra is the director-general of Sashastra Seema Bal (SSB). Subodh Kumar Jaiswal is the director-general of the Central Industrial Security Force (CISF).

Hence, the correct option is (B).

51. As Japan is related to Judo. In same ways, Spain is related to Bull's Fight.

Bullfighting is illegal in most countries, but remains legal in most areas of Spain and Portugal, as well as in some Hispanic American countries and some parts of southern France.

Hence, the correct option is (D).

52. As per the option,

(A) MIGE,

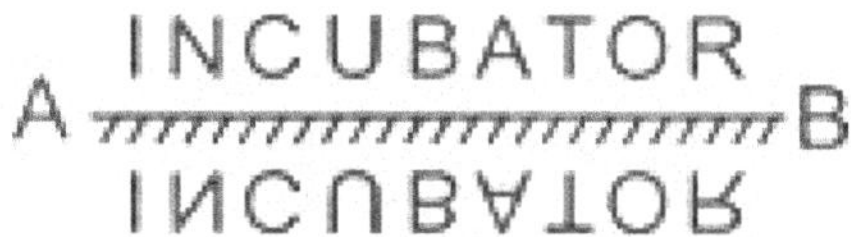

(B) XTRO,

$$X \xrightarrow{-4} T \xrightarrow{-3} Q \xrightarrow{-2} O$$

(C)
RNKT,

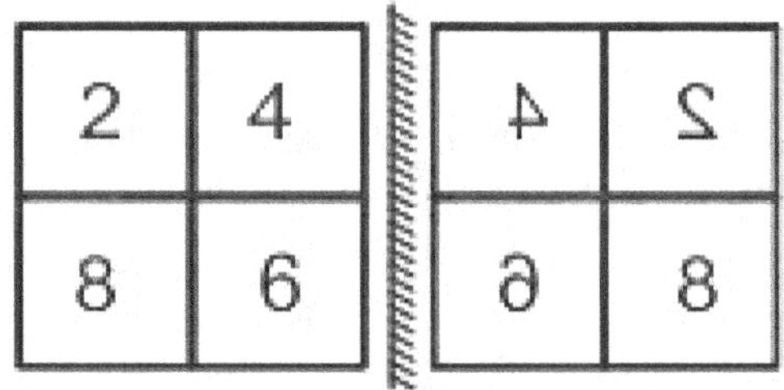

(D)
HDAY,

$$H \xrightarrow{-4} D \xrightarrow{-3} A \xrightarrow{-2} Y$$

Hence, the correct option is (A).

53. The mirror image will be as follows:

INCUBATOR

Hence, the correct option is (A).

54. The mirror image will be as follows:

Hence, the correct option is (B).

55. All the symbols move clockwise inside the square in each step i.e., they move one at a time. The symbols are replaced by new symbols sequentially in an anticlockwise direction. Thus, the answer figure is,

Hence, the correct option is (B).

56. In each step, the dot moves the given sphere one space clockwise and the arrow moves two spaces clockwise. Thus, the answer figure is,

Hence, the correct option is (A).

57.

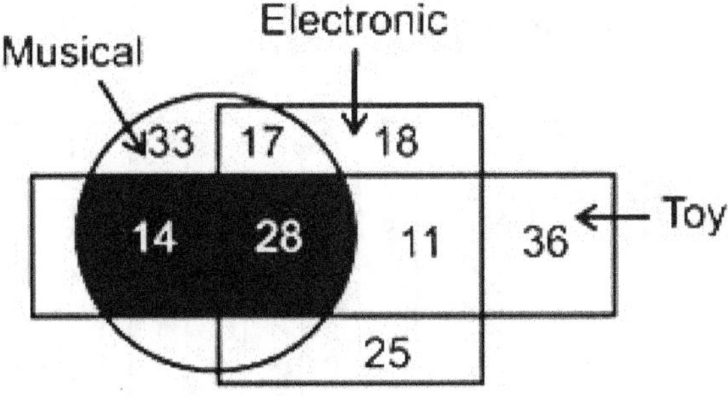

Musical toys: 28 + 14 = 42

Therefore, there are '42' musical toys.

Hence, the correct option is (C).

58. Some workers may be managers and vice – versa.

All workers and managers are staff.

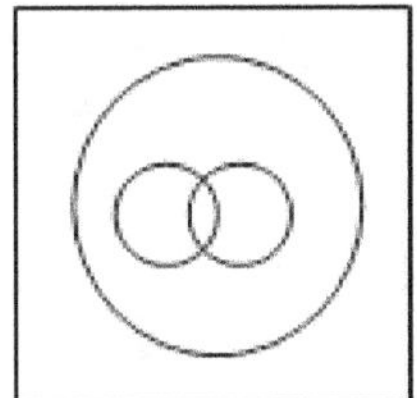

Hence, the correct option is (B).

59. Possible Venn diagram for the given statements is as follows:

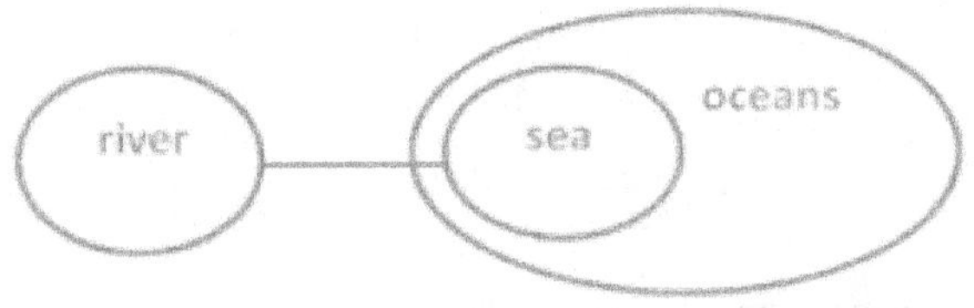

Conclusions:

I. All rivers are oceans. → False (There is no definite relation between rivers and oceans)

II. No river is oceans. → False (There is no definite relation between rivers and oceans)

Hence, the correct option is (C).

60. Possible Venn diagram for the given statements is as follows:

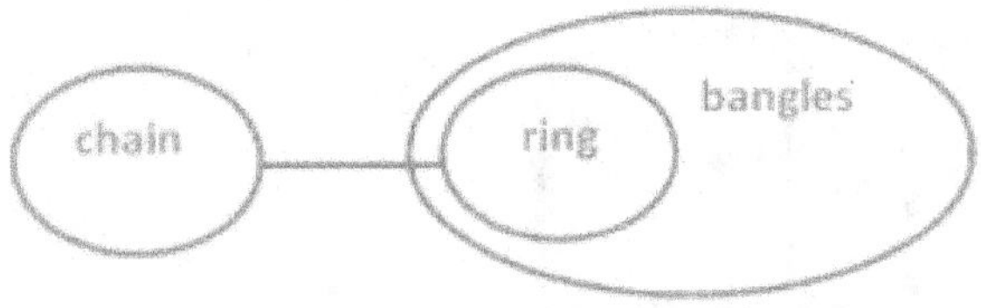

Conclusions:

I. Some bangles are rings. → True (As all rings are bangles.)

II. Some chains are bangles. → False (Possible but not definite.)

Hence, the correct option is (B).

61. This is a simple division series; each number is one-half of the previous number.

In other terms to say, the number is divided by 2 successively to get the next result.

$$\frac{4}{2} = 2$$

$$\frac{2}{2} = 1$$

$$\frac{1}{2} = \frac{1}{2}$$

$$\frac{\left(\frac{1}{2}\right)}{2} = \frac{1}{4}$$

$$\frac{\left(\frac{1}{4}\right)}{2} = \frac{1}{8} \text{ and so on.}$$

Hence, the correct option is (B).

62. In the above 2 × 2 matrices, the sum of all the four numbers of a matrix is 33.

In matrix 1 → 4 + 13 + 4 + 12 = 33

In matrix 2 → 7 + 5 + 20 + 1 = 33

Similarly,

In matrix 3 → ? + 9 + 2 + 19 = 33 → ? = 33 - 30 = 3

Hence, the correct option is (A).

63. Option(C) contains the figure.

Hence, the correct option is (C).

64. Option (A) is embedded in the given figure.

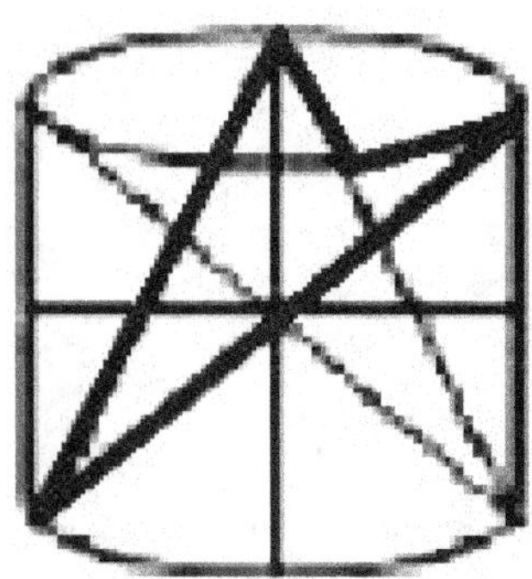

Hence, the correct option is (A)

65. Counting the years 1600 + 300 + 74

In 1600 years, there are zero odd days.

In 300 years, there is one odd day.

In 74 years, there are 18 leap years and 56 normal years, so the odd days are:

18(2) + 56(1) = 36 + 56 = 92,

Which are 13 weeks and 1 odd day.

In 25 days of January 1975, there are 3 weeks and 4 odd days.

Total odd days = 0 + 1 + 1 + 4

Six odd days, so it was a Saturday.

Hence, the correct option is (B).

66.

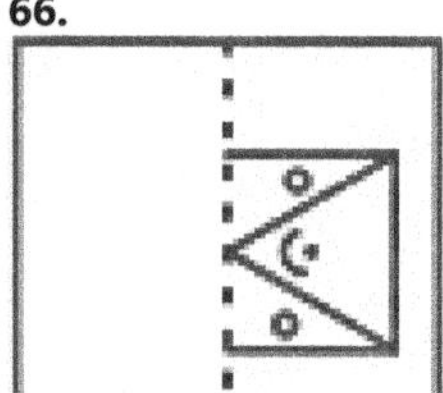 resembles the pattern formed after folding the sheet.

In the folding of the transparent sheet having design, the vertical dotted folding line can be considered as a mirror. So, after folding the transparent sheet, we will get the mirror image of the design on the other side of the sheet.

Design on the side toward which the sheet is folded will remain as it is and will be visible fully even after folding, as the sheet is transparent.

Hence, the correct option is (A).

67. The arrows indicated in the given figures are showing the direction of folding of the paper. Every unfolding line will act as mirror.

Since two punch holes are made in final folding so when it will be unfolded from Z to Y then 4 number of punch line holes will be visible.

After complete unfolding from Y to X, all 16 punch line holes will be visible on the given piece of paper and at the center of paper one circular type punch hole will be visible.

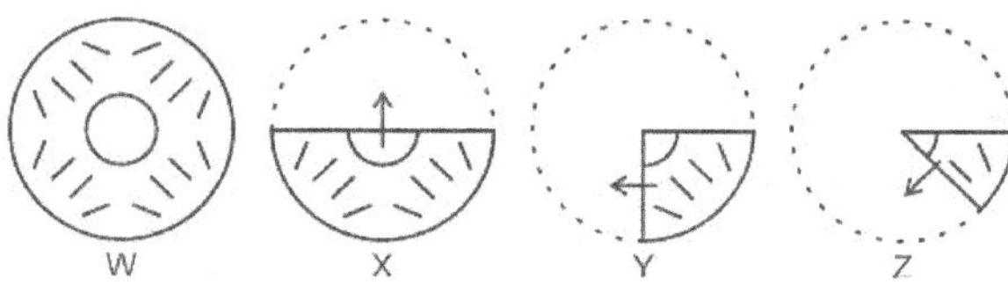

Hence, the correct option is (B).

68. We know that:

Alpha bets	A	B	C	D	E	F	G	H	I	J	K	L	M
Positional value	1	2	3	4	5	6	7	8	9	10	11	12	13
Positional value	26	25	24	23	22	21	20	19	18	17	16	15	14
Alpha bets	Z	Y	X	W	V	U	T	S	R	Q	P	O	N

Given,
MATERIAL is written as NDYLTMGT.
The pattern followed here is,

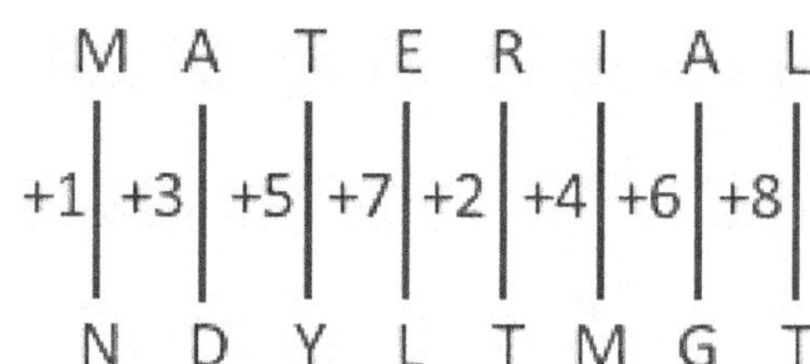

Similarly

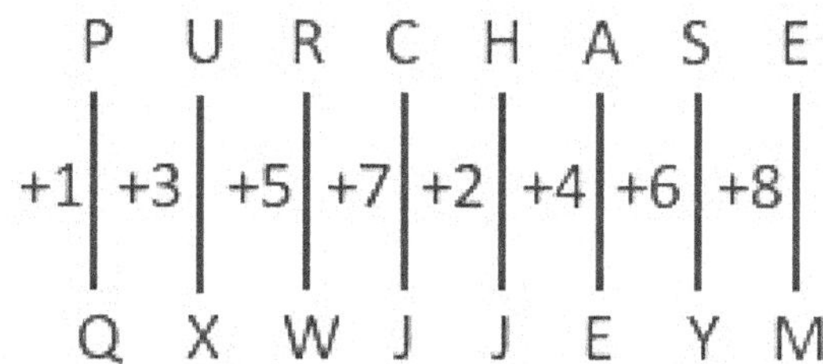

Therefore, the correct answer is QXWJJEYM.

Hence, the correct option is (B).

69. We know,

Alpha bets	A	B	C	D	E	F	G	H	I	J	K	L	M
Positional value	1	2	3	4	5	6	7	8	9	10	11	12	13
Positional value	26	25	24	23	22	21	20	19	18	17	16	15	14
Alpha	Z	Y	X	W	V	U	T	S	R	Q	P	O	N

Given,

SAILOR is written as 21414192631

The patter followed here is,

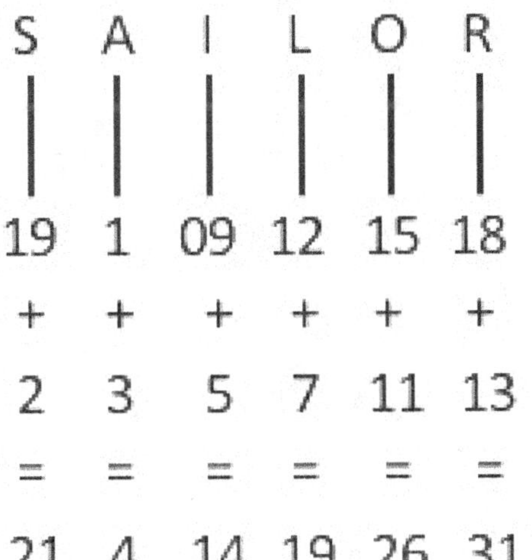

Symbol in Diagram	Meaning
○	Female
□	Male
══	Married Couple
——	Siblings
│	Difference of A Generation

Similarly,

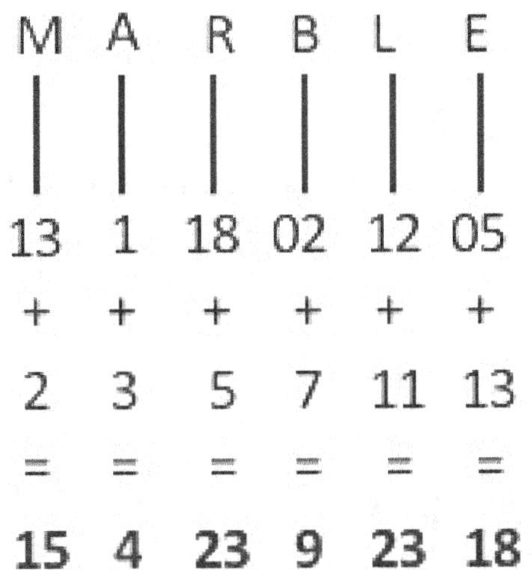

Therefore, the correct answer is 1542392318.

Hence, the correct option is (B).

70. The correct order of given words in the dictionary is:

Aquarium → Aquatic → Aqueous → Aquiline

So, the correct option is 2, 4, 1, 3.

Hence, the correct option is (C).

71. Alphabetical order is:

Abysmal → Accrue → Agility → Arise

So, the correct order is 2, 4, 3, 1.

Hence, the correct option is (D).

72. Preparing the family tree using the following symbols:

Possible tree diagram will be:

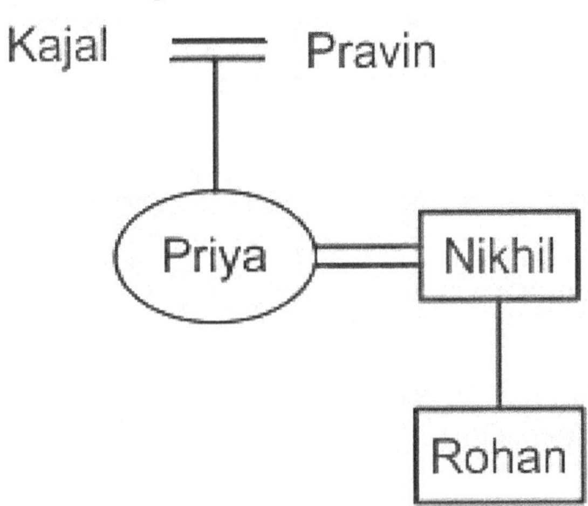

So, Priya is the wife of Nikhil.

Hence, the correct option is (D).

73. Preparing the family tree using the following symbols:

Symbol in Diagram	Meaning
○	Female
□	Male
═══	Married Couple
───	Siblings
│	Difference of A Generation

Possible tree diagram will be,

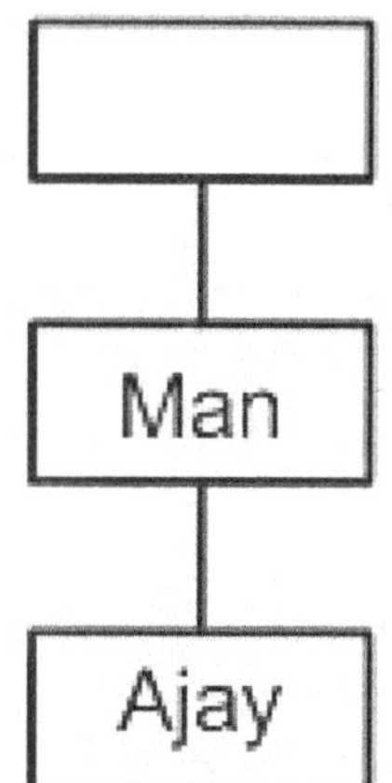

According to the tree diagram, Ajay is the son of that man.

So, son is the correct answer.

Hence, the correct option is (D).

75. Except option (D) the difference between the numbers in all others is 6.

Hence, the correct option is (D).

76. 30% discount on $2000 = 30\%$ of $2000 =$ Rs. 600

25% discount on $2000 = 25\%$ of $2000 =$ Rs. 500

Remaining amount $= 2000 - 500 =$ Rs. 1500

Second discount of $5\% = 5\%$ of $1500 =$ Rs. 75

Total discount $= 500 + 75 =$ Rs. 575

So, difference in discounts $= 600 - 575 =$ Rs. 25

Hence, the correct option is (B).

77. Given,

Average of 4 consecutive even numbers $= 47$

As we know,

$$\text{Average} = \frac{\text{Sum of all observations}}{\text{Total number of observations}}$$

Let the four consecutive even terms be $x, x + 2, x + 4, x + 6$

According to the question,

$$47 = \frac{(x+x+2+x+4+x+6)}{4}$$

$$\Rightarrow 47 = \frac{(4x+12)}{4}$$

$$\Rightarrow 188 = 4x + 12$$

$$\Rightarrow 4x = 176$$

$$\Rightarrow x = 44$$

Largest number $= x + 6$

$$= 44 + 6$$

$$= 50$$

Hence, the correct option is (A).

78. Marks obtained by Ragini in Chemistry and Biology together $= 45 + 38 = 83$

Marks obtained by Mohini in Physics and Mathematics together $= 55 + 82 = 137$

Required $\% = \frac{83}{137} \times 100 = 60.58\%$

Hence, the correct option is (B).

79. Marks obtained by all the students in Mathematics = 65 + 52 + 78 + 82 + 96 = 373

Marks obtained by all the students in Chemistry = 45 + 62 + 70 + 65 + 64 = 306

Required ratio = 373 : 306

Hence, the correct option is (B).

80. Total marks in all the subjects $= 75 + 100 + 75 + 75 + 120 = 445$

Marks obtained by Sohan in all the subjects $= 50 + 78 + 70 + 58 + 88 = 344$

Required $\% = \frac{344}{445} \times 100 = 77.3\%$

Hence, the correct option is (C).

81. Percentage of marks obtained by Mohan in English

$$= \frac{104}{120} \times 100 = 86.67\%$$

Percentage of marks obtained by Rohan in Physics

$$= \frac{60}{75} \times 100 = 80\%$$

Required difference $= 86.67 - 80 = 6.67\%$

Hence, the correct option is (A).

82. Sum of marks obtained by Rohan in all the subjects = 60 + 52 + 62 + 55 + 88 = 317

Hence, the correct option is (D).

83. Given:

Speed of train = 72 kmph

Time = 20 seconds

Speed of car = 18 kmph

Formula used:

Speed $= \dfrac{Distance}{time}$

1 kmph $= \dfrac{5}{18}$ m/s

Calculating length of train

$\Rightarrow$ 72 kmph $= \dfrac{72 \times 5}{18}$ m/s

$\Rightarrow$ Speed of train = 20 m/s

$\Rightarrow$ length of train = Speed × Time

$\Rightarrow$ length = 20 × 20

$\Rightarrow$ Length of train = 400 m

Now, calculate relative speed

$\Rightarrow$ car is moving in opposite direction as train hence relative speed = 72 + 18

$\Rightarrow$ Relative speed = 90 kmph

$\Rightarrow$ Relative speed = 25 m/s

$\Rightarrow$ Time taken to cross car $= \dfrac{400}{25}$

$\Rightarrow$ Time taken = 16 sconds

$\therefore$ Train takes 16 seconds to cross the car

Hence, the correct option is (B).

84. $? = 120 \div 40$ of $\dfrac{1}{4} + \dfrac{2}{5} \times 3\dfrac{1}{4}$

$\Rightarrow ? = 120 \div 40 \times \dfrac{1}{4} + \dfrac{2}{5} \times \dfrac{13}{4}$

$\Rightarrow ? = 120 \div 10 + \dfrac{2}{5} \times \dfrac{13}{4}$

$\Rightarrow ? = 12 + \dfrac{13}{10}$

$\Rightarrow ? = 13\dfrac{3}{10}$

Hence, the correct option is (A).

85. Given-

$$A : B = 7 : 3$$

Let $A = 7k,\ B = 3k$.

On putting the values of A and B,

$$\frac{AB + B^2}{A^2 - B^2}$$

$$= \frac{(7k \times 3k) + (3k)^2}{(7k)^2 - (3k)^2}$$

$$= \frac{21k^2 + 9k^2}{49k^2 - 9k^2}$$

$$= \frac{30k^2}{40k^2}$$

$$= \frac{3}{4}$$

Hence, the correct option is (A).

86. Anil + Bini $= 2 \times 20 = 40yr$

Bini + Chaya $= 2 \times 19 = 38yr$

Chaya + Anil $= 2 \times 21 = 42yr$

On adding all three,

2 (Anil + Bini + Chaya) $= 40 + 38 + 42 = 120$

$\Rightarrow$ Anil + Bini + Chaya $= 60$

$\therefore$ Anil $= ($ Anil + Bini + Chaya $) - ($ Bini + Chaya $) = 60 - 38 = 22yr$

Similarly,

Bini = (Anil + Bini) - Anil $= 40 - 22 = 18$ yr

Chaya $= ($ Chaya + Anil $) -$ Anil $= 42 - 22 = 20yr$

Hence, the correct option is (C).

87. Given:

Area of circular plot $= 144\pi m^2$

As we know, the area of circle $= \pi \times ($ Radius $)^2$

$\Rightarrow 144\ \pi m^2 = \pi \times ($ Radius $)^2$

Radius $= \sqrt{144} = 12\ m$

Now,

Width of path $= 5\ m$

Radius of circular plot including the path surrounding it $= 12 + 5 = 17\ m$

$\therefore$ Required area $= \pi \times (17)^2 = 289\pi m^2$

Hence, the correct option is (B).

88. Given that, due to shortage of labor in a factory, its production decrease $= 25\%$

Hence the working period $= \dfrac{25}{100-25} \times 100$

$\Rightarrow 33\dfrac{1}{3}\%$

Hence, the correct option is (D).

89. Given,

Wages of 20 days of 1 man and 1 woman = Rs. 1500

Let efficiency of 1 woman be 1 unit/day

Efficiency of 1 man $= 2$ unit/day

According to the question,

$2 + 1 = 3$ unit

$\Rightarrow 3$ unit $= 1500$

$\Rightarrow 1$ unit $= \dfrac{1500}{3} = 500$

20 day's wages of 1 woman = Rs. 500

Daily wages of 1 woman $= \dfrac{500}{20} = $ Rs. 25

Hence, the correct option is (A).

90. Given:

$I = a^2 + b^2 + c^2$, where a and b are consecutive integers and $c = ab$

Let a and b be 1 and 2 respectively (a and b are consecutive numbers)

So, $c = 1 \times 2 = 2$

Now

$\Rightarrow I = 1^2 + 2^2 + 2^2$

$\Rightarrow I = 9$

Now let the values of a and b be 2 and 3 respectively

So, $c = 2 \times 3 = 6$

Now,

$\Rightarrow I = 2^2 + 3^2 + 6^2$

$\Rightarrow I = 49$

In both cases, it is coming out to be the square of an odd integer.

Hence, the correct option is (D).

91. A header is the top margin of each page, and a footer is the bottom margin of each page. Headers and footers are useful for including material that you want to appear on every page of a document such as your name, the title of the document, or page numbers.

Hence, the correct option is (D).

92. Text-styling feature of MS word is WordArt. The Styles feature in Microsoft Word is one of a handful of tools that keep me from moving to the free LibreOffice suite.
Hence, the correct option is (C).

93. Both TEXT and IMAGE can be used as a watermark in a word document. It is important to note that watermarks can be inserted in all pages of a word document all at once.

Hence, the correct option is (C).

94. Footnotes appear at the bottom of the page and endnotes come at the end of the document. A number or symbol on the footnote or endnote matches up with a reference mark in the document. Click where you want to reference to the footnote or endnote. On the References tab, select Insert Footnote or Insert Endnote.

Hence, the correct option is (B).

95. Put the mouse pointer over the bottom right-hand corner of the cell until it's a black plus sign. Click and hold the left mouse button, and drag the plus sign over the cells you want to fill. And the series is filled in for you automatically using the AutoFill feature.

Hence, the correct option is (B).

96. 'Ctrl + Shift + S' Save current data under a different name. The file name associated with the data changes to the new name.
Hence, the correct option is (A).

97. The server is a computer device/program which provides functionality for other devices/program.

Servers can provide functions such as sharing data or resources among multiple clients or performing computation for a client.

It manages network resources.

It can serve data to systems on a local area network (LAN) or a wide area network (WAN) over the Internet.

Web servers, mail servers, and file servers, etc are examples of different types of servers.

An individual system can provide resources and use them from another system at the same time.

Client-server systems are today most frequently executed by (and often identified with) the request-response model.

The device that makes the request, and receives a response from the server, is called a client.

Hence, the correct option is (A).

98. A router is a device that enables the movement of data from one network to another network.

It receives, analyzes, and forwards data packets between computer networks.

A router is connected to at least two networks, commonly two LANs or WANs or a LAN and its ISP's network.

Cisco, HP, Juniper, and D-Link are the popular companies that develop routers.

A router shares information with other routers in networking.

It works on the third layer of the OSI model.

It provides high-speed internet connectivity with different types of ports.

It sends data based on the IP address of a device.

The router uses a routing table to send the data.

Hence, the correct option is (C).

99. Internet Explorer is a series of graphical web browsers developed by Microsoft and included in the Microsoft Windows line of operating systems, starting in 1995. It was first released as part of the add-on package Plus for Windows 95 that year.

Hence, the correct option is (A).

100. A modem is a hardware device that converts data so that it can be transmitted from computer to computer over telephone wires. A network interface card (NIC) is a circuit board or card that is installed in a computer so that it can be connected to a network.

Hence, the correct option is (B).

// Notes //

// Notes //